Sicily

Fionn Davenport

LONELY PLANET PUBLICATIONS
Melbourne • Oakland • London • Paris

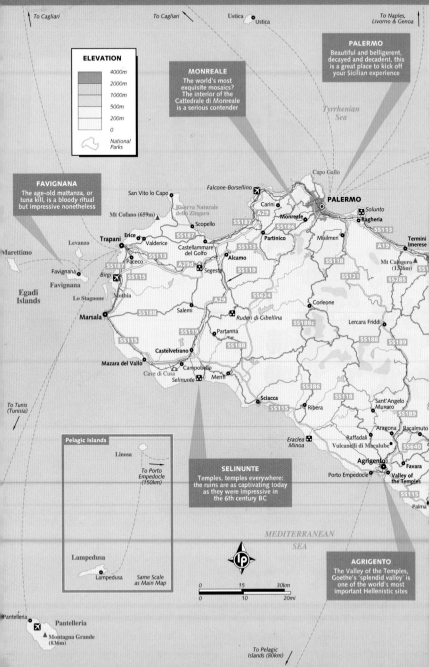

SICILY

ELEVATION

4000m
2000m
1000m
500m
200m
0

National Parks

To Cagliari

To Cagliari

Ustica
• Ustica

To Naples, Livorno & Genoa

PALERMO
Beautiful and belligerent, decayed and decadent, this is a great place to kick off your Sicilian experience

MONREALE
The world's most exquisite mosaics? The interior of the Cattedrale di Monreale is a serious contender

Tyrrhenian Sea

Capo Gallo

FAVIGNANA
The age-old mattanza, or tuna kill, is a bloody ritual but impressive nonetheless

San Vito lo Capo

Falcone-Borsellino ✈

PALERMO

Carini

Soluto
Bagheria

Mt Cofano (659m) ▲

Riserva Naturale dello Zingaro

Scopello

SS187

SS186

Monreale

A29

SS113

Partinico

Misilmeri

Termini Imerese

Erice

Trapani

Valderice

SS187

Castellammare del Golfo

SS113

Mt Calogero (1326m) ▲

SS1

Levanzo

Paceco

SS113

A29d

Alcamo

SS119

SS118

A19

Marettimo

Favignana

Birgi ✈

SS187

Segesta

SS121

SS285

Egadi Islands

Favignana

SS115

Mothia

SS624

Corleone

Lo Stagnone

Salemi

Ruderi di Gibellina

SS188c

Lercara Friddi

Marsala

SS119

Partanna

SS188

SS188

SS189

SS115

Castelvetrano

SS188

Mazara del Vallo

Campobello

Menfi

Cave di Cusa

Selinunte ✈

SS386

SS118

Sant'Angelo Muxaro

Sciacca

SS115

Ribera

SS189

Aragona

Racalmuto

Pelagic Islands

Linosa

Eraclea Minoa ✈

Raffadali

Vulcanelli di Macalube

SS640

To Porto Empedocle (150km)

Agrigento

Favara

SELINUNTE
Temples, temples everywhere: the ruins are as captivating today as they were impressive in the 6th century BC

Porto Empedocle

Valley of the Temples

SS115

Palma

Lampedusa

Lampedusa

Same Scale as Main Map

MEDITERRANEAN SEA

AGRIGENTO
The Valley of the Temples, Goethe's 'splendid valley' is one of the world's most important Hellenistic sites

0   15   30km
0   10   20mi

Pantelleria

Pantelleria

Montagna Grande (836m) ▲

To Pelagic Islands (80km)

To Tunis (Tunisia)

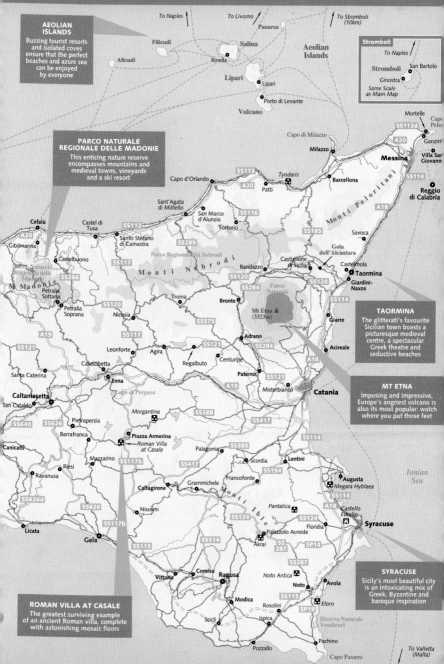

SICILY

AEOLIAN ISLANDS
Buzzing tourist resorts and isolated coves ensure that the perfect beaches and azure sea can be enjoyed by everyone

PARCO NATURALE REGIONALE DELLE MADONIE
This enticing nature reserve encompasses mountains and medieval towns, vineyards and a ski resort

TAORMINA
The glitterati's favourite Sicilian town boasts a picturesque medieval centre, a spectacular Greek theatre and seductive beaches

MT ETNA
Imposing and impressive, Europe's angriest volcano is also its most popular: watch where you put those feet

SYRACUSE
Sicily's most beautiful city is an intoxicating mix of Greek, Byzantine and baroque inspiration

ROMAN VILLA AT CASALE
The greatest surviving example of an ancient Roman villa, complete with astonishing mosaic floors

To Naples
To Livorno
To Stromboli (10km)

Panarea

Filicudi
Salina
Aeolian Islands

Alicudi
Rinella
Lipari

Lipari
Porto di Levante

Vulcano

Stromboli
To Naples
Stromboli
San Bartolo
Ginostra
Same Scale as Main Map

Mortelle
Capo Pelo
SS113d
Ganzirri
A20
Capo di Milazzo
Villa Sar Giovanni
Milazzo
Messina
SS113
Tyndaris
Barcellona
SS114
Capo d'Orlando
A20
Patti
Reggio di Calabria
Sant'Agata di Militello
San Marco d'Alunzio
SS116
A18
Monti Peloritani
Cefalù
Tortorici
SS185
Savoca
Castel di Tusa
SS113
Gola dell'Alcántara
Gibilmanna
Santo Stefano di Camastra
SS289
Parco Regionale dei Nebrodi
Castelmola
Castiglione di Sicilia
Taormina
Castelbuono
SS117
Monti Nebrodi
Giardini-Naxos
SS286
Randazzo
Mt Madonie
SS120
SS284
Parco Naturale dell'Etna
Petralia Sottana
Troina
Bronte
SS120
Petralia Soprana
SS120
Nicosia
SS575
Mt Etna (3323m)
SS114
Giarre
SS117
Adrano
Leonforte
SS121
Agira
SS284
Acireale
SS121
Regalbuto
Centuripe
A18
Calascibetta
Paternò
Santa Caterina
Enna
A19
Misterbianco
SS121
Catania
Caltanissetta
Lago di Pergusa
San Cataldo
Morgantina
SS640
SS626
SS288
Pietraperzia
SS417
Barrafranca
SS114
Canicattì
Piazza Armerina
Roman Villa at Casale
Palagonia
SS385
Riesi
Mazzarino
Palazzolo
SS417
SS114
Ravanusa
SS117b
Scordia
Augusta
SS626d
Grammichele
Francofonte
SS194
Megara Hyblaea
SS626
Caltagirone
SS114
Licata
SS117b
Niscemi
Pantalica
A18
Castello Euralio
Gela
SS115
SS124
SS124
Syracuse
Floridia
Vittoria
Comiso
Ragusa
Akrai
SS514
SS 287
SP14
Noto Antica
SS287
Modica
Palazzolo Acreide
Noto
Avola
Rosolini
SS115
Scicli
Eloro
SP19
Ispica
Riserva Naturale Vendicari
Pozzallo
Pachino

Ionian Sea

To Valletta (Malta)

Capo Passero

Sicily
1st edition – August 2000

Published by
Lonely Planet Publications Pty Ltd ABN 36 005 607 983
90 Maribyrnong St, Footscray, Victoria 3011, Australia

Lonely Planet Offices
Australia Locked Bag 1, Footscray, Victoria 3011
USA 150 Linden St, Oakland, CA 94607
UK 10a Spring Place, London NW5 3BH
France 1 rue du Dahomey, 75011 Paris

Photographs
Many of the images in this guide are available for licensing from
Lonely Planet Images.
email: lpi@lonelyplanet.com.au

Front cover photograph
A slice of Sicilian life, Lipari (Nicholas DeVore, Tony Stone Images)

ISBN 1 86450 099 9

Contents – Text

Contents – Maps

MAP LEGEND – SEE BACK PAGE

3

MAPS

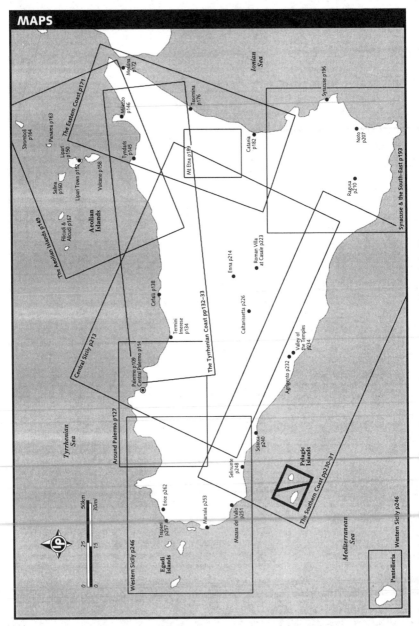

50km

30mi

25

15

0

The Author

Fionn Davenport
Fionn was born in and spent most of his youth in Dublin – that is, when his family wasn't moving him to Buenos Aires or Geneva or New York (all thanks to his Dad, whose job took him far and wide). Infected with the travel disease, he became a nomad in his own right after graduating from Trinity College, moving first to Paris and then to New York, where he spent five years as a travel editor and sometime writer. The call of home was too much to resist, however, so armed with his portable computer, his record collection and an empty wallet he returned to Dublin where he decided to continue where he left off in New York. Only it was quieter, wetter and a hell of a lot smaller. When he's not DJing in pubs and clubs throughout the city he's writing and updating travel guides. He has written about many destinations throughout the world. This is his fourth book for Lonely Planet, having worked already on the *Spain*, *Dublin* and *Ireland* guides.

FROM THE AUTHOR
Like all adventures, the pleasure of travelling through Sicily was made all the better – and all the more educational – thanks to the help and friendship of a large number of people. Firstly, the tourist offices, both large and small, were extremely helpful, even though most of them were unaware of my intentions. I didn't pose as a florist, or as any other profession, but simply as a fascinated traveller keen to explore the nooks and crannies of this wonderful place. Your help in opening all kinds of doors both physical and metaphorical is greatly appreciated. In particular, a big thanks to Loredana at the APT in Syracuse, for taking a couple of hours out of her day to share with me her knowledge of her splendid city and a box of very good chocolates!

In more than one way this book would not have been possible without the invaluable help of Dario Ferrante. Your patient answering of all my questions and your excellent contacts kicked off my trip on a good foot, but more importantly you introduced me to people whose company and friendship made all those months of trekking up and down the island seem like a holiday at home. In this, I owe a huge debt of gratitude to Michelangelo Marchingiglio and his family, who were among the nicest people I have met anywhere in the world. A big thank you also to Stephane Ladant and Fabio Hopps for their much-needed help, hospitality and concern.

In Palermo, I would have been lost without the help of Fernanda Brancatelli and Corradina Sapuppo. Their invaluable insights into the near impenetrable morass of Sicilian culture and politics have (hopefully) given me something more than a bird's eye view of these complexities. More to the point, however, I wanted to thank you both (and your friends) for making me feel welcome in Palermo and I look forward to seeing you all there again: *vi ringrazio dal profondo del cuore*. To Fernanda's brother, thanks for putting me up, even if you didn't really know anything about it!

No list of acknowledgements would be complete without mentioning Letizia Pipitone and her exceptional family. Poste restante, dinner invitations, long chats and Internet access were much appreciated (and greatly needed!) but more than all that I wanted to express my gratitude for your open hospitality and warm friendship.

A few friends from home made it over, including Laurie Kelliher (who was there for the first tentative steps!): I'm sorry you couldn't stay longer. Morgan Ferriter and Gertie Neary took their holidays in Sicily, as did Geoff 'Double' O'Sullivan: I hope the experience of following me from one sight to another and from one hostel to the next hasn't spoiled your notion of what a good relaxing holiday is about. For my part, thanks to you all for keeping me company and giving me some pretty good laughs along the way.

Finally, a word about the book itself. All of you mentioned above and many more besides made it possible for me to get it done: in particular I would like to mention the staff at LP in London, including Claire Hornshaw, David Wenk and Paul Bloomfield. Your patience and eagle eyes are greatly appreciated. I absolutely loved the island (I have recommended a trip there to anyone who would care to listen!) and have tried to carry my enthusiasm into every page, but not at the expense of being critical when it was necessary. There are far too many cliched, uninformed opinions about Sicily, and I have done my best not to fall into that category, but if there are mistakes or ill-conceived judgements then the fault is entirely mine.

This Book

This 1st edition of Sicily was researched and written by Fionn Davenport, using material from Lonely Planet's *Italy* guide.

From the Publisher

This edition of *Sicily* was edited and proofed in Lonely Planet's London office by Claire Hornshaw, with inestimable help from Amanda Canning; Christine Stroyan assisted with the proofing and produced the index, and Quentin Frayne compiled and updated the Language chapter. David Wenk coordinated the mapping and design, assisted by Paul Edmunds, Sara Yorke and Angie Watts; Jim Miller created the back cover map. Illustrations were drawn by Jane Smith, and Lonely Planet Images provided the photographs. Thanks to Imogen Franks, Jen Loy, Agata Sternalski, Sally O'Brien and Kate Daly for checking the travel information, and to Anna Sutton for giving the book a road test. Thanks also go to Tony Wheeler and Helen Gillman for their contributions. Many thanks to Fionn for all his hard work and good humour during a busy time.

Foreword

ABOUT LONELY PLANET GUIDEBOOKS

The story begins with a classic travel adventure: Tony and Maureen Wheeler's 1972 journey across Europe and Asia to Australia. Useful information about the overland trail did not exist at that time, so Tony and Maureen published the first Lonely Planet guidebook to meet a growing need.

From a kitchen table, then from a tiny office in Melbourne (Australia), Lonely Planet has become the largest independent travel publisher in the world, an international company with offices in Melbourne, Oakland (USA), London (UK) and Paris (France).

Today Lonely Planet guidebooks cover the globe. There is an ever-growing list of books and there's information in a variety of forms and media. Some things haven't changed. The main aim is still to help make it possible for adventurous travellers to get out there – to explore and better understand the world.

At Lonely Planet we believe travellers can make a positive contribution to the countries they visit – if they respect their host communities and spend their money wisely. Since 1986 a percentage of the income from each book has been donated to aid projects and human rights campaigns.

Updates Lonely Planet thoroughly updates each guidebook as often as possible. This usually means there are around two years between editions, although for more unusual or more stable destinations the gap can be longer. Check the imprint page (following the colour map at the beginning of the book) for publication dates.

Between editions up-to-date information is available in two free newsletters – the paper *Planet Talk* and email *Comet* (to subscribe, contact any Lonely Planet office) – and on our Web site at www.lonelyplanet.com. The *Upgrades* section of the Web site covers a number of important and volatile destinations and is regularly updated by Lonely Planet authors. *Scoop* covers news and current affairs relevant to travellers. And, lastly, the *Thorn Tree* bulletin board and *Postcards* section of the site carry unverified, but fascinating, reports from travellers.

Correspondence The process of creating new editions begins with the letters, postcards and emails received from travellers. This correspondence often includes suggestions, criticisms and comments about the current editions. Interesting excerpts are immediately passed on via newsletters and the Web site, and everything goes to our authors to be verified when they're researching on the road. We're keen to get more feedback from organisations or individuals who represent communities visited by travellers.

Lonely Planet gathers information for everyone who's curious about the planet – and especially for those who explore it first-hand. Through guidebooks, phrasebooks, activity guides, maps, literature, newsletters, image library, TV series and Web site we act as an information exchange for a worldwide community of travellers.

Research Authors aim to gather sufficient practical information to enable travellers to make informed choices and to make the mechanics of a journey run smoothly. They also research historical and cultural background to help enrich the travel experience and allow travellers to understand and respond appropriately to cultural and environmental issues.

Authors don't stay in every hotel because that would mean spending a couple of months in each medium-sized city and, no, they don't eat at every restaurant because that would mean stretching belts beyond capacity. They do visit hotels and restaurants to check standards and prices, but feedback based on readers' direct experiences can be very helpful.

Many of our authors work undercover, others aren't so secretive. None of them accept freebies in exchange for positive write-ups. And none of our guidebooks contain any advertising.

Production Authors submit their raw manuscripts and maps to offices in Australia, USA, UK or France. Editors and cartographers – all experienced travellers themselves – then begin the process of assembling the pieces. When the book finally hits the shops some things are already out of date, we start getting feedback from readers, and the process begins again...

WARNING & REQUEST

Things change – prices go up, schedules change, good places go bad and bad places go bankrupt – nothing stays the same. So, if you find things better or worse, recently opened or long since closed, please tell us and help make the next edition even more accurate and useful. We genuinely value all the feedback we receive. Julie Young coordinates a well-travelled team that reads and acknowledges every letter, postcard and email and ensures that every morsel of information finds its way to the appropriate authors, editors and cartographers for verification.

Everyone who writes to us will find their name in the next edition of the appropriate guidebook. They will also receive the latest issue of *Planet Talk*, our quarterly printed newsletter, or *Comet*, our monthly email newsletter. Subscriptions to both newsletters are free. The very best contributions will be rewarded with a free guidebook.

Excerpts from your correspondence may appear in new editions of Lonely Planet guidebooks, the Lonely Planet Web site, *Planet Talk* or *Comet*, so please let us know if you *don't* want your letter published or your name acknowledged.

Send all correspondence to the Lonely Planet office closest to you:

Australia: Locked Bag 1, Footscray, Victoria 3011
UK: 10A Spring Place, London NW5 3BH
USA: 150 Linden St, Oakland CA 94607
France: 1 rue du Dahomey, Paris 75011

Or email us at: talk2us@lonelyplanet.com.au

For news, views and updates see our Web site: www.lonelyplanet.com

HOW TO USE A LONELY PLANET GUIDEBOOK

The best way to use a Lonely Planet guidebook is any way you choose. At Lonely Planet we believe the most memorable travel experiences are often those that are unexpected, and the finest discoveries are those you make yourself. Guidebooks are not intended to be used as if they provide a detailed set of infallible instructions!

Contents All Lonely Planet guidebooks follow roughly the same format. The Facts about the Destination chapter or section gives background information ranging from history to weather. Facts for the Visitor gives practical information on issues like visas and health. Getting There & Away gives a brief starting point for researching travel to and from the destination. Getting Around gives an overview of the transport options when you arrive.

The peculiar demands of each destination determine how subsequent chapters are broken up, but some things remain constant. We always start with background, then proceed to sights, places to stay, places to eat, entertainment, getting there and away, and getting around information – in that order.

Heading Hierarchy Lonely Planet headings are used in a strict hierarchical structure that can be visualised as a set of Russian dolls. Each heading (and its following text) is encompassed by any preceding heading that is higher on the hierarchical ladder.

Entry Points We do not assume guidebooks will be read from beginning to end, but that people will dip into them. The traditional entry points are the list of contents and the index. In addition, however, some books have a complete list of maps and an index map illustrating map coverage.

There may also be a colour map that shows highlights. These highlights are dealt with in greater detail in the Facts for the Visitor chapter, along with planning questions and suggested itineraries. Each chapter covering a geographical region usually begins with a locator map and another list of highlights. Once you find something of interest in a list of highlights, turn to the index.

Maps Maps play a crucial role in Lonely Planet guidebooks and include a huge amount of information. A legend is printed on the back page. We seek to have complete consistency between maps and text, and to have every important place in the text captured on a map. Map key numbers usually start in the top left corner.

Although inclusion in a guidebook usually implies a recommendation we cannot list every good place. Exclusion does not necessarily imply criticism. In fact there are a number of reasons why we might exclude a place – sometimes it is simply inappropriate to encourage an influx of travellers.

Introduction

'The deepest mystery is always hidden in the midday sun,' wrote Nietzsche, 'not in the darkness.' He may not have had Sicily in mind when he wrote this, but he would have struggled to find a more compelling example of his theory. Today, the cloak of insularity is slowly being cast aside and the Sicilians, who for centuries spoke loudest through their enduring silence, have begun to open up to the outside world. Yet deep into the island's mountainous interior, away from the bustling cities and trendy beach resorts, change is not so evident, and that all-embracing shroud of mystery lives on. Hardly surprising considering that the burden of 6000 years of invasion and occupation weighs heaviest here.

Since prehistory Sicily has attracted the attention of outsiders, who recognised its extraordinary potential and its plentiful natural resources which could sustain even the most developed civilisation. And of those there were plenty, including the Greeks, the Romans, the Arabs, the Byzantines, the Normans, the French and the Spanish, who came, saw and conquered and in their wake left a trail of impressive ruins, monuments and buildings that draw ever-increasing gasps of admiration for their stunning beauty. Basking under the hot sun amid a lush, subtropical vegetation, Sicily is one of the garden spots of the Mediterranean, a garden where you can come to play and learn about three millennia of European history.

Yet so much beauty has a price, and Sicily is heavily in debt. Each occupier mercilessly stripped the island's wealth, leaving its inhabitants to struggle with endemic poverty, mass emigration and an almost crippling dependency on outside aid which has left the island isolated and marginalised only 3km from the shores of its latest 'occupier', Italy. Since WWII the government in Rome has poured trillions of lire into the island in the hope of kick-starting its moribund economy, but a huge percentage has been siphoned off through kickbacks and protection payments

to a home-grown oppressor: the Mafia. A rash of ill-conceived and often illegal construction during the boom years of the 1950s and '60s has scarred parts of the landscape with some phenomenally ugly buildings and stretches of industrial wasteland that stand in stark relief to the island's natural and man-made splendours. In the name of island-wide progress, these modern developments only benefited a powerful, self-interested few.

11

Such myopic greed, coupled with problems that were not of its own making, has led many Italians to dismiss Sicily as an albatross around Italy's neck. The island has slumped even further into isolation and resentment of the government in Rome, which is as foreign to many Sicilians as the emperors of ancient history, and not that different from the oppressive Spanish, whose 500-year rule ended with Italian unification.

Despite its many problems, the island still has plenty to offer the visitor. No matter where you are in Sicily there's always something to see, a little town to poke around or a beach to stretch out on. For all of its unifying elements, the island throws up an equal amount of diversity and contrast, from the crumbling grandeur of the capital, Palermo, to the high-flying resorts of Taormina and the Aeolian Islands, summer home to a chunk of Italy's glitterati – the have-yachts in the land of the have-nots. The more exotic west has a distinctly Tunisian feel about it, a stark contrast to the cosmopolitan, European flavours of Catania to the east. If traces of antiquity are what you seek, then you've come to the right place – Sicily's wealth of archaeological finds will have you planning a return visit before you've even left. The stunning baroque architecture of the south-west alone is worth making the trip for, while walkers will find plenty of paths in the island's nature reserves and on Sicily's most prominent natural feature, the ever-active but always-popular Mt Etna.

Fittingly, the last say goes to a Sicilian – the island's most famous modern painter, Renato Guttuso:

'In Sicily you can find dramas, pastorals, idylls, politics, gastronomy, geography, history, literature...in the end you can find anything and everything, but you can't find truth.'

Facts about Sicily

HISTORY

Strategically located at the heart of the Mediterranean basin, Sicily has been the target of colonisers and settlers from all sides of the sea for over 6000 years. Eager to establish their primacy over the rich waters of the Mediterranean, invaders from two continents – Africa and Europe – turned Sicily into a defensive bulwark intended to support their commercial and military interests in the region. Each conqueror has undoubtedly contributed to the make-up of modern Sicily, some leaving a rich cultural heritage still in evidence today. Yet much foreign occupation has also deeply scarred the island, whose inhabitants have always borne the brunt of the suffering heaped upon it by one coloniser after another. Even today, despite being part of a unified Italy, many Sicilians still feel that they are living through the latest cycle of occupation.

Earliest Settlers

The most compelling evidence of Sicily's first human settlers is found in a series of cave etchings that date from around 12,000 BC, located along the coastal areas of the western seaboard, most notably in the Grotta del Genovese on Levanzo and the Grotta dell'Addaura on Mt Pellegrino. Other than their ability to draw, little is known about these first settlers other than that they may have come from Africa in the late Pleistocene. The island was so far south as to make irrelevant the effects of the Ice Age, so it has proven difficult for palaeontologists to distinguish between the peoples of the successive prehistoric ages, from the Mesolithic to the Palaeolithic.

The first real evidence of an organised settlement familiar with rudimentary tools and the basic functions of farming, including animal husbandry and crop plantings, belongs to the Stentillenians, who originated from the Middle East and settled on the island's eastern shores sometime between 4000 and 3000 BC. They founded small colonies at Stentinello, Megara Hyblaea and on Lipari, where they began the highly lucrative business of trading crafted obsidian, a hard, glassy stone that served as an adequate substitute for metal.

According to the Athenian historian Thucydides (c. 460–404 BC), the island's prime location on the Mediterranean trading routes and the relative success of the Stentillenians in developing commerce made it a much sought-after prize for prehistoric colonists. Consequently, from the middle of the second millennium BC, new waves of settlers began appearing on its shores. From Hiberia (the Iberian peninsula) came the Sicanians, who settled around the coast; they were soon followed by the Elymians – thought by some historians, including Thucydides, to be refugees from Troy, although it is more likely that they were from Anatolia – who occupied the territory in and around Eryx (Erice) and Segesta. Trade with Mediterranean powers such as Mycenae and Minoa grew and brought prosperity to the island, resulting in the fortification of settlements and their transfer to inaccessible higher ground as they sought to protect their wealth from marauding pirates. The settlement on Filicudi's Capo Graziano dates from this period.

Around 1250 BC the first Siculians (or Sikels) arrived from the Calabrian peninsula, forcing settlers on the eastern coast to pack up and move inland. The Siculians (from whom the island takes its name) were particularly successful in establishing working colonies that engaged in agriculture and trading – the vast necropolis of Pantalica near Syracuse was created during this period.

The last of the pre-Hellenic colonists were the Phoenicians from the eastern Mediterranean, who established a number of trading posts along the western coast. According to Thucydides, the Phoenicians filled the gap left by the demise of the Mycenaean trading empire. Here they laid the foundations for a

The Symbol of Sicily

Triskele, the name for the ceramic bowl with three legs, stems from the ancient Greek word *thrinakrie* (*trinacria* in Italian), meaning trident-shaped, the name given to the island by Homer in The Odyssey. Sicily is also known as 'the island of the three promontories' – Capo Faro, north of Messina; Capo Boeo, near Marsala; and Capo Isola delle Correnti, south of Noto – which represent the islands extremities. Sicily's symbol, visible throughout the island, features three bent legs protruding outward from a central sun.

JANE SMITH

number of cities including Mothia, just off the coast from present-day Marsala. Eager to increase the potential for trading, they welcomed the arrival of the Greeks.

The Hellenisation of Sicily

There was no organised invasion of Sicily, nor did the Greeks that settled here all come from the one place. As the great city-states of Greece began flexing their imperialist muscles, so it seemed natural that they would try to carve up the Mediterranean pie between them. A group of Chalcidians landed on Sicily's eastern coast in 735 BC and founded a small settlement at Naxos. The following year a group of Corinthians followed suit and built their colony on the south-eastern island of Ortygia, calling it Syracoussai (Syracuse). In 729 BC the Chalcidians founded a second town south of

Naxos called Katane (Catania) – and so it went until three-quarters of the island was in Hellenic hands. In 728 BC Megara Hyblaea was founded, in 689 BC Gela and in 628 both Selinus (Selinunte) and Zankle (Messina) – the latter on the site of a Sicilian settlement. The last of the great cities to be founded was Akragas (Agrigento), established on the southern coast in 581 BC as a subcolony of Gela.

Initially, the Hellenic colonies lived pretty much at peace with their Phoenician and Elymian neighbours to the west, but the growing strength of Carthage in North Africa soon put an end to good relations. The Carthaginians were keen to establish a foothold in Sicily and, during the 7th century BC, created a string of alliances with the Phoenicians, which naturally aroused the suspicions of the island's Greek powers. By the middle of the next century, however, the Hellenisation of the island was deemed complete. The sole exception was the northwestern corner, still in the hands of the Phoenicians and the Elymians, whose continued presence was bolstered by a powerful Punic army sent from the ancient city of Carthage (on the north African coast), now a formidable force in the western Mediterranean. They created a network of small cities intended to halt the eventual advance of the Greeks.

Still, the colonies of Magna Graecia (Greater Greece) were in the ascendant. Close ties with mainland Greece assured them of profitable trading routes while the plentiful resources of Sicily – supplemented through the introduction of the grape and the olive – were certain guarantees that the colonies would always have something lucrative to trade. The cities they built were a testament to the architectural sophistication and cultural elegance they had brought with them from the Greek mainland, but as the settlements grew in size and importance the colonists sought to outdo the cities in the motherland. As the colonies became wealthier, however, so did greed and disaffection increase. Bitter rivalries, often reflecting those of the Greek city-states themselves, resulted in endless squabbling between the different cities. This sometimes spilled out into open warfare and led some of the more powerful colonies to seek a break from the political hold that the mother country had over them. Furthermore, in a pattern that would sadly become the norm for Sicily over the next 2500 years, the ordinary citizens (mostly Siculians who had been co-opted into working for their new Greek overlords) began to question the oligarchies that ruled them with almost no concern for their general welfare, leaving them in conditions of absolute squalor. In the midst of such upheaval and turmoil the era of the tyrants began.

The Tyrannies

Obliged to expand to stay afloat in an increasingly competitive market and troubled by popular uprising at home, Hippocrates of Gela (498–491 BC) decided in 494 BC that the only way of ensuring his city's continued prosperity was to establish a totalitarian regime with him as autocrat, or tyrant. A few years later Theron of Akragas followed suit, whereupon he decided that what the city really needed was not just the firm rule of law, but an outlet to the Tyrrhenian Sea. Consequently he sought a temporary alliance with Hippocrates and they led their combined forces into Phoenician-Punic territory and annexed the colony at Himera. The death of Hippocrates brought Gelon to power in Gela, and he also seized Syracuse and made it the capital of his dominion.

Deeply concerned by the developments in Hellenic Sicily, the Carthaginians were quick to initiate a counter-offensive. They formed a rapid alliance with a number of city-states alarmed by the expansionist tendencies of Syracuse and Agrigento and in 480 BC sent a massive army led by Hamilcar to Himera. On 4 September the Carthaginians met the combined armies of Theron and Gelon and were convincingly defeated. Although this didn't spell the end of Carthage's involvement in Sicilian affairs, it marked the dramatic rise in importance of Syracuse, which soon came to be the dominant power on the island.

The meteoric rise of Syracuse under suc-cessive tyrants stirred another of the Mediterranean's great powers into action, but this time the foe was mighty Athens herself. One hundred years earlier it would have been unthinkable for a Sicilian colony to challenge the hegemony of mainland Greece, but under the tyrants all the rules had changed. Syracuse was now a direct rival to Athenian power; in 415 BC Athens decided to punish the Sicilian 'upstart' by deploying the largest fleet ever assembled, to subdue Syracuse. The Great Expedition, as it was known, resulted in a crushing defeat for Athens two years later. Seven thousand soldiers were captured and imprisoned in Syracuse's notorious limestone quarries, where many died or were sold into slavery.

The victory over Athens marked the zenith of Syracusan power on the island. The rest of Sicily, however, was in a constant state of civil war, which provided the perfect opportunity for Carthage to seek its revenge for Himera. In 409 BC a new army, this time led by Hamilcar's bitter but very brilliant nephew Hannibal, wreaked havoc in the Sicilian countryside, completely destroying Selinunte, Himera, Agrigento and Gela. In 405 BC the Syracusan tyrant Dionysius I (405–367 BC) launched a counter-offensive which resulted in the complete destruction of the Phoenician city of Mothia between 398 and 397 BC.

Needless to say, Sicily was nothing short of a bloody battlefield throughout this period, and peace was very much in demand.

The Romans in Sicily

Although Timoleon (345–336 BC) did much to bring peace to the island, rebuilding cities and repopulating the island with a fresh wave of settlers from Greece and the Italian mainland, the days of Greek domination in Sicily were numbered. Under Agathocles (317–289 BC) Syracuse once again went on the rampage, fighting virtually everyone who stood in her way. Hieron II (265–215 BC) attempted to restore some order by forming an alliance with mainland Italy's newest power, Rome, but other than protect Syracuse during the First Punic War (264–241 BC), the alliance did little to stop the Roman tide that was sweeping its way across the Mediterranean basin. The end drew near in 213 BC when the Syracusans – caught between a rock and a hard place – made the disastrous mistake of siding with Carthage during the Second Punic War. Rome was unforgiving in victory and in 211 BC completed the conquest of Sicily which had begun in earnest after their victory in the First Punic War.

Under Roman rule Sicily was treated as a sub-colony whose inhabitants were not granted the right of citizenship. Consequently they were a largely dispossessed people whose only maintenance came from their service as indentured peasants and slaves on the large *latifondi* (landed estates) set up by their conquerors from the Italian mainland. The vast majority of Sicilians – most of them still Greek-speaking – were kept in conditions of such abject poverty that the rule of the most vicious of Syracusan tyrants seemed like a golden age. In 135 BC the first slave revolt occurred, led by Eunus of Henna (Enna) and involving tens of thousands of men, women and even children. No sooner had the Romans suppressed the first revolt than the Second Servile War broke out (104–101 BC), with the rebellious slaves supported by a large chunk of the island's peasant class. This too was suppressed with great severity.

As the need to feed an ever-expanding Rome grew, Sicily's forests were felled to make way for the plantation of grain, which then became the island's main export – with the vast majority of the profits being channelled directly into the pockets of the Romans themselves. Under the praetorship of Verres (73–71 BC) Sicily's temples (or, at least, those that were still standing) were stripped of all their treasures, an act which so provoked Cicero that he prosecuted the praetor, successfully condemning him in two orations delivered in the Senate in Rome.

Although treated as little more than the Roman breadbasket, Sicily was to play a key role in the final days of the Roman republic. Following the political vacuum that was created by the murder of Julius Caesar

in 44 BC, the popular and successful general Sextius Pompey sought to gain an advantage over his rivals to the seat of power – the triumvirate of Mark Antony, Lepidus and Octavius – by seizing the island and blocking all transfer of grain to the Italian mainland. Pompey held on for eight years, supported by a majority of Sicilians, but in 36 BC Octavius defeated his rival in a naval battle off the coast of Milazzo. Not forgetting Sicily's support of Pompey throughout the civil war, Octavius exacted a bloody retribution on the island which only ended when he was finally crowned as the emperor Augustus in 27 BC.

With the demise of the Republic, Sicily underwent a period of peace and relative prosperity as it once again became an important centre of trade within the Roman empire. Syracuse experienced a partial rebirth as an important commercial centre, and the period coincided with the construction of some of the finer monuments of the Roman occupation, including the Roman villa at Casale. In the 3rd century AD Sicilians were finally granted the right to citizenship, but the end was already in sight for the greatest empire the world had ever seen. The Barbarians were knocking at the door and were keen to come in.

The Byzantine Interlude

After Rome fell to the Visigoths in AD 410 Sicily was occupied by Vandals from North Africa, but their tenure was relatively brief. In 535 the Byzantine general Belisarius landed an army and was welcomed by a population that, despite over 700 years of Roman occupation, was still largely Hellenised, both in language and custom. The Byzantines had great plans for the island, and were eager to use it as a launching pad for the retaking of Saracen lands with a view towards building a Christianised empire under the rule of Rome and the papacy. In 663 Syracuse temporarily supplanted Constantinople as the capital of the empire, but dreams of Byzantine greatness were not to be realised. A new power was emerging in the Mediterranean and its sights were firmly set on Sicily.

Saracen Sicily

By AD 700 the Moors were already in control of the North African coast and Spain, and considered Sicily a strategic stepping stone in their territorial expansion and consolidation of the Mediterranean trading routes. Although the island had been subjected to repeated raids and Pantelleria had fallen under Arab control, it was not until 827 that a full-scale invasion took place. A combined army of Arabs, Berbers and Spanish Muslims – collectively termed Saracens – landed at Mazara del Vallo at the invitation of a Byzantine general rebelling against the emperor. In 831 Palermo fell, followed by Syracuse in 878, its resistance punished by the wholescale massacre of its citizens and the stripping of all its wealth. Yet despite this the Saracen occupation of Sicily can be considered one of the better periods of its history, a time when a substantial section of the Sicilian population reaped a share of the rewards accrued from the renewed prosperity.

First and foremost, the Saracens introduced widespread agrarian reform. The large estates were broken up and the lands put under the direct control of the peasants with a view towards encouraging free trade. New crops were introduced, including citrus trees, date palms and sugar cane. More importantly, the Saracens developed and perfected a system of water supply and irrigation that was based on the maintenance of large tracts of woodland in the interior and marshlands along the coast, thereby preserving a moist micro-climate from which water could be drawn. Existing bridges and aqueducts were reinforced and new ones built, while the Saracens applied their skill in urban planning to redraw and redesign the layouts of cities and towns.

Sicily became an important centre for the expansion of Islam, but a policy of religious tolerance towards non-Muslims was also exercised. This was largely down to the taxation system which, although more equitable than at any other time in Sicily's history, was designed so that non-Muslims would pay higher taxes than Muslims. Consequently, it was not in the Saracens'

interest to convert the population – though many Sicilians converted of their own accord to avoid paying higher taxes.

After the invasion, Palermo was chosen as the capital of the emirate and, over the next 200 years, became one of the most splendid cities in the Arabic world, a haven of culture and commerce rivalled only by Córdoba in Spain.

The Norman Invasion

By 1040, however, Arab Sicily was in crisis. The Kalbidi (or Aghlabid) dynasty of Tunisia, which had ruled the emirate without interruption since 947, were replaced by the Egyptian Fatimid clan who chose Cairo as their new capital, once more leaving Sicily on the periphery of power. Meanwhile, the Normans had begun a steady campaign of conquest and expansion in southern Europe, primarily through the efforts of the Hauteville brothers: the eldest, William 'Bras de Fer', defeated the Byzantine Greeks who controlled Apulia in 1042, whereupon he was elected count of Apulia. Four years later, he was succeeded by his brother Drogo. Norman activity in southern Italy aroused the fears of the papacy who, although eager to be rid of the Byzantines, were equally suspicious of the Normans (they were considered by Pope Leo IX to be little more than destabilising anarchists establishing a foothold along the southern frontier of the papal territories). The arrival in 1047 of William and Drogo's half-brother Robert Guiscard eventually settled matters in favour of the Normans. For six years he wreaked havoc in Calabria and southern Campania, burning, looting and holding the people to ransom. Such mercenary activity, however, disguised a shrewd and capable military mind, and in 1053 he comprehensively defeated the combined forces of the Calabrian Byzantines, the Lombards and the papal forces an Civitate.

Robert's control of southern Italy, however, was threatened by internal strife bought on by the deaths of his brothers William, Drogo and the recently arrived Humphrey, so Robert returned to Apulia in 1057 to wrest control of the territory from

Humphrey's sons. Having established his supremacy, Robert turned his attentions to expanding the territories under his control. To achieve this, however, he had to deal with the Vatican.

Robert's relationship with the Vatican underwent a radical turn following the Great Schism of 1054, which resulted in the complete break between the Byzantine and Latin churches and forced the papacy into an uncertain alliance with the Normans. In 1059 Pope Nicholas II and Robert signed a concordat at Melfi, which invested Robert with the titles of duke of Apulia and Calabria. In return, Robert agreed to chase the Saracens out of Sicily and restore Christianity to the island; as backup he summoned his younger brother Roger from Normandy in 1060. Roger landed his troops at Messina in 1061 and captured the port after a siege lasting several months. In 1064 he tried to take Palermo but was repulsed by a well-organised Saracen army; it wasn't until Robert arrived in 1071 with substantial reinforcements that the city fell into Norman hands.

Roger was never willing to play second fiddle to his older brother but after their joint capture of Palermo he recognised Robert's role as supreme overlord in return for the title of count of Sicily and Calabria in 1072. Eager to make the most of this new role, Roger set about conquering the entire island, although it was to be another 20 years before the conquest of Sicily was complete. In the meantime, he began to reform the areas under Norman control, beginning with Palermo. The city was fortified, its streets were widened and a number of building projects undertaken. Lacking the personnel to completely replace the Arab system of government, Roger wisely went for a policy of partial assimilation between the two cultures, adopting elements of the efficient Saracen bureaucracy and encouraging the employment of Arab engineers and architects to aid in his construction projects. Roger's dalliance with the Arabs notwithstanding, the Normans did introduce a policy of Latinisation. By 1200 the Christianity had replaced Islam as the official religion and

Italian and French had supplanted Arabic as the island's language.

Roger ruled Sicily with a firm hand, maintaining a permanent army and a fleet at the ready in case there was any opposition to his rule. Robert's death in 1085 conveniently removed him as a potential rival to Roger's control of the island, though in fact Robert had had his sights on larger fry – the capture of the Byzantine throne.

Roger's death in 1101 brought his nine-year-old son Roger (1105–54) to the seat of power after a short interregnum which saw the island ruled by the young Roger's mother, Adelaide of Savona. Unlike his father, Roger was a Mediterranean lord brought up in a cosmopolitan environment. He spoke Greek and Arabic, and was – despite assuming power at a young age – supremely gifted in the art of diplomacy. He used the skill with great success in fending off the local barons, who considered the Hautevilles little more than upstarts attempting to usurp total authority in Sicily. When his cousin William, duke of Apulia, died in 1127 he laid claim to the duchy against the wishes of the barons. He sought the support of Pope Honorius II, who duly invested him with the title of duke of Apulia, Calabria and Sicily in 1128. The pope's death in 1130 resulted in a dispute between two rivals to the papal throne. Pope Innocent II was supported by most of Europe, but Roger supported the antipope Anacletus II; in return Anacletus crowned him king of the Two Sicilies. Eight years later Anacletus died and a brief war between Roger and Innocent II resulted in the pope's capture at Galluccio in Calabria, whereupon Roger forced his captive to confirm his title of king.

The Two Sicilies

Roger II was a brilliantly gifted monarch, a keen intellectual who studied the science of government and built an efficient civil service that was the envy of Europe. He assigned key posts to a number of non-Norman advisers: his finances and army were controlled by Arabs while his increasingly powerful navy was controlled by a Greek, George of Antioch. His court was unrivalled for exotic splendour and learning, while

Roger flaunted his multicultural heritage by wearing Arabic and Byzantine robes and even keeping a substantial harem. His enlightened rule was remarkable not only for his patronage of the arts but also for the creation of the first written legal code in Sicilian history and his success in enlarging his kingdom to include Malta, most of southern Italy and even parts of North Africa.

His death in 1154 left the kingdom in the hands of his son William I (1154–66), known as 'William the Bad', who had none of his father's attributes save a propensity for self-indulgence. During his rule the pope managed to organise the election of his English ally Walter of the Mill (Gualtiero Offamiglia) as archbishop of Palermo, a move that would prove to be a thorn in the side of the Hautevilles for over 20 years. William's successor to the throne was William II (1166–89), who issued a direct challenge to the growing power of the pope on the island when he ordered that a second archbishopric be created at Monreale, only 10km from Palermo. The cathedral he ordered was decorated with some of the finest mosaics ever seen and to this day a visit remains one of the main highlights of a trip to Sicily (see the boxed text 'The Battle of the Two Cathedrals' in the Palermo chapter for details). It is perhaps fitting that his moniker was 'William the Good'.

William's premature death at the age of 36 left the throne in the hands of his illegitimate son Tancred, who was elected king by an assembly of barons. His rule was challenged by the German Hohenstaufen (or Swabian) king Henry VI, who laid claim to the throne by virtue of his marriage in 1186 to Roger II's posthumous daughter Constance. Tancred had a pretty torrid time of it all: apart from resisting the claims of the Hohenstaufens, he had to deal with the barons' decision to purge the island of all Arabs, which forced many of them to leave Sicily for good, and the sacking of Messina in 1190 by the English king Richard I ('the Lion-Heart'), who stopped here on his way to the Third Crusade.

Tancred died in 1194. No sooner had his young son William III been installed as king

than the Hohenstaufen fleet docked in Messina. On Christmas Day of that year Henry declared himself king and young William was imprisoned in the castle at Caltabellotta in Southern Sicily, where he eventually died.

Sicily under the Hohenstaufens

As Holy Roman Emperor Henry chose to pay scant attention to his Sicilian kingdom, and he died prematurely of malaria in 1197. The previous year Henry had attempted to convince the German barons to make the emperor's crown hereditary, but to no avail. His young heir Frederick had to make do with the German crown in 1196 and that of Sicily in 1198. It wasn't until 1220 that the pope crowned him Holy Roman Emperor.

Frederick's rule has been the subject of much debate in recent years, with some historians arguing that he was an enlightened and gifted ruler who managed to impose order on the kingdom after years of uncertain rebellion, while others insist that he was little more than a totalitarian despot who filled his court with some of Europe's great minds. Frederick was certainly a tough and unforgiving ruler, but he had also inherited many of his grandfather's qualities and, like Roger II before him, had a keen intellectual mind and a penchant for political manoeuvring.

In 1231 he issued the anti-feudal Constitution of Melfi, which stripped the feudal barons of much of their power in favour of a more centralised authority – his own. He drew up the Liber Augustales, which created a unified legal system based on the legal code promulgated by the Roman emperor Augustus 1200 years earlier. This guaranteed certain rights to the citizenry while reinforcing the unquestionable authority of the monarch. He became an avid patron of the arts and the first official champion of vernacular Italian. In his *Divine Comedy* Dante devoted an entire canto to the glory of Frederick's court and the marvellous poetry produced therein – to this day Sicilians will insist that the dialect that was the basis for Italian was not Tuscan in origin but Sicilian.

In the latter years of his reign Frederick took to calling himself Stupor Mundi, 'Wonder of the World', a none-too-humble recognition of his successful rule which had brought glory and stability to the island. Sicily had become a homogenised, centralised state which played a key commercial and cultural role in European affairs. Throughout the 13th century Palermo was recognised as the continent's most important city, a centre of learning that was unrivalled in the Western world. Yet Frederick's rule left substantial scars on the island, most notably in the restriction of free trade, the supplanting of rural settlements in favour of massive landed estates, and a heavy tax burden brought on by the pressures of maintaining the empire. Frederick's death in 1250 left the disaffected barons and their foreign allies, most notably the pope, in open rebellion against the Hohenstaufens. Frederick's son Manfred tried desperately to hold on to power, but his rule was seriously challenged when the throne was surreptitiously offered to Prince Edmund of Lancaster, who adopted the title of king of Sicily despite the fact that he had never actually set foot on the island – and never would.

The Sicilian Vespers

The French pope Urban IV decided that Edmund was not the right man for the job and in 1263 offered the crown to Charles of Anjou, brother of the French King Louis IX (later St Louis). In 1266 the Angevin army defeated and killed Manfred at Benevento on the Italian mainland. Two years later, another battle cost the life of Manfred's 15-year-old nephew and heir Conradin, who was publicly beheaded in a final attempt to end the Hohenstaufen line.

Under the Angevins Sicily was weighed down by an onerous tax burden (to pay for the expensive business of defeating the Hohenstaufens) and their rule was marked by the general oppression of the average Sicilian (mainly agricultural labourers), who had sided firmly with the Germans in the war of succession. Many of the baronial fiefs were awarded to French aristocrats, much to the chagrin of the Norman barons, but the break-

ing point drew near when Naples was made the capital of the kingdom over Palermo.

The story goes that it was the rape of a Sicilian girl by a gang of French troops on Easter Monday 1282 that sparked a popular revolt, known as the Sicilian Vespers, by the people of Palermo, who lynched every French soldier they could get their hands on. The revolt spread to the countryside and was supported by the barons, who had formed an alliance with pro-imperial Peter of Aragon, who landed at Trapani and was proclaimed king. For the next 20 years the Aragonese and the Angevins were engaged in the War of the Sicilian Vespers, but it was almost immediately clear that the Angevins had permanently lost their foothold in Sicily. The island was to remain in Spanish hands for nearly all of the next 500 years.

The Spanish Occupation

Once the war between the pro-imperial Aragonese and the pro-Vatican Angevins was concluded with the Peace of Caltabellotta in 1302, the kingdom of the Two Sicilies was divided with the Spaniards taking Sicily and the French retaining control over the mainland territories. Until 1458 Sicily was ruled directly by the Aragonese kings, but their general lack of interest in the island's welfare coupled with the strength of the barons meant that Sicily reverted to a pre-Hohenstaufen feudal regime, with a largely ineffectual central government in Palermo and all the real power concentrated in the hands of the Sicilian nobility, who maintained huge estates on the island. The Sicilian peasantry, which had borne the brunt of most of the fighting of the previous 100 years, suffered greatly, and the decimating effect of the Black Death along with chronic periods of starvation hastened their descent into a state of desperate poverty.

By the end of the 14th century Sicily was marginalised with no commercial or political allies except Spain. The eastern Mediterranean was sealed off by the Ottoman Turks, while the Italian mainland was off limits on account of Sicily's political ties with Spain. The Spanish king Alphonse II (1416–58) attempted to regain a foothold in Italy by retaking Naples from the Angevins, but after his death the city was recaptured by the French and Sicily slid once more into semi-isolation. Even Spain began to lose interest in the island as it concentrated its efforts on the Reconquista (Reconquest) of the peninsula from the Arabs, and started to turn its attentions away from the Mediterranean to the Atlantic as a preferred channel of trade. After 1458 the Spaniards ruled the island through viceroys – the only king to set foot on the island over the next 200 years was Charles V, who docked here for a few days in 1535 on his way home from a crusade.

Culturally, Sicily was almost completely barren and the Renaissance that was sweeping throughout the republics and kingdoms of Italy was barely noticed in this feudal backwater. There were, however, some exceptions, not least in the Catalan-Gothic style that became all the rage in architecture and the fostering of some good local artistic talent, most notably Antonello da Messina (c. 1430–79). See the special section 'Art & Architecture' for details.

Sicily's isolation was to continue unabated for another 300 years. By the end of the 15th century Spain had discovered America and was no longer a major participant in the affairs of the Mediterranean, now the preserve of the Ottomans to the east and the great naval republics of Pisa, Genoa and Venice to the west. The viceroy's court was a den of corruption and mismanagement serving only the interests of the favoured nobility at the expense of everyone else. With the expulsion of the Jews in 1492 the era of religious tolerance was at an end. The most influential body on the island became the Catholic Church (whose archbishops and bishops were mostly Spaniards), which exercised draconian powers through a network of Holy Office tribunals, otherwise known as the Inquisition.

The Rise of Brigandry

Faced with restricted commercial opportunities, even the feudal nobility were forced to make changes in order to survive. They initiated a policy of resettlement that forced thousands of peasant families off the land and into new towns, with a view towards streamlining crop growth on their terrain. Many others moved to the big cities such as Palermo and Messina, leaving their estates in the hands of *massari* or *gabellotti*, bailiffs who were charged with collecting ground rents. The first murmurs of discontent gave way to sporadic uprisings against the overlords, but the most widespread protest against Spanish rule came in the form of brigandry, where small gangs of armed peasants began robbing from the large estates and generally causing mayhem, from burning crops to butchering livestock and killing bailiffs. The local authorities were usually inept at dealing with the brigands, who would disappear into the brush only to reappear and strike again. These bands struck a mixture of fear and admiration into the hearts of the peasantry, who supported any efforts to destabilise the feudal system and were often willing accomplices in protecting the outlaws. Their revolutionary fervour, however, was held in check by the conservative Church, who declared every outlaw an enemy of Christianity. Although it would be another 400 years before crime became 'organised', the 16th and 17th centuries witnessed a substantial increase in the activities of brigand bands, who were referred to by the name 'mafia'. They protected themselves from prosecution by what was to become the modern Mafia's most important weapon, the code of silence, or *omertà*.

The 17th & 18th Centuries

The 17th century brought nothing but disaster to Sicily in the form of plague, cholera and two cataclysmic natural disasters: the eruption of Mt Etna in 1669 and the devastating earthquake of 1693, which destroyed most of the cities on the eastern coast and killed more than 5% of the island's population. Reeling under the weight of natural destruction and state oppression, ordinary Sicilians demanded reform and the major cities, particularly Palermo and Messina, became centres of protest and unrest. The Spanish suppressed every attempt at revolt, but international politics were about to play a part in dislodging the Spanish from Sicily. In 1713, following the death of Charles II of Spain, the island passed into the hands of the House of Savoy as a result of the Treaty of Utrecht, but was traded to the Austrians for Sardinia in 1720. The Spanish reclaimed the island in 1734, this time under the Bourbon king Charles I (1734–59), whose meagre attempts at reform through his viceroy (in keeping with tradition, Charles only ever visited the island once) were cut short when he gave up the Sicilian throne to become King Charles III of Spain. Under the reign of his successor Ferdinand IV – who ruled Sicily indirectly as Ferdinand IV of Naples until 1806 and directly as Ferdinand I of the Two Sicilies from 1816 to 1825 – the landed gentry vetoed any attempts at liberalisation and turned the screws even tighter on the peasantry. The spread of the revolutionary spirit after the demise of France's *ancien régime* in 1789 stopped well short of Sicily's shores, as the island's aristocracy and parasitic bourgeoisie sought to maintain their privileged position through increased repression.

The Napoleonic Wars & the End of Feudalism

Although Napoleon never occupied Sicily, his capture of Naples in 1799 forced Ferdinand to move to Sicily under the protection of the British. Ferdinand returned to Naples in 1802 but was forced out again in 1806, when Napoleon awarded the crown to his brother Joseph. Spanish domination of Sicily was becoming increasingly untenable and Ferdinand's ridiculous tax demands were met with open revolt by the peasantry and the more far-sighted nobles, who believed that the only way to maintain the status quo was to usher in limited reforms. After strong pressure from Lord William Bentinck, commander of the British forces, Ferdinand reluctantly agreed in 1812 to the drawing up of a constitution modelled on the British one. A two-chamber parliament was formed, feudal privileges were abolished, the king was forbidden to enlist foreign troops without the permission of parliament and a court was set up in Palermo that was to be independent of the one in Naples.

Revolution & Unification

With the final defeat of Napoleon in 1815 Ferdinand returned to Naples and abrogated the constitution. He united the two states into the kingdom of the Two Sicilies and took the title Ferdinand I, but the writing was on the wall. The first real uprising against Bourbon rule occurred in Palermo between 1820 and 1821. It was suppressed but followed by another in Syracuse in 1837, when citizens rose up during a cholera epidemic they believed had been spread by Bourbon officials. On 12 January 1848 conspirators in Palermo launched a new uprising which spread around the entire island. On 13 April they declared a provisional government but it soon collapsed under international pressure when Ferdinand of Savoy refused the crown that was offered to him. For the next 12 years the island was divided between a minority who sought an independent Sicily and the reactivation of the old Norman line of kings (one of Roger's descendants was involved in the provisional government, where he took the name Roger VII) and a majority who believed that the island's survival could only be assured as part of a unified Italy.

On 4 April 1860 the revolutionary committees of Palermo gave orders for a widespread revolt against the tottering Bourbon state. News of the uprising reached Giuseppe Garibaldi, who decided that this was the perfect moment to begin his war for the unification of Italy. He landed in Marsala on 11 May 1860 with about 1000 soldiers – the famous *mille* – and set about conquering Sicily. His brilliant command of tactics coupled with a friendly peasantry assured his success: he defeated a Bourbon army of 15,000 at Calatafimi on 15 May and took Palermo two weeks later. His victory at Milazzo on 20 July more or less completed his Sicilian campaign. Incredibly, the island was free of the Spanish for the first time since 1282.

If the Sicilian peasantry held high hopes of finally getting their hands on the land that had been denied them for so long they were sorely disappointed. Despite the revolutionary fervour, Garibaldi was not a revolutionary in the social sense, and his soldiers blocked every attempt at a land grab on the part of the ordinary worker. On 21 October a referendum was held which – incredibly – saw Sicily opt for unification with Savoy by a staggering 99%. According to many Sicilians (most of whom didn't have the right to vote), the island had a new foreign occupier.

From Unification to Fascism

Sicily struggled to adapt under the Piedmontese House of Savoy. Despite unification, Sicily still laboured under a system that was imposed on it by outsiders. Under the new constitution only one percent of the population had the right to vote, as voting rights were linked with property holdings, of which the majority of Sicilian people had none. The old aristocracy by and large maintained all of their privileges and land rights. All hopes of social reform were soon dashed as the new government was either too poor or too ignorant of the situation to affect any real change. Its efforts to centralise power, accompanied by burdensome taxes and military conscription – never before introduced to Sicily – intensified resentment. In 1866 a popular uprising in Palermo was brutally crushed by the Turin authorities who were wrongly convinced that what Sicily needed was a firm dose of law and order to bring it into line.

What the island needed, however, was a far-reaching policy of agrarian reform, including a redistribution of land, which was still in the hands of a tiny minority. The large estates had been partially broken up after the abolition of feudalism but the only beneficiaries were the bailiffs – the traditional gabellotti – who leased land from the owners and then exacted prohibitive ground rents from the peasants who lived and worked on it. To assist them with their rent collections the bailiffs enlisted the help of local gangs, who then took on the role of intermediaries between the tenant and the owner, sorting out disputes and regulating affairs in the absence of an effective judicial system. These individuals were called *mafiosi* and they formed the basis of what

would later become the Mafia of today (see The Mafia later in this chapter).

In 1894 the government (which had moved to Rome from Turin in 1870) responded to the growing threat of an agrarian trade union movement – a loose collection of representative groups known as *fasci* – with the imposition of martial law. What was particularly galling to the Sicilians was that the prime minister who made the decision was Francesco Crispi, himself a Sicilian and a one-time leader of the island's independence movement. Crispi sent 15,000 troops to Palermo to suppress any attempt at revolt on the part of the fasci. His repressive tactics were followed by an offer of mild reform, but this was eventually discarded by the ruling gentry who felt that the government was meddling in their affairs.

By the turn of the 20th century the gap between the south and the north of Italy was wider than ever. Emigration was draining Sicily and the rest of the south of millions of its inhabitants, and despite localised efforts at land reform the situation was going from bad to worse. In 1908 the Messina earthquake left the city in ruins, over 80,000 people dead and tens of thousands of others homeless. By the time Italy entered WWI in 1915 the island was on its figurative knees.

Sicily under Mussolini

In 1925 Mussolini addressed the problem of Sicily by despatching his prefect Cesare Mori to Palermo with orders to crush lawlessness and insurrection on the island once and for all. Nobody was yet willing to admit openly that the Mafia held any kind of power in Sicily, but his intent was clear: upon his arrival, he ordered the round-up of thousands of individuals suspected of involvement in 'illegal organisations'. Free from the constraints of democratic law, Mori's roughhouse tactics were brutally effective, forcing the once ever-present Mafia to run for cover. To help him in his efforts Mori drew on the support of the landed gentry, who were rewarded for their efforts with the reversal of all agrarian reforms achieved in the previous 50 years. Incredibly, Sicily in the late 1920s was still feudal in all but name.

In the 1930s, however, things began to change. Mussolini's drive to gain a foothold in Africa resulted in a massive increase in the demand for grain, and Sicily was declared by the propaganda machine as instrumental to Italy's quest for empire. As the whole island was prodded and encouraged to do its bit for Fascist glory, promises were made (but never kept) of widespread reform that would return land to its rightful owners. WWII put an end to all that. With the help of the Mafia, who were keen to see the back of the Fascist regime, the Allies took the island in just over a month. Few towns escaped heavy bombardment, the scars of which are still visible today.

Post-War Sicily

Following the war Sicily was in a state of upheaval. There was widespread support for the separatist movement, which called for a totally independent Sicily. The Communist Party were also extremely active on the island, organising discontented labourers and peasants into protest groups that called for radical reforms and a total redistribution of land. In response to demands for change, the government decided to grant partial autonomy to Sicily in 1946, but while the new status was met with general approval at a bureaucratic level, it did little to resolve the island's age-old problems. The Mafia, freed from the oppressive attentions of the Fascist regime, were enlisted by the ruling classes to help suppress the spread of left-wing ideologies in the countryside. On 1 May 1947, a May Day celebration at Portella della Ginestra, near Palermo, was fired upon by a gang of bandits led by Salvatore Giuliano, recently defected from the separatist movement – 11 people were killed and 65 wounded in what became a powerful symbol of the Sicilian tragedy.

The most powerful force in Sicilian politics in the latter half of the twentieth century was the Democrazia Cristiana (Christian Democrats, or DC), a centre-right, Catholic party that appealed to the island's traditional conservatism. Allied closely with the Church, the DC promised wide-ranging reforms while at the same time demanding vigilance against Europe's latest threat, godless communism. They were greatly aided in their efforts by the Mafia, whose grassroots control of the countryside had been firmly re-established. They were thus in a position to ensure that the local DC mayor or councillor would always top the poll. In return, the system of *clientilismo*, or political patronage, that became a key feature of Sicily's political activities, guaranteed that Mafia business interests would be taken care of through the granting of favourable contracts in the massive reconstruction projects undertaken after 1950. Inevitably, much of the funding poured into the new Cassa del Mezzogiorno (Southern Italy Development Fund) found its way into Mafia pockets, never to be seen again.

Sicily today is better off than at any other time in history, but the island still has enormous economic, social and political problems. The Mafia, despite an all-out campaign by the government in the 1980s and 90s, is still a powerful presence and the system of political patronage still lives on, irrespective of the demise of the DC (see Government & Politics later in this chapter). Feudal society may be a thing of the past, but the scars it left are still visible: the countryside is dominated by large estates and small towns depopulated through emigration struggle to make ends meet in the face of a demanding economy and the constant presence of the Mafia.

GEOGRAPHY

Extending over 25,708 sq km, triangular-shaped Sicily is the largest island in the Mediterranean. It occupies a central and strategic location, about halfway between Gibraltar and the Suez Canal. Sicily's position just off the western tip of the Calabrian peninsula (Italy's 'toe') has likened it to a football being 'kicked' by the large Italian boot. Physically, the largely mountainous island (83% of the total surface can be described as either hilly or mountainous) straddles two continental shelves: the northern and eastern half is considered to be an extension of the Calabrian Apennines while the southern and western half is topographically similar to the Atlas mountains of North Africa. Scholars have cast some doubt over the popular theory that the island was once part of the Italian mainland and that a rise in the level of the sea caused its separation. Despite being only 3km from the Calabrian tip at its closest point, an alternative theory has suggested that the island was formed immediately following the split between the European and African land masses between 80 and 90 million years ago; as evidence they point to the fact that Sicily is inching its way *closer* to the mainland, not farther away.

The topography of the island is a combination of mountain, plateau and fertile coastal plain. In the north-east, the mountains are made up of three distinct ranges: the Nebrodi and Madonie ranges, which skirt along virtually the entire length of the Tyrrhenian coast up to Palermo; and the Peloritani, which rise above the length of the eastern coast. The interior is mostly hills and plateaux that extend and slope downwards to the southern coast. Sicily's population is concentrated mainly on the fertile coastal plains, largely due to the island's historical importance as a centre of maritime trade. The coasts are an alternating panorama of rugged cliffs and low sandy shores that make up some of the island's most beautiful scenery.

Of the several island groups that are also contained within the Sicilian territory the largest is the Aeolian archipelago, off the north-eastern coast. Off the western coast are the three Egadi Islands of Favignana, Levanzo and Marettimo, while 60km north of the coast of Palermo is the island of Ustica. The islands off the southern coast – Pantelleria and the Pelagic archipelago – are even further away, closer to Tunisia than they are to Sicily.

GEOLOGY

Sicily is renowned for its volcanic activity and the eastern half of the island is dominated by the imposing cone of Mt Etna (3323m), Europe's largest active volcano. Of the 135 recorded eruptions, the last began in September 1999 and was still continuing at the time of research. Although the annals of Sicilian

history are littered with tales of the volcano's destructive capabilities, the last devastating eruption occurred in 1669, when Catania was engulfed in lava. Sicily's two other active volcanoes are both in the Aeolian archipelago. Although both Stromboli (924m) and Vulcano (500m) appear to be smaller than Mt Etna, they are actually both roughly the same size: both are rooted at a depth of about 2000m below sea level, with only their cones breaking the surface of the sea.

Sicily's precarious position between two continental plates has resulted in the island being a major centre for seismic activity. Although most of the Italian peninsula is at risk, earthquakes largely strike the southern half of the country, including Sicily. The most recent quake occurred in 1968, when the western Belice valley was flattened by a powerful tremor. Before that, a cataclysmic quake followed by giant tidal waves levelled Messina and half of Calabria in 1908.

CLIMATE

Sicily is deemed to have a mild Mediterranean climate, which in layperson's terms can be defined as hot, dry summers followed by mild winters with light rainfall. Even the intermediate seasons – spring and autumn – are usually characterised as an extension of the summer, so short is the Sicilian winter. This, however, is far from the whole picture, as the island has a surprising variation of climatic conditions. The finest weather is usually found around the coast, where summer temperatures hover around the mid-30s and in even the coldest winter the thermometer never falls below 7°C, maintaining an average of between 10° and 13°C. The southern and western coasts, however, due to their

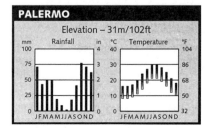

proximity to Africa, are hotter than anywhere else on Sicily, and for six months of the year are affected by the sirocco wind that carries Saharan sand onto the island. In the most uncomfortable months, July and August, it is reputed to make visitors and locals alike tired and cranky. The Tyrrhenian coast is usually shielded by the mountainous interior from the worst effects of the sirocco, while the eastern coast is considered to have the best weather of all, with manageably hot summers and relatively dry winters.

In summer, the cities can a nightmare, especially Palermo and Catania where the oppressive heat combines with the smog to make conditions uncomfortable at best and downright insufferable at worst. Although the 'true' temperature taken at the weather station may be in the mid-30s, the traffic and tall buildings in the cities trap the heat and push the mercury up a few degrees; it is not unusual to get a reading of 40°C or more in July and August. Like most anywhere else, the best place to be in high season is on the quieter stretches of coastline, where a sea breeze usually takes the edge off the worst of the heat.

Sicily's interior presents a different story. Summer days are extremely dry and hot, with little or no respite until sundown, when an evening breeze cools the land – at altitude it can even get quite nippy. During the short winters (December to February, with the coldest month being January), the weather can be bitterly cold, especially after dark. There are two winter resorts on the island, in the Madonie mountains and on Mt Etna, both of which can see substantial snowfall in January.

ECOLOGY & ENVIRONMENT

Sicily is a dramatically beautiful country, with some of the most splendid scenery to be found anywhere in Europe. Yet humans seem to have done their level best to spoil the natural legacy of the island, both on land and off it. Throughout most of the 20th century industrialisation and urbanisation resulted in pollution problems that have yet to be dealt with adequately. In Palermo and Catania car emissions poison the atmosphere with carbon monoxide and lead that on a summer's day is clearly visible as a yellow pall of smog floating in the skies above. The seas surrounding the island, and therefore many of the beaches, have been fouled to some extent, particularly in the industrialised areas around Gela, Porto Empedocle, Augusta and Trapani, where it is inadvisable to go swimming. Aesthetically, these areas represent shameful scars on the island's otherwise pristine coastlines, industrial eyesores that stand in stark relief to the countryside around them.

Sicilians as a whole do not help matters greatly. Although deeply proud of their island, they have an extraordinarily lax attitude towards discarding rubbish where and when they please, something that will undoubtedly alarm most litter-conscious visitors.

Since the end of WWII, another major problem on the island has been that of illegal construction, known here as *case abusive* (literally 'abusive houses'). It is widely believed that the Mafia are involved in most construction projects, which are used to launder ill-gotten money from the drugs trade. Many of the more modern houses built throughout the island, including most of the ugly suburbs that plague Sicily's cities, were constructed illegally. Once the authorities got around to checking whether the builders had permits or not, they were presented with a *fait accompli* and thus could do nothing about the situation. Perhaps the most appalling example of this is in the famed Conca d'Oro valley around Palermo, which at one time was thought of as a type of Eden, overflowing with citrus trees and olive groves. Today many of the trees have disappeared and the valley is ruined by overdevelopment.

Throughout the rural interior you will undoubtedly see plenty of houses that look half-built, with exposed brick and large metal girders jutting out through the top of the roof. Plaster facades are intentionally left off to avoid incurring taxes on 'finished' houses, while the ugly girders exist in the eventuality that the owner's children might need an extension when they decide to marry: a second floor is added to the house and the newlyweds simply move upstairs. Although these practices spoil the environment, it must be remembered that they are often born of necessity. Sicilians are by and large not a wealthy people so they must make do with what they have, especially in the poorer rural communities.

The government's record on ecology is frankly a poor one. The Ministry for the Environment was only created in 1986, and many environmental laws are either badly enforced or ignored altogether. Recycling is almost completely unheard of in Sicily, although in the larger cities you will find the occasional bottle bank – far too few to make any considerable difference, however. The one bright spot is in the recent creation of national parks and nature reserves. See that section under Flora & Fauna for details.

FLORA & FAUNA

The long presence of humans in Sicily has had a significant impact on the island's environment, most notably in the widespread deforestation of the territory that began during Roman times. Enormous tracts of forest – important humid micro-climates that provided water for the land – were stripped to make way for the large-scale cultivation of grain, particularly in the interior, where virtually all of the land was divided up into massive estates to produce wheat for Rome. Along the western coast you will see plenty of vineyards. These were introduced by the Greeks, along with the olive tree, which grows throughout the island. You will also see plenty of citrus groves and – in the west – palm dates, both of which were brought here by the Arabs. Along the length of the southern coast the terrain is characterised by the presence of a North African brush, or *maquis*, interspersed with the occasional vineyard or olive grove.

Sicily's density of population, coupled with deforestation, has had an adverse effect on the island's fauna. Outside of the nature reserves it is most unlikely that you will see any creatures other than sheep on your travels, while the coastlines are home to a regular selection of birds, mostly seagulls and cormorants. Sicily's only poisonous snake,

the viper, can be found slithering around the undergrowth throughout the south of the island – watch out for it at archaeological sites. Even the great schools of tuna, which for centuries were to be found off the western coasts, are fast disappearing into the nets of large Japanese trawlers far offshore.

National Parks & Nature Reserves

Despite their poor track record on the environment, Sicilian authorities have gone to great lengths to protect large tracts of land from the bulldozer through the designation of specially protected nature reserves. The two coastal reserves of Zingaro, north-west of Palermo (see the Western Sicily chapter) and Vendicari on the southern coast (see the Syracuse & the South-East chapter) are areas of extraordinary beauty that are well-run and easily accessible on foot. Here you will find a plethora of birdlife, including the rare Bonelli eagle, the Imperial crow and a species of wild dove in Zingaro; and black-winged stilts, slender-billed gulls and Audoin's gulls in Vendicari.

The Parco Naturale Regionale delle Madonie was set up in 1989 to protect a vast area of mountainous woodland east of the

JANE SMITH

The rare Bonelli eagle is to be found safe and sound in Sicily's nature reserves.

capital (see The Tyrrhenian Coast chapter). It is the only reserve on the island where people actually live, in small towns dotted throughout the hills. Farther west is the Parco Regionale dei Nebrodi (see the Central Sicily chapter), where the San Fratello breed of horses, unique to Sicily, can be found roaming free along with all kinds of farmyard animals including sheep, pigs and cattle.

The island's only national park is the Parco Naturale dell'Etna (see The Eastern Coast chapter), which was set up to protect the volcano from the spread of development threatening its slopes up to the late 1980s. Although there is still a sizeable amount of unwelcome construction on the mountain, the area appears to be in good hands.

The saltpans of Trapani and Marsala are partially protected by the Regione Sicilia, while the long beach at Capo Bianco, near Eraclea Minoa, was purchased by the Worldwide Fund for Nature in 1991.

GOVERNMENT & POLITICS

In 1946, Sicily was declared an autonomous region within the Italian state, one of five to be granted partial or complete autonomy under the post-war constitution (the others are Sardinia, the mostly German-speaking Trentino-Alto Adige, Friuli-Venezia Giulia and Valle d'Aosta), much in the same way as Great Britain devolved powers to Scotland, Wales and Northern Ireland in 1999. The local parliament is known as the Assemblea Regionale Siciliana and is made up of 89 deputies and led by a regional president. The president selects the cabinet *(giunta)* from the deputies, who in turn are responsible for the various departments of state, such as health, the environment, finance and so on.

At the time of research the leading force within the Assemblea was media-magnate Silvio Berlusconi's Forza Italia (meaning 'Go Italy'), a centre-right party that more or less picked up where the DC left off after they were dismantled following the Tangentopoli scandal of the early 1990s (see Political Skulduggery later in this section). Their leader in Sicily is the Agrigento-born Angelino Alfano. There are 11 other parties represented in

the assembly, all of whom have between two and 13 seats. Apart from Forza Italia (which is currently represented with 18 seats), the biggest parties are the neo-Fascist Alleanza Nazionale (a more public-friendly version of the old Movimento Sociale Italiano, the direct successors to Italian Fascism) and the Partito Popolare Italiano, a populist, centrist collection of disaffected socialists and DC. It is difficult to tell the difference between the other parties represented; even their names tend to consist of the same key words but in different combination (for example: Cristiani Democrati Uniti, Centro Cristiano Democratico and I Democrati). The Left has never held much sway in traditional Sicily, hence parties such the Rifondazione Communista (Refounded Communists, formerly the old guard of the Italian Communist Party), Gruppo Communista (Communist Group) and even the Partito Socialista Sicilia (the Sicilian branch of the Italian Socialist Party) figure towards the bottom of the representative scale.

At the time of going to press Italian politics was in a state of flux. Local elections in March 2000 resulted in a shift of power within Italy's centre-left governing party. In April the leader of the oppostion, Berlusconi was calling for an early general election.

Political Skulduggery

Since WWII and autonomy the political system of Sicily has been mired in corruption, graft and cronyism. Dozens of books have been written on the multi-layered webs of scandal and intrigue that have plagued the island over the last 50 years, and it would take more than a couple of paragraphs to begin to sift through the quagmire that is Sicilian politics. Simply put, the two main players in the island's affairs over the last 50 years have been the Mafia and the driving force behind Italy's political oligarchy, the DC, which dominated every Italian government from 1948 to 1994.

More so in Sicily than in the rest of Italy did the one-party domination of the political system, known in Italian as *partitocrazia*, play such a decisive role. It is widely believed that there existed between the Mafia

The Day of the Fox

Giulio Andreotti's troubles with the law started in 1993 when Baldassare Di Maggio, driver to Sicily's Mafia godfather Totò Riina, testified to the anti-Mafia commission that he had witnessed Andreotti and Riina exchanging a kiss on the cheek in the familiar style of two men who know – and trust – each other well. This remarkable statement shook the very foundations of Italian politics, for it was the first time that Andreotti, for decades the untouchable embodiment of the Italian political system, was directly implicated in the Mafia's affairs. Without needing an explanation, most Italians and Sicilians recognised the symbolic importance of *il bacio* (the kiss): if Di Maggio's statement was true, then there could be no doubt about it; Andreotti was indeed in league with the Mafia.

Andreotti was arrested and charged with Mafia association, and in 1994 went on trial in Palermo. Throughout the five-year trial Andreotti displayed an extraordinary forgetfulness about meetings and events at which he was shown to be involved, yet the wily old man – whose nickname was *la volpe* (the fox) because of his ability to manoeuvre himself and his party through the most difficult situations relatively unscathed – never once crumbled under the barrage of interrogation. His most damning admission was that of course he had had dealings with the Mafia – it was impossible to maintain a career in Italian politics without doing so – but that he had never knowingly helped the Mafia in any way nor did he serve as their political godfather in Rome.

Over the course of the trial Andreotti's lawyers did much to destroy Di Maggio as a credible witness, which raised key questions about the policy of pursuing the Mafia through the confessions of its former members, the so-called *pentiti* (literally the 'repented'); after all, argued Andreotti's counsel, why would the court take the word of a convicted murderer and gangster over that of a respected international politician? In a sense, the prosecution didn't just have Andreotti in the dock but the course of Italian history over the previous 50 years, and considering that the country was only beginning to recover from the widespread revelations of the *Tangentopoli* scandal (the institutionalisation of kick-backs and bribes which had been the country's *modus operandi* since WWII), most commentators felt that the country could not stomach the possibility of the charges being proven. On 23 October 1999 the court returned a verdict of 'not guilty' and Andreotti walked out a free man.

and the island's most influential party, the DC, a Machiavellian pact whereby the Mafia would play its part in ensuring that the electorate would vote for the 'right' candidate come election time and, in return, they would largely leave the Mafia alone. Most of the island's governments adopted a 'hear no evil, see no evil' approach to Mafia affairs. On the few occasions that the authorities decided to curb the organisation's activities, their willingness soon faded and the situation carried on as before.

Things, however, are beginning to change. The Tangentopoli (Bribesville) scandal that broke in Milan in early 1992 eventually implicated thousands of politicians, public officials and businesspeople, many of whom were charged with a host of criminal activities ranging from bribery, making illicit political payments and receiving kickbacks to blatant theft. Although largely focused on the industrial north, the repercussions of the widespread investigation into graft (known as Mani Pulite, or Clean Hands) were inevitably felt in Sicily, where politics, business and the Mafia were long-time bedfellows.

Palermo's outspoken mayor *(sindaco)*, Leoluca Orlando, has been the most vocal political opponent of the Mafia's activities for many decades, and for the time being he remains incredibly popular, sponsoring a wide-ranging program of reform and restoration in the capital.

The demise of the DC has thrown the cosy arrangement between political parties and the Mafia – known as Il Terzo Livello, the Third Level – into disarray, as witnessed by the Mafia's wild attempts to assert their illicit authority over the island's affairs in 1992 by murdering the former DC mayor of

Palermo, Salvatore Lima (who despite serving as a Euro MP was later revealed to have been a sworn-in member of the Mafia), and anti-Mafia magistrates Giovanni Falcone and Paolo Borsellino. For more details see The Mafia section later in this chapter.

Italy's most important post-war politician was DC leader Giulio Andreotti, whose brilliant political mind and extraordinary capacity to survive even the most damning scandal will assure him a place alongside Machiavelli in the pantheon of Italian political strategists and thinkers. In 1994 he was charged with Mafia association and in 1995 put on trial in Palermo. In October 1999 he was sensationally acquitted, bringing an end to a trial that had electrified the entire country for five years (for more details see the boxed text 'The Day of the Fox' on the previous page).

ECONOMY

There are two commonly held opinions on the state of the Sicilian economy. While both concur that it is nothing short of a shambolic mess, one view – widely held in the more prosperous north of Italy – is that Sicily is an endless black hole of corruption, laziness and mismanagement that has swallowed without trace the trillions of lire that have been poured into the island via a plethora of development funds. The second view, more common in the poorer south, is that ordinary Sicilians have always been the victims of outsiders' narrow-minded greed, and while the industrialised north may have poured money into reviving the south's economy, there are no 'quick-fix' solutions to a problem that has been 2500 years in the making.

The truth of the matter lies somewhere in between. Of all the southern regions, Sicily is the most troubled economically, mostly because it is so populous. Unemployment stands at an alarming 27%, which is more than double the national average and triple that of the industrialised north. The average wage is just over half of the national average, and less than 40% of the wage earned north of Florence. Poverty is endemic, making Sicily the poorest of all Italian regions and one of Eur-ope's most glaring economic black spots. With Sicily lagging so far behind economically, it comes as a surprise that the island is second only to the United States as a producer of sulphur; that one quarter of Italy's fishing vessels operate out of the island (most of them out of Mazara del Vallo, home to Italy's largest fishing fleet); and that the petrochemical industry is one of Sicily's biggest enterprises, operating huge plants along the south-eastern and eastern coasts, at Catania, Syracuse, Ragusa and Gela.

Despite the growing importance of the tourist and services industries, Sicily remains a largely agricultural region, with wheat the most important crop. Cereal grains are grown on the larger estates in the interior and along the southern coast, while smaller holdings are devoted principally to the cultivation of olives, almonds, grapes, citrus fruit, beans and sumac, which is used in the tanning industry as a dye.

Smaller industries are given over to a variety of other enterprises, including canning and the production of wine and olive oil. In the larger urban centres you will find a thriving cottage industry engaged in the creation of glassware, metalware, ceramics and even matches (thanks to the presence of sulphur).

Such limited industrial activity, coupled with the age-old reliance on agriculture as a source of income, has spelt certain disaster for Sicily. Despite continuous efforts to modernise the island's economy, Sicily remains tied to the economic model created by the Romans over 2000 years ago. For almost its entire history of occupation the island has been methodically stripped of all its wealth, and whatever profits were generated in Sicily were almost always spirited abroad, with little or no money being reinvested back into the economy.

After WWII the government in Rome began to make serious efforts to address the enormous economic gap between the prosperous north and the poor south. In 1950 the Cassa del Mezzogiorno was set up with a view towards rebuilding the south's pitiful economy. Sicily was one of the main beneficiaries of the fund, which poured gigantic amounts of state money into all kinds of projects – from road building to the development of the petrochemical industry – aimed at kick-starting an economic recovery. Enormous amounts of money also came from the European Economic Community's (EEC; now the European Union) regional development fund, which helped finance a road-building project that saw the construction of Sicily's limited network of motorways. In response to the growing northern frustration with the disappearance of so much of the cash into the pockets and bank accounts of the Mafia, the government decided to scrap the Cassa del Mazzogiorno in 1992 and leave most subsides in the hands of the EU.

At the beginning of the 21st century Sicily remains in deep economic trouble. The petrochemical industry suffered an enormous collapse in the 1970s due to the oil wars that resulted from the Organisation of Petroleum-Exporting countries' (OPEC) landmark decision to raise oil prices in 1973. The citrus industry has virtually collapsed in the face of increased competition from Spain, Israel, South Africa and even the United States, who have flooded the Italian markets with cheaper produce. The once-powerful fishing fleets that provided much of Europe's canned tuna have been challenged by the more efficient and mass-producing Japanese, whose nets now catch the majority of the Mediterranean's schools of tuna fish, leaving the local fleets with almost nothing to catch. To add insult to injury, the tuna is taken to Japan where it is canned and then sold back to Sicily.

Although all of these factors play a key role in determining the state of Sicily's economy, the picture is far from complete without a mention of the island's single most powerful economic, political and social force: the Mafia (see The Mafia section later in the chapter for further details).

POPULATION & PEOPLE

According to 1998 estimates the population of Sicily is 5.19 million, 9% of the national population. The birth rate was put at 12.35 per thousand the same year, a little more than the European Union (EU) average of about 12 per thousand – surprising given the Sicilians' preoccupation with children and family.

Most of the island's population lives on or near the coast. Palermo is by far the largest city, with 730,000 inhabitants (over a million if one includes the surrounding hinterland), followed by Catania (376,000), Messina (268,000), Syracuse (125,900), Marsala (80,000) and Trapani (72,500). The largest city in the interior is Caltanissetta, with a population of 61,300. The rest of the interior is relatively unpopulated.

Since the end of the 19th century Sicily has suffered an enormous drain of human resources through emigration. Between 1880 and 1910 over 1.5 million Sicilians left for the United States, and in 1900 the island was the world's main area of emigration. In the 20th century, Sicilians in their tens of thousands moved northward to work in the factories of Piedmont, Lombardy and farther afield in Switzerland and Germany. Even today emigration continues to be a problem, with over 10,000 people leaving the island for pastures greener each year.

With an economy in such dire straits, it is hardly surprising that Sicily does not figure as a port of call for the hundreds of thousands of *extracommunitari* (immigrants from outside the EU) that have flooded into Italy. The only town on the island to have any kind of immigrant population is Mazara del Vallo, which is home to a substantial Tunisian population (around 9000), most of whom work in the fishing industry.

EDUCATION

Sicily's educational system is the same as the rest of Italy's, consisting of a state-school system divided into several levels. Attendance is compulsory from the ages of six to 14 years, although children can attend a *scuola materna* (nursery school) from the ages of three to five years before starting the *scuola elementare* (primary school) at six. After five years they move on to the *scuola media* (secondary school) until they reach the age of 14.

The next level, the *scuola secondaria* superiore (higher secondary school), is voluntary and lasts a further five years until the student is 19 years old. It is, however, essential if young people want to go on to university. At higher-secondary level there are several options: four types of technical school, four types of *liceo* (humanities-based school), and teacher-training school.

The government is in the process of re-forming the education system. The standards of education in the state-run system compare well with those in other countries, although the system does have its problems, compounded by relatively low standards in teacher training and poor government management. Officially at least, only 3% of Sicilians over the age of 15 cannot read or write, although the real figure is probably closer to 5%.

University courses usually last from four to six years, although students are under no obligation to complete them in that time. In fact, students often take many more years to fulfil their quota of exams and submit their final thesis. Attendance at inevitably over-crowded lectures is optional and for scientific courses practical experimentation is rare. Students therefore tend to study at home from books. All state-school and university examinations are oral, rather than written. There are universities in Palermo, Catania, Syracuse and Messina.

ARTS
Literature

Until the 19th century, there was a relative dearth of great Sicilian literature. It all began so promisingly in the 13th century, however, with the birth of the Sicilian school of poetry at the court of Frederick I, which pre-dated Dante and Petrarch in the use of Italian rather than the more accepted language of high literature, Latin. It is a little-known fact (but one acknowledged by Dante) that the first official literature in Italian was born in Palermo. Its authors were the jurists, notaries, captains and officials of the court, who sought relief from their roles as state functionaries in the composition of poems essentially about courtly love, using the traditional Provençal lyric and fitting it to a new metric mould.

One of the earliest exponents of the new school was Jacopo de Lentini (c. 1215–90), known as Il Notaro (The Notary), who invented the sonnet, the school's most impor-

tant and original metric innovation. Other notables included Guido delle Colonne (1210–80), a judge, and Rinaldo d'Aquino, whose splendid *Lamento dell'Amante del Crociato* (Lament of the Crusading Lover) is about the only thing we know of him. Unfortunately, the school petered out with the death of Frederick in 1250.

With few exceptions, such as Antonio Veneziano (1543–93), whose style was a worthy imitation of Petrarch, there were no truly great authors writing in Sicily until the 19th century, when the literary colossus that was Giovanni Verga (1840–1922) emerged onto the scene. His early novels gave little indication of the impact he would later have on Italian literature. It is worth mentioning that his timing was certainly spot on, as he lived and wrote through some of the most intense historical vicissitudes of modern Italian history: the unification of Italy, WWI and the rise of Fascism. His greatest novel is *I Malavoglia* (1881), the first novel of the Realist school, the Italian equivalent of the French Naturalists, whose greatest success was Emile Zola. Verga's classic, essentially a story about a family's struggle for survival through desperate times in Sicily, is a permanent fixture on every schoolchild's reading list.

The 20th century has been kind to Sicilian literature. Playwright and novelist Luigi Pirandello (1867–1936) was awarded the Nobel Prize for Literature in 1934 for a substantial body of work that included *Sei Personaggi in Ricerca di un Autore* (Six Characters in Search of an Author) and *Enrico IV* (Henry IV). Poet Salvatore Quasimodo (1901–68) won the award in 1959 for his exquisite lyric verse, which included delightful translations of Shakespeare and Pablo Neruda. Elio Vittorini (1908–66) captured the essence of the Sicilian migration north in his masterpiece *Conversazione in Sicilia* (1941), the story of his return to the roots of his personal, historical and cultural identity.

Sicily's most famous novel of the 20th century was a one-off by an aristocrat whose intent was to chronicle the social upheaval caused by the end of the old regime and the unification of Italy. Giuseppe Tomasi di

A Sicilian Iconoclast

Acclaimed and criticised throughout his life, Leonardo Sciascia (1921–89) is one of the most important Italian writers of the 20th century. He proudly claimed to have been the first Sicilian writer to directly tackle the contentious subject of the Mafia (in *The Day of the Owl*, published in 1961), a subject that fascinated and tormented him until the day he died. Although radically opposed to the activities of organised crime, he was sensitive to the paradoxical nature of Cosa Nostra, which he considered to be against Sicily yet an intangible part of its social and cultural fabric.

In his later years, he developed an almost irrational dislike for the activities of Giovanni Falcone's anti-Mafia commission, accusing the magistrate of being vainglorious and nothing more than a headline chaser. A committed left-winger, he dallied with the extremist elements during the 1970s and in 1979 published a famous pamphlet called *Il Caso Aldo Moro* (The Aldo Moro Affair) in which he subtly accused the ruling Democrazia Cristiana (Christian Democrats, or DC) of collusion in the kidnapping of the Italian prime minister Aldo Moro by the Red Brigades. Although the popular press derided him at the time, much of what he believed was subsequently proven to be at least partially true, and Sciascia consolidated his position as a hero of the anti-establishment opposition.

Despite his vocal political activities, Sciascia is still best remembered as one of the most extraordinary writers to have emerged from Sicily. His other great novels include *A Ciascuno il Suo* (To Each his Own; published 1966), *Il Consiglio d'Egitto* (The Council of Egypt) and *Todo Modo* (One Way or Another), both published in 1974. His simple and direct approach to narrative marked him as one of the great stylists of the 20th century, while his often black humour made him one of the most widely read authors of his generation.

JANE SMITH

The power of the pen: Leonardo Sciascia confronted Sicily's most volatile issues.

Lampedusa (1896–1957) published *Il Gattopardo* (The Leopard) in 1957 and it was an immediate success with both critics and the public. Although it is strictly a period novel, it is of great relevance to the modern day, as its insightful observations into every stratum of Sicilian society prove the old French adage of *plus ça change, plus ça reste le même* ('the more things change, the more they stay the same').

Leonardo Sciascia (1921–89) used contemporary themes for the body of his work and is recognised as one the great writers of the latter half of the 20th century (see the boxed text 'A Sicilian Iconoclast'). Another contemporary writer worth mentioning is Gesualdo Bufalino (1920–96), whose novel *Le Menzogne della Notte* (Night's Lies) won the prestigious Strega Prize in 1988. It tells the story of four condemned men in a Bourbon prison who spend the eve of their execution recounting the most memorable moments of their lives.

Music

Vincenzo Bellini (1801–35) reigns supreme in the pantheon of great Sicilian composers (see the boxed text 'The Master of Song' in The Eastern Coast chapter), but before him came the versatile Alessandro Scarlatti (1660–1725). Along with the Venetian Apostolo Zeno and the Roman Pietro Trapassi (or Matastasio) he is credited with creating the kind of lyrical opera that later became known as the 'Neapolitan' style. He wrote more than 100 works, including the oratorios *Il Trionfo dell'Onore* (The Triumph of Honour; 1718) and *La Griselda* (1721).

In contemporary terms, there are virtually no writers of good music in Sicily. Aldo Clementi (born 1925) is a classical composer whose name will be unknown to all but serious students of the avant-garde.

Cinema

Sicily has not produced any directors of note with the exception of Giuseppe Tornatore (born 1956). Tornatore followed up on the incredible success of *Cinema Paradiso* (1990) with *La Leggenda del Pianista sull'Oceano* (The Legend of the Pianist Over the Ocean; 1998), a quirky tale of a genius piano player born and raised in the bowels of a huge ocean-going liner. His current project is a film entitled *Malena* which will be released sometime towards the end of 2000.

Puppet Theatre

Sicily's most typical form of traditional entertainment is the puppet theatre, which was first introduced to the island by the Spanish in the 18th century. It provided ordinary people with a chance to attend a 'theatre' of sorts as nearly everything else was closed off to them. The puppeteers re-enacted the old tales of knights and damsels within a modern context, and despite their names – such as Angelica, Orlando, Rinaldo, Astolfo – the characters represented Sicilians in everyday life. The puppets themselves were the creation of a number of extraordinary artisans; in Palermo there was Gaetano Greco, the first of a long line of puppeteers; in Catania there was Giovanni Grasso and his lifelong rival Gaetano Crimi. The last of the great puppeteers was Emanuele Crimi, who died in 1974. Performances are still running at the puppet theatre in Palermo (see Entertainment in the Palermo chapter).

SOCIETY & CONDUCT

It is difficult to make blanket assertions about Sicilian culture, if only because there are huge differences between the more modern-minded cities and the traditional, conservative countryside.

Stereotypes

Foreigners may think of Sicilians as passionate, animated people who gesticulate wildly when speaking, love to eat, drive like maniacs and never forget a grudge. There's a little bit more to it than that, however.

Coming closer to the truth than the traditional stereotype is a description by journalist Luigi Barzini. He has defined the Italians as a hard-working, resilient and resourceful people, optimistic and with a good sense of humour. Sicilians are also passionately loyal to their friends and families – all-important qualities, noted Barzini, since 'a happy private life helps people to tolerate an appalling public life'.

Yet initially Sicilians can be incredibly mistrustful of strangers, particularly those who ask a lot of questions. At first meeting they may appear guarded and somewhat taciturn – a common attribute in the countryside – regarding the newcomer with suspicion and responding to queries with a shrug of the shoulders and a monosyllabic grunt. Remember that this is the land of omertà, which, despite its connotations with the Mafia, is ingrained in the very character of the Sicilian people, an understandable response (or lack of!) to centuries of foreign intrusion. Once the ice has broken, however, Sicilians are as friendly and embracing as any people in Europe; it is not uncommon to be invited into their homes to share in a family meal.

They have a strong distrust of authority and, when confronted with a silly rule, an unjust law or a stupid order (and they are regularly confronted with many of them), they do not complain or try to change it, but rather try to find the quickest way around it.

Family

The family remains of central importance in the fabric of Sicilian society. Young Sicilians tend to stay at home until they marry, a situation partly exacerbated by the lack of affordable housing. At the centre of the family is *la madre*, the mother, the most venerated of all Sicilians. She is considered second only to the Virgin Mary, who many jokingly believe must have been an islander; after all, the son she adored lived with her until he was 30 and when he was killed by the authorities she maintained an air of dignified composure as she mourned!

Still, modern attitudes have begun to erode the traditions. In the larger cities such as Palermo and Catania you will find a vibrant youth culture that has rejected many traditional values as antiquated and out-of-date, although the sexual revolution that has gripped northern Italy is viewed upon with more than a mild hint of suspicion.

Dos & Don'ts

Sicilians tend to be tolerant but, despite an apparent obsession with (mostly female) nakedness, especially in advertising, they are not excessively free and easy. Women, for instance, are sure to be verbally harassed if they wear skimpy or see-through clothing.

Topless sunbathing, while not uncommon on some Sicilian beaches (especially on the islands), is not always acceptable and can often offend. Take your cue from other sunbathers. Walking the streets near beaches in a bikini or skimpy costume is also not on.

In churches you are expected to dress modestly. This means no shorts (for men or women) or short skirts, and shoulders should be covered. Churches that are also major tourist attractions, such as the cathedrals at Monreale and Palermo, enforce strict dress codes. If you visit one during a service (which preferably you should refrain from doing), try to be as inconspicuous as possible.

The police and *carabinieri* (see under Police in Legal Matters in the Facts for the Visitor chapter) may well be used to handling brusque Sicilians, but they don't take kindly to discourteous treatment by foreigners (and have the power to arrest you if they feel you have insulted them) so be diplomatic in your dealings with them!

THE MAFIA
Its Origins

There is no other word in Italy as contentious as 'mafia'. It took over 110 years of common usage before it was officially acknowledged as referring to an actual organisation. Although formally recorded by the Palermitan prefecture in 1865, the term was not included in the Italian penal code until 1982. Even the Oxford English Dictionary, the doyen of impartial opinion, defined the word in the 1970s as 'often erroneously supposed to constitute an organised secret society existing for criminal purposes'. Today, the first five words have been eliminated from the definition.

The origins of the word have been much debated. The author Norman Lewis has suggested that it derives from the Arabic *mu'afah* or 'place of refuge'. Nineteenth-century etymologists proposed *mahjas*, the Arabic word for 'boasting'. A more fanciful suggestion is that it originates from the Sicilian Vespers uprising of 1282; when the French soldiers raped a young girl her mother was said to have cried out *ma fille* and her desperate cry provoked the rebellion against the French. Whatever the origin, the term mafioso existed long before the organisation known as the Mafia, and was used to describe a character that was elegant and proud, with an independent vitality and spirit, much in the same way as the Neapolitan word *guapo*, from the Spanish for 'handsome', was used to describe a dangerous but likeable rogue.

Although mafiosi had been involved in sporadic acts of brigandry since the 13th century – usually to punish a feudal baron guilty of treating his serfs unfairly – their role did not become defined until after 1812 and the abolition of feudalism, when local mafiosi were used as bailiffs or *gabellotti* by landowners to strong-arm ground rents out of the peasantry (see The Rise of Brigandry in the earlier History section).

After the unification of Italy in 1861 the mafiosi, by now organised into small territorial gangs drawn up along family lines, were able to fill the vacuum that existed between the people and the state; the new government was largely ignorant of Sicilian affairs and did not have the means at its disposal to reorganise Sicilian society from a grassroots level. Although evidence of the Mafia's early rise to power is sketchy, it is believed that by 1890 the Sicilian countryside had two distinct authorities: the legitimate forces of law and order, whose presence was largely inconspicuous and in-effectual – as well as grievously resented by most of the peasantry – and a rural Mafia, who comfortably slotted into the role of local power brokers in a land that was well used to taking the law into its own hands.

Up to WWII the Mafia operated almost exclusively in the countryside, controlling rents and extorting a percentage of each crop yield in return for its protection. Their role and presence was never spoken of pub-licly, with every small town and village under their control adhering steadfastly to the ancient code of omertà. Much to the frustration of the authorities, Sicilians kept quiet about every aspect of the Mafia's ac-tivity, denying their existence as much out of fear of reprisal as out of mistrust for what they viewed as a 'foreign' occupier.

It is reputed that Sicily's first real 'god-father' was Don Vito Cascio Ferro, who de-veloped close ties with the American Black Hand, the earliest form of Italian Mafia op-erating from New York at the turn of the 20th century. It would be another 50 years, however, before US–Sicilian cooperation was to radically change the make-up and goals of the Sicilian mob.

The arrival of Mussolini's prefect of police Cesare Mori in Palermo in 1925 was the be-ginning of a 20-year hiatus in the history of the Mafia. Mori's ruthless pursuit of anyone vaguely associated with illegal activities (the word 'Mafia' was never officially mentioned) resulted in the jails being crammed with pris-oners convicted on the most meagre scraps of evidence. While Mori's efforts did not even come close to eliminating the Mafia, it forced their activities so far underground that they were unable to operate as before.

The 'New' Mafia

The liberation of Sicily in 1944 coincided with the freeing of the Mafia from the con-straints of Fascist authority. The Mafia played a key role in the Allied landings, guiding the troops through the mountains and generally ensuring that their passage through the island was relatively untroubled. The fact that Sicily was taken from the Ger-mans in only 39 days was testament to the Mafia's influence in the countryside. After the war, the prisons were emptied of all those unfairly convicted under Fascism, and Mafia activity picked up where it had left off. Or so everyone thought. It was impossi-ble to predict in 1945 that within the next ten years the Mafia would undergo a radical ex-pansion into the cities where it would con-trol a huge percentage of the island's economy; and it was unthinkable to suggest that within 20 years the organisation's dons would be controlling a multi-billion-dollar narcotics empire spread throughout the world.

In 1982 a leading mafioso named Tom-maso Buscetta was arrested in Brazil and extradited to Italy, where he was charged with a litany of Mafia-related crimes, in-cluding murder, money-laundering, extor-tion and drug trafficking. A Palermitan magistrate called Giovanni Falcone (see the boxed text 'Palermo & the Mafia' in the Palermo chapter) led Buscetta's interroga-tion, and after nearly four years the impos-sible occurred: Buscetta broke the code of silence and decided to talk. His revelations shocked and fascinated the Italian nation, as he revealed the innermost workings of La Società Onorata ('The Honoured Society', the Mafia's chosen name for itself) includ-ing how it was organised and who its main characters were. In response to his confes-sion Buscetta was given a new identity and relocated in the USA by the witness protec-tion program. He died, aged 71, in April 2000.

He told of how after the war the Mafia began its expansion into the cities, where it took over the construction industry, chan-nelling funds into its bank accounts and cre-ating an elaborate network of kickbacks and pay-offs that were factored into every project undertaken on the island. In 1953, a meeting between representatives of the Sicilian and US Mafias resulted in the creation of the first Sicilian Commission, or Cupola, on which were represented the six main Mafia families (or *cosche*, literally meaning 'artichoke'), so as to efficiently run their next expansion into the ultra-lucrative world of narcotics. At the head of the commission was Luciano Liggio from Corleone, whose 'family' had played a vital role in developing US–Sicilian relations.

Throughout the 1960s and '70s the Mafia earned billions of dollars from the drugs trade (*narcodollari* in Italian), the profits of which were laundered through a variety of sources, including real estate, urban development projects and – it is claimed – in state treasury bonds, which helped Italy tackle its enormous national debt in the 1980s. Inevitably, the raised stakes made the different Mafia families greedier for a greater share of the spoils, and from the late 1960s onwards Sicily was awash with vicious feuds that left hundreds dead (see also the boxed text 'Where Fact & Fiction Meet' in the Palermo chapter).

In 1982 Pio La Torre, Regional Secretary of Sicily's Communist Party, was gunned down in Palermo as a punishment for having proposed a law in parliament that would have allowed prosecutors greater access to private bank accounts. Three months later, the recently appointed chief prefect of police, General Dalla Chiesa – fresh from his successful pursuit of Italy's Red Brigade terrorist group – met his death when he was ambushed in the heart of the capital along with his wife. In his diary, Dalla Chiesa revealed that he was wary of his appointment as prefect, not because he was daunted by the challenge of confronting the Mafia, but because he felt that the government in Rome was 'isolating' him in Sicily without the effective means to tackle the Mafia. In his abbreviated tenure he had uncovered evidence of corruption at the highest levels of government and suspected that the Mafia's interests were being protected by the upper echelons of the political system. He reserved judgement about the real intentions of prime minister Giulio Andreotti, whom he suspected of having other agendas with regard to crime-fighting in Sicily. These revelations, along with a long list of admissions by Mafia informers, raised the question of what is commonly termed Il Terzo Livello (the Third Level: the arrangement between Mafia and government), an issue that is as contentious today as it was scandalous when it was first revealed.

Dalla Chiesa's brutal murder was only one in a long line of *cadaveri eccellenti* (excellent corpses). His death led to prosecutors and magistrates being granted wider powers of investigation, and in 1986, 500 top mafiosi were put on trial in the first *maxi-processo*, or super-trial, in a specially constructed bunker near Palermo's Ucciardone prison. The trial resulted in 347 convictions, of which 19 were life imprisonments and the others jail terms totalling a staggering 2065 years.

The Mafia responded to the convictions with typical brutality. The murder of Salvatore Lima in 1992 (see Political Skulduggery under Government & Politics earlier in the chapter) was treated in informed circles as a warning to the government to curb the prosecuting magistrates' vigour.

The tidal wave of disgust and anger that followed these brutal murders is arguably the most important development in the fight against the Mafia. For the first time ordinary people spoke out against organised crime in powerful public displays of emotion. The funerals attracted tens of thousands of mourners, and all around the island there was a tangible sense that the people had reached the end of their tether and would tolerate no more. In January 1993 the authorities arrested Totò Riina, who had been living openly in Palermo since 1969. He was charged with a host of murders and sentenced to life imprisonment for all of them, including those of Falcone and Borsellino. At the time of research there were still four charges pending against him, and it is unlikely that he will ever see the light of day again.

The Mafia Today

Following Riina's conviction, other top mafiosi have followed him behind bars, most notably his successor Leoluca Bagarella, arrested in 1995, and vicious killer Giovanni Brusca, arrested in 1996. In 1998 top bosses Vito Vitale and Mariano Troia were arrested and prosecuted, as well as Mafia accountant Natale d'Emmanuele, thought to be the main number-cruncher for Catania's mob. The authorities proudly declared that the Mafia were on the run and that their organisation was permanently damaged.

Yet many questions remain, particularly about the circumstances of the arrest of Totò Riina. Journalists and commentators alike have wondered how was it possible for the most wanted man in Italy, one of the most dangerous criminals in the whole world, to live so openly in Palermo without benefiting from some kind of official protection? When he was finally revealed to the world in court, it startled many to observe that this criminal mastermind was actually a diminutive figure with a hesitant command of Italian, much in the tradition of the typical, old-style Sicilian peasant; furthermore, the arresting officers found a dog-eared notebook in his pocket full of sums and figures roughly scribbled in with a pencil. Is it possible, people asked, that the world's largest drug syndicate could be efficiently run by a semi-literate man whose accounts were kept in a shoolchild's notebook? Surely, they proclaimed, there was somebody (or bodies) behind him?

Nobody has been able to answer these questions convincingly one way or the other. The Mafia, however, are far from dead and buried. An English journalist once noted: 'Everyone knows that the Mafia and the establishment are intertwined, and that this marriage is one of the pillars of political life in Italy. The Mafia is not only omnipotent, it is omnipresent.'

Indeed, according to the late Tommaso Buscetta the state has lost the will to fight the Mafia, even despite the tragedies of 1992, and has inadvertently made the Mafia a political reality, a role it never possessed before.

RELIGION

Religion is a big deal in Sicily. With the exception of the small Muslim communities of Palermo and the larger community of Tunisian Muslims in Mazara del Vallo, the overwhelming majority of the islanders consider themselves practising Catholics. Even before the 1929 Lateran Treaty between the Vatican and the Italian state, where each recognised the legitimacy of the other and Roman Catholicism became the

> ## Stray Flock
>
> Most Sicilians claim to be Catholic, but ask them about the *malocchio* (evil eye) and see what happens. Most will make a simple hand movement (index and little finger pointing down, with the middle and ring fingers folded under the thumb) which is designed to ward off evil spirits. Others, if pressed, might admit to wearing amulets. A pregnant woman might wear a chicken's neck hanging around her own neck to ensure that her child is not born with the umbilical cord around its neck. Insurance agents can have difficulty discussing life insurance policies with clients, as many of them don't want to discuss their eventual death, or the possibility of suffering serious accidents. This phenomenon is known to sociologists as Catholic paganism.
>
> **Helen Gillman**

official religion of the land, Sicily was incontrovertibly Catholic, mostly due to 500 years of Spanish domination. In 1985 the treaty was renegotiated whereby Catholicism was no longer the state religion and compulsory religious education was dropped, but this only reflected the reality of mainland Italy north of Rome. In the south, the Catholic Church remains strong and extremely popular. Most young people – usually the first to fall away from the Church – still attend Mass once a week.

Some of the older traditions, such as a widow wearing black for a full year after her husband's death, have been largely confined to the small communities of the interior. Here too you will also find that the mix of faith and superstition that for centuries dictated Sicilian behaviour is still strong, and that the local curate is still considered the most important person in the community. Pilgrimages remain a central part of the religious ritual, with thousands of Sicilians travelling to places like the Santuario della Madonna Nera at Tyndaris or the church at Gibilmanna in the Madonie mountains. The younger, more cosmopolitan sections of society living in the cities tend to dismiss their elders' deepest expressions of religious devotion, but most everyone still maintains an air of respect.

LANGUAGE

The official language is Italian, which is spoken by everyone but a minority in the backwaters of the interior. Most Sicilians also speak Sicilian dialect, a rich patois comprised of words of Arabic, Greek, French, Italian and Spanish origin – basically a linguistic amalgam of 3500 years of history. When speaking to outsiders, Italian is used, but when speaking amongst themselves, Sicilians largely revert to dialect. For more information about the Italian language and the Sicilian dialect, some useful words and phrases and food glossary, see the Language chapter later in this book.

ART & ARCHITECTURE

BETHUNE CARMICHAEL

It is no exaggeration to claim that Sicily is a living museum of nearly 10,000 years of Mediterranean art and architecture. Its location at the heart of the Mediterranean brought waves of occupiers to its shores and, while they most certainly wreaked all kinds of havoc, each colonising force also left its cultural stamp in the form of some of the most spectacular buildings and works of art to be found anywhere in Europe – from cave paintings to Doric temples to the glory of the Sicilian baroque. While the particular styles of the colonisers are ever-present, it is also possible to detect the influences of local craftworkers, architects and painters, allowing for a hybrid style that is unique to the island. The problem is that while Sicily is indeed a rich museum, it is a very badly maintained one. A series of devastating earthquakes, volcanic eruptions and a short but spectacularly effective spate of bombing in WWII has left many of Sicily's more noteworthy buildings in an alarming state of disrepair. Although in recent years the relevant authorities have initiated a number of restoration projects, there is still much work to be done, such as finding effective means to curb the pilfering of works of art – a favourite Mafia cash cow – which are smuggled abroad or disappear into the private collections of some very dubious aficionados.

Prehistoric Art

Of all the important prehistoric art discovered in Sicily, the most extraordinary examples are on the island of Levanzo, off the western coast. In 1949, in the Grotta del Genovese, locals uncovered a series of cave paintings and incised outlines made up of 32 separate animal figures depicted in a lifelike style, including cattle, deer and horses. The paintings are thought to date to the Neolithic period (c. 4000–2400 BC) and the incisions to the Upper Palaeolithic (c. 40,000–12,000 BC). On Mt Pellegrino (606m) just north of Palermo, the Grotta dell'Addaura are home to another set of incised drawings dating from the Upper Palaeolithic period. They are remarkable for the presence of human figures as well as the usual representations of animals. There are some fine examples from the Neolithic period, including finds of pottery and basic tools made on Lipari and in the Megara Hyblaea area, north of Syracuse.

Hellenistic Art

Although Sicily has plenty of examples of early Hellenistic art and architecture – including the rock-cut chamber tombs at Sant'Angelo Muxaro and a plethora of pottery on view in most of the island's archaeological museums – it was the founding of Syracuse in 735 BC that marked the beginning of the Hellenistic world's extraordinary contribution to Sicily's artistic patrimony. Undoubtedly, the apogee of their creative talents is the Doric temple, splendid examples of which can be seen at Selinunte, Segesta, Syracuse and at Agrigento's Valley of the Temples, one of the most breathtaking repositories of Greek architecture in the world.

Traditionally, the Doric temple was built to a rectangular plan with a divided interior, often with an end space which was occupied by the main altar. Most were colonnaded, although variations can be seen at Agrigento, such as the now ruined Tempio di Giove (Temple of Jupiter), where you can still make out the half columns and telamons (oversized human figures) which once topped them and supported the roof. The unusual temple at Segesta is a peristyle (a court surrounded by a columned portico) at the centre of which is an altar (although experts disagree on whether it was ever finished). The temple's slightly stunted appearance was an aesthetic choice, made with its location atop a hill in mind.

CHRISTOPHER WOOD

The best examples of the Sicilian Doric style, however, can be seen at Selinunte, whose temples show a break with the classic Greek model. The imposing Temple C once featured sculpted reliefs on the metopes and a Gorgon's head on the tympanum (the area above the main doorway), additions that were rare in Greece and not present on any of Sicily's other Doric temples (these can now be viewed in the Museo Archeologico Regionale in Palermo). Furthermore, the architects designed it so that the spacing of the columns at both the sides and the ends is the same, an aesthetic deviation from the standard model where the side columns are usually built closer together.

Above right: Built in the 5th century BC, Temple E is the crowning glory of the archaeological site at Selinunte.

The Greek theatre is another highlight of Hellenistic architecture, even

BETHUNE CARMICHAEL

though most of them were either modified or completely rebuilt during the Roman occupation. The best example of an original temple is at Segesta. It is relatively intact and benefits from the most spectacular natural setting on the island, with panoramic views of the valley below and the sea acting as a breathtaking backdrop to the stage. Other outstanding examples can be seen at Syracuse (perhaps the island's most famous theatre) and at Taormina, although both were heavily altered to allow the Romans to stage gladiatorial battles instead of plays.

The artistic achievement of the Sicilian Greeks was not limited to architecture alone. They produced a phenomenal amount of pottery, including the particularly beautiful red-and-black *kraters* (vases) which came from Gela. The world's most important collection of these vases is exhibited at the archaeological museum in Gela.

Roman Architecture

The Romans were less interested than the Greeks in enhancing Sicily's artistic wealth, and most of their contributions were public buildings, such as the theatre in Catania and the aqueduct at Termini Imerese. One outstanding exception is the Roman villa (Villa Romana) at Casale, just outside Piazza Armerina. This fantastic complex made up of four separate groups and totalling 50 rooms, galleries and corridors once belonged to the co-emperor Maximian, who ruled jointly with Diocletian in the 3rd century AD. The villa's ruins are mightily impressive, but the real draw are the extensive polychrome floor mosaics. These finely executed mosaics testify to the wonderful skill of the craftsmen (almost certainly imported from North Africa) in creating a variety of realistic and natural episodes in minute detail, from an exhaustive portrayal of a great hunt to scenes from Greek mythology and even ten female figures clad in what must be the world's first bikinis.

Above: A spectacular 3rd century BC Greek theatre overlooks the glitzy resort town of Taormina.

From the Byzantines to the Normans

The Byzantines limited themselves to converting some of Sicily's Doric temples to Christian basilicas. The best example of this crossover can be seen in Syracuse's cathedral, which clearly shows both styles. Ironically, it would be another 300 years before the Byzantines left their indelible mark on the island's architectural treasures, after the Arab occupation when the Byzantines were invited back to Sicily by the island's latest conquerors, the Normans.

Little too remains of Arab rule on the island. Their contribution was mainly to urban planning: they developed the 'branching tree' style of street grid, with main roads having minor offshoots that ended in blind alleys. Again, Arab art did not truly flourish until Norman times, when the Arab craftworkers and designers were actively encouraged to express themselves as part of a grander, symbiotic style that was particular to Sicily. This Arab-Norman collaboration perhaps represents its greatest period of artistic development.

Sicilian Romanesque

The Normans were a clever bunch and by the middle of the 11th century their domination of Sicily was virtually complete. The early stages of their rule were characterised by an intense period of artistic creativity and construction that resulted in the Sicilian Romanesque style, an intoxicating fusion of Byzantine, Arabic and Norman design and building. The defeat of the Arabs and the wisdom of the Normans in not turning their backs on the substantial skills and aesthetic sense of the Saracen period, coupled with the return of many Byzantine craftsmen who had fled the island during the Arab occupation, created an exciting, multi-cultural atmosphere. This was actively encouraged and patronised by the clergy, who along with the Norman barons were responsible for commissioning the period's most important buildings – the cathedrals. Indeed, it is in ecclesiastical architecture that we can see the best of what the Normans had to offer.

Although there are a myriad of fine examples of Norman cultural expression in Sicily, including plenty of fortified strongholds and a plethora of churches, the apotheosis of the Hauteville rule can be seen in the cathedrals at Monreale and Cefalù, along with the Palazzo dei Normanni in Palermo. The first great cathedral was commissioned by Roger II (1131–54) at Cefalù in classic Romanesque style – with a chevron pattern and a Latin-cross plan made up of a long, tall nave, a deep choir stall and two flanking chapels – although typically Sicilian touches can be detected, such as the use of pointed arches and angled columns. The decoration of the interior, however, stands out as one of the finest anywhere in Europe. The extensive mosaics – with the dominant figure of the long-faced Christ Pantokrator (all-powerful) at the centre – were created in classical style by Byzantine craftsmen. Yet despite their beauty they fall somewhat short of the mosaics at Monreale, which represent

Sicily's greatest contribution to European art in the Middle Ages. It is the sheer scale of the decoration that at first overwhelms, but the closer one examines them the more one appreciates their unsurpassed beauty and profound spiritual effect. Here, unlike the mosaics at Cefalù, one can detect a break with the rules of Byzantine representative art: the stories of the Bible are executed starting at the church's main entrance and proceed in chronological order from the Creation to the Last Judgement – a tacit indication of the Norman barons' desire to see the Roman west dominant over the Orthodox east. Their iconography was also influenced by contemporary events, hence the appearance of the recently canonised Thomas à Becket as one of the key saints. In the cloister is the largest collection of Norman sculpture in Sicily, consisting of over 200 colonnettes with twin capitals and each featuring a singular composition.

The third building of this magnificent trio is the enormous Palazzo dei Normanni in Palermo, the stronghold of Norman power in Sicily and the seat of the Hauteville dynasty. The palace was originally built by the Arabs in the 9th century but was enlarged by the Normans between 1132–40. The real attraction at the heart of this monolithic structure is the exquisite Cappella Palatina (Palatine Chapel), which features an Egyptian-style cupola and a wooden honeycomb ceiling

Below: Detail from the Capella Palatino, Palazzo dei Normanni, Palermo.

that is undoubtedly inspired by Arabic screen designs. The chapel itself is devoted to Christian worship though decorated with scenes from a variety of sources, including Greek, Persian and Indian myths as well as visual representations of key moments in the Bible. It was largely designed, constructed and decorated by local workers and is a perfect example of the fusion of styles that sets the Sicilian Romanesque apart from other forms used in mainland Italy.

The key buildings of secular architecture can be found in and around Palermo, and include the graceful palace of La Zisa, summer residence of the Hauteville kings. Again the Arab influence is noteworthy, and it is fitting that today the palace serves as the city's museum of Arabic art. It is likely that the palace was also decorated in mosaic, but these have largely disappeared.

With the demise of the Hautevilles and the arrival of the Hohenstaufen (Swabian) dynasty in the 13th century, the emphasis shifted from the creative arts to the erection of mighty castles and fortifications. It would be another 400 years before Sicily witnessed as rich a period of architectural genius, and then only in response to a devastating earthquake that flattened half the island.

BETHUNE CARMICHAEL

The Renaissance

Although Sicily did not figure too much in the new learning and aesthetic principles that swept first through Italy and then Europe during the Renaissance – under Spanish occupation, Sicily was often excluded from events on the Italian mainland – Sicilian painting and sculpture was very much in the ascendancy, only its influences were mostly Spanish and Flemish. The first of the great Sicilian artists was Antonello da Messina (1430–79) who trained in the Flemish style but later allowed his work to show influences of Piero della Francesca, one of the earliest luminaries of Renaissance art. In sculpture and architecture, the dominant school of the 15th and 16th centuries was founded by Domenico Gagini (1420–92), a student of the Quattrocento (1400s) Florentine style who almost single-handedly dragged Sicilian design out of the Middle Ages and created a style that fused local designs with those more popular on the Italian mainland. Another important sculptor was Francesco Laurana (1430–1502) who, like Gagini, was heavily influenced by the early Renaissance. Although Laurana spent only a brief period of his prolific career in Sicily, his influence on Sicilian artists was considerable. Traditional styles persisted, particularly in the construction of fortified homes, which copied the Arab-Norman model – which was medieval in appearance, with plenty of rustication and squinches (a narrow slit window at a corner) – rather than contemporary forms.

Sicilian Baroque

The most important artistic and architectural development since the early Middle Ages was the explosion of the baroque style, which became widespread throughout the south-east of the island following the devastating earthquake of 1693. Towns that were almost entirely destroyed were rebuilt in this elegant new style; these included Noto, Modica, Ragusa, Catania and large parts of Syracuse. The dominant figure at this time was Rosario Gagliardi (1700–70), the engineer and architect considered to be the father of Sicilian baroque. He was the designer of the splendid Cattedrale San Giorgio at Ragusa Ibla as well as the Chiesa di San Giorgio in Modica. GB Vaccarini (1702–68) introduced the Roman baroque to Catania and his work shows the distinctive influence of Francesco Borromini. In Syracuse, Andrea Palma (1664–1730) designed the wonderful facade of the city's cathedral, adding yet another cultural layer to the church and its history.

Modern Art

There is an alarming dearth of good modern art in Sicily. The island's greatest modern painter, Renato Guttuso (1912–87), was renowned for painting in a visceral style that reflected his Sicilian 'nature'; consequently, his paintings are bursting with colour and portray the island and its personalities in all their harshness and beauty.

Facts for the Visitor

SUGGESTED ITINERARIES

You could cover quite a bit of ground in a week, especially if you have your own vehicle, but unless you plan a 'click-and-run' tour you will have to limit yourself to a handful of towns and sights. Ten days or two weeks is plenty of time to acclimatise yourself and to get the most out of what Sicily has to offer. If you plan a longer stay you can explore the island at your leisure, stopping at length in various towns, cities and offshore islands; only then will you begin to understand the often contradictory nature of this extraordinary place, which can infuriate and charm at the same time. Below are a couple of itineraries that might help you organise your trip. These are merely suggestions, however; while in Sicily you may find yourself sitting tight in one or two particular places because the thought of leaving them is too much: the island can have that effect!

One Week

You should devote at least one day to exploring Palermo. Make sure you put a few hours aside to get to the Cattedrale di Monreale. Your next objective should be Agrigento, within easy striking distance of the capital, from where you could head east along the coast to Syracuse. Once you're done with the baroque south-east, Mt Etna is next. If you're fixed on incorporating a little sun-worshipping you could make the short trip up the coast from Catania to the resort town of Taormina. Alternatively, if beaches and bronzing are not your thing, you could go inland from Catania towards Enna, and on to Piazza Armerina and the Villa Romana (Roman villa) at Casale. From the capital you can also travel along the Tyrrhenian coast to Milazzo and the Aeolian Islands.

Two Weeks

Two weeks should give you enough time to explore some of the island's less touristy areas. From Palermo you can move in a westerly arc that will take in small coastal resorts and the Riserva Naturale dello Zingaro. From there you could move south to Trapani, a good base for visiting the province. The medieval hill town of Erice, near Trapani, is perhaps Sicily's most picturesque town. While in the west, you shouldn't

Highlights

Sicily is crammed with great things to see and do, from ancient Greek sites to mountain walks. Below is our guide to the top sights and activities on this diverse island. Don't leave Sicily without having experienced them!

- The breathtaking mosaics in the cathedral at Monreale, the Byzantine equivalent of Michelangelo's Sistine Chapel
- The extraordinary ruins of the Valley of the Temples in Agrigento, the highlight of Goethe's 18th-century trip to Sicily and still one of the island's greatest crowd-pleasers
- The spectacular eruptions of Stromboli's volcano when viewed at dusk
- Walking to the summit of Mt Etna, which on a clear day affords views of virtually half the island
- The island of Ortygia in Syracuse: the graceful elegance of Piazza del Duomo makes it one of Sicily's finest squares
- The magnificent polychrome mosaics of the Roman villa at Casale just outside Piazza Armerina, still captivating after 700 years spent buried in mud
- The Greek theatre at Segesta, an incomparable combination of architectural elegance and wonderful natural setting, with great views of the surrounding countryside
- A summer recital in the ruins of the Chiesa di Santa Maria dello Spasimo in Palermo; there is no better setting for good music
- The medieval hill town of Erice near Trapani, perhaps Sicily's prettiest town
- Lying on the beach at Cefalù in September: the crowds are gone but the sun shines on

miss Segesta and Selinunte which, along with the Valley of the Temples in Agrigento, are Sicily's premier ancient Greek sites. Next you can move on to Agrigento itself, perhaps stopping at Eraclea Minoa where you can relax on the gorgeous beach. If you're a classical buff you might want to visit the top-notch archaeological museum in Gela. From there you can either head into the interior or continue east. Moving along the eastern coast you might want to spare a day for Catania. Next head for Mt Etna by bus. Taormina and the Aeolian Islands are the next obvious destinations. From Cefalù you can visit the hill towns to the south and the Parco Naturale Regionale delle Madonie, one of the most impressive landscapes on the island.

PLANNING
When to Go
The best time to visit Sicily is in the low season, from April to June and September and October, when the weather is usually good, prices are lower and there are fewer tourists. Late July and August are the times to avoid the place: the sun broils, prices are inflated and the island's top attractions are awash with a tide of holidaymakers. Most of Italy goes on holiday in this period – especially August – and a chunk of them choose Sicily as their preferred destination.

The sunshine spots – the beaches and offshore islands – warm up relatively early, usually around mid-April, and stay hot well into October, so you can still enjoy a sea-and-sun holiday when the rest of Italy is dusting off their heavy sweaters. The same is true of the natural parks, particularly Madonie and Mt Etna: these are best visited in the months surrounding July and August. The dramatic effect of climbing Mt Etna is somewhat spoilt by having to wait an hour in a queue to board the cable car.

You may prefer to organise your trip to coincide with one or more of the many festivals that festoon the Sicilian calendar – Easter is a particular highlight, with the whole island given over to the celebrations. Turn to the Special Events section later in this chapter for more information.

What Kind of Trip
There are several ways to organise your trip around Sicily other than simply touring the main towns and cities. If you fancy a sea-and-sun holiday, there are fewer places in the whole of Italy that are better, with plenty of resorts, beachfront towns and offshore islands expressly given over to that purpose. The island is rich in tradition and culture, and has a long and varied history, so you could easily organise your trip according to a theme. Sicily is also small enough to allow you to combine themes.

An increasingly popular option is *la vacanza agrituristica* in the island's interior, which involves renting a house or lodging in a farming community in the countryside (for details see under Agriturismo in the later Accommodation section). In winter, you can even go skiing in the Madonie or on Mt Etna, although the resorts here are small and, while there is usually snow, it is difficult to predict how much there will be, especially during mild winters.

Maps
Small-Scale Maps The best map of Sicily is published by the Touring Club Italiano (TCI) at a scale of 1:200,000. It costs L9500 and you can buy it at all bookshops, airports and at cafes along the motorways in Sicily. Michelin also has a good fold-out map (No 432) of Sicily and the offshore islands at a scale of 1:400,000.

Road Atlases The AA's *Big Road Atlas – Italy*, available in the UK for £9.99, includes Sicily; the scale is 1:250,000. De Agostini's *Atlante Turistico Stradale della Sicilia* (1:250,000) contains city plans and tourist itineraries and costs L34,000. It is available in bookshops throughout the island.

What to Bring
Pack as little as possible. A backpack is an advantage since petty thieves prey on luggage-laden tourists with no free hands. Backpacks with straps and openings that can be zipped inside a flap are less awkward and more secure than the standard ones.

Suitcases with portable trolleys may be fine in airports but you won't get far on foot with them. If you must carry a suitcase/bag, make sure it is lightweight and not too big. Remember that most everyday necessities can be found easily in Sicily – there is no need to stock up in advance and drag it all around with you.

A small pack (with a lock) for day trips and sightseeing is preferable to a handbag or shoulder bag.

Clothes Sicily is scorching hot in summer, with temperatures in the high 30s or even low 40°s Celsius. Consequently, you should stick to the lightest fabrics, such as thin cotton T-shirts and shorts. If you plan on entering churches or other religious buildings – and sightseeing in Sicily involves a lot of them – be sure to wear something to cover your shoulders and down to below your knees; it is considered an insult to enter a place of worship with bare shoulders. Remember also to bring protection for your head, such as a light cotton hat, to lessen the risk of sunstroke. It is pleasantly warm in spring and autumn, so you won't need anything other than a jacket or a light sweater for the cooler evenings. Winter is usually mild so a lined raincoat should do the trick.

If you plan on travelling in the interior or go walking in the mountains, make sure you bring the necessary clothing and equipment, in particular a pair of walking boots (lightweight and waterproof). Even in high summer you would be advised to have some warm clothing on long walks – it can get chilly at high-altitude spots like Mt Etna.

Like most Italians, Sicilians tend to pay attention to their clothes. Although not nearly as obsessive about their dress as on the mainland, they still like to make an effort when going out, and usually put on something that is casually dressy. You should consider doing the same.

Unless you plan to spend large sums of money in dry-cleaners and laundrettes, pack a portable clothes-line. Many *pensioni* (guesthouses) and hotels ask guests not to wash clothes in the room, but such rules are rarely enforced. Consider packing a light travel iron or crease-proof clothes.

Useful Items In addition to any special personal needs, consider taking the following:

- an under-the-clothes moneybelt or shoulder wallet, useful for protecting your money and documents

- a towel and soap, which are sometimes lacking in cheap accommodation
- a small Italian dictionary and/or phrasebook
- a Swiss army knife
- a medical kit (see Health later in this chapter)
- a padlock or two to secure your luggage to racks and to close hostel lockers
- a sleeping sheet to save on sheet rental costs if you're using youth hostels (a sleeping bag is unnecessary unless you're camping)
- an adaptor plug for electrical appliances
- a torch (flashlight)
- an alarm clock
- sunglasses and a hat
- a universal sink plug

Basic drugs are widely available and indeed many items requiring prescriptions in countries such as the USA can be obtained easily over the counter in Sicily. If you require specific medication, it's easier to bring it with you. Condoms can cost between L12,000 and L30,000 for 12 depending where you shop (supermarkets are generally cheapest).

RESPONSIBLE TOURISM

It would be nice to see more travellers wandering around with an awareness of local sensibilities. Visitors all too often seem to leave manners and common sense at home. In the main tourist centres, locals are by now used to the sight of men wandering around in little more than a pair of shorts and (maybe) sandals. Bear in mind that sunscorched bellies do not a pretty sight make, and less still to a people known for their preoccupation with dressing well.

When visiting sites such as the Valley of the Temples in Agrigento or, indeed, any of the many other Greek and Roman ruins dotted throughout the island, don't go clambering where you are asked not to or have no need to. By leaving things alone you do your little bit to help preserve them. On an immediately practical level, if you're visiting the sites of ancient cities such as Eraclea Minoa or Selinunte, stay on the well-marked paths: there are snakes in the undergrowth whose bite, although not fatal, will require medical treatment.

Don't use flash when photographing artworks in museums, churches and so on. The burst of light can damage the art.

Respect for tradition and religion is deeply rooted in Sicily, so when visiting churches be sure to show the proper decorum. Sicilians do not take kindly to anyone who does otherwise and will not think twice about letting their thoughts on the matter be known. If you must talk in churches, do so in a whisper so as not to disturb those who have come to pray.

The moral of the story is, simply, respect the monuments and works of art, the towns and their people, as you would your own prized possessions. Tread softly. And enjoy.

TOURIST OFFICES
Local Tourist Offices

The quality of tourist offices in Sicily can vary quite dramatically. As you would expect, the tourist offices in popular destinations such as Palermo, Catania, Taormina, Syracuse and the Aeolian Islands are used to dealing with visitors from all over the world, so they are usually well-stocked with information and staffed by employees who often have a working command of at least one foreign language, usually English but often also French, German and others. As Sicilians are by nature a pretty friendly bunch, they will often go out of their way to help you no matter where you are.

The main tourist office for the entire region of Sicily is the Assessorato Regionale del Turismo, delle Communicazioni e dei Trasporti (ARTCT), which is generally concerned with promotion, planning, budgeting and other projects far removed from the daily concerns of the humble tourist. Otherwise, tourist offices in Sicily are divided into two tiers: provincial and local. Regional offices are known as the Azienda di Promozione Turistica (APT). They run efficient tourist offices with plenty of up-to-date information on both the province and the town or city. Local offices in Sicily are known by a variety of names that change according to the town, but the most common are Azienda Autonoma di Soggiorno e Turismo (AAST) or Azienda Soggiorno e Turismo (AST). They only have information on their town,

but are the place to go if you want specific information such as bus routes or museum openings. In many small towns and villages the local tourist office is called a Pro Loco, often similar to the AAST or AST offices but on occasion little more than a room with a small desk where locals hang out and chat.

Although most offices of the APT, AAST or AST usually respond to written or telephone requests for information, you can sometimes draw a blank with the smaller offices or bureaux in places that are off the tourist path, usually because of lack of staff or funding.

Tourist offices are generally open from 9 am to 12.30 or 1 pm and 3 to 7 pm Monday to Friday. Hours are extended during the summer (usually from May to September, but sometimes even Easter to October) when many of the offices in popular tourist destinations are open part or all of Saturday and occasionally even Sunday.

All APT offices and most of the larger AAST and AST offices provide an excellent accommodation guide called the *Guida dell'Ospitalità nella Provincia*. These are updated annually and include every hotel, camp site, hostel and other rented accommodation within each of Sicily's nine provinces.

Information booths at most major train stations and in locations throughout the bigger cities tend to keep similar hours but in most cases only operate during the summer. Here you can usually pick up a map *(pianta della città)*, a photocopied list of hotels *(elenco degli alberghi)* and information on the major sights *(informazioni sulle attrazioni turistiche)*.

The address and telephone number of local tourist offices are listed under towns and cities throughout this book.

Tourist Offices Abroad

Information on Sicily is available from the Italian State Tourist Office (ENIT; Web site at www.enit.it) in the following countries:

Australia
(☎ 02-9262 1666, fax 9262 5745)
c/o Italian Chamber of Commerce, Level 26,
44 Market St, Sydney, NSW 2000

Austria
(☎ 01-505 16 39) Kaerntnerring 4,
1010 Vienna
Canada
(☎ 514-866 7669, ✉ initaly@ican.net)
Suite 1914, 1 Place Ville Marie, Montreal,
Que H3B 2C3
France
(☎ 01 42 66 66 68, ✉ 106616.131@compuserve
.com) 23 rue de la Paix, 75002 Paris
Germany
Berlin: (☎ 030-247 83 97, ✉ enit-berlin@
tonline.de) Karl Liebknecht Strasse 34,
10178 Berlin
Frankfurt: (☎ 069-25 93 32, ✉ enit.ffm@
tonline.de) Kaisertstrasse 65, 60329
Frankfurt am Main
Munich: (☎ 089-53 13 17) Goethe Strasse 20,
80336 Munich
Netherlands
(☎ 020-616 82 44) Stadhouderskade 2,
1054 ES Amsterdam
Spain
(☎ 91 559 9750) Gran Via 84, Edifico Espagna,
28013 Madrid
Switzerland
(☎ 01-211 7917, ✉ enit@bluewin.ch) Urania-
strasse 32, 8001 Zurich
UK
(☎ 020-7408 1254, 0891 600 280, ✉ enitlond@
globalnet.co.uk) 1 Princes St, London
W1R 9AY
USA
Chicago: (☎ 312-644 0996, ✉ enitch@
italiantourism.com) 500 North Michigan Ave,
Chicago, IL 60611
Los Angeles: (☎ 310-820 1890) Suite 550,
12400 Wilshire Blvd, Los Angeles, CA 90025
New York: (☎ 212-245 4822, ✉ enitny@bway
.net) Suite 1565, 630 Fifth Ave, New York,
NY 10111

Sestante CIT (Compagnia Italiana di Turismo), Italy's national travel agency, has offices worldwide (known as CIT or Citalia
outside Italy). Staff can provide extensive
information on travelling in Sicily and will
organise tours, as well as book individual
hotels. CIT staff can also make train bookings and sell Eurail passes and discount passes for train travel in Sicily. Offices include:

Australia
Melbourne: (☎ 03-9650 5510) Level 4,
227 Collins St, Melbourne 3000

Sydney: (☎ 02-9267 1255) 263 Clarence St,
Sydney, NSW 2000
Canada
Montreal: (☎ 514-845 4310, toll-free 800 361
7799) Suite 750, 1450 City Councillors St,
Montreal, Que H3A 2E6
Toronto: (☎ 905-415 1060, toll-free 800 387
0711) Suite 401, 80 Tiverton Court, Markham,
Toronto, Ont L3R 0G4
France
(☎ 01 44 51 39 00) 5 blvd des Capucines,
Paris 75002
Germany
(☎ 0211-69 00 30) Geibelstrasse 39,
40235 Dusseldorf
UK
(☎ 020-8686 0677, 8686 5533) Marco Polo
House, 3–5 Lansdowne Rd, Croydon, Surrey
CR9 1LL
USA
Los Angeles: (☎ 310-338 8615) Suite 980,
6033 West Century Blvd, Los Angeles,
CA 90045
New York: (☎ 212-730 2121) 10th Floor,
15 West 44th St, New York, NY 10036

Italian cultural institutes in major cities
throughout the world have extensive information on the study opportunities available
in Sicily.

VISAS & DOCUMENTS
Passport
Citizens of the 15 European Union (EU)
member states can travel to Sicily with their
national identity cards alone. People from
countries that do not issue ID cards, such as
the UK and Ireland, must have a valid passport. All non-EU nationals must have a full
valid passport.

If you've had the passport for a while,
check that the expiry date is at least some
months off, otherwise you may not be
granted a visa (if you need one). If you
travel a lot, keep an eye on the number of
pages you have left in the passport. US consulates will generally insert extra pages into
your passport if you need them, but other
consulates require you to apply for a new
passport.

If your passport is stolen or lost while in
Sicily, notify the police and obtain a statement, and then contact your embassy or
consulate as soon as possible.

Visas

Italy is one of 15 countries that have signed the Schengen Convention, an agreement whereby all EU member countries (except the UK and Ireland) plus Iceland and Norway have agreed to abolish checks at common borders by the end of 2000. The other EU countries are Austria, Belgium, Denmark, Finland, France, Germany, Greece, Luxembourg, the Netherlands, Portugal, Spain and Sweden. Legal residents of one Schengen country do not require a visa for another Schengen country. Citizens of the UK and Ireland are also exempt from visa requirements for Schengen countries. In addition, nationals of a number of other countries, including Canada, Japan, New Zealand and Switzerland, do not require visas for tourist visits of up to 90 days to any Schengen country.

Various other nationals not covered by the Schengen exemption can also spend up to 90 days in Sicily without a visa. These include Australian, Israeli and US citizens. However, all non-EU nationals entering Italy for any reason other than tourism (such as study or work) should contact an Italian consulate, as they may need a specific visa. They should also insist on having their passport stamped on entry as, without a stamp, they could encounter problems when trying to obtain a *permesso di soggiorno* (resident permit; see under Permits later in the section). If you are a citizen of a country not mentioned in this section, you should check with an Italian consulate whether you need a visa.

The standard tourist visa issued by Italian consulates is the Schengen visa, valid for up to 90 days. A Schengen visa issued by one Schengen country is generally valid for travel in all other Schengen countries. However, individual Schengen countries may impose additional restrictions on certain nationalities. It is, therefore, worth checking visa regulations with the consulate of each Schengen country you plan to visit.

It is mandatory that you apply for a visa in your country of residence. You can apply for no more than two Schengen visas in any 12-month period and they are not renewable inside Italy. It's worth applying early for your visa, especially in the busy summer months.

Study Visas Non-EU citizens who want to study at a university or language school in Sicily must have a study visa. These visas can be obtained from your nearest Italian embassy or consulate. You will normally require confirmation of your enrolment, proof of payment of fees and adequate funds to support yourself before a visa is issued. The visa will cover only the period of the enrolment. This type of visa is renewable within Sicily but, again, only with confirmation of ongoing enrolment and proof that you are able to support yourself – bank statements are preferred.

Permits

EU citizens do not require permits to live, work or start a business in Sicily. They are, however, advised to register with a police station *(questura)* if they take up residence, in accordance with an anti-Mafia law that aims at keeping a watch on everyone's whereabouts in the country. Failure to do so carries no consequences, although some landlords may be unwilling to rent out a flat to you if you cannot produce proof of registration. Those considering long-term residence will eventually want to consider getting a work permit (see later in the section), a necessary first step to acquiring a *carta d'identitá* (ID card). While you're at it, you'll need a *codice fiscale* (tax-file number) if you wish to be paid for most work in Sicily.

Work Permits Non-EU citizens wishing to work in Sicily will need to obtain a *permesso di lavoro* (work permit). If you intend to work for an Italian company and will be paid in lire, the company must organise the permit and forward it to the Italian embassy or consulate in your home country – only then will you be issued with an appropriate visa.

If non-EU citizens intend to work for a non-Italian company, will be paid in foreign currency or wish to go freelance, they must organise the visa and permit in their country of residence through an Italian embassy or consulate. This process can take several months – so look into it early.

It is in any case advisable to seek detailed information from an Italian embassy or consulate on the exact requirements before attempting to organise a legitimate job in Sicily. Many foreigners, however, don't bother with such formalities, preferring to try and work illegally (*al nero*, literally 'in black'). See the Work section later in the chapter for details.

Permesso di Soggiorno If you intend to stay at the same address for more than one week, you are technically obliged to report to a police station and obtain a permesso di soggiorno. Tourists who are staying in hotels do not need to do this, because hotel owners are required to register all guests with the police.

A permesso di soggiorno only becomes a necessity if you plan to study, work (legally) or live in Sicily. Obtaining one is never a pleasant experience, although for EU citizens it is fairly straightforward and success is guaranteed. Other nationals may find it involves long queues, rude police officers and the frustration of arriving at the counter (after a two-hour wait) to find that you don't have all the necessary documents.

The exact requirements, such as documents and *marche da bollo* (official stamps), can vary from one place to another. In general, you will need a valid passport containing a visa stamp indicating your date of entry into Italy, a special visa issued in your own country if you are planning to study, four passport-style photographs, and proof of your ability to support yourself financially.

It is best to go to the police station to obtain precise information on what is required.

Travel Insurance
Medical costs might already be covered through reciprocal healthcare agreements (see Medical Cover under Health later in this chapter) but you'll still need cover for theft or loss and for unexpected changes in travel plans (such as ticket cancellation).

You may prefer a policy that pays doctors or hospitals directly rather than you having to pay on the spot and claim later. If you have to claim for anything later, make sure you keep all documentation. Some policies ask you to reverse the charges (call back) to a centre in your home country where an immediate assessment of your problem is made.

Check that the policy covers ambulances or an emergency flight home.

Driving Licence & Permits
EU member states' pink-and-green driving licences are recognised in Sicily. If you hold a licence from other countries you are supposed to obtain an International Driving Permit too. See under Car & Motorcycle in the Getting There & Away chapter for more information.

Hostel Cards
A valid Hostelling International (HI) hostelling card is required in all associated youth hostels (Associazione Italiana Alberghi per la Gioventù) in Sicily. You can get this in your home country or at youth hostels in Sicily. In the latter case you apply for the card and must collect six stamps on it at L5000 each. You pay for a stamp on each of the first six nights you spend in a hostel. With six stamps you are considered a full international member. HI is on the Web at www.iyhf.org.

Student, Teacher & Youth Cards
The International Student Identity Card (ISIC), for full-time students, and the International Teacher Identity Card (ITIC), for full-time teachers and professors, are issued by more than 5000 organisations around the world – mainly student travel-related, and often also selling student air, train and bus tickets. The cards entitle you to a range of discounts, from reduced museum entry charges to cheap airfares. You also get use of an international helpline and can call reverse charges to the UK (☎ 020-8666 9205).

Student travel organisations such as STA (Australia, the UK and USA), Council Travel (the UK and USA) and Travel CUTS /Voyages Campus (Canada) can issue these cards. See under Air in the Getting There & Away chapter for some addresses, phone numbers and Web sites.

Anyone aged under 26 can get a Euro<26

card. This gives similar discounts to the ISIC and are issued by most of the same organisations. The Euro<26 has a variety of names including the Under 26 Card in England and Wales.

Centro Turistico Studentesco e Giovanile (CTS) youth and student travel organisation branches in Sicily can issue ISIC, ITIC and Euro<26 cards. You have to join the CTS first, however, which costs L45,000.

Seniors Cards

Seniors over 60 or 65 (depending on the reductions they're seeking) can get many discounts simply by presenting their passport or ID card as proof of age. For discounted international rail travel in Europe, you could apply for a Rail Europe Senior card.

Copies

Be sure to make photocopies of all important documents (passport data page and visa page, credit cards, travel insurance policy, air/bus/train tickets, driving licence and so on) before you go; leave one copy with someone at home and keep another with you, separate from the originals.

There is another option for storing details of your vital travel documents before you leave – Lonely Planet's online Travel Vault. Storing details of your important documents in the vault is safer than carrying photocopies. It's the best option if you travel in a country with easy Internet access. Your password-protected travel vault is accessible online at anytime. You can create your own travel vault free of charge at www.ekno.lonelyplanet.com.

EMBASSIES & CONSULATES
Your Own Embassy or Consulate

It's important to realise what your own embassy – the embassy of the country of which you are a citizen – can and can't do to help you if you get into trouble.

Generally speaking, it won't be much help in emergencies if the trouble you're in is remotely your own fault. Remember that you are bound by the laws of the country you are in. Your embassy will not be sympathetic if you end up in jail after committing a crime locally, even if such actions are legal in your own country.

In genuine emergencies you might get some assistance, but only if other channels have been exhausted. For example, if you need to get home urgently, a free ticket home is exceedingly unlikely – the embassy would expect you to have insurance. If you have all your money and documents stolen, it might assist with getting a new passport, but a loan for onward travel is out of the question.

Italian Embassies & Consulates

The following is a selection of Italian diplomatic missions abroad. As a rule, you should approach the consulate rather than the embassy (where both are present) on visa matters. Also bear in mind that in many of the countries listed below there are further consulates in other cities.

Australia
Embassy: (☎ 02-6273 3333, fax 6273 4223, ✉ ambital2@dynamite.com.au) 12 Grey St, Deakin, Canberra, ACT 2600
Consulate: (☎ 03-9867 5744, fax 9866 3932, ✉ itconmel@netlink.com.au) 509 St Kilda Rd, Melbourne, Vic 3004
Consulate: (☎ 02-9392 7900, fax 9252 4830, ✉ itconsyd@armadillo.com.au) Level 43, The Gateway, 1 Macquarie Place, Sydney, NSW 2000

Austria
Embassy: (☎ 01-712 51 21, fax 713 97 19, ✉ ambitalviepress@via.at) Metternichgasse 13, Vienna 1030
Consulate: (☎ 01-713 5671, fax 715 40 30) Ungarngasse 43, Vienna 1030

Canada
Embassy: (☎ 613-232 2401, fax 233 1484, ✉ italcomm@trytel.com) 21st Floor, 275 Slater St, Ottawa, Ontario K1P 5H9
Consulate: (☎ 514-849 8351, fax 499 9471, ✉ consitmtl@cyberglobe.net) 3489 Drummond St, Montreal, Que H3G 1X6
Consulate: (☎ 416-977 1566, ✉ consolato.it@toronto.italconsulate.org) 136 Beverley St, Toronto, Ontario M5T 1Y5

France
Embassy: (☎ 01 49 54 03 00, fax 01 45 49 35 81, ✉ stampa@dial.oleane.com) 7 rue de Varenne, Paris 75007
Consulate: (☎ 01 44 30 47 00, fax 01 45 66 41 78) 5 blvd Augier, Paris 75116

Germany
  Embassy: (☎ 0228-82 20, fax 82 22 10,
  @ italia.ambasciata.bonn@t-online.de) Karl
  Finkelnburgstrasse 49–51, Bonn 53173
  Consulate: (☎ 030-25 44 00, fax 25 44 01 00,
  @ italcons.berlino@t-online.de) Hiroshima-
  strasse 1–7, Berlin 10785
Ireland
  Embassy: (☎ 01-660 1744, fax 668 2759,
  @ italianembassy@tinet.ie)
  63–65 Northumberland Rd, Dublin 4
Netherlands
  Embassy: (☎ 070-302 1030, fax 361 4932,
  @ italemb@worldonline.nl) Alexanderstraat 12,
  2514 JL The Hague
  Consulate: (☎ 020-550 2050, fax 626 2444,
  @ consital@euronet.nl) Herengracht 581,
  1017 Amsterdam
New Zealand
  Embassy: (☎ 04-473 53 39, fax 472 72 55,
  @ ambwell@xtra.co.nz) 34 Grant Rd,
  Thorndon, Wellington
Slovenia
  Embassy: (☎ 061 126 21 41, fax 125 33 02)
  Snezniska Ulica 8, Ljubljana 61000
Spain
  Embassy: (☎ 91 577 6529, fax 575 7776,
  @ ambital.sp@nauta.es) Cale de Lagasca 98,
  Madrid 28006
Switzerland
  Embassy: (☎ 031-352 41 51, fax 351 10 26,
  @ ambital.berna@soectraweb.ch)
  Elfenstrasse 14, Bern 3006
  Consulate: (☎ 022-839 67 44, fax 839 67 45)
  14 rue Charles Galland, Geneva 1206
UK
  Embassy: (☎ 020-7312 2209, fax 7312 2230,
  @ emblondon@embitaly.org.uk) 14 Three
  Kings Yard, London W1Y 2EH
  Consulate: (☎ 020-7235 9371, fax 7823 1609)
  38 Eaton Place, London SW1X 8AN
USA
  Embassy: (☎ 202-328 5500, fax 328 5593,
  @ itapress@ix.netcom.com) 1601 Fuller St NW,
  Washington DC 20009
  Consulate: (☎ 213-820 0622, fax 820 0727,
  @ cglos@aol.com) Suite 300, 12400 Wilshire
  Blvd, West Los Angeles, CA 90025
  Consulate: (☎ 212-737 9100, fax 249 4945,
  @ italconsny@aol.com) 690 Park Ave,
  New York, NY 10021-5044
  Consulate: (☎ 415-931 4924, fax 931 7205)
  2590 Webster St, San Francisco, CA 94115

Embassies in Rome

Most countries have an embassy in Rome,
but several also maintain consulates in

Palermo. Passport enquires should be addressed to the Rome-based offices:

Australia (☎ 06 85 27 21) Via Alessandria 215
Canada (☎ 06 44 59 81, fax 06 445 98 912) Via
  Zara 30
France (☎ 06 68 60 11) Piazza Farnese 67
Germany (☎ 06 49 21 31) Via San Martino della
  Battaglia 4
Ireland (☎ 06 697 91 21) Piazza Campitelli 3
Netherlands (☎ 06 322 11 41) Via Michele
  Mercati 8
New Zealand (☎ 06 441 71 71, fax 06 440 29 84)
  Via Zara 28
Slovenia (☎ 06 808 10 75) Via L Pisano 10
Spain (☎ 06 68 32 168) Largo Fontella
  Borghese 19
Switzerland (☎ 06 80 95 71) Via Barnarba
  Oriani 61
UK (☎ 06 4 67 41) Via XX Settembre 80/a
USA (☎ 06 4 67 41) Via Vittorio
  Veneto 119a–121

Consulates in Palermo

It may be handier for some to go to a consulate in Palermo. Office hours are from
9 am to 12.30 pm and 2.30 to 3.30 pm Monday to Friday. Offices include:

France (☎ 091 58 50 73) Via Segesta 9, 90139
  Palermo
Germany (☎ 091 34 25 75, fax 091 34 70 34)
  Viale Scaduto 2d, 90144 Palermo
Netherlands (☎ 091 58 15 21, fax 091 58 12
  30) Via Roma 489, 90139 Palermo
Tunisia (☎ 091 32 89 96) Piazza Ignazio
  Florio 2, 90144 Palermo
UK (☎ 091 58 25 33, fax 091 58 42 40) S
  Tagiavia & Co, Via Cavour 121, 90133 Palermo
USA (☎ 091 611 00 20) Via Re Federico 18b,
  90141 Palermo

CUSTOMS

On 1 July 1999, duty-free sales within the
EU were abolished. Under the rules of the
single market, goods bought in and ex-
ported within the EU incur no additional
taxes, provided duty has been paid somewhere within the EU and the goods are for
personal consumption.

Travellers entering Italy from outside the
EU are allowed to bring in duty free: 200
cigarettes, 1L of spirits, 2L of wine, 60mls
of perfume, 250mls of toilet water, and

other goods up to a total value of L340,000
(€175); anything over this limit must be
declared on arrival and the appropriate duty
paid (it is advisable to carry all your receipts with you).

MONEY
A combination of travellers cheques and
credit or cash cards is the best way to take
your money.

Currency
Until the euro notes and coins are in circu-
lation (see the boxed text 'Introducing the
Euro'), Italy's currency will remain the *lira*
(plural: *lire*). The smallest note is L1000.
Other denominations in notes are L2000,
L5000, L10,000, L50,000, L100,000 and
L500,000. Coin denominations are L50,
L100 (two types of silver coin), L200, L500
and L1000.

Like other continental Europeans, Italians indicate decimals with commas and
thousands with points.

Exchange Rates

country	unit		lire
Australia	A$1	=	L1233
Canada	C$1	=	L1422
euro	€1	=	L1936
France	1FF	=	L295
Germany	DM1	=	L990
Ireland	IR£1	=	L2459
Japan	¥100	=	L1976
New Zealand	NZ$1	=	L1022
UK	UK£1	=	L3305
USA	US$1	=	L2097

Exchanging Money
You can exchange money in banks, at post
offices or in currency exchange booths (bureaux de change). Banks are generally the
most reliable and tend to offer the best rates.
However, you should look around and ask
about commissions. These can fluctuate
considerably and a lot depends on whether
you are changing cash or cheques. While
post offices charge a flat rate of L1000 per
cash transaction, banks charge L2500 or
even more. Travellers cheques attract
higher fees. Some banks charge L1000 per

Introducing the Euro

Since 1 January 1999, the *lira* and the euro –
Europe's new currency in 11 EU countries –
have both been legal tender in Italy. Euro
coins and banknotes have not been issued
yet, but you can already get billed in euros
and opt to pay in euros by credit card. Essentially, if there's no hard cash involved, you can
deal in euros. Travellers should check bills
carefully to make sure that any conversion
has been calculated correctly.

The whole idea behind the current paper-
less currency is to give euro-fearing punters a
chance to limber up arithmetically before euro
coins and banknotes are issued on 1 January
2002. The same euro coins (one to 50 cents,
€1 and €2) and banknotes (€5 to €500) will
then be used in the 11 countries of what has
been dubbed Euroland: Austria, Belgium, Finland, France, Germany, Ireland, Italy, Luxembourg, the Netherlands, Portugal and Spain.
The lira will remain legal currency alongside
the euro until 1 March 2002, when it will be
hurled on the scrapheap of history.

Until then, the 11 currencies have been
fixed to the euro at the following rates:
AS13.76, BF40.34, 5.95 mk, 6.56FF, DM1.96,
IR£0.79, L1936, flux40.34, f2.2, 200$48 and
166.39 ptas. The Lonely Planet Web site at
www.lonelyplanet.com has a link to a currency converter and up-to-date news on the
integration process. Alternatively, have a look
at europa.eu.int/euro/html/entry.html.

Euro exchange rates include:

Australia	A$1	=	€0.64
Canada	C$1	=	€0.72
Japan	¥100	=	€0.99
New Zealand	NZ$1	=	€0.52
UK	UK£1	=	€1.68
USA	US$1	=	€1.05

cheque (L3000 minimum), while post offices charges a maximum L5000 per transaction. Currency exchange booths often
advertise 'no commission', but the rate of
exchange is usually inferior to that of
banks.

Cash Don't bring wads of cash from home (travellers cheques and plastic are much safer). Bag snatchers and pickpockets – a problem in Sicily's more crowded areas – prey on cash-flashing tourists, so your best bet is to never carry more than you need for a day or two. It is, however, an idea to keep an emergency stash separate from other valuables in case you should lose your travellers cheques and credit cards. You will need cash for many day-to-day transactions (many small guesthouses, eateries and shops do not take credit cards).

Travellers Cheques These are a safe way to carry your money because they can be replaced if lost or stolen. They can be cashed at most banks and exchange offices. American Express (Amex) and Thomas Cook are widely accepted brands. If you lose your Amex cheques, you can report your loss by phoning a 24-hour toll-free number (☎ 800 87 20 00) from anywhere in Italy.

If you buy your travellers cheques in lire there should be no commission charge when cashing them. Buying cheques in a third currency (such as US dollars if you are not coming from the USA), means you pay commission when you buy the cheques and again when cashing them in Sicily.

It's vital to keep your initial receipt, a record of your cheque numbers and the ones you have used, separate from the cheques themselves. Take your passport when you go to cash travellers cheques.

Credit/Debit Cards Carrying plastic is the simplest way to organise your holiday funds. You don't have large amounts of cash or cheques to lose, you can get money after hours and at weekends and the exchange rate is sometimes better than that offered for travellers cheques or cash exchanges. By arranging for payments to be made into your card account while you are travelling, you can avoid paying interest.

Major cards, such as Visa, MasterCard, Eurocard, Cirrus and Eurocheque cards, are accepted throughout Sicily. They can be used for many purchases (including in some supermarkets) and in hotels and restaurants.

Credit cards can also be used in Automatic Teller Machines (ATMs) displaying the appropriate sign or (if you have no PIN number) to obtain cash advances over the counter in many banks – Visa and MasterCard are among the most widely recognised for such transactions. Check charges with your bank but, as a rule, there is no charge for purchases on major cards and a minimum charge on cash advances and ATM transactions in foreign currencies. For larger withdrawals this charge rarely exceeds 1.5%.

It is not uncommon for ATMs in Sicily to reject foreign cards. Don't despair or start wasting money on international calls to your bank. Try a few more ATMs displaying your credit card's logo before assuming the problem lies with your card rather than with the local system.

If your credit card is lost, stolen or swallowed by an ATM, you can telephone toll-free to have an immediate stop put on its use. For MasterCard the number in Sicily is ☎ 800 87 08 66, or make a reverse-charges call to St Louis in the USA on ☎ 314-275 66 90; for Visa, phone ☎ 800 87 72 32 in Sicily.

Amex is also widely accepted (although not as commonly as Visa or MasterCard). There is no full-service office in Sicily as Amex is represented by a number of travel agents throughout the island. If you lose your Amex card you can call ☎ 800 86 40 46 in Sicily or contact the office in Rome on ☎ 06 7 22 82, which runs a 24-hour cardholders service.

International Transfers One reliable way to send money to Sicily is by 'urgent telex' through the foreign office of a large Italian bank, or through major banks in your own country, to a nominated bank in Sicily. It is important to have an exact record of all details associated with the money transfer. The money will always be held at the head office of the bank in the town to which it has been sent. Urgent telex transfers should take only a few days, while other means, such as telegraphic transfer, or draft, can take weeks. It is also possible to transfer money through Amex and Thomas Cook.

A speedier option is to send money

through Western Union (toll-free ☎ 800 46 44 64/22 00 55). The sender and receiver have to turn up at a Western Union outlet with passport or other form of ID and the fees charged for the virtually immediate transfer depend on the amount sent. For sums up to US$400, Western Union charges the sender US$20; the money can supposedly be handed over to the recipient within 10 minutes of being sent. This service functions through several outlets in Sicily.

Another service along the same lines is MoneyGram, which operates mainly through Thomas Cook. Like Western Union they are expanding their network of agents.

Security
Keep only a limited amount of your money as cash, and the bulk in more easily replaceable forms, such as travellers cheques or plastic. If your accommodation has a safe, use it. If you have to leave money in your room, divide it into several stashes and hide them in different places.

For carrying money on the street the safest thing is a shoulder wallet or under-the-clothes money belt. An external money belt attracts rather than deflects attention from your valuables.

Costs
Sicily isn't as cheap as many travellers assume, but it is one of the few destinations in Italy where the budget-minded can have a relatively comfortable time. You should bear in mind that Sicily is essentially a warm-weather destination, and a key factor to consider is the often wild difference in costs between the summer months (usually Easter to the end of September) and the rest of the year. Even the most popular tourist resorts, such as Cefalù, the Aeolian Islands and Taormina drop their prices dramatically out of season; in effect the sunshine can often double your costs.

The less-visited areas of the island – the west and parts of the interior – generally offer cheaper accommodation and eating options; even prices in supermarkets are lower than in the tourist Meccas. Admission fees to all the major archaeological sites and museums run by the Regione Sicilia are set at the same price, which at the time of research was L4000. Even the more expensive museums and galleries don't cost more than L8000 and most offer a discount to students, OAPs and children.

A very prudent backpacker might scrape by on L50,000 per day, but only by staying in youth hostels or camp sites, eating one simple meal a day, buying a sandwich or a pizza slice for lunch, travelling slowly to keep transport costs down and minimising visits to museums and galleries.

One rung up, you can get by on L90,000 per day if you stay in the cheaper guesthouses or small hotels, and keep sit-down meals and museum visits to one a day. Lone travellers may find even this budget hard to maintain.

If money is no object, you'll find plenty of ways to get rid of it, especially in the cities and resorts where there's no shortage of luxury hotels, expensive restaurants and shops to wave wads at. Realistically, a traveller wanting to stay in comfortable lower-to mid-range hotels, eat two square meals a day, not feel restricted to one museum a day and be able to enjoy the odd drink and other minor indulgence should reckon on a minimum daily average of L150,000 – more if you have a car.

Ways to Save If you could, it would be nice to avoid paying the extra charged by many guesthouses for compulsory breakfast – a coffee and brioche in a cafe cost less and taste better. The sad reality is that most places only offer one price on rooms and that includes breakfast.

In bars, prices can double (sometimes even triple) if you sit down and are served at the table. Stand at the bar to drink your coffee or eat a sandwich.

Read the fine print on menus (usually posted outside eating establishments) to check the cover charge (*coperto*) and service fee (*servizio*).

Tipping & Bargaining
You are not expected to tip on top of restaurant service charges, but it is common to leave a small amount. If there is no service

euro currency converter   L10,000 = €5.16

charge, the customer might consider leaving a 10% tip, but this is by no means obligatory. In bars, Sicilians usually leave small change as a tip, often as little L100 or L200. Tipping taxi drivers is not common practice, but you should tip the porter at higher-class hotels.

Bargaining or haggling is less commonplace than it once was, but it still goes on at Sicilian markets and is considered quite an art form. Most traders and stallholders work on the premise that the foreign tourist always has more money than the local, so if they spot you for an outsider (and they will!) you'll have a harder time of it than if you were a local. Never accept the first price quoted and counter-offer with half the amount. Don't be deterred by stallholders who dismiss you with a wave of the arm: the person at the next stall may well accept your offer after a brief (and obligatory) haggle. While bargaining in shops is not acceptable, you might find that the proprietor is disposed to give a discount if you are spending a reasonable amount of money.

It is quite acceptable (and advisable) to ask if there is a special price for a room in a guesthouse if you plan to stay for more than a few days.

Taxes & Refunds
A value-added tax (known as Imposta di Valore Aggiunto or IVA) of around 19% is slapped onto just about everything in Sicily. Tourists who are residents of countries outside the EU may claim a refund on this tax if the item was purchased for personal use and costs more than a certain amount (L300,000 in 1999). The goods must be carried with you and you must keep the fiscal receipt.

The refund only applies to items purchased at retail outlets affiliated to the system – these shops display a 'Tax-free for tourists' sign. Otherwise, ask the shopkeeper. You must fill out a form at the point of purchase and have the form stamped and checked by Italian customs when you leave the country. You then return it by mail within 60 days to the vendor, who will make the refund, either by cheque or to your credit card. At major airports and some border crossings you can get an immediate cash refund at specially marked booths.

For more information call ☎ 0332 87 07 70, or consult the rules brochure available in affiliated stores.

Receipts
Laws aimed at tightening controls on the payment of taxes in Italy mean that the onus is on the buyer to ask for and retain receipts for all goods and services. This applies to everything from a litre of milk to a haircut. Although it rarely happens, you could be asked by an officer of the fiscal police (*guardia di finanza*) to produce the receipt immediately after you leave a shop. If you don't have it, you may be obliged to pay a fine of up to L300,000.

POST & COMMUNICATIONS
Sicily's postal service is notoriously slow, unreliable and expensive.

Stamps (*francobolli*) are available at post offices and authorised tobacconists (look for the official *tabacchi* sign: a big 'T', often white on black). Main post offices in the bigger cities are generally open from around 8 am to at least 5 pm. Many open on Saturday mornings too. Tobacconists keep regular shop hours.

Postal Rates
Postcards and letters up to 20g sent airmail (*via aerea*) cost L1400 to Australia and New Zealand, L1300 to the USA and L800 to EU countries (L900 to the rest of Europe). Aerograms are a cheap alternative, costing only L900 to send anywhere. They can be purchased at post offices only.

A new service, *posta prioritaria* (priority post – a little like the UK's first-class post), began in 1999. For L1200 postcards and letters weighing up to 20g, posted to destinations within Italy, the EU, Switzerland and Norway, are supposed to arrive the following day.

Sending letters express (*espresso*) costs a standard extra L3600, but may help speed a letter on its way.

If you want to post more important items by registered mail (*raccomandato*) or by insured mail *(assicurato)*, remember that they will take as long as normal mail. Registered mail costs L4000 on top of the normal cost of the letter. The cost of insured mail depends on the value of the object being sent (L6000 for objects up to L100,000 value) and is not available to the USA.

Sending Mail

If you choose not to use priority post (see Postal Rates in the previous section) an airmail letter can take up to two weeks to reach the UK or the USA, while a letter to Australia will take between two and three weeks.

The service within Sicily is not much better: local letters take at least three days to arrive, intercity letters take up to a week.

Parcels *(pacchetti)* can be sent from any post office. You can buy posting boxes or padded envelopes from most post offices. Stationery shops *(cartolerie)* and some tobacconists also sell padded envelopes. Don't tape up or staple envelopes – they should be sealed with glue. Your best bet is not to close the envelope or box completely and ask at the counter how it should be done. Parcels usually take longer to be delivered than letters. A different set of postal rates applies.

Express Mail Urgent mail (maximum 20kg for international destinations) can be sent by the post office's express mail service, known as CAI Post or *posta celere*. Letters up to 500g cost L30,000 within Europe, L46,000 to the USA and Canada and L68,000 to Australia. A parcel weighing 1kg will cost L34,000 within Europe, L54,000 to the USA and Canada, and L80,000 to Australia and New Zealand. CAI Post is not necessarily as fast as private services. It will take three to five days for a parcel to reach the USA, Canada or Australia and one to three days to European destinations. Generally only the main post offices receive CAI Post.

Couriers Several international couriers operate in Sicily: for DHL call toll-free ☎ 800 34 53 45; for Federal Express call toll-free ☎ 800 12 38 00; for UPS call toll-free ☎ 800

82 20 54. Look in the telephone book for addresses. Note that if you are having articles sent to you by courier in Sicily, you might be obliged to pay IVA of up to 20% to retrieve the goods.

Receiving Mail

Poste restante is known as *fermo posta*. Letters marked thus will be held at the counter of the same name in the main post office in the relevant town. Poste restante mail should be addressed as follows:

John SMITH,
Fermo Posta,
Posta Centrale,
90100 Palermo
Italy

You will need to pick up your letters in person and present your passport as ID.

Amex card or travellers-cheque holders can use the free client mail-holding service at Amex offices. Take your passport when picking up mail.

Telephone

The partly privatised Telecom Italia is the largest phone company in the country and its orange public pay phones are liberally scattered all over the place. The most common accept only telephone cards *(carte/ schede telefoniche)*, although you will still find some that accept both cards and coins (L100, L200 and L500). Some card phones now also accept special Telecom credit cards and even commercial credit cards.

Phones can be found in the streets, train stations and some big stores as well as in unstaffed Telecom centres, a few of which also have telephone directories for other parts of the country.

You can buy phonecards at post offices, tobacconists, newspaper stands and from vending machines in Telecom offices. To avoid the frustration of trying to find fast-disappearing coin telephones, always keep a phonecard on hand. They come with a value of L5000, L10,000 and L15,000. Remember to snap off the perforated corner before using them.

euro currency converter L10,000 = €5.16

Emergency Numbers

Military Police (Carabinieri)	☎ 112
Police (Polizia)	☎ 113
Fire Brigade (Vigili del Fuoco)	☎ 115
Highway Rescue	
(Soccorso Stradale)	☎ 116
Ambulance (Ambulanza)	☎ 118

Public phones operated by a new telecommunications company, Infostrada, can be found in airports and train stations. These phones accept Infostrada phonecards (available from post offices, tobacconists and newspaper stands), which come with a value of L3000, L5000 or L10,000. Infostrada's rates are slightly cheaper than Telecom's for long-distance and international calls, but you cannot make local calls from these phones.

Costs Rates, particularly for long-distance calls, are among the highest in Europe. Peak time for domestic calls is from 8 am to 6.30 pm Monday to Friday and from 8 am to 1 pm Saturday. Cheap rates apply from 6.30 pm to 8 am Monday to Friday, on Saturday afternoon and on Sunday and public holidays. For international calls, different times apply. Cheap rates to the UK apply from 10 pm to 8 am Monday to Saturday and all day Sunday, to the US and Canada from 7 pm to 2 pm Monday to Friday and all day Saturday and Sunday, and to Australia from 11 pm to 8 am Monday to Saturday and all day Sunday.

A local call *(comunicazione urbana)* from a public phone will cost L200 for three to six minutes, depending on the time of day you call. Peak call times are from 8 am to 6.30 pm Monday to Friday and from 8 am to 1 pm Saturday.

Rates for long-distance calls within Sicily *(comunicazione interurbana)* depend on the time of day and the distance involved. At the worst, one minute will cost about L340 in peak periods.

If you need to call overseas, beware of the cost, even a call of five minutes to Australia after 10 pm will cost around L10,000 from a private phone (more from a public phone). Calls to most of the rest of Europe (except the UK, which is cheaper) cost L1245 for the first minute and L762 thereafter (it's closer to L1200 from a public phone).

Domestic Calls Since July 1998 area codes have become an integral part of the telephone number. The codes all began with 0 and consisted of up to four digits. You must now dial this whole number, even if calling from next door. Thus, any number you call in the Palermo area will begin with 091.

Toll-free numbers *(numeri verdi)* all begin with the prefix 800. The prefix 147 indicates a national number charged at a local rate.

Mobile-telephone numbers begin with a four digit prefix, such as 0330, 0335 or 0347.

For directory enquiries dial ☎ 12.

Note Not content to make the area code part of the phone number, it is planned to convert the initial 0 into a 4 by the end of 2000. Thus any number in the Palermo area will start with 491.

International Calls Direct international calls are easily made from public telephones by using a phonecard. Dial 00 to get out of Sicily, then the relevant country and city codes, followed by the telephone number.

Useful country codes are: Australia 61, Canada and the USA 1, New Zealand 64 and the UK 44. Codes for other countries in Europe include: France 33, Germany 49, Greece 30, Ireland 353 and Spain 34. Other codes are listed in Italian telephone books.

To make a reverse-charge (collect) international call from a public telephone, dial ☎ 170.

It is easier, and often cheaper, to use the Country Direct service in your country. You dial the number and request a reverse-charge call through the operator in your country. Numbers for this service include:

Australia	(Optus)	☎ 172 11 61
	(Telstra)	☎ 172 10 61
Canada	(AT&T)	☎ 172 10 02
	(Teleglobe)	☎ 172 10 01
France		☎ 172 00 33

Germany		☎ 172 00 49
Ireland		☎ 172 03 53
Netherlands		☎ 172 00 31
New Zealand		☎ 172 10 64
UK	(BT)	☎ 172 00 44
	(BT Automatic)	☎ 172 01 44
USA	(AT&T)	☎ 172 10 11
	(IDB)	☎ 172 17 77
	(MCI)	☎ 172 10 22
	(Sprint)	☎ 172 18 77

For international directory enquiries call ☎ 176.

International Phonecards The Lonely Planet eKno Communication Card is aimed specifically at independent travellers and provides budget international calls, a range of messaging services, free email and travel information – for local calls, you're usually better off with a local card. You can join online at www.ekno.lonelyplanet.com, or by phone from Sicily by dialling ☎ 800 97 56 91. Once you have joined, to use eKno from Sicily dial ☎ 800 87 56 83. Check the eKno Web site for joining and access numbers from other countries and updates on super budget local access numbers and new features.

A growing army of private companies now distribute international phonecards, some linked to US phone companies such as Sprint and MCI. The cards come in a variety of unit sizes and are sold in some bars, tobacconists, newspaper stands and other shops – look out for signs advertising them.

Telecom has brought out its own Welcome Card, which costs L25,000 for 100 units. It's certainly cheaper than making international calls on a standard phonecard, but may not stand up to some of the competition.

Infostrada sells various cards, some of which are only good in the very limited number of Infostrada phones around. The best for international calls cost L20,000 and can be used from private or public phones (you dial a toll-free access number and then key in a provided code).

Calling Sicily from Abroad Dial the international access code (00 in most coun-

tries), followed by the code for Italy (39) and the full number including the initial zero (for example – 00 39 091 555 55 55). If calling a mobile phone you must drop the initial 0.

Telegram
These dinosaurs can be sent from post offices or dictated by phone (☎ 186) and are an expensive, but sure, way of having important messages delivered by the same or next day.

Fax
There is no shortage of fax offices in Sicily's cities and larger towns, but the country's high telephone charges make it an expensive mode of communication. Some offices charge per page and others charge per minute, and still others charge for both! In all cases, prices vary considerably from one office to another. However, in general, to send a fax within Sicily you can expect to pay L4000 for the first page and L1500 for each page thereafter, or L3000 for the first minute and L1500 for subsequent minutes. International faxes can cost from L8000 for the first page and L5000 per page thereafter, depending on the destination. A fax to an EU country can cost L7000 for the first minute and L3500 thereafter; to the USA it can cost L9000 for the first minute and L4500 thereafter. Faxes can also be sent from some Telecom public phones. It usually costs about L1000 per page to receive a fax.

Email & Internet Access
Italy has been a little slower than some parts of Western Europe to march down the information highway, and Sicily has been slower still. Nevertheless, email has definitely arrived. If you plan to carry your notebook or palmtop computer with you, buy a universal AC adaptor, which will enable you to plug it in anywhere without frying the innards. You'll also need a plug adaptor (the standard European two round-pin variety) – it's easiest to buy these before you leave home.

Your PC-card modem may or may not work once you leave your home country –

and you won't know for sure until you try. The safest option is to buy a reputable 'global' modem before you leave home, or buy a local PC-card modem if you're spending an extended amount of time in Sicily. The telephone socket will sometimes be different from that at home, so have at least a US RJ-11 telephone adaptor that works with your modem. You can almost always find an adaptor that will convert from RJ-11 to the local variety. For more information on travelling with a portable computer, see Web sites www.teleadapt.com or www.warrior.com.

Major Internet service providers (ISPs), such as CompuServe (www.compuserve .com) and IBM Net (www.ibm.net), have dial-in nodes in Sicily (Palermo only); you can download a list of the dial-in numbers before you leave home. Be sure to read the fine print – often you pay an extra fee for use of a local node.

If you intend to rely on cybercafes, you'll need to carry three pieces of information with you to enable you to access your Internet mail account: your incoming (POP or IMAP) mail server name, your account name and your password. Your ISP or network supervisor will be able to give you these. Armed with this information, you should be able to access your Internet mail account from any net-connected machine in the world. Another option to collect mail through cybercafes is to open a free eKno Web-based email account online at www .ekno.lonelyplanet.com. You can then access your mail from anywhere in the world from any net-connected machine running a standard Web browser.

There aren't too many cybercafes in Sicily, but new ones are opening all the time. There are a few in Palermo, Catania, Taormina (see those chapters for details) and other well-visited spots; ask at the local tourist office for the addresses. You can expect to pay between L10,000 and L15,000 an hour.

INTERNET RESOURCES

The World Wide Web is a rich resource for travellers. You can research your trip, hunt down bargain air fares, book hotels, check on weather conditions or chat with locals

and other travellers about the best places to visit (or avoid!).

One of the best places to start your Web explorations is the Lonely Planet Web site at www.lonelyplanet.com. Other sites you might like to surf include:

CTS Village This site provides useful information from CTS, Italy's leading student travel organisation. It's in Italian only.
www.cts.it

Excite Call this site up and key in Sicily; it will give you a wide selection of related sites, as well as brief reviews and ratings.
www.excite.com

Excite Travel This site contains a farefinder and booking facilities and links to maps, restaurant tips and the like.
city.net/countries/italy/sicily

Ferrovie dello Stato This is the official site of the Italian railways. You can look up fare and timetable information here, although it can be a little complicated to plough through.
www.fs-on-line.com

Internet Café Guide At this site you can get a list of Internet cafes in Sicily. It's not as up-to-date as you might expect, but it is a start.
www.netcafeguide.com

Parks.it This is the place to look for basic information on all of Sicily's national and regional parks, along with any other protected areas.
www.parks.it

BOOKS

Over the centuries Sicily has been a source of endless fascination to a stream of foreign visitors, who have come to soak up the beauty and express an opinion. Some of these are little more than uninformed, prejudiced twaddle, but those that have taken the time to delve a little deeper have left us with some penetrating insights that are worth checking out, if only to aid your own interpretations. The Mafia is a red-hot subject that has spawned a thousand and one books, most of which are a thinly veiled attempt to get to the summit of the bestseller list, but there are a few that offer well-considered, informative and thoughtful analyses of a highly complex issue.

Most books are published in different editions by different publishers in different countries. Your local bookshop or library is best placed to advise you on the availability of the following recommendations.

Lonely Planet

Travellers planning to move around more widely should consider *Italy*. The *Italian Phrasebook* lists all the words and phrases you're likely to need when travelling in Italy. Lonely Planet's *World Food Italy* is a full-colour book containing information on the whole range of Italian food and drink, including Sicilian cuisine and a useful language section with the definitive culinary dictionary.

Guidebooks

The ultimate guide is the red hardback *Sicily*, published in English and Italian by the Touring Club Italiano. The TCI also puts out a green soft cover series (Italian only) divided by province; look out for *Siracusa e Provincia*. So far this is the only provincial guide pertinent to Sicily.

Travel

The grand touring classic is Johann Wolfgang von Goethe's *Italienische Reise* (Italian Journey, 1786–8), which includes a substantial section on Sicily. Another interesting travel book is *A Traveller in Southern Italy* by HV Morton. Although written in the 1960s – Sicily has changed enormously since then – it remains a valuable guide to the island and its people. The narrative of Vincent Cronin's *The Golden Honeycomb* is organised as a trip in search of Daedalus's honeycomb but is actually an account of a sojourn in Sicily in the 1950s. Again it may seem out of date but the insight into the ways and attitudes of the Sicilians, especially in the interior, is still relevant today.

Sicily by Russell King, part of the *Islands* series, is well-written and contains informed chapters on all of Sicily's high- and lowlights, including architecture, ancient history and the Mafia. *Sicily: An Archeological Guide* by Margaret Guido is an in-depth guide to the island's network of prehistoric and classical sites. Be aware that it hasn't been revised since the late 70s, so all practical information is out of date.

History & Politics

Giuliano Procacci's *History of the Italian People* and Paul Ginsborg's *A History of Contemporary Italy* are absorbing and very well-written books with good sections on Sicily. In *Frederick II: A Medieval Emperor* David Abulafia delves into the life and times of the greatest of the Hohenstaufen rulers of Sicily and finds that he did have chinks in his formidable armour. John Julius Norwich's *The Normans in Sicily* (which also includes an earlier title, *Kingdom in the Sun*) is a detailed account of the Norman takeover of the island. *The Sicilian Vespers* by Steven Runciman is the best book on the popular 13th-century uprising against the French Angevin dynasty. It's a pretty heavy read.

The Mafia

Norman Lewis' *The Honoured Society* is a good introduction to the subject, even though his lack of confirmed sources make the book a little dated. The best book on the subject is Giancarlo Caselli's *A True History of Italy* which, with almost surgical precision, chronicles the rise of the Mafia and its nefarious influence on the apparatus of state. The author was one of Sicily's leading anti-Mafia magistrates and his book benefits from some extraordinary testimony by recalcitrant mobsters. *Men of Honour* by Giovanni Falcone is in a similar vein, and is an essential read for anyone looking to understand the state of the Mafia today. Falcone paid for his knowledge with his life.

Peter Robb's *Midnight in Sicily* is a well-written and immensely enjoyable treatise on the four pillars of Sicilian society: art, culture, food and the Mafia. Renate Siebert's *Secrets of Life and Death: Women and the Mafia* has been translated by Liz Heron and provides first-hand accounts of the role of women within this patriarchal structure.

Art & Architecture

Anthony Blunt's classic *The Sicilian Baroque* is the key read on the subject, containing a detailed and precise history of the style as well as illustrations and black and white photos of buildings and churches. The book is out of print in the US but you might find it in the public library.

FILMS

Sicily has been the subject of a number of great Italian films, including Luchino Visconti's *La Terra Trema* (The Earth Trembles; 1948), which is a brilliant adaptation of Giovanni Verga's *I Malavoglia*, and the wonderful *Il Gattopardo* (The Leopard; 1963), Visconti's take on Lampedusa's novel of the same name.

The Taviani brothers, Paolo (born 1931) and Vittorio (born 1929) brought Sicily to life in *Kaos* (1984), which was based on several of Luigi Pirandello's short stories. Nanni Moretti (born 1953), who first came to the silver screen in the late 1970s, has proven to be a highly individualistic actor-director. His *Caro Diario* (Dear Diary), a whimsical, self-indulgent, autobiographical three-part film largely set on the Aeolian Islands, won the prize for best feature film at Cannes in 1994.

Il Postino (The Postman; 1995), starring Massimo Troisi, was one of the most striking Italian films of the 1990s. It tells the story of a shy village postman on the island of Salina who comes in contact with the great Chilean poet Pablo Neruda, a meeting that opens the postman's heart to the beauty of poetry.

Of all the films with a link to Sicily, easily the best known is Francis Ford Coppola's epic trilogy *The Godfather*, based on Mario Puzo's best-seller of the same name. Excellent performances by a host of actors, among them Al Pacino, Marlon Brando, James Caan, Robert Duvall and Talia Shire, were awarded with a heap of Oscars, including two for Best Film (for the first two pictures). This largely romanticised tale of the rise to power of a New York Mafia crime family from its humble origins in the Sicilian town of Corleone is worth watching because it's an expertly crafted story, but it will teach you very little about the Mafia itself. A chunk of each instalment is set in Sicily, including the famous wedding scene from the first film (set in Savoca on the east-

ern coast) and the opera scene from the third film (set in Palermo's Teatro Massimo).

Roberto Rossellini's *Stromboli* (1950, also known as *Stromboli, La Terra di Dio*) was filmed on the eponymous island and tells the story of Karen (played by Ingrid Bergman), a young refugee from a POW camp who marries a local fisherman (Mario Vitale) to escape imprisonment. The film's drama – a good example of the Italian Neo-Realist school of cinema – is played out against the ever-present threat of the volcano.

Woody Allen's *Mighty Aphrodite* (1995) is set in New York and has nothing to do with Sicily, but the scenes of the Greek chorus were shot in Taormina's Greek theatre.

Lonely Planet produces the video *Corsica, Sicily and Sardinia*.

NEWSPAPERS & MAGAZINES

It can be difficult to find a selection of national daily newspapers from around Europe in Sicily. In larger tourist resorts you can usually pick up the *International Herald Tribune* and either the *Guardian* or the *Independent*, both at least one day old. In Taormina and Lipari during the high season a wider selection is usually available, including French and German magazines and newspapers.

The only Sicilian daily is *Il Giornale di Sicilia*, which is sold everywhere. It is uncompromisingly tough on corruption and political scandals (an almost daily occurrence), and has a good (if limited) section on international news and a terrific listings page with details of all cinemas, theatres, festivals and other events. It is published in provincial editions, so the Palermo edition will have different listings than, say, Catania or Agrigento. It is also the cheapest newspaper around at L1100.

So-called 'national' papers – actually important dailies published out of three major Italian cities – are also sold throughout Sicily. These include Milan's *Corriere della Sera*, Turin's *La Stampa* and Rome's *La Repubblica*. This trio forms what could be considered to be the nucleus of a national press, each publishing Sicilian editions. Politically speaking, they range from establishment-right *(La Stampa)* to centre-

An island of contrasts: Sicily is crammed with spectacular scenery that ranges from rumbling volcanoes to rolling fields and almost everything in-between.

Food is a serious business in Sicily – whether you are making it, selling it or having a little rest on the way home from buying it.

left (La Repubblica). These cost L1500, unless containing a weekly magazine inserto (supplement), in which case the cost sometimes rises to L2200.

RADIO & TV
You can pick up the BBC World Service on medium wave at 648kHz, on short wave 6195kHz, 9410kHz, 12095kHz, 15575kHz, and on long wave at 198kHz, depending on where you are and the time of day. Voice of America (VOA) can usually be found on short wave at 15205 kHz.

The three state-owned stations are: RAI-1 (1332 AM or 89.7 FM), RAI-2 (846 AM or 91.7 FM) and RAI-3 (93.7 FM). They combine classical and light music with news broadcasts and discussion programs.

The three state-run TV stations, RAI-1, RAI-2 and RAI-3 are run by Radio e Televisione Italiane. Historically, each has been in the hands of one of the main political groupings in the country, although allegiances are less clear these days.

Of the three, RAI-3 tends to have some of the more interesting programmes. Generally, however, these stations and the private Canale 5, Italia 1 and Rete 4, tend to serve up a diet of indifferent news, appalling variety hours and equally terrible game shows. Talk shows, some interesting but many nauseating, also abound.

Other stations include Telemontecarlo (TMC), on which you can see CNN if you stay up late enough (starting as late as 5 am), and a host of local channels.

VIDEO SYSTEMS
If you want to record or buy video tapes to play back home, you won't get a picture if the image registration systems are different. TVs and nearly all pre-recorded videos on sale in Italy use the Phase Alternation Line (PAL) system common to most of Western Europe and Australia, incompatible with France's SECAM system or the NTSC system used in North America and Japan.

PHOTOGRAPHY
A roll of 100 ASA Kodak film costs around L7000/8000 for 24/36 exposures. Develop-

ing costs around L11,000/14,000 for 24/36 exposures in standard format. A roll of 36 slides costs L10,000 to buy and L8000 for development.

TIME
Italy (and hence Sicily) is one hour ahead of GMT/UTC during winter and two hours ahead of GMT/UTC during the daylight-saving period, from the last Sunday in March to the last Sunday in October. Most other Western European countries have the same time as Italy year-round, the major exceptions being Britain, Ireland and Portugal, which are one hour behind.

When it's noon in Sicily, it's 3 am in San Francisco, 6 am in New York and Toronto, It's 11 am in London, 9 pm in Sydney and 11 pm in Auckland. Note that the changeover to/from daylight saving usually differs from the European date by a couple of weeks in North America and Australasia.

ELECTRICITY
Voltages & Cycles
Electric current in Sicily is 220V, 50Hz, as in the rest of continental Europe. Several countries outside Europe (such as the USA and Canada) use 110V, which means that appliances with electric motors (such as some CD- and tape-players) from those countries may perform poorly. It is always safest to use a transformer.

Plugs & Sockets
Plugs have two round-pins, again as in the rest of continental Europe.

WEIGHTS & MEASURES
Sicily uses the metric system. Basic terms for weight include un etto (100g) and un chilo (1kg). Like other continental Europeans, the Italians indicate decimals with commas and thousands with points.

LAUNDRY
There are a couple of coin laundrettes in Palermo where you can do your own washing. A load will cost around L8000. The alternative is to wash your underclothes and T-shirts yourself and send your delicates to

a dry cleaner. Dry-cleaning *(lavasecco)* charges range from around L6000 for a shirt to L12,000 for a jacket.

TOILETS
Public toilets are not exactly widespread in Sicily. Most people use the toilets in bars and cafes – although you might need to buy a coffee first!

HEALTH
Medical Services & Emergencies
The quality of medical treatment in public hospitals is not great in Sicily. Overcrowding, underfunding and staff shortages can all add up to a nightmare experience that you would do best to avoid if you can.

Private hospitals and clinics throughout the region generally provide excellent services but are expensive for those without medical insurance. That said, certain treatment in public hospitals may also have to be paid for, and in such cases can be equally costly.

Your embassy or consulate in Italy can provide a list of recommended doctors in major cities; however, if you have a specific health complaint, it would be wise to obtain the necessary information and referrals for treatment before leaving home.

The public health system is administered along provincial lines by centres generally known as Unità Sanitarie Locali (USL) or Unità Soci Sanitarie Locali (USSL). Increasingly they are being reorganised as Aziende Sanitarie Locali (ASL). Through them you find out where your nearest hospital, medical clinics and other services are. Look under 'U' or 'A' in the telephone book (sometimes the USL and USSL are under 'A' too, as Azienda USL).

Under these headings you'll find long lists of offices – look for Poliambulatorio (Polyclinic) and the telephone number for Accetazione Sanitaria. You need to call this number to make an appointment: there is no point in just rolling up. Clinic opening hours vary widely, with the minimum generally being about 8 am to 12.30 pm Monday to Friday. Some open for a couple of hours in the afternoon and on Saturday mornings too.

Each ASL/USL area has its own Consul-

Medical Kit Check List

Following is a list of items consider including in your medical kit – consult your pharmacist for brands available in your country.

- ☐ **Aspirin** or **paracetamol** (acetaminophen in the USA) – for pain or fever
- ☐ **Antihistamine** – for allergies, eg, hay fever; to ease the itch from insect bites or stings; and to prevent motion sickness
- ☐ **Cold and flu tablets, throat lozenges** and **nasal decongestant**
- ☐ **Multivitamins** – consider for long trips, when dietary vitamin intake may be inadequate
- ☐ **Antibiotics** – consider including these if you're travelling well off the beaten track; see your doctor, as they must be prescribed, and carry the prescription with you
- ☐ **Loperamide** or **diphenoxylate** – 'blockers' for diarrhoea
- ☐ **Prochlorperazine** or **metaclopramide** – for nausea and vomiting
- ☐ **Rehydration salts** – to prevent dehydration, which may occur, for example, during bouts of diarrhoea; particularly important when travelling with children
- ☐ **Insect repellent, sunscreen, lip balm** and **eye drops**
- ☐ **Calamine lotion, sting relief spray** or **aloe vera** – to ease irritation from sunburn and insect bites or stings
- ☐ **Antifungal cream** or **powder** – for fungal skin infections and thrush
- ☐ **Antiseptic** (such as povidone-iodine) – for cuts and grazes
- ☐ **Bandages, Band-Aids (plasters)** and other wound dressings
- ☐ **Water purification tablets** or **iodine**
- ☐ **Scissors, tweezers** and a **thermometer** – note that mercury thermometers are prohibited by airlines

torio Familiare (Family Planning Centre) where you can go for contraceptives, pregnancy tests and information about abortion (legal up to the 12th week of pregnancy).

For emergency treatment, go straight to the *pronto soccorso* (casualty) section of a public hospital, where you can also get emergency dental treatment. If you need an ambulance call ☎ 118. Sometimes hospitals are listed in the phone book under Aziende Ospedaliere. In major centres you are likely to find doctors who speak English. Often, first aid is also available at train stations, airports and ports.

Medical Cover

Citizens of EU countries are covered for emergency medical treatment in Sicily on presentation of an E111 form. Treatment in private hospitals is not covered and charges are also likely for medication, dental work and secondary examinations, including X-rays and laboratory tests. Ask about the E111 at your local health services department a few weeks before you travel (in the UK, the form is available at post offices). Australia also has a reciprocal arrangement with Italy so that emergency treatment is covered – Medicare in Australia publishes a brochure with the details. Advise medical staff of any reciprocal arrangements *before* they begin treating you. Most travel insurance policies include medical cover. See Travel Insurance under Documents earlier in the chapter.

Pre-Departure Preparations

Make sure you are healthy before you leave home. If you are embarking on a long trip, have a check-up to make sure your teeth are OK, because dental treatment is particularly expensive in Sicily.

Basic Rules

Stomach upsets are the most likely travel health problem, but in Sicily the majority of these will be relatively minor and probably due to overindulgence in the local food. Some people take a while to adjust to the regular use of olive oil in the food.

Water Tap water is drinkable throughout much of Sicily, although Sicilians themselves have taken to drinking the bottled stuff. The sign *acqua non potabile* tells you that water is not drinkable (you may see it in trains and at some camp sites). Water from drinking fountains is safe unless there is a sign telling you otherwise.

Environmental Hazards

Motion Sickness Eating lightly before and during a trip will reduce the chances of motion sickness. If you are prone, try to find a place that minimises disturbance – near the wing on aircraft, close to midships on boats, near the centre on buses. Fresh air usually helps; reading and cigarette smoke don't. Commercial anti-motion-sickness preparations, which can cause drowsiness, have to be taken before the trip commences. Ginger (available in capsule form) and peppermint (including mint-flavoured sweets) are natural preventatives.

Prickly Heat Caused by excessive perspiration trapped under the skin, prickly heat is an itchy rash. It usually strikes people who have just arrived in a hot climate. Keep cool by bathing often and use a mild talcum powder. You may find that resorting to air-conditioning will help until you become acclimatised.

Sunburn In Sicily you can get sunburnt surprisingly quickly, even through cloud. Use a sunscreen, a hat and some barrier cream for your nose and lips. Calamine lotion is good for soothing mild sunburn. Always protect your eyes with good-quality sunglasses.

Sexually Transmitted Diseases HIV/AIDS and hepatitis B can be transmitted through sexual contact. Other STDs include gonorrhoea, herpes and syphilis; sores, blisters or rashes around the genitals and discharges or pain when urinating are common symptoms. In some STDs, such as wart virus or chlamydia, symptoms may be less marked or not observed at all, especially in women. Chlamydia infection can cause infertility in men and women before any symptoms have been noticed. Syphilis symptoms eventually disappear completely but the disease continues and can cause severe problems in later years. While abstinence from sexual contact is the only 100% effective prevention, using condoms is also effective. The treatment of gonorrhoea and syphilis is with antibiotics. Each of the different sexually transmitted diseases requires treatment with specific antibiotics.

Insect-Borne Diseases

Leishmaniasis This is a group of parasitic diseases transmitted by sandflies and found in coastal parts of Sicily. Cutaneous leishmaniasis affects the skin tissue, causing ulceration and disfigurement; visceral leishmaniasis affects the internal organs. Avoiding sandfly bites by covering up and using repellent is the best precaution against this disease.

Lyme Disease Lyme disease is an infection transmitted by ticks. It can be acquired throughout Europe, including in the forested areas of Sicily. The illness usually begins with a spreading rash at the site of the tick bite and is accompanied by fever, headache, extreme fatigue, aching joints and muscles and mild neck stiffness. If untreated, these symptoms usually resolve over several weeks but, over subsequent weeks or months, disorders of the nervous system, heart and joints may develop. Treatment works best early in the illness. Medical help should be sought.

Bites & Stings

Jellyfish Sicilian beaches are occasionally inundated with jellyfish. Their stings are painful but not dangerous. Dousing in vinegar will deactivate any stingers that have not fired. Calamine lotion, antihistamines and analgesics may reduce the reaction and relieve the pain. If in doubt about swimming, ask locals if any jellyfish are in the water.

Snakes Italy's only dangerous snake, the viper, is found throughout Sicily. To minimise your chances of being bitten, always wear boots, socks and long trousers when walking through undergrowth where snakes may be present – especially at archaeological sites. Don't put your hands into holes and crevices and do be careful when collecting firewood.

Viper bites do not cause imediate death and an antivenene is widely available in pharmacies. Keep the victim calm and still,

wrap the limb tightly, as you would for a sprained ankle, and attach a splint to immobilise it. Then seek medical help, if possible with the dead snake for identification. Don't attempt to catch the snake if there is even a remote possibility of being bitten again. Tourniquets and sucking out the poison are now comprehensively discredited.

WOMEN TRAVELLERS

Sicily is not an especially dangerous region for women, but women travelling alone will often find themselves receiving unwanted attention from men. This attention usually involves staring, catcalls, hisses and whistles and, as such, is more annoying than anything else. Also to be considered is the particular role of women in Sicilian society; although this in the process of changing, there's still a long way to go before Sicily catches up with the more progressive north of Italy (see the boxed text 'Standing on a Pedestal' on the following page)

Lone women may at times also find it difficult to remain alone. It is not uncommon for Sicilian men to harass women in the street, while drinking a coffee in a bar or trying to read a book in a park. On an island where the sanctity of marriage is still held in the highest regard – second only to the sanctity of the Virgin Mary and one's own mother – a wedding ring is often as garlic to a vampire. Otherwise, position yourself near a family group, or group of women, or tell them that you're waiting for your boyfriend *(fidanzato)*. Ignoring them and, if necessary, walking away will also do the trick. As frustrating and annoying though it may be, remember that no real harm is meant: it's just that, more so than in the rest of Italy, 'courting' is the man's responsibility. Avoid becoming aggressive as this almost always results in an unpleasant confrontation. If all else fails, approach the nearest member of the police or *carabinieri* (military police).

Basically, most of the attention falls into the nuisance category. However, women on their own should use their common sense. Avoid walking alone on deserted and dark streets and look for centrally located hotels

Standing on a Pedestal

The role of women in Sicilian society is a traditional and often conflicting one. The conflict is the product of two distinct cultures – Arab and Catholic – that for over 1000 years have seen women cast in the dual role of subservient homemaker and symbol of Catholic purity, worshipped as the embodiment of the Virgin Mary. To the modern thinker such attitudes smack of oppression, because a woman on a pedestal can easily be torn down when she does not live up to the impossible ideals imposed upon her by Sicilian men.

You would be mistaken, however, to assume that women meekly perform this role. Even in the traditional interior, women are recognised as the central force of the family and have adapted to their constricted position with admirable strength and vigour. More often than not it is they who dictate the course of a community's affairs and have exploited the position that has been foisted upon them to their own advantage.

Things are changing, albeit slowly. In the larger, more cosmopolitan cities, such as Palermo and Catania, a younger and better-educated generation has rejected traditional mores in favour of an attitude more in keeping with 21st-century Western values, and it is not uncommon to see groups of women sitting at the bar alongside everyone else. In the fight against the Mafia, women have taken a leading role, organising protest marches and generally involving themselves at every level in the struggle to rid the island of the nefarious influence of organised crime. Sicily is not Sydney, however, and while the struggle for equality of the sexes has come in leaps and bounds, it still lags some way behind.

within easy walking distance of places you can eat at night. It is highly recommended that women should not hitch alone.

Recommended reading is the *Handbook for Women Travellers* by M & G Moss.

GAY & LESBIAN TRAVELLERS

Although homosexuality is legal in Sicily and the age of consent is 16, it is not particularly well tolerated anywhere. There are almost no gay and/or lesbian clubs and bars, and overt displays of affection by homosexual couples can attract a negative response. Yet physical contact between men (and women), such as linking arms and kissing on the cheek, are commonplace and very much part of Sicilian life. It is best to bear this strange dichotomy in mind when travelling throughout the island and – depressing though it may be – to avoid open displays that might incite locals. Again, as with attitudes to women (see Women Travellers earlier in this chapter), the views on homosexuality are changing, at least in cities such as Palermo and Catania, but progress seems to be even slower than it is with women's rights.

The annual *Guida Gay Italia* is available at many news-stands in Palermo and Catania. Also worth checking out is the national monthly gay magazine *Babilonia*, which you can check out on the Internet at www.babilonia.net. If you want to track down the small (but growing) gay scene in Palermo, you can take a look at the Internet at www.palermogay.it or visit the office of Arci Gay (☎ 091 33 56 88) at Via Genova 7.

International gay and lesbian guides worth checking out are the *Spartacus International Gay Guide* (the Spartacus list also includes the comprehensive *Spartacus National Edition Italia*, in English and German), published by Bruno Gmünder Verlag, Mail Order, PO Box 11 07 29, D-1000 Berlin 11, Germany, and *Places for Women*, published by Ferrari Publications, Phoenix, Arizona, USA.

DISABLED TRAVELLERS

The Italian State Tourist Office in your country may be able to provide advice on Italian associations for the disabled and the help available in Sicily (for contact details see Tourist Offices Abroad in the earlier Tourist Office section). It may also carry a small brochure, *Services for Disabled People*, published by the Italian state railway company, Ferrovie dello Stato (FS), which details facilities at stations and on trains. Some of the better trains, such as the

euro currency converter L10,000 = €5.16

ETR460 and ETR500 trains, have a carriage for passengers in wheelchairs and their companions.

The Italian travel agency CIT can advise of hotels with special facilities, such as ramps. It can also request that wheelchair ramps be provided on arrival of your train if you book travel through CIT.

The UK-based Royal Association for Disability & Rehabilitation (RADAR) publishes a guide called *Holidays & Travel Abroad: A Guide for Disabled People*, which provides a useful overview of the facilities that are available for disabled travellers throughout Europe. Contact RADAR (☎ 020-7250 3222) Unit 12, City Forum, 250 City Rd, London EC1V 8AS.

Another organisation worth calling is Holiday Care Service (☎ 01293-774 535). They produce an information pack on Italy (including Sicily) for disabled people and others with special needs.

In Sicily itself you may also be able to get help. Cooperative Integrate (Co.In.) is a national voluntary group with links to the government and branches all over the country. They publish a quarterly magazine for disabled tourists, *Turismo per Tutti* (Tourism for All) in Italian and English. They have information on accessible accommodation, transport and attractions. Co.In. (☎ 06 232 67 505) is at Via Enrico Giglioli 54a, Rome. Its Web site is at andi.casaccia.enea.it/hometur.htm.

SENIOR TRAVELLERS

Seniors are entitled to discounts on public transport and on admission fees at some museums. It is always important to ask. The minimum qualifying age is generally 60 years. You should also seek information in your own country on travel packages and discounts through seniors organisations and travel agencies.

TRAVEL WITH CHILDREN

Discounts are available for children (usually under 12 years of age) on public transport and on admission to museums, galleries and other sites.

Always make a point of asking at tourist offices if they know of any special family or children's activities; these may come in handy if the children (and adults!) have had enough of museums and galleries. Also ask for details on the hotels that cater for kids. Families should book accommodation in advance, wherever possible, to avoid inconvenience.

Chemists *(farmacie)* sell baby formula in powder or liquid form as well as sterilising solutions, such as Milton. Disposable nappies are widely available at supermarkets, chemists (where they are more expensive) and sometimes in larger stationary stores. A pack of around 30 disposable nappies (diapers) costs around L18,000. Fresh cow's milk is sold in cartons in bars (which have a 'Latteria' sign) and in supermarkets. If it is essential that you have milk you should carry an emergency carton of UHT milk, since bars usually close at 8 pm. In many out-of-the-way areas in Sicily the locals use only UHT milk. For more information, see Lonely Planet's *Travel with Children* by Maureen Wheeler.

USEFUL ORGANISATIONS

The Istituto Italiano di Cultura (IIC), with branches all over the world, is an organisation sponsored by the government aimed at promoting Italian culture and language. They put on classes in Italian and provide a library and information service. This is a good place to start your search for places to study in Sicily. The library at the London branch – 39 Belgrave Square, London SW1 (☎ 020-7235 1461) – has an extensive reference book collection, with works on art and history, a range of periodicals and videos. Other IIC branches include:

Australia
(☎ 03-9866 5931) 233 Domain Rd, South Yarra, Melbourne, VIC 3141
(☎ 02-9392 7939) Level 45, Gateway 1, Macquarie Place, Sydney, NSW 2000
Web site: www.iicmelau.org
Canada
(☎ 416-921 3802) 496 Huron Street, Toronto, Ontario M5R 2R3
(☎ 514-849 3473) 1200 Penfield Drive, Montreal, Que H3A 1A9
Web site: www.iicto-ca.org/istituto.htm

France
  (☎ 01 44 39 49 39) Hotel Galliffet,
  50 rue de Varenne, 75007 Paris
  Web site: www.italynet.com/cultura/istcult
Germany
  (☎ 030-261 78 75) Hildebrandstrasse 1,
  10785 Berlin
  (☎ 089-76 45 63) Hermann Schmidtstrasse 8,
  80336 Munich
Ireland
  (☎ 01-676 6662) 11 Fitzwilliam Square,
  Dublin 2
Switzerland
  (☎ 01-202 48 46) Gotthardstrasse 27, 8002
  Zurich
USA
  (☎ 212-879 4242) 686 Park Ave,
  New York, NY 10021-5009
  (☎ 310-443 3250) 1023 Hildegard Ave,
  Los Angeles, CA 90024
  (☎ 202-387 5261) 1717 Massachussets Ave
  S104 NW, Washington, DC 20036
  Web site: www.italcultny.org

Centro Turistico Studentesco e Giovanile
(CTS) is the main Italian student and youth-
travel organisation. They act mainly as a
travel agent, but you can also obtain ISIC,
Euro<26 and Youth Hostel cards at their
branches. Note, however, that you will generally be obliged to pay a joining fee of
L45,000. CTS has branches in the main
centres across Sicily, including Palermo,
Catania and Agrigento.

DANGERS & ANNOYANCES
Theft
This is the main problem for travellers in
Sicily, where a plague of pickpockets and
bag-snatchers operate in the most touristy
parts of the bigger cities and some of the
coastal resort towns.

Prevention is better than cure. Wear a
money belt under your clothing. Keep all
important items, such as money, passport,
other papers and tickets, in your money belt
at all times. If you are carrying a bag or
camera, wear the strap across your body
and have the bag on the side away from the
road to deter snatch thieves who operate
from motorcycles and scooters, an all too
common plague in Palermo. Many of the
perpetrators are young teenagers whose

sorry destiny is to be swallowed up into the
lower ranks of the Mafia – if they haven't
been so already.

Motorists are not immune to thieves either. If you're in traffic, make sure that your
window is rolled up (and hope that you
have air-conditioning!) and that all your
valuables are out of view. A common ploy
by assailants is to accost cars blocked in on
all sides and reach in and grab whatever is
available before speeding off (some thieves
even carry crowbars to smash the window
if they see something of particular value).

Parked cars are the easiest prey for
thieves, particularly those with foreign
number plates or rental company stickers.
Naturally, *never* leave valuables in your car
– in fact, try not to leave anything in the car
if you can help it.

In the case of theft or loss, always make a
report at the police station within 24 hours
and ask for a statement, otherwise your travel
insurance company won't pay out. For emergency numbers see the boxed text under Post
& Communications earlier in this chapter.

Traffic
Sicilian traffic – particularly in Palermo – is
second only to Naples as the most chaotic
in Europe. The unprepared tourist is likely
to be in for a shock when first confronted
with the sheer lunacy of local motorists,
who do not wear seatbelts and have seemingly never heard of the rules of the road.
The honking of car horns is incessant and –
for the most part – without purpose other
than to make noise or greet pedestrian ac-
quaintances passing by. Nearly every car
you will see has a dent on it – these are battle scars, for driving here is truly like a war.
If you must drive in the city, you'll need to
develop nerves of steel pretty quickly and
remember the golden rule: if there's a gap,
go for it, because if you don't someone else
will and everyone behind you will start
honking their disapproval.

Drivers are not keen to stop for pedestri-
ans, even at pedestrian crossings. Sicilians
simply step off the footpath and walk
through the (swerving) traffic with determination – it is a practice which seems to

work, so if you feel uncertain about crossing a busy road, wait for the next Sicilian. In the major cities, roads that appear to be for one-way traffic have special lanes for buses travelling in the opposite direction – always look both ways before stepping out.

LEGAL MATTERS

For many Sicilians, finding ways to get around the law (any law) is a way of life. They are likely to react with surprise, if not annoyance, if you point out that they might be breaking the law. No-one bats an eyelid about littering or dogs pooping in the middle of the footpath – even though many municipal governments have introduced laws against these things.

The average tourist will probably have a brush with the law only if robbed by a bag-snatcher or pickpocket.

Drugs

Sicily's drug laws are lenient on users and heavy on pushers. If you're caught with drugs that the police determine are for your own personal use, you'll be let off with a warning – and, of course, the drugs will be confiscated. If, instead, it is determined that you intend to sell the drugs, you could find yourself in prison. It's up to the police to determine whether or not you're a pusher, since the law is not specific about quantities. The sensible option is to avoid illicit drugs altogether.

Drink Driving

The legal limit for blood alcohol level is 0.08% and breath tests are now in use. Penalties for driving under the influence of alcohol can be severe.

Police

The police (polizia) are a civil force and take their orders from the Ministry of the Interior, while the carabinieri fall under the Ministry of Defence. There is a considerable duplication of their roles, despite a 1981 reform intended to merge the two forces.

The carabinieri wear a dark-blue uniform with a red stripe and drive dark-blue cars with a red stripe. They are well-trained and tend to be helpful. Their police station is called a caserma (barracks). Although innocent queries are always dealt with politely, the carabinieri's role in Sicily is an especially sensitive and difficult one, as along with the regular army (recently confined to barracks) they are the vanguard in the fight against the Mafia; consequently they have a reputation for being harsh and sometimes heavy-handed.

The police wear powder-blue trousers with a fuchsia stripe and a navy-blue jacket and drive light blue cars with a white stripe, with 'polizia' written on the side. Tourists who want to report thefts, and people wanting to get a residence permit, will have to deal with them. They are based at the questura (police station).

Other varieties of police in Italy include the vigili urbani, basically traffic police who you will have to deal with if you get a parking ticket or if your car is towed away; and the guardia di finanza, who are responsible for fighting tax evasion and drug smuggling. Their role in Sicily is vastly inflated compared to the rest of Italy and are given wide berth by many Sicilians; the ordinary tourist, however, will have almost no occasion to deal with them.

BUSINESS HOURS

Generally shops open from around 9 am to 1 pm and 3.30 to 7.30 pm (or 4 to 8 pm) Monday to Friday. Some stay closed on Monday mornings. Big department stores, such as COIN and Rinascente, and most supermarkets have continuous opening hours, from 9 am to 7.30 pm Monday to Saturday. Some even open from 9 am to 1 pm on Sunday. Smaller shops open on Saturday morning until about 1 pm.

Business hours have become more flexible since opening times were liberalised under new trading hours laws that went into effect in April 1999. At the time of writing it was difficult to determine what effect this would have on day-to-day practicalities. As a rule travel agencies open 9 am to 12.30 or 1 pm and 4 to 7 pm.

Banks tend to open from 8.30 am to 1.30 pm and 3.30 to 4.30 pm Monday to

Friday, although hours can vary. They are closed at the weekend, but it is always possible to find an exchange office open in the larger cities and in major tourist areas.

Major post offices open from 8.30 am to 6 or 7 pm Monday to Saturday. Smaller post offices generally open from 8.30 am to 2 pm Monday to Friday and from 8.30 am to midday on Saturday.

Pharmacies are usually open from 9 am to 12.30 pm and 3.30 to 7.30 pm. They are always closed on Sunday and usually on Saturday afternoon. When closed, pharmacies are required to display a list of pharmacies in the area which are open.

Bars (in the Italian sense, that is, coffee-and-sandwich places) and cafes generally open from 7.30 am to 8 pm, although some stay open after 8 pm and turn into pub-style drinking and meeting places. Discos and clubs might open around 10 pm, but often there'll be no-one there until midnight. Restaurants open roughly from midday to 3 pm and 7.30 to 11 pm. Restaurants and bars are required to close for one day each week, (the day varies between establishments).

Museum and gallery opening hours vary, although there is a trend towards continuous opening hours from around 9.30 am to 7 pm. Many close on Monday.

PUBLIC HOLIDAYS

Most Sicilians take their annual holiday in August, deserting the cities for the cooler seaside or mountains. This means that many businesses and shops close for at least a part of the month, particularly during the week around Feast of the Assumption (Ferragosto) on 15 August. The Easter break (Settimana Santa) is another busy holiday period for Sicilians. To give you an idea of when this period will fall in the next few years, Good Friday is April 13 in 2001 and March 29 in 2002.

National public holidays in Sicily include the following:

New Year's Day (Anno Nuovo) 1 January – Celebrations take place on New Year's Eve (Capodanno)
Epiphany (Befana) 6 January
Good Friday (Venerdì Santo) March/April

Easter Monday (Pasquetta/Giorno dopo Pasqua) March/April
Liberation Day (Giorno della Liberazione) 25 April – Marks the Allied victory in Italy and the end of the German presence and Mussolini
Labour Day (Giorno del Lavoro) 1 May
Feast of the Assumption (Ferragosto) 15 August
All Saints' Day (Ognissanti) 1 November
Feast of the Immaculate Conception (Concezione Immaculata) 8 December
Christmas Day (Natale) 25 December
St Stephen's Day (Boxing Day, Festa di Santo Stefano) 26 December

Individual towns also have public holidays to celebrate the feasts of their patron saints. See the following section.

SPECIAL EVENTS

Sicily's calendar is full to bursting with events, ranging from colourful traditional celebrations, with a religious and/or historical flavour, through to festivals of the performing arts, including opera, music and theatre. Some appear in the following list:

January
Epiphany (Befana)
The town of Piana degli Albanesi, near Palermo, celebrates the festival of *La Befana* with a colourful parade that culminates in a fireworks' display.

February
Carnevale
During the week before Ash Wednesday many towns stage carnivals and enjoy their last opportunity to indulge before Lent (the name derives from the Latin for 'goodbye meat'). The popular festivities in Sciacca are renowned throughout Sicily for imaginative floats, which are usually made up along allegorical themes. The party in Taormina is also pretty good.
Feast of St Agatha (Festa di Sant'Agata)
From the third to the fifth of the month Catania celebrates the feast of its patron saint with the procession of the saint's relics amid foodstalls, fireworks and all-round mayhem.

April
Easter (Pasqua)
Holy Week in Sicily is a very big deal, and is marked by solemn, slow-moving processions and passion plays. Trapani's procession of the

Misteri is the island's most famous, but there are similar processions worth checking out in Enna and in towns throughout the island.

Motor Racing (Corsa Automobilistica)

The circuit is around Lago di Pergusa near Enna. Racing begins its season on the last weekend of April and runs to the end of September.

July

Feast of St Rosalia (Festa di Santa Rosalia)

From the 11th to the 15th Palermo pulls out all the stops in the celebration of one of its patron saints; amid the street celebrations – music, food, dancing and partying – the saint's relics are brought through the Quattro Canti.

August

Medieval Pageant (Palio dei Normanni)

On the 14th and 15th of the month Enna is almost completely given over to a wonderful celebration of its Norman past as it commemorates Count Roger's taking of the town from the Arabs in the 13th century. There are costumed parades, a procession into the town and even a joust.

September

Pilgrimages (Pelegrinaggi)

This is the month for many of Sicily's pilgrimages. The most important are on the 4th to Mt Pellegrino, north of Palermo, and to the church at Gibilmanna in the Madonie on the 8th.

ACTIVITIES

If the museums, galleries and sights are not enough for you there are numerous options to get you off the beaten track.

Cycling

This is a good option for people who can't afford to hire a car but want to see some of the more out-of-the-way places, particularly in the interior. You'll need some serious stamina and a good bike to tame the mountains and hills though. You can either bring your own bike or buy or hire one in Sicily. Bike hire costs between L20,000 and L30,000 per day.

Skiing

Strange as it may seem, Sicily has two winter ski resorts, in the Parco Naturale Regionale delle Madonie (see the Tyrrhenian Coast chapter) and on Mt Etna (see the Eastern Sicily chapter). Skiing in Sicily tends to be cheaper than in northern Italy.

Walking

The serious walker will relish the chance to climb a volcano or two, both on the mainland and on the Aeolian Islands. The Nebrodi (see the Central Sicily chapter) and Madonie nature reserves (see the Tyrrhenian Coast chapter) also have well-marked and challenging trails.

If you plan on walking to Mt Etna, remember that this is an active volcano and walkers are strongly advised not to proceed beyond the safety zone (usually marked out with ropes). See the Mt Etna section in the Eastern Coast chapter for details.

If you plan on doing a little walking while in Sicily, especially on the island's volcanoes, you should pick up *Walking in Italy* by Lonely Planet, which has in-depth chapters on climbing both Stromboli and Mt Etna.

Water Sports

Scuba-diving, snorkelling, windsurfing and sailing are extremely popular at Sicily's beach resorts, where you will have no problem renting boats and equipment. On Lipari (see the Aeolian Islands chapter) you will find plenty of outfits willing to relieve you of your money in exchange for diving courses and windsurfing instruction.

WORK

It is illegal for non-EU citizens to work in Sicily without a work permit, but trying to obtain one can be time-consuming. EU citizens are allowed to work in Sicily, but they still need to obtain a resident permit from the main police station in the town where they have found work. See Work Permits in the Documents section earlier in the chapter for more information. The main challenge, however, will not be bureaucracy but the economy, which has unemployment in Sicily at 27%, the highest of any region in Italy. Frankly, other than being sent here by a company or teaching a little English, you won't have much luck securing employment.

English Tutoring

Virtually the only source of work available to foreigners in Sicily is teaching English, but even with full qualifications an American, Australian, Canadian or New Zealander might find it difficult to secure even a temporary position. There are language schools in Palermo, Catania and a few larger towns, but teaching positions don't often come up. Most of the more reputable schools will only hire people with a work permit and will require at least a Teaching English as a Foreign Language (TEFL) certificate. It is advisable to apply for work early in the year, in order to be considered for positions that become available in October (language school years correspond roughly to the Italian school year: late September to the end of June).

Some schools hire people without work permits or qualifications, but the pay is usually low (around L15,000 an hour). It is more lucrative to advertise your services and pick up private students (although rates vary wildly, ranging from as low as L15,000 up to L50,000 an hour). Most people get started by placing advertisements in shop windows and on university notice boards Although you can get away with absolutely no qualifications or experience, it might be a good idea to bring along a few English grammar books (including exercises) to help you at least appear professional.

ACCOMMODATION

Prices for accommodation quoted in this book are intended as a guide only and generally reflect the cost of a room during high season (April to September). There tends to be a fair degree of fluctuation in hotel prices, depending on the season and, sometimes, whim. It is not unusual for prices to remain fixed for years on end and, in some cases, they even go down. It is more common that they rise by around 5% or 10% annually. Always check room charges before putting your bags down.

Reservations

It's a good idea to book a room in advance if you are planning to travel during peak tourist periods. Hotels usually require confirmation by fax or letter, as well as a deposit. Tourist offices will generally send out information about hotels, camping, apartments and so on.

Camping

Camp sites in Sicily vary in terms of facilities: some are well-organised and well-laid out, others are simply an empty space where you can pitch a tent and facilities comprise of little more than a toilet-and-shower block.

Even the most basic camp sites can be surprisingly dear once you add up the various charges for each person and the site for your tent or caravan and a car, but they generally still work out cheaper than a double room in a one-star hotel. Prices range from L6000/6000 per adult/child aged under 12, to L18,000/12,000, plus L7000 to L18,000 for a site. You'll also often have to pay to park your car and there is sometimes a charge for use of the showers, usually around L2000.

Independent camping is generally not permitted and you might find yourself disturbed during the night by the carabinieri. But, out of the main summer tourist season, independent campers who choose spots not visible from the road, don't light fires, and who try to be inconspicuous, shouldn't have too much trouble. Always get permission from the landowner if you want to camp on private property. Camper vans are popular in Italy.

Touring Club Italiano publishes an annual book which lists all the camp sites in Sicily, *Campeggi in Italia* (L32,000), and the Istituto Geografico de Agostini publishes the annual *Guida ai Campeggi in Europa*, which is sold together with *Guida ai Campeggi in Italia* (L29,900). These guides are in Italian only and are available in all major bookshops.

Hostels

Youth hostels *(ostelli per la gioventù)*, of which there are only a handful in Sicily, are run by the Associazione Italiana Alberghi per la Gioventù (AIG), which is affiliated to Hostelling International (HI). You need to be a member, but can join at one of the hostels. For details on how to get a card see Hostel Cards in the Visas & Documents section earlier in the chapter. Nightly rates vary from L16,000 to L24,000 including breakfast. A meal will cost L14,000. Check out the AIG Web site at www.hostels-aig.org for details of facilities on offer.

Accommodation is in segregated dormitories, although some hostels offer family rooms (at a higher price per person).

Hostels are generally closed from 10 am to 3.30 pm. Check-in is from 6 to 10.30 pm, although some hostels will allow you a morning check-in before they close for the day (it is best to confirm beforehand). Curfew is 11.30 pm or midnight. It is usually necessary to pay before 9 am on the day of your departure, otherwise you could be charged for another night.

Guesthouses & Hotels

Hotels (albergi) and guesthouses (pensioni) are allowed to increase their prices twice a year, although many don't. Travellers should always check on prices before deciding to stay. Make a complaint to the local tourist office if you believe you're being overcharged. Many proprietors employ various methods of bill-padding, such as charging for showers, or making breakfast compulsory.

There is often no difference between a guesthouse and a hotel; in fact, some establishments use both titles. However, a hotel will generally be of one to three-star quality, while a guesthouse can be awarded up to five stars.

Inns (locande, similar to pensioni) and affittacamere (rooms to rent, also known as alloggi) are generally, but not always, cheaper. Inns and affittacamere are not included in the classification system.

Quality of accommodation can vary a great deal. One-star hotels/guesthouses tend to be basic and usually do not have an en-suite bathroon. Standards at two-star places are often only slightly better, but rooms will generally have a private bathroom. Once you arrive at three stars you can assume that standards will be reasonable, although quality still varies dramatically between establishments. Four- and five-star hotels are sometimes part of a group of hotels and offer facilities such as room service, laundry and dry-cleaning.

Prices are highest in Taormina, on the Aeolian Islands (especially Lipari, Vulcano and Stromboli) and in Cefalù.

A single room (camera singola) will always be expensive. Although there are a few pokey exceptions, you should reckon on a minimum of L30,000, while a double room with twin beds (camera doppia) and a double with a double bed (camera matrimoniale) cost from around L50,000. It is much cheaper to share with two or more people. Proprietors will often charge no more than 15% of the cost of a double room for each additional person.

Tourist offices have booklets listing accommodation, including prices (although they might not always be up to date).

Agriturismo

Agriturismo is a holiday on a working farm, and is an idea that is gaining in popularity in Sicily. Traditionally the idea was that families rented out rooms in their farmhouses, and it is still possible to find this type of accommodation. However, more commonly now the term refers to a restaurant in a restored farm complex, which has rooms that are available for rent. All agriturismo establishments are operating farms and you will usually be able to sample the local produce.

They are becoming an increasingly popular choice with travellers wanting to enjoy the peace and quiet of the countryside. Generally you will need to have your own transport to get to and away from these places. Check with local tourist offices for information on agriturismo options available in the area.

Rental Accommodation

Finding rental accommodation in the cities can be difficult and time-consuming, but not impossible. Rental agencies will assist, for a fee. A one-room apartment with kitchenette in Lipari will cost from L600,000 to L1,000,000 a month (long term). Renting in other towns can be considerably cheaper.

Short-term rental is inevitably more expensive, but many locals are keen to rent to foreigners for brief periods.

EATING *ALLA SICILIANA*

CHRISTOPHER WOOD

Sicily is recognised throughout Italy for the high quality of its cuisine, which has evolved over 25 centuries of foreign occupation and influence. In a country where preparing even the simplest meal is treated as an art form and each region proudly proclaims its superiority over the others, Sicilian cooking is granted a seat at the table of honour. As you would expect from an island, the emphasis is on fish – and in Sicily you will find the day's catch in virtually everything you see on a menu – but meat should not be ignored either. Their greatest achievement, the incredible variety of imaginatively created cakes and pastries: an ideal way to top off any meal.

The secret of Sicilian cuisine lies in the island's climate and history. Due to the warm weather, vegetables grow pretty much year-round, and they are usually fresher, juicier and more abundant than those grown in the seasonal climates up north – eat a Sicilian tomato and you'll notice the difference. You will also notice that the cooking is spicier than elsewhere in Italy: this is a legacy of the Arabs, who more than any other foreign occupier left their stamp on the Sicilian kitchen, particularly in the west, where a popular substitute for pasta is couscous (a fish-based version, rather than the more common meat-based North African variety). Other cultures have also played their part: the Greeks introduced the olive and the vine, the Romans turned the island over to the wholesale planting of wheat, while Spanish rule saw an imaginative and varied approach to the preparation of fish.

Recommended further reading includes Lonely Planet's full-colour World Food Italy, which incorporates information on the cuisine of Sicily. For assistance deciphering the menu turn to the glossary at the back of this book.

You can find details of a cooking course under Organised Tours in the Getting There & Away chapter.

Antipasti

Sicilians aren't big on *antipasti* (literally 'before pasta'), or hors d'oeuvres, but in recent decades they have started making an appearance on the Sicilian table. In Palermo, the most common dish is *panelle*, chickpea fritters cooked in olive oil and flavoured with parsley. In the east a popular titbit is *olive fritte*, olives fried in olive oil, crushed garlic, vinegar and marjoram. The Spanish introduced the white bean to the island (appositely called *fagioli Spagnoli* here), which you will find boiled and flavoured with garlic, celery and chunks of mint leaves – hence the dish *fagioli alla menta*.

Pasta

Not surprisingly, many of the island's pasta dishes lean heavily on the use of fish and vegetables. The simplest of all pasta dishes – available on virtually every menu on the island – is *pasta a picchi pacchiu*, the

A Sicilian Meal

Most travellers leave Sicily with a taste for Sicilian cuisine. To help you recreate the experience of a fine meal in the comfort of your own home, there follows a set of recipes, from *antipasto* to *dolce* (sweet). The servings are for four people.

Panelle

200g of chickpea flour
a fistful parsley (chopped)

2 tablespoons of olive oil
salt

Mix the flour with ½ litre of cold, salted water and place in a pot. Cook on a medium to high flame, stirring continuously until the water has evaporated and you're left with a dough-like, solid lump. Add the parsley and remove from the flame. Knead the mixture into moulds, which traditionally are flat, wooden rectangles 9cm long, 4cm wide and ½cm thick (but any mould will do). When the mixture has cooled, detach the pieces from the moulds and fry in hot olive oil.

Pasta con le Sarde

2 onions (finely sliced)
4 anchovy fillets
1kg fennel
1kg fresh sardines (boned)
50g raisins (softened)

50g pine nuts
a few strands of saffron
½ a wine glass of olive oil
bucatini (long, hollow tubes of pasta)
salt and pepper

First, boil the fennel in a pot of well-salted water. After approximately seven minutes drain in a colander by pressing with the back of a spoon, squeezing out all the moisture. Keep the water in which you boiled it. Mince the fennel and set aside. Lightly-fry the onions in the olive oil, and add the anchovies. Next, chop the sardines (pilchards are the best type to use) into small pieces and add to the onions. Add salt, pepper and the fennel and cook the lot for about five minutes. Then add raisins (first, let them soak in water for about 20 minutes to soften), pine nuts and some saffron thinned with a little water. Once you've done this, turn to your pot of boiling water and half-cook the bucatini (this should take no more than six or seven minutes; you can also use *penne*, *rigatoni* or any other type of short pasta), drain, and add to the sauce. Cook the mixture until the pasta is *al dente* (firm to the bite) and serve.

Pesce Spada alla Messinese

4 thick slices of
   boned swordfish

1 wine glass of olive oil
a fistful of salted capers

A Sicilian Meal

1 garlic clove (crushed)
1 onion (finely sliced)
750g tomatoes
  (peeled and chopped)
75g green olives
  (stoned and chopped)
20g pine nuts
1 stick of celery (sliced)
20g of raisins (softened)
1 basil leaf
fish/vegetable stock
pinch of salt and pepper

Coat the swordfish with flour and fry lightly in a deep pan with olive oil. Once cooked (it'll take about seven minutes), drain, transfer to a flameproof pan and keep hot. Using the same oil, fry the onion and add the rest of the ingredients. Cook for about five minutes on a medium flame and then pour over the fish. Thin with a ladle of stock and place in a preheated oven where it should be cooked at 180°C for about ten minutes. Remove, let it cool slightly and serve.

Cannoli
dough
250g white flour
1 egg-white
knob of lard
1 tablespoon of sugar
1 teaspoon of coffee powder
1 teaspoon of bitter cocoa
1½ cups of white wine
pinch of salt

filling
250g ricotta cheese (sieved)
150g sugar
50g candied fruits (diced)
50g cooking chocolate

Sicily's most famous pastry was originally made with orange rind, but the modern version can be made using flour. Pile flour onto a surface and make a hole in the middle of the mound. Into this put egg-white, lard, sugar, coffee powder, cocoa and a pinch of salt. Gradually add wine to make a solid dough. Knead the dough, wrap it in a towel and let it rest for about one hour. Then remove the towel and spread the dough across the surface to a thickness of approximately ¼cm. Cut circles of about 10cm in diameter and then wrap them around a cylinder greased with lard – a cane or tin cylinder about 13cm long and 2cm wide will do – ensuring that the joints have been sealed with egg white. Place the cylinder with the dough into hot oil and cook until browned. Remove the cylinders and let the 'tubes' drain.

   To prepare the filling, knead ricotta cheese with sugar, candied fruits and cooking chocolate. Blend the mixture, stuff the tubes and serve.

Sicilian version of pasta with tomato and chilli sauce. Sicilian tomatoes are renowned throughout Italy for their rich, fulsome flavour, and it is unlikely you'll eat a better version of the dish anywhere else in the country. Unlike the mainland, which uses parmesan almost exclusively, Sicilians like to spread liberal helpings of a strong cheese called *caciocavallo* on their pasta dishes (despite the name *cavallo*, which means horse, the cheese is actually made from cow's milk) – although you will find parmesan served in most restaurants.

The most famous and typical of all Sicilian pasta dishes is *pasta con le sarde* (pasta with sardines), which can be found most anywhere along the coast. It is a heavy dish that can look less than appetising, but the liberal use of wild mountain fennel (unique to Sicily), onions, pine nuts and raisins give the sardines a wonderfully exotic flavour. Catania is home to *pasta alla Norma*, whose rich combination of tomatoes, aubergine and grated ricotta cheese was named in tribute to the city's most famous son, the composer of *Norma*, Vincenzo Bellini. High tribute indeed. In the interior you will find a dependency on meat (mostly mutton and beef) and cheese rather than fish in the preparation of pasta dishes. Baroque Modica is where the island's best lasagne (*lasagne cacate*) are made, with two kinds of cheese – ricotta and *pecorino* (sheep's cheese) – added to minced beef and sausage and spread between layers of home-made pasta 'squares'.

Fish

One could devote an entire book to the use of fish in Sicilian cuisine. The extensive development of underwater fishing and – until recent years – the widespread presence of bluefish (including sardines, tuna and mackerel) off the island's shores have ensured that fish is a staple of most meals, at least anywhere near a coastline. Each town and city has its own specialities, even though the tourist boom has seen a spread of local dishes on to menus throughout Sicily.

In Palermo, a local favourite is *sarde a beccafico alla Palermitana* (Palermitan-style stuffed sardines), which are best eaten in the fried-fish shops around the traditional Vucciria market. Here in the capital you can also try the *polpette di nunnata* (fishballs), which in recent years have been increasingly difficult to find due to the largely illegal use of freshly-hatched anchovies, sardines and red mullet. The fish are pounded into a pulp and fried with parsley, garlic and

Below: Fish is a fundamental ingredient in the island's cuisine.

JANE SMITH

grated pecorino cheese. In Messina, *agghiotta di pesce spada* is a local classic which you will also see labelled as *pesce spada alla Messinese* (Messinese-style swordfish), a mouth-watering dish flavoured with pine nuts, sultanas, garlic, basil and tomatoes. The western Egadi Islands are home to two splendid fish dishes, *tonno 'nfurnatu* (oven-baked tuna with tomatoes, capers and pale olives) and *alalunga di Favignana al ragù*, fried albacore which is served in a spicy sauce of tomatoes, red chilli peppers and garlic; it is not uncommon to see the sauce appear as part of your pasta dish either. Finally, a popular food throughout the island is *calamari* and *calamaretti* (squid and baby squid) which are prepared in a variety of ways: stuffed, fried, or sauteed in a tomato sauce.

Meat

Although you can find a limited number of meat dishes along the coast, you won't see the best dishes until you move further inland. The province of Ragusa is perhaps the most renowned for its superb and imaginative uses of meat, particularly mutton, beef, pork and rabbit. Its most famous dish is *falsomagro*, a stuffed roll of minced beef, sausages, bacon, egg and pecorino cheese. Another local speciality is *coniglio all-agrodolce* (sweet-and-sour rabbit), which is marinated in a sauce of red wine flavoured with onions, olive oil, onions, bay leaves and rosemary. In the Madonie mountains, Castelbuono is the home of *capretto in umido* (stewed kid) and *agnello al forno all Madonita* (Madonie-style roast lamb). The latter is left to soak in a marinade of oil, lemon juice, garlic, onion and rosemary which gives it a particularly delicious flavour.

Desserts

Sicilians are justifiably proud of their desserts, which are perhaps the island's culinary highlight. Of the dessert cakes, pride of place goes to the *cassata*, made with ricotta cheese, sugar, vanilla, diced chocolate and candied fruits. In a restaurant always ask if it is home-made *(fatto in casa)* to ensure that what you get isn't a supermarket imitation of the real thing. In the west you can find *cuccia*, an Arab cake made with grain, honey and ricotta. Most will have heard of the famous *cannoli* (cream horns), which are found throughout the island but are best in Palermo. Sicily's extraordinary pastries – rich in colour and elaborately designed – may well be the best you'll ever find. Any decent *pasticceria* (pastry shop) will have an enormous spread of freshly made cakes and little pastries that are a perfect accompaniment to after-dinner coffee. It is very common for Sicilians to have their meal in a restaurant and then go to a pastry shop where they have their coffees and cakes while standing at the bar. Chocoholics will salivate at the displays of little buns overflowing with rich chocolate cream.

If you are in Palermo around late October, before the festival of Ognissanti (All Saints' Day, 1 November) you will see plenty of stalls selling and displaying the famous almond confectioneries known as *frutti della Martorana* (fruit of the Martorana), named after the church which first began producing them. There's nothing fruity about them other than their appearance, but this almond paste biscuit is part of a Sicilian tradition that dates back to the Middle Ages. Today the 'fruits' are sold all over the island pretty much throughout the year, but only during the week preceding All Saints' Day will you appreciate their wonderful array of colour and shape.

JANE SMITH

Left:
It would be a Sicilian heaven for the sweet-toothed. Cassata and cannoli are specialities.

Wines

Sicily is not famous for its wines, but there are a few that can compete with the more renowned wines of the Italian mainland. The island's most prized producer is Regeleali, which produces robust reds and some delicious whites that go perfectly with almost any dish. The wine you'll see on most menus, however, is the Corvo di Salaparuta, a velvety red that is an ideal companion to falsomagro, while the whites are usually quite fresh and slightly fruity. The island's most popular white wine is Rapitalà from Alcamo, a soft, neutral white that goes well with most whitefish dishes. If you're looking for something a little more flavoured you might try one of the Etna whites, whose mild fragrance of wine flowers sits well with the spicier bluefish dishes. Other excellent reds include Ceravasuolo (produced around Ragusa and Comiso) and Donnafugata – ask for that produced at the Vigna di Gabri.

Messina produces the strong Faro red which goes well with most meat dishes, while also from the area is a good white called Capo Bianco. Grapes cultivated on the volcanic soil around Etna are used in the production of Etna reds, rosés and whites. Another good choice from the area is the rosé Ciclopi – it is known as the best wine to drink with rabbit dishes.

From the south-west, the best-known wines are the red Terreforti produced near Catania and the Anapo white, Eloro and Pachino reds, all produced near Syracuse. In recent years the three wines from the Agrigento region – Drepano, Draceno and Saturno – have made an impact on the American market. From the west, Belice (red and white) and Capo Boeo (white) are good choices. Segesta reds and whites are also popular for their well-balanced body and generous taste.

Sicilian dessert wines are excellent. Top of the list is Marsala, the sweet wine from the western port city. Sweet Malvasia from the Aeolians is a fruity wine whose best producer is Carlo Hauser – just look for his name on the bottle and you'll know you have a good one. Italy's most famous Muscat is the Moscato di Pantelleria, which also comes as a table red.

There are three main classifications of wine – DOCG (*denominazione d'origine controllata e garantita*), DOC (*denominazione di origine controllata*) and *vino da tavola* (table wine) – which will be marked on the label. A DOC wine is produced subject to certain specifications, although the label does not certify quality. DOCG is subject to the same requirements as normal DOC but it is also tested by government inspectors. While there are table wines better left alone, there are also some that are of excellent quality, notably the Sicilian Corvo red and white.

For hints on particular vineyards you might want to invest in a wine guide. Burton Anderson's hardback guide *Wines of Italy* is a handy little tool to have in your back pocket.

FOOD

Eating is one of life's great pleasures for Sicilians and, though they have stiff competition from other Italian regions, they pride themselves on being at the top of the pile when it comes to dining well. See the previous special 'Eating alla Siciliana' section for information on when, where and what to eat, plus some pointers on Sicilian wine.

Lonely Planet's *World Food Italy* is a full-colour book with information on the whole range of Italian food and drink, including Sicily. It incorporates a useful language section, with the definitive culinary dictionary and a handy quick-reference glossary.

Vegetarian Food

Vegetarians will have few problems eating in Sicily, although vegans may make heavier weather of it. While few restaurants are strictly vegetarian, vegetables are a staple of the Italian diet. Most eating establishments serve a good selection of vegetable *antipasti* (starters) and *contorni* (vegetable side orders prepared in a variety of ways).

Self-Catering

If you have access to cooking facilities, it is best to buy fruit and vegetables at open markets, and salami, cheese and table wine at *alimentari* (grocery store), which are a cross between grocery stores and delicatessens. *Salumerie* sell sausages, meats and sometimes cheeses. For quality wine, search out an *enoteca*. For fresh bread go to a *forno* or *panetteria* (bakeries that sell bread, pastries and sometimes groceries)r or an alimentari. Most towns also have supermarkets.

DRINKS
Nonalcoholic Drinks

Coffee The first-time visitor to Sicily is likely to be confused by the many ways in which the locals consume their caffeine. Sicilians take their coffee seriously; some say even more seriously than in the rest of Italy, which is quite a feat.

First is the pure and simple *espresso* – a tiny cup of very strong black coffee. *Doppio-espresso* is a double shot of the same. You could also ask for a *caffè lungo*, but this may end up being more like the watered-down version with which Anglos will be more familiar. If you want to be quite sure of getting the watery version, ask for a *caffè americano*.

Enter the milk. A *caffè latte* is coffee with a reasonable amount of milk. To most locals it is a breakfast or morning drink. A stronger version is the *caffè macchiato*, basically an espresso with a dash of milk. Alternatively, you can have *latte macchiato*, a glass of hot milk with a dash of coffee. The *cappuccino* is basically a frothy version of the caffé latte. You can ask for it *senza schiuma* (without froth), in which case the froth is scraped off the top. It tend to comes lukewarm, so if you want it hot, ask for it *molto caldo*.

In summer, the local version of an iced coffee is a *caffè freddo*, served in a long glass and sometimes helped along with ice cubes.

To warm up on those winter nights, a *corretto* might be for you – an espresso 'corrected' with a dash of *grappa* (grape liqueur) or some other spirit. Some locals have it as a heart-starter.

After lunch and dinner it wouldn't occur to Italians to order either caffè latte or a cappuccino – espressos, macchiatos and correttos are perfectly acceptable. Of course, if you want a cappuccino there's no problem – but you might have to repeat your request a couple of times to convince disbelieving waiters that they have heard correctly.

An espresso or macchiato can cost from an island-wide standard of L1400 or L1500 standing at a bar to L3500 sitting outside at the Teatro Massimo in Palermo.

Granita Sicily's greatest contribution to summer thirst-quenchers is *granita*, a drink made of crushed ice with fresh lemon or other fruit juices, or with coffee topped with fresh whipped cream. Like the Irish with Guinness, Sicilians treat it as the creation of a skilled artisan and will be glad to recommend where the best *granite* are to be had in their town.

Latte di Mandorla The cultivation of almonds is widespread throughout Sicily, so the Sicilians have invented a delicious cold drink that is basically almond pulp and water. It is drunk mostly in the west, where you can also buy it in supermarkets, but the best place to get it is in a bar, where it is freshly made.

Tea Sicilians don't drink a lot of tea *(tè)* and, if they do, generally only in the late afternoon, when they might take a cup with a few *pasticcini* (small cakes). You can order tea in bars, though it will usually arrive in the form of a cup of warm water with an accompanying tea bag. If this doesn't suit your taste, ask for the water molto caldo or *bollente* (boiling). In places where there is a substantial Arab influence (Mazara del Vallo, for instance), you might find *tè ai pinoli* (pine-nut tea), often spruced up with a mint leaf. You can find a range of herbal teas in herbalist's shops *(erboristeria)*, which will sometimes also stock health foods.

Soft Drinks The usual range of international soft drinks are available in Sicily, although they tend to be expensive if bought outside a supermarket (anywhere between L1500 and L3000).

Water While tap water is reliable throughout the country, most Sicilians prefer to drink bottled mineral water *(acqua minerale)*. It will be either sparkling *(frizzante)* or still *(naturale)* and you will be asked in restaurants and bars which you would prefer. If you want a glass of tap water, ask for *acqua dal rubinetto*, although simply asking for *acqua naturale* will also suffice.

Alcoholic Drinks
Beer The main domestic labels are Peroni, Dreher and Moretti, all very drinkable and cheaper than the imported varieties.

Sicily imports beers from throughout Europe and the rest of the world. Several German beers, for instance, are available in bottles or cans; English beers and Guinness are often found on tap *(alla spina)* in *birrerie* (bars specialising in beer).

Wine See the separate special section 'Eating *alla Siciliana*' earlier in the chapter for details.

Liqueurs Sicily's most famous dessert wine is Marsala, made exclusively in and around the city of the same name. It is basically a heavy sweet wine that is the Sicilian equivalent to port. The best (and most widely known) label is Florio. After dinner try a shot of grappa, a strong, clear brew made from grapes. Or you could go with an *amaro*, a dark liqueur prepared from herbs. For a sweeter liqueur, try an almond-flavoured *amaretto* or the aniseed *sambuca*.

ENTERTAINMENT
Bars & Pubs
Italians cannot be said to have a 'drinking culture' but, especially in the bigger cities, you'll find plenty of bars. You can get a beer, wine or anything else at practically any bar where you can also get coffee. They range from workaday grungy to chic places to be seen. Places operating first and foremost as nocturnal drinking establishments generally stay open until about 1 am.

Perhaps one reason why Italians don't tend to wander out of bars legless is the price of a drink. A tiny glass of beer can start at around L4000! For a pint you are looking at an average of L8000.

Discos & Clubs
Discos (what Brits think of as clubs) are expensive: entrance charges hover around L20,000, which may include a drink. Sicily is not the most happening clubland but you'll find some reasonable places in Palermo and coastal spots such as Cefalù and Taormina. Some are huge, with several dance spaces catering to various tastes.

Outside the big cities and the summer resorts the pickings are slim. Often the clubs are out in the countryside and if you aren't in the know and don't have wheels they can remain pretty much out of reach. The theory is that at least the city- and town-dwellers don't have their sleep ruined.

Jazz
The number of jazz fans is growing in Sicily. A real treat is to see live jazz at the Chiesa di Santa Maria dello Spasimo in Palermo, a wonderful venue that is free to

all (see Lo Spasimo in the Palermo chapter for more details).

Classical Music
Palermo is the place for classical concerts, either at the Teatro Massimo or at the Teatro Politeama-Garibaldi. See the Palermo chapter for details.

Cinemas
There is no shortage of cinemas in Sicily, but unless the film is an Italian production, none of them show films in their original language. It costs about L13,000 to see a movie, although that can come down to L6000 on the cheap day (often Wednesday).

Theatre
If you can understand Italian, you'll have several theatres to choose from in places such as Palermo, Syracuse, Catania and Enna. Performances in languages other than Italian are hard to come by. Tourist offices should be able to help out with information.

SPECTATOR SPORT
Football
Il calcio excites Sicilian souls more than politics, religion, good food and dressing up all put together. Unfortunately, no Sicilian team has been in the premier league (Serie A) for quite a while; Palermo are perennial strugglers around the middle of Serie C. Most Sicilians, though, are fanatical supporters of Italy's most successful team of the last 40 years, Juventus of Turin, who on those rare occasions when they are forced to play a home match away from home (usually as a punishment imposed by soccer authorities on account of crowd trouble), always play in Palermo's La Favorita stadium. Tickets for matches at La Favorita can be bought from newspaper kiosks in Palermo.

SHOPPING
Shopping in Sicily is probably not what you are used to back home. Most shops are small businesses, and large department stores and supermarkets tend to be thin on the ground.

If you need necessities such as underwear, tights, pyjamas, T-shirts or toiletries head for one of the large retail stores such as COIN or Rinascente, found in most major cities. Otherwise, you can pick up underwear, tights and pyjamas in a haberdashery *(merceria)*, toiletries and condoms in a pharmacy or sometimes in an alimentari, and items such as T-shirts in a normal clothing store. Supermarkets also stock toiletries and condoms. For stationary such as airmail paper, notepads, pens, greeting cards and so on try a paper-goods shop *(cartoleria)*.

The most interesting place to shop in Sicily are at the markets, and every town worth its salt has at least one. Palermo's Vucciria is probably the most famous of all, but it is no longer what it once was and most Palermitans shop in one of the city's two other markets. Catania has a fine produce market, as does Syracuse. At most markets you can pick up virtually everything you need, from fish to frocks and all things in between. These are also the places to go to buy the best in imitation gear, as most Sicilians like to dress well but can't afford to buy the real McCoy.

Ceramics
Since the days of the ancient Greeks, Sicily has deservedly maintained a reputation for high-quality ceramics. The best places to buy them are in Caltagirone, Santo Stefano di Camastra and Sciacca, the main centres of production.

Souvenirs & Handicrafts
Sicily does a roaring trade in souvenirs and handicrafts, particularly as most of the traditional crafts are fast disappearing, leaving the past in the hands of souvenir sellers. One of the most popular souvenirs is a miniature model of the traditional Sicilian cart, which once ruled the countryside before the advent of sealed roads. Pain stakingly decorated with all kinds of colourful features, the originals are now collector's items in high demand. Also popular are Sicilian puppets from the island's most typical form of entertainment, the puppet theatre.

Getting There & Away

Sicily is not the easiest place in Europe to get to. The best (and fastest) way to get there is by air, which can often be cheaper than the long overland route, which involves travelling the length of Italy. Competition between airlines on intercontinental routes means you should be able to pick up a reasonably priced fare, even if you are coming from as far away as Australia or New Zealand, to one of Italy's main airports in Rome or Milan, from where it's no problem to pick up a connecting flight to Sicily. There are a limited number of direct flights from the rest of Europe as well as some interesting charter options to either Palermo or Catania. If you plan on travelling overland you can get on a train in Milan, Florence, Rome, Naples and most major cities in between. A third alternative is to arrive by boat from Naples, Genoa or Livorno.

AIR
Airports & Airlines
Sicily has two main airports, Falcone-Borsellino outside Palermo and Fontanarossa in Catania. There is also a small airport at Birgi, near Trapani, which is only used for domestic flights within Sicily (see the Getting Around chapter). Neither of the main airports are served by intercontinental flights, and only a limited number of airlines fly into the island; if you're coming from outside Italy you'll more than likely have to pick up a connecting flight (and probably change airlines) in either Rome or Milan. Palermo and Catania are served by flights from a number of Italian destinations. Alitalia is the main carrier to and from Sicily, serving both Palermo and Catania; British Airways also has scheduled flights, although these are routed through Milan, Pisa or Rome. During the summer months (usually May to October) both airports are served by a number of charter flights, although airline schedules can be restrictive.

Buying Tickets
World aviation has never been so competitive, making air travel better value than ever, but you have to research the options carefully to make sure you get the best deal. The Internet is a useful resource for checking air fares: many travel agencies and airlines have Web sites (included later in the chapter).

Some airlines sell discounted tickets direct to the customer, and it's worth contacting them anyway for information on routes and timetables. However, there is sometimes nothing to be gained by going direct to the airline – specialist discount agencies often offer fares that are lower and/or carry fewer conditions than the airline's published prices. You can expect to be offered a wider range of options than a single airline would provide and, at worst, you will just end up paying the official airline fare.

The exception to this rule is the new breed of 'no-frills' carriers, which mostly sell direct. Unlike the 'full-service' airlines, the no-frills carriers often make one-way tickets available at around half the return fare, meaning that it is easy to stitch together an open-jaw itinerary. Regular airlines may also offer open jaws, particularly if you are flying in from outside Europe.

If you're booking a charter flight, remember to check what time of day or night you'll be flying: many charter flights arriving in Sicily do so late at night. Bear in mind too, if you miss your charter flight, you've lost your money.

Round-the-World (RTW) tickets are another possibility and are comparable in price to an ordinary return long-haul ticket. RTWs start at about UK£800, US$1300 or A$1800 and can be valid for up to a year. They can be particularly economical if you're flying from Australia or New Zealand. Special conditions might be attached to such tickets (such as not being able to backtrack on a route). Also, beware of cancellation penalties for these and other tickets.

You may find that the cheapest flights are being advertised by obscure agencies. Most such firms are honest and solvent, but there are some rogue fly-by-night outfits around. Paying by credit card generally offers protection, since most card issuers will provide refunds if you don't get what you've paid for. Similar protection can be obtained by buying a ticket from a bonded agent, such as one covered by the Air Transport Operators Licence (ATOL) scheme in the UK. If you feel suspicious about a firm, it's best to steer clear, or only pay a deposit before you get your ticket, then ring the airline to confirm that you are actually booked on the flight before you pay the balance. Established outfits, such as those mentioned in this book, offer more security and are about as competitive as you can get.

For Sicily, the cheapest deals tend to be available out-of-season (between October and April) and when travelling on weekdays. Always ask about the route: it may be that the cheapest tickets involve an inconvenient stopover. Don't take schedules for granted either: airlines usually change their schedules twice a year, at the end of March and the end of October.

Ticketless travel, whereby your reservation details are contained within an airline computer, is becoming more common.

Student and Youth Fares Full-time students and people aged under 26 have access to better deals than other travellers. The better deals may not always be cheaper fares but can include more flexibility to change flights and/or routes. You have to show a document proving your date of birth or a valid International Student Identity Card (ISIC) when buying your ticket and sometimes when boarding the plane.

Frequent Fliers The majority of airlines offer frequent-flier deals that can earn you a free air ticket or other goodies. To qualify, you have to accumulate sufficient mileage with the same airline or airline alliance. Many airlines have 'blackout periods', or times when you cannot fly for free on your frequent flier points (such as Christmas).

Courier Flights Courier flights are a great bargain if you're lucky enough to find one. Air freight companies expedite delivery of urgent items by sending them with you as your baggage allowance. You are permitted to bring along a carry-on bag, but that's all. In return, you get a steeply discounted ticket. There are other restrictions and you should be sure before you fly which ones apply to your ticket.

Booking a courier ticket takes some effort. They are not readily available and arrangements have to be made a month or more in advance. Courier flights are occasionally advertised in newspapers, or you could contact air freight companies listed in the phone book, although they aren't always keen to give out information over the phone. *Travel Unlimited* (PO Box 1058, Allston, MA 02134, USA) is a monthly travel newsletter that publishes many courier flight deals from departure points worldwide. A 12-month subscription to the newsletter costs US$25, or US$35 for those resident outside the USA.

Travellers with Special Needs

If you are on crutches or in a wheelchair, are a vegetarian or require a special diet (such as kosher food) or have some other special need, let the airline know so that they can make arrangements. You should call to remind them of your requirements at least 72 hours before departure and again when you check in at the airport. It may also be worth ringing round the airlines before you make your booking to find out how they can handle your particular needs. Some airlines publish brochures on the subject. Ask your travel agency for details.

Guide dogs for the blind will often have to travel in a specially pressurised baggage compartment and are subject to quarantine laws (six months in isolation and so on) when entering, or returning to, countries currently free of rabies, such as Australia or the UK. Travellers with a hearing impairment can ask for airport and in-flight announcements to be written down for them.

Children aged under two travel for 10% of the standard fare (or free on some airlines), as long as they don't occupy a seat.

Air Travel Glossary

Cancellation Penalties If you have to cancel or change a discounted ticket, there are often heavy penalties involved; insurance can sometimes be taken out against these penalties. Some airlines impose penalties on regular tickets as well, particularly against 'no-show' passengers.

Courier Fares Businesses often need to send urgent documents or freight securely and quickly. Courier companies hire people to accompany the package through customs and, in return, offer a discount ticket which is sometimes a phenomenal bargain. However, you may have to surrender all your baggage allowance and take only carry-on luggage.

Full Fares Airlines traditionally offer 1st class (coded F), business class (coded J) and economy class (coded Y) tickets. These days there are so many promotional and discounted fares available that few passengers pay full economy fare.

Lost Tickets If you lose your airline ticket an airline will usually treat it like a travellers cheque and, after inquiries, issue you with another one. Legally, however, an airline is entitled to treat it like cash and if you lose it then it's gone forever. Take good care of your tickets.

Onward Tickets An entry requirement for many countries is that you have a ticket out of the country. If you're unsure of your next move, the easiest solution is to buy the cheapest onward ticket to a neighbouring country or a ticket from a reliable airline which can later be refunded if you do not use it.

Open-Jaw Tickets These are return tickets where you fly out to one place but return from another. If available, this can save you backtracking to your arrival point.

Overbooking Since every flight has some passengers who fail to show up, airlines often book more passengers than they have seats. Usually excess passengers make up for the no-shows, but occasionally somebody gets 'bumped' onto the next available flight. Guess who it is most likely to be? The passengers who check in late.

Promotional Fares These are officially discounted fares, available from travel agencies or direct from the airline.

Reconfirmation If you don't reconfirm your flight at least 72 hours prior to departure, the airline may delete your name from the passenger list. Ring to find out if your airline requires reconfirmation.

Restrictions Discounted tickets often have various restrictions on them – such as needing to be paid for in advance and incurring a penalty to be altered. Others are restrictions on the minimum and maximum period you must be away.

Round-the-World Tickets RTW tickets give you a limited period (usually a year) in which to circumnavigate the globe. You can go anywhere the carrying airlines go, as long as you don't backtrack. The number of stopovers or total number of separate flights is decided before you set off and they usually cost a bit more than a basic return flight.

Transferred Tickets Airline tickets cannot be transferred from one person to another. Travellers sometimes try to sell the return half of their ticket, but officials can ask you to prove that you are the person named on the ticket. On an international flight tickets are compared with passports.

Travel Periods Ticket prices vary with the time of year. There is a low (off-peak) season and a high (peak) season, and often a low-shoulder season and a high-shoulder season as well. Usually the fare depends on your outward flight – if you depart in the high season and return in the low season, you pay the high-season fare.

They don't get a baggage allowance. Sky-cots, baby food and nappies (diapers) should be provided by the airline if requested in advance. Children aged between two and 12 years can usually occupy a seat for half to two-thirds of the full fare and do get a baggage allowance. Pushchairs (strollers) can often be carried as hand luggage.

Departure Tax
The departure tax payable when you leave Sicily (or Italy) by air is factored into your airline ticket.

Other Parts of Italy
The Italian domestic airline Meridiana (☎ 06 478 041 in Rome) flies between Milan and Palermo for around L330,000 and to Catania for around L260,000. If your Italian is up to it check out their Web site at www.meridiana.it. Air Europe (☎ 02 675 791 140) also flies from Milan to Palermo and Catania; flights cost around L290,000 to both destinations. Air One (☎ 06 488 800 in Rome) flies from Rome and Milan to Pantelleria and Lampedusa. The flights from Rome start at around L390,000; the flights from Milan are more expensive, starting at around L514,000.

Continental Europe
It's worth considering air travel between Sicily and other countries in continental Europe if you are pushed for time. Short hops can be expensive, but good deals are available from some major hubs.

Several airlines, including Alitalia, Qantas Airways and Air France, offer cut-rate fares between cities on the European legs of long-haul flights. These are usually cheap, but often involve flying at night or early in the morning.

France The student travel agency OTU Voyages (☎ 01 44 41 38 50; ☎ 01 40 29 12 12 for reservations) has a central Paris office at 39 ave Georges Bernanos and another 42 offices around the country. The Web address is www.otu.fr. Usit Voyages (☎ 01 42 44 14 00) is a safe bet for reasonable student and cut-price travel. They have

four addresses in Paris, including 85 blvd St Michel, and other offices around the country. STA Travel's Paris agent is Voyages Wasteels (☎ 01 43 25 58 35).

Alitalia flies directly between Paris and Palermo. At the time of research a return flight cost around 2100FF. Sabena (☎ 820 830 830) flies to Catania via Brussels and flights cost 1600FF return. There is a Sabena office at Orly airport in Paris. There are regular flights between Paris and Rome or Milan. The train is generally an easier bet for Milan (see under Train in the Land section later in the chapter), but to Rome you can occasionally find good air deals. A low-season return flight with Alitalia costs around 1300FF – cheaper than the train.

OUT Voyages offers charter flights from Paris to Palermo. Flights depart on Friday and Saturday and cost around 940FF.

Germany Munich is a haven of bucket shops and more mainstream budget travel outlets. Council Travel (☎ 089-39 50 22), Adalbertstrasse 32, near the university, is one of the best. STA Travel (☎ 089-39 90 96), Königstrasse 49, is also good.

In Berlin, try Kilroy Travel-ARTU Reisen (☎ 030-310 00 40), Hardenbergstrasse 9, near Berlin Zoo (with three more branches around the city). There's also a branch of STA Travel (☎ 030-311 09 50, fax 313 09 48 14) at Goethestrasse 73. In Frankfurt-am-Main, you could try STA Travel (☎ 069-70 30 35, fax 77 70 600), Bockenheimer, Landstrasse 133.

Alitalia flies from Munich to Palermo and Catania via either Rome or Milan. At the time of research a discount return flight cost DM600. KLM-Royal Dutch Airlines flies from Munich to Rome via Amsterdam from around DM600 return (non-refundable and non-exchangeable). Lufthansa flies direct to Rome for around DM460 return. Keep an eye out for special deals which can bring prices down as low as DM380.

The Netherlands The student travel agency NBBS Reiswinkels (☎ 020-620 5071), Rokin 38, Amsterdam, offers reliable and reasonably low fares. Compare with the bucket shops along Rokin before making your decision. Another recommended travel agency in Amsterdam is Malibu Travel (☎ 020-626 3230), Prinsengracht 230.

Alitalia flies to both Palermo and Catania via Rome; return flights cost around fl900. Meridiana (☎ 020-316 4224), Westelijke Randweg 59, 1118 CR, Lucht Haven Schipol, offers flights between Amsterdam and Catania, via Rome, for f1781 return; and Palermo via Florence for around f1400 return.

Spain In Madrid, one of the most reliable budget travel agencies is Viajes Zeppelin (☎ 91 547 7903), Plaza de Santo Domingo 2.

Alitalia flies to both Palermo and Catania via Rome and Milan; return flights cost around 68,000 ptas. Return flights to Rome in the low season start at about 30,000 ptas. Flights to Milan tend to be pricier. In Barcelona, Meridiana (☎ 93 487 5775), Paseo Gracia 55, flies to Palermo via Bologna. A return costs 62,000 ptas.

The UK & Ireland
Discount air travel is big business in London. Advertisements for many travel agencies appear in the travel pages of the weekend broadsheet newspapers, as well as in publications such as *Time Out*, the *Evening Standard* and *TNT*.

For students and for travellers aged under 26, popular travel agencies in the UK include STA Travel (☎ 020-7361 6161), 86 Old Brompton Rd, London SW7, which has offices throughout the UK. Visit its Web site at www.statravel.co.uk. Usit Campus (☎ 0870 240 1010), 52 Grosvenor Gardens, London SW1, also has branches throughout the UK. Check out their Web site at www.usitcampus.com. Both of these agencies sell tickets to all travellers, but cater especially to young people and students.

Other recommended agencies include: Trailfinders (☎ 020-7937 5400), 215 Kensington High St, London W8, with a Web site at www.trailfinders.co.uk; Bridge the World (☎ 020-7734 7447), 4 Regent Place, London W1, Web site at www.b-t-w.co.uk; and Flightbookers (☎ 020-7757 2000), 177–178 Tottenham Court Rd, London W1, Web site at www.ebookers.com.

As fare competition in Europe grows, a gaggle of small airlines jostles for custom, but only the Irish airline Ryanair (☎ 0870 333 1250 in the UK, ☎ 050 50 37 70 in Italy) flies anywhere near Sicily, to Reggio di Calabria (a short hop across the straits from Messina) from Stansted, with one flight daily. At the time of writing, a one-way mid-week fare cost around UK£140, including taxes. Visit the Web site at www.ryanair.ie.

Alitalia (☎ 08705 448 259), 4 Portman Square, London W1H 9PS, operates frequent flights (usually several a day) to Rome and Milan, from where you can pick up regular connections to Palermo (10 daily from Rome, 7 daily from Milan) and Catania (11 daily from Rome, 8 daily from Milan). Standard returns cost from UK£250. However, watch out for special deals and you should not need to resort to standard fares. For example, at the time of writing, British Airways (BA; ☎ 020-7434 4700, ☎ 0345 222 111 for 24-hour local-rate line), 156 Regent St, London W1R, offered a return to Rome for as little as UK£120, with certain conditions, while Alitalia offered discount deals on its domestic flights with one-way fares from Rome to Palermo or Catania starting at UK£40 and one-way fares from Milan to the same destinations starting at UK£60.

Meridiana (☎ 020-7839 2222), at 15 Charles II St, London SW1, flies from Gatwick to Catania and Palermo, via Florence, for around UK£230 return. Italy Sky Shuttle (☎ 020-8748 1333), 227 Shepherd's Bush Rd, London W6, specialises in charter flights to 22 destinations in Italy. The best return flight in the high season from London to Palermo or Catania (via Rome or Milan) costs around UK£230. LAI Travel (☎ 020-837 8492), 185 King's Cross Rd, London W6, has return flights to Palermo and Catania that cost around UK£220. The Charter Flight Centre (☎ 020-7565 6755), 15 Gillingham St, London SW1, has return flights to Palermo or Catania via Rome or Milan for around UK£250.

There are no direct scheduled flights to Sicily from Ireland, so you will need to pick up a connection in Milan or Rome. It might be worth comparing the cost of flying to Italy directly from Dublin and the cost of flying to London first and then on to Italy. Sunway Travel (☎ 01 288 6828), 114 Lower George's St, Dun Laoghaire, Co Dublin, has charter flights to Catania every Friday between May and September. Return flights, with a maximum stay of two weeks, costs around IR£350.

Youth Passes Alitalia offers people aged under 26 (and students aged under 31 with a valid ISIC) a Europa Pass from London and Dublin. The pass is valid for up to six months and allows unlimited one-way flights (with a minimum of four flights per pass and a minimum stay of seven days per flight) to all the airline's European and Mediterranean destinations for around UK£60 per flight. The first flight has to be to Italy and the last flight back to the UK or Ireland from Italy. Internal flights in Italy on this pass cost UK£53 a pop. In the UK contact CTS (☎ 020-7636 0031) for more details.

The USA

The North Atlantic is the world's busiest long-haul air corridor and the flight options are bewildering. Several airlines fly direct to Italy, landing at either Rome or Milan. These include Alitalia, Lufthansa, Air France, TWA and Delta Air Lines.

Discount travel agencies in the USA are known as consolidators (although you won't see a sign on the door saying 'Consolidator'). San Francisco is the ticket consolidator capital of America, although some good deals can be found in Los Angeles, New York and other big cities. Consolidators can be found through the *Yellow Pages* or the major daily newspapers. The *New York Times*, the *Los Angeles Times*, the *Chicago Tribune* and the *San Francisco Examiner* all produce weekly travel sections where you will find travel agency ads. Look out for an SOT number: if they have one of these they are probably legitimate.

Council Travel (☎ 800 226 8624), 205 E 42 St, New York, NY 10017, America's largest student travel organisation, has around 60 offices in the USA. Call for the

office nearest you or visit the Web site at www.counciltravel.com. STA Travel (☎ 800 777 0112) has offices in Boston, Chicago, Miami, New York, Philadelphia, San Francisco and other major cities. Call the toll-free ☎ 800 number for office locations or visit the Web site at www.statravel.com.

At the time of writing, you could get return fares with Lufthansa from Los Angeles to Rome or Milan via Frankfurt for around US$500 in the low season (roughly January to March). With a little luck you can do better still from the east coast. KLM, for instance, was offering return fares of around US$300 from New York to Milan in the low season. After March, prices begin to rise rapidly and availability declines.

Discount and rock-bottom options from the USA include stand-by fares, charter and courier flights. Stand-by fares are often sold at 60% of the normal price for one-way tickets. Airhitch (☎ 212-864 2000, ☎ 800 326 2009 toll-free), 2641 Broadway, New York, NY 10025, specialises in this. Have a look at their Web site at www.airhitch.org. You will need to give a general idea of where and when you need to go, and a few days before your departure you will be presented with a choice of two or three flights.

A New York to Rome return on a courier flight can cost about US$300 (more from the west coast). Now Voyager (☎ 212-431 1616), Suite 307, 74 Varrick St, New York, NY 10013, specialises in courier flights, but you must pay an annual membership fee (around US$50) that entitles you to take as many courier flights as you like. Colorado-based Air Courier Association (☎ 800 983 8333) is similar. Check out their Web site at www.aircourier.com.

Also worth considering are Europe by Air coupons (☎ 888 387 2479). Check out the Web site at www.eurair.com. You purchase a minimum of three US$90 coupons before leaving North America. Each coupon is valid for a one-way flight within the combined system of 10 participating regional airlines in Europe (exclusive of local taxes, which you will be charged when you make the flight). The coupons are valid for 120 days from the day you make your first flight. A few words of caution – using one of these coupons for a one-way flight won't always be better value than local alternatives, so check them out before committing yourself to any given flight.

If you can't find a particularly cheap flight, it is always worth considering a cheap transatlantic hop to London to prowl around the bucket shops there. See The UK & Ireland earlier in the section.

Canada

Both Alitalia and Air Canada have direct flights to Rome and Milan from Toronto and Montreal. Scan the budget travel agencies' ads in the *Toronto Globe & Mail*, the *Toronto Star* and the *Vancouver Province*.

Canada's main student travel organisation is Travel CUTS (☎ 800 667 2887), which has offices in all major cities. It is known as Voyages Campus in Quebec. The Travel CUTS Web address is www.travelcuts.com.

For courier flights originating in Canada, contact FB on Board Courier Services (☎ 514-631 2077).

Low-season return fares from Toronto to Rome or Milan start from around C$630 for students and other young types. From Montreal, KLM had a student deal for C$540 at the time of writing.

Australia

There is generally some special fare deal on offer for travel from Australia to Italy, but only Alitalia and Qantas offer direct flights; the alternative is to fly to Rome or Milan and buy a separate ticket on to Sicily. Other flights from Australia and New Zealand to Italy are usually via Asia or another European city. Low season return fares to Palermo, via Rome, cost from around A$1370 to A$1650 with Alitalia. Singapore Airlines flies to Rome, via Singapore, with connections on Italian domestic airlines to Palermo; return fares start from A$2100 in the low season.

Quite a few travel offices specialise in discount air tickets. Some travel agencies, particularly smaller ones, advertise cheap air fares in the travel sections of weekend newspapers, such as the *Age* in Melbourne and the *Sydney Morning Herald*.

Two agencies that are well known for cheap fares are STA Travel and Flight Centre. STA Travel (☎ 03-9349 2411), 224 Faraday St, Carlton, Melbourne 3053, has offices in all major cities and on many university campuses. Call ☎ 131 776 Australia-wide for the location of your nearest branch or visit its Web site at www.statravel.com.au. Flight Centre (☎ 131 600 Australia-wide), 82 Elizabeth St, Sydney, has dozens of offices throughout Australia. Its Web address is www.flightcentre.com.au. Compagnia Italiana di Turismo (CIT) can also help out with cheap fares (see Tourist Offices Abroad in the Facts for the Visitor chapter for details of its offices in Australia).

For courier flights try Jupiter (☎ 02-9317 2230), Unit 3, 55 Kent Rd, Mascot, Sydney 2020.

New Zealand

From New Zealand, Qantas or Alitalia flights from Australia are the most direct way to get to Palermo. Expect to pay around NZ$2115 for a return flight in the low season.

The *New Zealand Herald* has a travel section in which travel agencies advertise fares. Flight Centre (☎ 09-309 6171) has a large central office in Auckland at National Bank Towers (corner of Queen and Darby Sts) and many branches throughout the country. STA Travel (☎ 09-309 0458), 10 High St, Auckland, has other offices in Auckland, as well as in Hamilton, Palmerston North, Wellington, Christchurch and Dunedin. Its Web address is www.statravel.com.au.

LAND

Located at the southern extremity of the Italian peninsula, getting to Sicily overland involves travelling the entire length of the country, which can either be an enormous drain on your time or, if you have plenty to spare, a wonderful way of seeing Italy on your way to Sicily. There are plenty of options for entering Italy by train, bus or private vehicle. Bus is generally the cheapest, but services are less frequent and considerably less comfortable than the train.

If you are travelling by bus, train or car to Italy it will be necessary to check whether you require visas to the countries you intend to pass through.

Bus

There is no direct service to Sicily from outside Italy – even Eurolines, Europe's main carrier, only goes as far as Rome. If you are sold on arriving by bus, your only option involves changing buses and carriers in Rome. To get to Rome, Eurolines is your best bet. See their Web site at www.eurolines.com. You can contact them in your own country (see under The UK or Continental Europe later in this section) or in Rome (☎ 06 440 40 09) c/o Agenzia Elios, Circonvallazione Nomentana 574, Lato Stazione Tiburtina.

Other Parts of Italy From Rome, Segesta (☎ 06 481 96 76), c/o Agenzia Saiatour, Piazza della Repubblica 42, has two departures daily from Piazza Tiburtina serving Messina (L55,000, 9 hours), Palermo (L66,000, 12 hours) and Syracuse (L66,000, 12 hours).

Continental Europe You will find Eurolines' main European offices at:

Austria
  (☎ 01-712 04 53) Schalter 2 (Window 2),
  Autobusbahnhof Wien-Mitte, Hauptstrasse 1b,
  Vienna
France
  (☎ 08 36 69 52 52) 28 ave du Général
  de Gaulle, Paris
Germany
  (☎ 089-545 87 00) Deutsche Touring GmbH,
  Arnulfstrasse 3 (Stamberger Bahnhof), Munich
Netherlands
  (☎ 020-627 5151) Rokin 10, Amsterdam
Spain
  (☎ 91 528 1105) Estación Sur de Autobuses,
  Calle de Méndez Alvaro 83, Madrid
Switzerland
  (☎ 01 431 57 24) Carplatz am Sihlquai, 8005
  Zurich

The UK Eurolines (☎ 0990 143 219), 52 Grosvenor Gardens, Victoria, London SW1, runs buses to Rome (33 hours) at 9 am on Wednesday and Saturday. At the time of research, under 26/adult return fares from London to Rome cost about UK£129/139. To Milan, under 26/adult return fares cost

UK£112/123. Prices rise in the peak summer season (July and August) and in the week before Christmas.

Train

Not quite as tough going as travelling by bus, one major advantage of getting to Sicily by train is the greater options you have en route, including more frequent departures and the possibility of breaking up your journey so that it isn't one long slog. If you plan to travel extensively by train in Europe it might be worth getting hold of the *Thomas Cook European Timetable*, which has a complete listing of train schedules. It is updated monthly and available from Thomas Cook offices and agencies worldwide.

On overnight hauls you can book a couchette for around UK£10 to UK£15 on most international trains. In 1st class there are four bunks per cabin and in 2nd class there are six bunks.

It is always advisable, and sometimes compulsory, to book seats on international trains to and from Sicily. Some of the main international services include transport for private cars – an option worth examining to save wear and tear on your vehicle before it arrives in Sicily.

Rail Passes & Discount Tickets Wasteels offers several rail passes for travel in Italy. The Italy Railcard allows either eight, 15, 21 or 30 days unlimited travel. Prices range from UK£128 to UK£220 for 2nd-class tickets. The Italy Flexicard is valid for either four, eight or 12 days travel within one month; prices range from UK£100 to UK£178. If you are under 26 the Freedom Pass offers between three and eight days travel and costs from UK£79 to UK£109.

If you have lived outside Europe for the past six months you are eligible for the Europass. The pass is valid for two months and includes travel in France, Germany, Italy, Spain and Switzerland with the option of several 'add-on' countries. Prices range from UK£163/208 to UK£359/434 youth/adult.

Rail Inclusive Tours, available from Citalia (see Tourist Offices Abroad in the Facts for the Visitor chapter), offer up to

30% discounts on train tickets, but only as part of an accommodation package.

Ferrovie dello Stato (FS, the Italian state railway) passes include the Carta Verde, for people aged between 12 and 26. It costs L40,000, is valid for one year and entitles you to a 20% discount on all train travel, but you'll need to do a fair bit of travelling to get your money's worth. The Carta d'Argento entitles people aged 60 and over to a 20% discount on 1st- and 2nd-class travel for one year. It also costs L40,000.

A *biglietto chilometrico* (kilometric card) is valid for two months and allows you to cover 3000km, with a maximum of 20 trips. It costs L206,000 (2nd class) and you must pay a supplement if you catch an Intercity train. Its main attraction is that it can be used by up to five people, either singly or as a group.

Always ask about discounts for children. As a rule, toddlers aged under four go for free. Kids aged four to 11 travel for half the adult fare.

Other Parts of Italy A one-way adult fare from Rome to Palermo on a mainline or Intercity train costs L200,000 1st class and L130,000 2nd class (11 hours, four daily). The equivalent from Milan costs L240,000/150,000 (19 hours, one daily). The train from Rome to Catania costs L180,000/120,000 (9 hours and 40 minutes, three daily); from Milan to Catania costs L230,000/150,000 (17 hours, two daily).

Continental Europe If you're travelling to Sicily from anywhere outside Italy you'll have to change trains somewhere along the line in Italy; the handiest place is Rome, although there are also trains for Sicily that depart from Milan and Turin (and travel via Rome).

From Paris to Palermo your options include the overnight sleeper which goes via Milan. The journey costs 90/1200FF for travellers aged under/over 26 and takes aobut 27 hours. Other sample fares include Vienna (AS2300, 28 hours), Amsterdam (f900, around 36 hours) and Barcelona (24,000 ptas, 33 hours).

The UK The Channel Tunnel allows for land transport links between Britain and continental Europe. The Eurostar passenger train (☎ 0990 186 186) travels between London and Paris and London and Brussels. Visit its Web site at www.eurostar. com.

Alternatively, you can get a train ticket that includes the Channel crossing by ferry, SeaCat or hovercraft. After that, you can travel via Paris and southern France or by swinging from Belgium down through Germany and Switzerland.

The cheapest standard fares to Palermo on offer at the time of writing were around UK£100/200 one-way/return for those aged under 26, while the full adult fares were UK£130/260. You need to add the price of a couchette onto this.

For the latest fare information on journeys including the Eurostar, call the Rail Europe Travel Centre (☎ 0990 848 848). For information on trips using normal trains and ferries only, call Wasteels Travel (☎ 020-7834 7066), Victoria Station, London, SW1.

Car & Motorcycle

Driving to Sicily is an expensive proposition, especially once you cross the border into Italy, which has the highest motorway tolls (from the French or Swiss borders to Naples it'll cost around L80,000, from Naples to Sicily they are free) as well as the most expensive petrol in Europe (see the Car & Motorcycle section in the Getting There & Around chapter). Furthermore, it's quite a drive to get to the ferry embarkation point at Villa San Giovanni, from where you'll cross the Straits of Messina into Sicily: you might make the trip from the French or Swiss borders in around 17 hours, but only if you keep to the motorways, drive flat out (remember that the speed limit in Italy is 130kmph), and avoid the worst of the traffic – during the holiday seasons it'll be a minor miracle if you do.

From the UK, you can take your car across to France either by ferry or the Channel Tunnel car train, Eurotunnel (☎ 0990 353 535). Check out their Web site at www.eurotunnel.com. The latter runs 24-hours, with up to four crossings (35 minutes) each hour between Folkestone and Calais in the high season. You pay for the vehicle only and fares vary according to the time of day and season. The cheapest economy fare (January to May) is around UK£170 return (valid for a year) and the most expensive (May to late September) around UK£220, if you depart during the day Friday to Sunday.

The main points of entry to Italy are: the Mt Blanc tunnel from France at Chamonix (closed at the time of writing following a fire in March 1999 and not due to reopen until autumn 2000 at the earliest), which connects with the A5 for Turin and Milan; the Grand St Bernard tunnel from Switzerland (SS27), which also connects with the A5; and the Brenner pass from Austria (A13), which connects with the A22 to Bologna. Mountain passes in the Alps are often closed in winter and sometimes in autumn and spring, making the tunnels a less scenic but more reliable way to arrive in Italy. Make sure you have snow chains in winter.

An interesting Web site loaded with advice for people planning to drive in Europe is at www.ideamerge.com/motoeuropa. If you want help with route planning, try www.euroshell.com.

Paperwork & Preparations Proof of ownership of a private vehicle should always be carried (Vehicle Registration Document for UK-registered cars) when driving through Europe. All EU member states' driving licences (not the old-style UK green licence) are fully recognised throughout Europe, regardless of your length of stay. Those with a non-EU licence are supposed to obtain an International Driving Permit (IDP) to accompany their national licence. In practice, you will probably be OK with national licences from countries such as Australia, Canada and the USA. If you decide to get the permit, your national automobile association can issue them.

Third-party motor insurance is a minimum requirement in Italy and throughout Europe. The Green Card, an internationally recognised proof of insurance obtainable from your insurer, is mandatory. Also ask your insurer for a European Accident Statement form, which can simplify matters in the event of an accident. Never sign statements you can't read or understand – insist on a translation and sign that only if it's acceptable.

A good investment is a European breakdown assistance policy, such as the AA Five Star Service (☎ 0990 500 600) or the RAC's Eurocover Motoring Assistance (☎ 0990 722 722) in the UK. In Italy, assistance can be obtained through the Automobile Club Italiano. See Organisations under Car & Motorcycle in the Getting Around chapter for details.

Every vehicle travelling across an international border should display a nationality plate of its country of registration (GB for Great Britain, F for France and so on). A warning triangle (to be used in the event of a breakdown) is compulsory throughout Europe. The following accessories are recommended: a first-aid kit, a spare-bulb kit and a fire extinguisher.

Rental There is a mind-boggling variety of special deals, and terms and conditions attached to car rental. Here are a few pointers to help you through.

Multinational agencies – Hertz, Avis, Budget and Europe's largest rental agency, Europcar – will provide a reliable service and good standard of vehicle. However, if you walk into an office and ask for a car on the spot, you will always pay high rates, even allowing for special weekend deals. National and local firms can sometimes undercut the multinationals, but be sure to examine the rental agreement carefully (although this might be difficult if it is in Italian).

Planning ahead and pre-booking a rental car through a multinational agency before leaving home will enable you to find the best deals. Pre-booked and prepaid rates are always cheaper. Fly/drive combinations and other packages are worth looking into. You will simply pick up the vehicle on your arrival in Italy and return it to a nominated point at the end of the rental period. Ask your travel agency for information, or contact one of the major rental agencies.

Holiday Autos often has good rates for Europe, for which you need to pre-book; its main office is in the UK (☎ 0870 400 0011).

Monreale's magnificent 12th-century cathedral

Norman-Arabic Chiesa di San Cataldo, Palermo

Palermo's gateway between old and new

The Normans left a rich architectural legacy.

Art that tells of times gone by: intricate mosaics in Monreale's cathedral and Palermo's Capella Palatino, art deco on the market wall and the city's historical puppets.

FERDINANDO III ET M. CAROLINAE REGINAE
PIISSIMIS CLEMENTISSIMIS
INTER AMORES ET VOTA SICILIAE

At the time of writing, they were charging around UK£300 (all-inclusive) for a small car (such as a Renault Twingo) for two weeks, with the option of one-way rental. Car Rental Direct (☎ 020-7625 7166) is another possibility. Have a look at their Web site at www.car-rental-direct.com.

If you don't know exactly when you will want to rent, you could call back home from Sicily (more or less affordable to the UK and the US) and reserve through an agency there, thus reaping the benefits of booking at home when abroad.

If you do wait until you are travelling before deciding on car hire, a possible option would be to include Switzerland in your driving itinerary. Car-hire costs can be much lower than anywhere in Sicily, and generally there is no problem with cross-border travel in rental cars (confirm this before signing on the dotted line).

No matter where you hire your car, make sure you understand what is included in the price (unlimited kilometres, tax, insurance, collision damage waiver and so on) and what your liabilities are. Insurance can be a vexed issue. Are you covered for theft, vandalism and fire damage? Since the most common and convenient way to pay for rental is by credit card, check whether or not you have car insurance with the credit card provider and what the conditions are. The extra cover provided may pick up the slack in any local cover.

The minimum rental age in Sicily is 21 years. A credit card is usually required.

Purchase It is illegal for non-residents to purchase vehicles anywhere in Italy, including Sicily. The UK is probably the best place to buy second-hand cars (prices are not so competitive for new cars). Bear in mind that you will be getting a right-hand-drive car (with the steering wheel on the right, for driving on the left-hand side of the road).

If you want a left-hand-drive car and can afford to buy new, prices are relatively low in Belgium, the Netherlands and Luxembourg. Paperwork can be tricky wherever you buy.

Camper Vans Travelling in a camper van can kill several birds with one stone, taking care of eating, sleeping and travelling in one package.

London is a good place to buy. Look in *TNT* magazine or the ads paper *Loot*, or go to the daily van market in Market Rd, London N7 (near Caledonian Rd tube station). Expect to spend at least UK£2000. The most common camper is the VW based on the 1600cc or 2000cc Transporter, for which spare parts are widely available in Europe.

There are drawbacks. Campers can be expensive to buy in spring and hard to get rid of in autumn. They are difficult to manoeuvre around towns. A car and tent may do just as well for some people.

If you want to rent, organise it before reaching Sicily, as it is impossible to hire vans there.

SEA

Unless you're flying, you'll have to board a ferry or a hydrofoil at some point to get to Sicily (usually to Messina). The easiest and most common point is at Villa San Giovanni on the mainland from where there are regular ferries connections, or from Reggio di Calabria, 15 minutes farther south at the end of the A3, where you can pick up a hydrofoil as well as a ferry. You can, however, also board a ferry in Naples bound for Palermo.

Although boarding a ferry to Sicily is almost as easy as getting on a bus, you might want to consider pre-booking your passage if you are travelling in the high season, especially if you have a vehicle. Viamare (☎ 020-7431 4560), Graphic House, 2 Sumatra Rd, London NW6 1PU, is the official representative for Grandi Navi Veloci. In London, Tirrenia is represented by SMS (☎ 020-7373 6548), 40–42 Kenway Rd, London SW5 0RA.

From Villa San Giovanni

FS (☎ 090 67 52 34) operates between 20 and 25 car-and-passenger ferries daily between Villa San Giovanni and Messina (25 minutes, hourly). At the time of research, prices for a one-way ticket were L1800 for foot passengers and L28,000 for cars (depending on size). Caronte (☎ 090 4 14 15) runs ferries to Messina every 20 minutes (every hour between midnight and 6 am) daily; the journey takes 35 minutes. Cars cost the same as the FS ferries but foot passengers travel for free. Tickets can be purchased at kiosks at the respective terminals by the ferry dock.

From Reggio di Calabria
FS runs 20 hydrofoils daily from Monday to Saturday and 10 on Sunday. The 20-minute trip costs L5500/8000 one-way/return. Meridiano runs 25 car ferries daily from May to September and 15 daily the rest of the year. Prices start at L13,000 for a car (including passengers) and L6500 for foot passengers. Tickets can be bought from a kiosk at the ferry dock.

From Naples
Tirrenia (☎ 081 251 47 63), Stazione Marittima, has a daily service to Palermo departing at 8 pm and arriving at 6 am. High season fares cost L88,000 one way in an airline-style seat *(poltrona)*; L115,000 for a bed in a 2nd cabin; L170,000 for a small car. SNAV (☎ 081 761 23 48), Via Caracciolo 10, Naples, runs one daily ferry to the Aeolian Islands, departing at 5.30 pm and arriving at 9.30 pm from April to October. Tickets cost L96,000 one way (L120,000 in July, August and September). The ferry terminal is at Mergellina, to the west of the city centre.

From Genoa
Grandi Navi Veloci (☎ 010 58 93 31), Via Fieschi 1, Genoa, runs daily (except Sunday) ferries to Palermo during the high season (two per week between October and April). The 20-hour journey costs from L150,000 for foot passengers and L190,000 for a car. The ferries depart from the Nuovo Terminale Traghetti.

From Livorno
Grandi Navi Veloci (☎ 0586 89 61 13), Varco Galvali, has three departures a week for Palermo. The trip takes 17 hours and costs from L128,000 for a foot passenger; cars from L175,000. Sicil Ferry (☎ 0586 40 98 04), Varco Galvani, has an infrequent ferry service to Palermo. Prices start at L130,000 for a foot passenger. The ferries depart from Stazione Marittima in Calata Carrara, north-west of the city centre.

ORGANISED TOURS
Options for organised travel to Sicily are increasing all the time. The Italian State Tourist Office (see Tourist Offices Abroad in the Facts for the Visitor chapter) can provide a list of tour operators, noting what each specialises in. Tours can save you a lot of hassle, but they rob you of independence and generally do not come cheap.

General
Sestante CIT (known as CIT or Citalia outside Italy), with offices worldwide (see Tourist Offices Abroad in the Facts for the Visitor chapter), organises a variety of tours.

A couple of big specialists in the UK are Magic of Italy (☎ 020-8748 7575), 227 Shepherd's Bush Rd, London W6, and Alitalia's subsidiary, Italiatour (☎ 01883-621 900). Between them they offer a wide range of tours, city breaks and resort-based holidays covering most of the island. Magic of Italy runs 'Discover Sicily', a seven-night package that covers all of the island's major sights, the tour includes Palermo, Syracuse, Taormina, Agrigento and the western coast. Tours run from April to June and September to October; prices start at around UK£760 including air fare.

Italia nel Mondo (☎ 020-7828 9171), 6 Palace St, London SW1, offers a variety of week-long tours, which range from a self-catering trip for UK£449 to accommodation in five-star hotels for UK£1279.

Tours for Seniors
For people aged over 60, Saga Holidays offers holidays ranging from cheap coach tours to luxury cruises. Of particular interest is the 'Sicilian Seduction' tour, which is a nine-day trip with the possibility of a three-day extension. Prices (from the UK) start at UK£629; the extension adds an extra UK£149 to the price. Saga has offices in Britain (☎ 0800 300 456), Saga Building, Middelburg Square, Folkestone, Kent CT20 1AZ; the

USA (☎ 800 343 0273), 222 Berkeley St, Boston, MA 02116; and Australia (☎ 02-9957 4266), Level 1, Suite 2, 110 Pacific Highway, North Sydney, Sydney 2061.

Walking Tours

Several companies offer organised walking tours in selected areas. Explore Worldwide (☎ 01252-319 448), 1 Frederick St, Aldershot, Hants GU11 1LQ, offers a guided walk around Sicily's volcanoes. The trip takes eight days and costs around UK£700 including flights and accommodation. Also in the UK, Alternative Travel Group (☎ 01865-315 678), 69–71 Banbury Road, Oxford, OX2 6PE, offers a series of walking tours in various areas of the island, including Mt Etna and the nature reserves at Nebrodi and Madonie. Eight-day tours cost from between UK£670 and UK£1100 (excluding flights). A cheaper option for one- and two-week guided walking holidays is Ramblers Holidays (☎ 01707-331 133), Box 43, Welwyn Garden City, Herts, AL8 6PQ. All-inclusive tours cost UK£450 for eight days and UK£700 for two weeks.

Other Tours

Tasting Places (☎ 020-7460 0077), Unit 40, Buspace Studios, Conlan St, London W10 5AP, offers one-week trips led by cooking instructors, perhaps the best means of getting to the island's heart – through its stomach. You cook and eat your way to a better understanding at their base in Menfi, near Selinunte. Prices start at UK£1075 (excluding flights).

Warning

The information in this chapter is particularly vulnerable to change: prices for international travel are volatile, special deals come and go, and routes, schedules and visa requirements change. Airlines and governments seem to take a perverse pleasure in making price structures and regulations as complicated as possible. You should check with the airline or a travel agency to make sure you understand how a fare (and ticket you may buy) works. The travel industry is highly competitive and there are many lurks and perks.

Get quotes and advice from as many airlines and travel agencies as possible before you part with your hard-earned cash. The pointers in this chapter are no substitute for your own careful research.

Getting Around

You can reach all of the major – and most of the minor – destinations in Sicily by train or bus, but it always seems to take a lot longer than it should, especially considering the size of the island. Trains are the most efficient means of public transport, linking all of the major cities and connecting most of the coastline, but they tend to chug along in no real rush to get to their destination. Some train stations in the interior are inconveniently located a bus ride or long walk out of town.

Bus travel can be a little more difficult to work out because there are so many different companies (though you can never seem to get a bus on a Sunday), but it is a cheap way to get around. Your own wheels give you the most freedom and flexibility, and you can stray off the main routes to discover out-of-the-way hill towns or deserted beaches. The limited motorway *(autostrada)* system is toll-free except for certain tracts between Messina and Catania and Palermo and Messina, which is a huge bonus, but the extensive network of state roads can be a traffic nightmare. You should also be aware that, like the rest of Italy, petrol is expensive and that the stress of driving and parking your car in the bigger Sicilian cities could easily ruin your trip.

AIR

The best way of getting to the distant offshore island of Pantelleria is by air. Otherwise, you won't need to go anywhere near an airport until you're actually leaving Sicily.

Flights can be bought at the airport or booked through any travel agency, including Sestante CIT (☎ 091 58 63 33), Via della Libertà 12, Palermo, and Centro Turistico Studentesco e Giovanile (CTS; ☎ 091 611 07 13), Via Nicolò Garzilli 28G, Palermo. For further addresses see Travel Agencies under individual cities in the regional chapters.

Air Sicilia (☎ 091 625 05 66) and Alitalia fly twice daily to Lampedusa from Palermo (L180,000 one way). They also have departures for Pantelleria from Birgi airport, south of Trapani, priced at L160,000 one way.

BUS

Bus services within Sicily are provided by a variety of companies and vary from local routes linking small villages to intercity connections. By utilising the local services, it is possible to get to just about any location on the island. Buses are usually a more reliable and faster way to get around if your destination is not on a main train line (on major routes, trains tend to be cheaper).

It is possible to get bus timetables for the provincial and intercity services from local tourist offices, although these are often incomplete or out of date. In larger cities, most of the main intercity bus companies have ticket offices or operate through agencies. Details are provided in the individual town and city sections. In some smaller towns and villages, tickets are sold in bars – just ask for *biglietti per il pullman* – or on the bus. Note that in Sicily some minor bus routes are linked to market requirements and Sicily's all-round early-morning habits: this can often mean leaving incredibly early or finding yourself stranded after 4 pm because the bus has stopped running for the day!

Reservations & Costs

It is not usually necessary to make reservations on buses, although it is advisable in the high season for overnight or long-haul trips. Phone numbers and addresses of major bus companies are listed throughout this book. Bus travel can be less expensive than train travel: the price of a ticket from Palermo to Catania is L20,000.

TRAIN

Travelling by train in Sicily may be slow, but it is simple, cheap and generally efficient. The Ferrovie dello Stato (FS) is the partially privatised state train system. There are five types of train. Intercity (IC) trains are the fastest, stopping only at major stations. The *diretto*, *interregionale* and *espresso* stop at all but the most minor stations, while the *regionale* (also called *locale*) is the slowest of all, making every stop on the line – to be avoided if at all possible. There is one private line in Sicily, the Circumetnea, which does a circuit of Mt Etna (see the Eastern Coast chapter for details). Eurostar Italia (ES), Italy's equivalent of the French TGV, does not run in Sicily.

Travellers should note that all tickets must be validated before you board your train. You simply punch them in the yellow machines installed at the entrance to all train platforms. If you don't validate them, you risk a large fine. The rule does not apply to tickets purchased outside Italy.

There are left-luggage facilities at all train stations. They are often open 24 hours but, if not, they usually close only for a couple of hours after midnight. They are open seven days and charge from L5000 per day for each piece of luggage.

Rail Passes

It is not worth buying a rail pass if you are only travelling in Sicily, since train fares are reasonably cheap and the network isn't big enough to justify the expense. However, it might be a worthwhile investment if you plan to get to and from Sicily by train (see under Rail Passes & Discount Tickets in the Getting There & Away chapter for information).

Classes

There are 1st and 2nd classes on all Italian trains, with a 1st-class ticket costing a bit less than double the price of 2nd class.

Reservations

It is recommended that you book your train tickets for long trips, particularly if you're travelling at the weekend or during holiday periods, otherwise you could find yourself standing in the corridor for the entire journey. You can get timetable information and make train bookings at most travel agencies, including CTS and Sestante CIT, or you can simply buy your ticket on arrival at the station. If you are doing a reasonable amount of travelling, it is worth buying a train timetable. There are several available, including the official FS timetables, which can be bought at newspaper stands in or near

train stations for L7500. A thinner Sicily-only booklet is available free at some major train stations and tourist offices: ask for the *orario ufficiale dei treni Siciliani.*

Costs

To travel on IC trains you are required to pay a *supplemento*, an additional charge determined by the distance you are travelling, usually between 20 and 25% of the ticket price. If you don't buy a supplement before you board you can get one from the conductor, but it will cost you closer to 40% of the ticket price. It is possible to take your bicycle in the baggage compartment on some trains (L10,000).

Sample prices for one-way train fares are as follows (return fares are double the one-way fare):

from	to	fare (L)
Palermo	Agrigento	24,000
	Syracuse	29,500
Catania	Palermo	26,000
	Agrigento	19,500
	Syracuse	13,000
	Messina	12,500

At the time of writing the FS services and fare structures were about to be revised. This will probably result in more expensive fares and the introduction of peak and off-peak travel, bringing train travel in Italy in line with other EU countries. Changes could be introduced from early 2000. Check at the information office at any train station or have a look at the FS Web site at www.fs-on-line.com.

CAR & MOTORCYCLE
Documents

If you want to hire a car or motorcycle, you will generally need to produce your driving licence. Certainly you will need to produce it if you are pulled over by the police or *carabinieri* (military police), who, if it's a non-EU licence, may well want to see an International Driving Permit (IDP). For further details see Paperwork & Preparations under Car & Motorcycle in the Getting There & Away chapter.

euro currency converter L10,000 = €5.16

Road Distances (km)

	Agrigento	Caltanissetta	Catania	Cefalù	Enna	Erice	Marsala	Mazara	Messina	Palermo	Ragusa	Sciacca	Syracuse	Taormina	Trapani
Agrigento	---														
Caltanissetta	58	---													
Catania	183	125	---												
Cefalù	158	100	180	---											
Enna	91	33	92	133	---										
Erice	182	231	318	176	264	---									
Marsala	132	219	305	192	252	48	---								
Mazara	91	190	324	211	223	67	19	---							
Messina	283	225	100	176	258	352	396	387	---						
Palermo	126	113	208	73	246	112	141	126	249	---					
Ragusa	124	137	101	237	170	308	256	215	201	250	---				
Sciacca	57	115	240	215	148	125	109	64	340	183	181	---			
Syracuse	218	231	60	331	264	378	350	309	160	268	94	275	---		
Taormina	230	172	47	229	205	365	362	321	53	255	157	287	107	---	
Trapani	174	225	312	168	258	6	50	69	344	104	298	127	392	359	---

Roads

Roads are generally good throughout the island and there is a limited network of motorways. The main west–east link is the A19, which extends from Palermo to Catania. The A18 runs along the eastern coast between Messina and Catania, while the A29dir goes from Palermo to the western coast, linking the capital with Trapani and – through the western interior – Mazara del Vallo along the A29. The A20 runs from Palermo to Messina; at the time of writing it was still incomplete between Cefalù and Sant'Agata Militello. Drivers usually travel at very high speeds in the fast (left-hand) lane on motorways, so use that lane only to pass other cars.

There's a toll to use the A18 and A20 motorways. Depending on the size of car, it costs approximately L7500 from Messina to Catania and L17,000 from Palermo to Messina. For more information call the Società Autostrade (☎ 06 436 32 121).

To really explore the island, travellers will need to use the system of state and provincial roads. *Strade statali* (state roads) are single-lane highways and are toll-free; they are represented on maps as 'S' or 'SS'. *Strade provinciali* (provincial roads) are sometimes little more than country lanes, but provide access to some of the more beautiful scenery and the many small towns and villages. They are represented as 'P' or 'SP' on maps.

Road Rules

Published in the UK by the RAC, *Motoring in Europe* (UK£4.99) gives an excellent summary of European road rules, including parking regulations. Motoring organisations in other countries have similar publications.

In Sicily, as throughout continental Europe, drive on the right-hand side of the road and overtake on the left. Unless otherwise indicated, you must always give way to cars coming from the right. It is compulsory to wear seat belts if fitted to the car (there are front seat belts on all cars and rear seat belts on cars produced after 26 April 1990). If you are caught not wearing a seat belt, you will be required to pay an on-the-spot L58,000 fine, although this doesn't seem to deter Sicilians, many of whom use them only on motorways.

Random breath tests now take place in Sicily. If you're involved in an accident while under the influence of alcohol, the penalties can be severe. The blood-alcohol limit is 0.08%.

Speed limits, unless otherwise indicated by local signs, are as follows: on motorways 130km/h for cars of 1100cc or more, 110km/h for smaller cars and for motorcycles under 350cc; on all main, non-urban highways 110km/h; on secondary, non-urban highways 90km/h; and in built-up areas 50km/h. Speeding fines follow EU standards and are L59,000 for up to 10km/h over the limit, L235,000 for up to 40km/h, and L587,000 for more than 40km/h. Running a red light will set you back L117,000.

You don't need a licence to ride a moped under 50cc, but you should be aged 14 or over; a helmet is compulsory for those aged under 18. You can't carry passengers or ride on motorways. The speed limit for a moped is 40km/h. To ride a motorcycle or scooter up to 125cc, you must be aged 16 or over and have a licence (a car licence will do). Helmets are compulsory when riding a motorcycle bigger than 50cc, although this is a rule that Italians choose to ignore. For motorcycles over 125cc you need a motorcycle licence.

On a motorcycle you will be able to enter restricted traffic areas in Sicilian cities without any problems, and traffic police generally turn a blind eye to motorcycles parked on footpaths. There is no lights-on requirement for motorcycles during the day.

City Driving

Driving in Sicilian towns and cities is quite an experience and may well present the unprepared with a few headaches. The Sicilian attitude to driving bears little similarity to the English concept of traffic in ordered lanes (a normal two-lane road in Sicily is likely to carry three or four lanes of traffic). Instead, the main factor in determining right of way is whichever driver is more *prepotente* (forceful). If you must drive in a Sicilian city, particularly in Palermo or Catania, remain calm and keep your eyes on the road and you should be OK. Once you arrive in a city or village, follow the *centro* (city centre) signs. Most roads are well signposted.

Parking

Be extremely careful where you park your car, especially in major cities. If you leave it in an area marked with a sign reading *Zona Rimozione* (Removal Zone) and featuring a tow truck, it will almost certainly be towed away and you will pay a heavy fine to retrieve it. It is a good idea to leave your car in a supervised car park if you have luggage, but even then it is a risk to leave your belongings in an unattended car. One feature of the non-metered parking in Sicily is that no matter where you stick your car – even on the street – there is usually someone around to help you squeeze into the tightest spots (even if you don't think you'll fit). These unofficial supervisors will usually expect a L1000 'tip' for watching your car while you're away. If you want to avoid the possibility of minor damage to your car – such as a broken wing mirror, a scrape or even slashed tyres – pay up.

Car parks in major cities are indicated throughout the book. In Sicily they are denoted on signs by a white 'P' on a blue background. There are parking meters in most cities and even in the historic centres of small towns. You are likely to have to pay in advance for the number of hours you think you will stay. Per hour, they can cost anything from L500 to L2000.

Petrol

The cost of petrol in Sicily is very high – ranging from around L1800 to L1900 per litre (slightly less for unleaded petrol). Petrol is called *benzina*, unleaded petrol is *benzina senza piombo* and diesel is *gasolio*. If you are driving a car that uses LPG (liquid petroleum gas), you will need to buy a special guide to service stations that have *gasauto* or GPL. By law these must be in non-residential areas and are usually in the country or on city outskirts, although you'll find plenty on the motorways. GPL costs around L900 per litre.

Rental

Rental agencies are listed under the major cities in this book. Most tourist offices can provide information about car or motorcycle rental; otherwise, look in the local *Pagine Gialle* (Yellow Pages).

Car It is cheaper to arrange car rental before leaving your own country, for instance through some sort of fly/drive deal. For more information see Rental under Car & Motorcycle in the Getting There & Away chapter).

You have to be aged 21 or over (23 or over for some companies) to hire a car in Sicily and you will find the deal far easier to organise if you have a credit card. Most firms will accept your standard licence, sometimes with an Italian translation (which can usually be provided by the agencies themselves), or IDP.

At the time of writing, Avis offered a special weekend rate for unlimited kilometres which compared well with rates offered by other firms: L285,000 for a Fiat Uno or Renault Clio, or L320,500 for a Fiat Brava, from 9 am Friday to 9 am Monday. Maggiore Budget offered a weekend deal of L147,000 for a Renault Clio, with a limit of 300km. The same car for five to seven days, with a limit of 1400km, costs L497,000. If you pick up or drop off the car at an airport there is a 12% surcharge.

Motorcycle You'll have no trouble hiring a small motorcycle such as a scooter (Vespa) or moped. There are numerous rental agencies in the cities (where you'll also usually be able to hire larger motorcycles for touring) and at tourist destinations such as seaside resorts. The average cost for a 50cc scooter (for one person) is around L40,000/250,000 per day/week. For a 125cc (for two people) you will pay from around L70,000/380,000 per day/week. For a moped (virtually a motorised bicycle) you'll pay around L35,000/200,000 per day/week. Most agencies will not rent motorcycles to people aged under 18. Note that many places require a sizeable deposit and that you could be responsible for reimbursing part of the cost of the bike if it is stolen. Always check the fine print in the contract. See Road Rules earlier in this section for more details about age, licence and helmet requirements.

Purchase

Car It's illegal for non-residents to buy a car in Sicily, as the law requires that you be a resident to own and register one. You can get round this by having a friend who is resident in Sicily buy one for you.

It is possible to buy a cheap, small 10-year-old car for as little as L1,500,000, rising to around L7,000,000 for a reasonable five-year-old Fiat Uno and up to around L10,000,000 for a two-year-old Fiat Uno. The best way to find a car to buy is to look in the classified section of local newspapers.

Motorcycle The same laws apply to owning and registering a motorcycle as apply to purchasing a car. The cost of a second-hand Vespa ranges from L500,000 to L1,500,000, and a moped will cost from L300,000 to L1,000,000. Prices for more powerful bikes start at L1,500,000.

Organisations

The Automobile Club Italiano (ACI) no longer offers free roadside assistance to tourists. Residents of the UK and Germany should organise assistance through their own national organisations, which will entitle them to use ACI's emergency assistance number ☎ 116 for a small fee. Without this entitlement, you'll pay a minimum fee of L150,000 if you call ☎ 116. ACI has offices at Via delle Alpi 6, Palermo (☎ 091 30 04 68) and Via Sabotino 1, Catania (☎ 095 53 33 24).

Rental Warning

Be careful when signing a rental agreement in Sicily. Some travellers have reported that the charges on their credit cards far exceeded the sum they expected to pay – even on cars that were booked from home – and it is difficult to query the charges as they don't show up until after your return home. Sicilian operators – even representatives of internationally recognised firms – have been known to slap all kinds of unforeseen charges onto the agreed price, after the keys have been returned. To avoid any hassle, make sure you know exactly how much the price of the car is when you pick it up, as plenty of rental agencies do not factor in such charges as local taxes when quoting a price, and be sure to find out exactly how much will be charged to your credit card as you return the keys.

BICYCLE

Cycling can be a great way to see the countryside as well as get around busy town centres. There are no special road rules for cyclists. Helmets and lights are not obligatory, but you would be wise to equip yourself with both. You cannot cycle on motorways.

If you plan to bring your own bike, check with your airline for any additional costs. The bike will need to be disassembled and packed for the journey.

Bikes can be taken very cheaply on trains (L10,000), although only certain trains will actually carry them. Fast trains will generally not accommodate them and they must be sent as registered luggage, which can take a few days. Check with the FS for more information. Bikes can be transported free on ferries to Sicily.

A primary consideration on a cycling tour is to travel light, but you should take a few tools and spare parts, including a puncture-repair kit and a spare inner tube. Panniers are essential to balance your possessions on either side of the bike frame. A bike helmet is a very good idea, as is a very solid bike lock and chain, although even that might not prevent your bike from being stolen if you leave it unattended. Theft of mountain bikes is a major problem in the big cities.

Rental

Bikes are available for hire in most Italian towns and many places have both city and mountain bikes. Rental costs for a city bike start at L15,000/100,000 per day/week. A good mountain bike will cost more. See Getting Around in individual cities for more information.

Purchase

If you shop around, bargain prices start at L190,000 for a ladies bike without gears and up to L400,000 for a mountain bike with 16 gears, but you will pay a lot more for a very good bike.

Organisations

There are organisations that can help you plan your bike tour or through which you can organise guided tours. In England, you should contact the Cyclists' Touring Club (☎ 01483-417 217), Cotterell House, 69 Meadrow, Godalming, Surrey GU7 3HS. Their Web site is at www.ctc.org.uk. The club can supply members with information on conditions, itineraries and cheap insurance. Membership costs £25 per year or £15 for seniors, students and those aged under 18.

HITCHING

Hitching is never safe in any country and we don't recommend it. Travellers who decide to hitch should understand they are taking a small, but potentially serious, risk. People who do choose to hitch will be safer if they travel in pairs and let someone know where they are planning to go. A man and a woman travelling together is probably the best combination. Women travelling alone should be extremely cautious about hitching anywhere.

In Sicily it can be pretty tough to get a lift, as most motorists tend to be mistrustful of anyone standing on the side of the road. It is illegal to hitch on Sicily's motorways, but quite acceptable to stand near the entrance to the toll booths. Never hitch where drivers can't stop in good time or without causing an obstruction. You could also approach drivers at petrol stations and truck stops. Look presentable, carry as little luggage as possible and hold a sign in Italian indicating your destination.

It is sometimes possible to arrange lifts in advance – ask around at youth hostels. Dedicated hitchhikers might also like to get hold of Simon Calder's *Europe – A Manual for Hitchhikers*.

BOAT

Sicily's offshore islands are served by *traghetti* (ferries) and *aliscafi* (hydrofoils). The main embarkation point for the Aeolian Islands is Milazzo; for the Egadi Islands the main point is Trapani; for the Pelagic Islands you'll have to go to Porto Empedocle near Agrigento; Ustica is served from Palermo. See the Getting There & Away sections in the relevant regional chapters for details.

Tirrenia Navigazione is the major company servicing the Mediterranean and it has offices throughout Sicily. The FS operates ferries to the Italian mainland (for more information see under Sea in the Getting There & Away chapter).

On overnight services (such as to the Pelagic Islands), travellers can choose between cabin accommodation (men and women are usually segregated in 2nd class, although families will be kept together) or a *poltrona*, an airline-type armchair. Deck class is available only in summer and only on some ferries, so ask when making your booking. Restaurant, bar and recreation facilities are available on the larger ferries. All ferries carry vehicles.

LOCAL TRANSPORT

All major cities and towns have good transport systems, with buses and – in Palermo's case – a metro.

Bus & Metro

City bus services are usually frequent and reliable. You must always purchase bus tickets before you board the bus and validate them once aboard. It is common practice among Sicilians and many tourists to ride on the buses for free by not validating their tickets – just watch how many people rush to punch their tickets when an inspector boards the bus. However, if you get caught with an unvalidated ticket, you will be fined on the spot (up to L50,000 in Palermo and Catania). Efficient provincial and regional bus services also operate between towns and villages. Tourist offices will provide information on bus routes.

There is a metro system in Palermo, but it is limited and does not service any destinations of real interest to the majority of tourists. You must buy tickets and validate them before getting on the train. You can get a map of the network from tourist offices in Palermo.

Tickets You can buy tickets at most *tabaccherie* (tobacconists), at many newspaper stands and at ticket booths. Tickets generally cost from L1500 for one hour to 90 minutes (it varies from city to city). Most cities offer 24-hour tourist tickets which can mean big savings.

Taxi

Taxis in Sicily are expensive so, if possible, it's preferable to catch a bus instead. If you need a taxi, you can usually find them in taxi ranks at train and bus stations or you can telephone (radio-taxi phone numbers are listed in the Getting Around sections of the major cities). However, if you book a taxi by phone, you will be charged for the trip the driver makes to reach you. Taxis will rarely stop when hailed on the street and generally will not respond to telephone bookings made from a public phone.

Rates vary from city to city. A good indication of the average is Palermo, where the minimum charge is L3000 for the first 3km, then L1000 per kilometre thereafter. There are supplements of L4000 from 10 pm to 7 am, and L2000 from 7 am to 10 pm on Sunday and public holidays. No more than four or five people will be allowed in one taxi, depending on the size of the car.

Watch out for taxi drivers who take advantage of new arrivals and stretch out the trip, and consequently the size of the fare.

ORGANISED TOURS

People wanting to travel to Sicily on a fully organised package tour have a wide range of options and it is best to discuss these with your travel agency. A selection of companies that offer tours of Sicily can be found in the Organised Tours section of the Getting There & Away chapter.

Once in Sicily, it is often less expensive and usually more enjoyable to see the sights independently, but if you are in a hurry or prefer guided tours, go to the Sestante CIT office (Palermo and Catania). They organise city tours for an average price of L40,000. They also offer an eight-day Sicily tour costing L1,230,000; prices include twin-share accommodation, transport and some meals.

The CTS, which has offices in all of Sicily's major cities, offers six- or seven-day tours of the island for around L1,500,000. The price includes twin-share accommodation, half board, transport by bus, and admission to museums and sites.

Tourist offices can generally assist with information on local agencies that offer tours.

Palermo

postcode 91100 • pop 730,000

Sicily's capital and largest city is a place of compelling contradictions. Difficult to define yet impossible to ignore, Palermo is bold, blaring and enticing. At one time an Arab emirate and seat of a Norman kingdom, and in its heyday regarded as the grandest city in Europe, Palermo today is in a remarkable state of decay, a city noted more for its crumbling buildings and crime-ridden neighbourhoods than its glorious past and cultural wealth. Noisy, intense and sometimes belligerent, Palermo is a place the first-time visitor might well be forgiven for avoiding. They would be missing out. The capital demands an effort but rewards those willing to give it the attention it deserves.

Behind the decay, Palermo is a beautiful city with a reserve of cultural, architectural and historical wealth to rival any of Europe's great capitals. With a long history of occupation by various Mediterranean powers, Palermo's role as a crossroads between east and west has resulted in an intoxicating cultural cross-fertilisation. This finds its best expression in the city's architectural mix, a fusion of diverse styles that include Byzantine, Arab, Norman, Renaissance and baroque.

Severely criticised for allowing its architectural heritage to languish following the heavy bombing of WWII and their general disinterest during the post-war years, the authorities have recently begun a number of sizeable restoration projects. Not least was that of the Teatro Massimo, which reopened to much fanfare in 1997. Some quarters of the historic centre, for years abandoned to crime that turned them into night-time no-go zones, have been given a new lease of life with the opening of some great bars, cafes and restaurants. This has created a scene to rival the more established and up-market nightlife centred around the grander streets north of Piazza Verdi.

Palermo's most interesting attraction, however, is its populace. Like their city, Palermi-

Highlights

- Appreciate the breathtaking beauty of the Cappella Palatina in the Palazzo dei Normanni

- Take a walk through the historic city's colourful markets on a weekday morning

- Visit the adjacent churches of La Martorana and San Cataldo, symbols of the city's multicultural past

- Enjoy a summer recital in the ruins of the Chiesa di Santa Maria dello Spasimo

- Have a drink amid the decaying elegance of the city's baroque past at one of the bars on Piazza Olivella or Via Candelai

- Marvel at the golden mosaics of the Cattedrale di Monreale, perhaps the most splendid work of art on the island

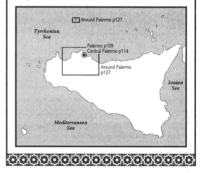

tans are a demanding lot. You will find that they are also warm and friendly, consumers of life's pleasures (both simple and sophisticated) and full of energy and passion.

Finally, a word on Palermo's most enduring shadow. Although still a powerful and ominous presence, the Mafia's activities took a substantial battering during the 1990s, especially following the 1992 killings. The army, called on to the streets after the murders of anti-Mafia magistrates Giovanni Falcone and Paolo Borsellino (see the boxed text 'Palermo & the Mafia' later in

PALERMO

the chapter), were removed in the summer of 1999, and the city has resumed an air of normality. Organised crime presents no real threat to the visitor save for the occasional incident of scooter-powered bag-snatching.

HISTORY

Palermo's superb position by the sea at the foot of Mt Pellegrino (606m), with the fertile Conca d'Oro valley behind it, has long made it a rich prize for Sicily's colonisers. Around the 8th century BC the Phoenicians established the town of Ziz here, on the site of a prehistoric village. It remained a relatively minor town under Roman, and later Byzantine, control and it was not until AD 831, when it was conquered by the Arabs, that the city truly flourished and became a jewel of the Islamic world.

When the Normans took control in 1072, things only improved. The seat of the kingdom of Roger I of Hauteville, Palermo was hailed as one of the most magnificent and cultured cities of 12th-century Europe. For more than 50 years after Roger's death the monarchy foundered. It eventually passed to the German Hohenstaufens and the Holy Roman Emperor Frederick I, still remembered as one of Sicily's most enlightened rulers and a pioneer of the Italian language (Dante devoted an entire canto of his *Divine Comedy* to Frederick and his patronage of early Italian poetry). After Frederick's death, Palermo and all of Sicily passed to the French Anjou family, themselves later deposed following the Sicilian Vespers revolt, which started in Palermo. By then eclipsed by Naples, Palermo sank into a long, slow decline, which continued right up to the 20th century.

Following WWII, the city expanded substantially as its population swelled through the influx of rural labourers looking for better-paid work. The old city sank into greater disrepair as Palermitans moved out from the centre into newly built housing estates that did little for Palermo's aesthetic charm (but allegedly filled the Mafia's coffers). Violence once made the city a European pariah, but a slow process of restoration and rehabilitation has begun. As Palermo be-

gins the new millennium, things look brighter than they have done for centuries.

ORIENTATION

Palermo is a large but manageable city. The historic centre is divided into four quarters *(canti)* – La Kalsa, Il Ballaro, Il Capo and La Vucciria – which meet at the crossroads of Corso Vittorio Emanuele and Via Maqueda. Although a maze of winding streets and minuscule alleyways, the historic centre is relatively small in comparison with the expanse of the modern city. Bordered to the west by the Palazzo dei Normanni and the Porta Nuova, to the east by the old port of La Cala, to the south by the train station (Stazione Centrale) and to the north by Piazza Verdi, here you will find the bulk of Palermo's sights of interest as well as the most authentic taste of Palermitan life, including the all-important markets and some of the city's cheapest restaurants and hotels.

Most of the cheaper *pensioni* (guesthouses) and hotels are around the train station. It's a grimy and chaotic area, but behind the decaying mansions lining the main streets is a fascinating maze of narrow lanes and tiny squares – though you can also, unfortunately, get a better idea here of just how decrepit parts of Palermo still are. It's not nearly as bad as it was even a few years ago, but visitors should be on their guard in the quieter, less-lit side streets.

The decision (made in September 1999) to ban all traffic except for buses and taxis from Via Maqueda will go a long way towards helping the street to re-establish itself as one of the city's most elegant boulevards, ensuring that boutique-gazers and windowshoppers aren't choked by traffic fumes. Via Roma, home of the budget stores and snack bars, has had no such luck and continues to deal with the plague of gridlock that grips it from 8 am to 8 pm daily.

North of Piazza Verdi is the newer and more modish part of the city, a mixture of late-19th-century elegance and post-WWII development, some parts a little more eyecatching than others. From the modern Piazza Castelnuovo, Via della Libertà cuts a swanky swathe north to the Giardino Inglese

PALERMO

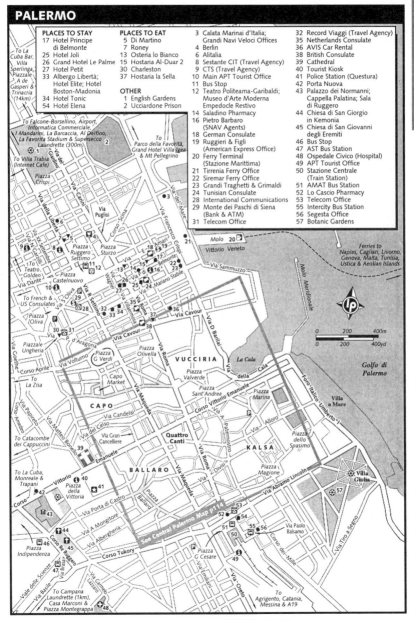

PLACES TO STAY
17 Hotel Principe
   di Belmonte
25 Hotel Joli
26 Grand Hotel Le Palme
27 Hotel Petit
33 Albergo Libertà;
   Hotel Elite; Hotel
   Boston-Madonia
34 Hotel Tonic
54 Hotel Elena

PLACES TO EAT
5 Di Martino
7 Roney
13 Osteria lo Bianco
15 Hostaria Al-Duar 2
30 Charleston
37 Hostaria la Sella

OTHER
1 English Gardens
2 Ucciardone Prison

3 Calata Marinai d'Italia;
   Grandi Navi Veloci Offices
4 Berlin
6 Alitalia
8 Sestante CIT (Travel Agency)
9 CTS (Travel Agency)
10 Main APT Tourist Office
11 Bus Stop
12 Teatro Politeama-Garibaldi;
   Museo d'Arte Moderna
   Empedocle Restivo
14 Saladino Pharmacy
16 Pietro Barbaro
   (SNAV Agents)
18 German Consulate
19 Ruggeri & Figli
   (American Express Office)
20 Ferry Terminal
   (Stazione Marittima)
21 Tirrenia Ferry Office
22 Siremar Ferry Office
23 Grandi Traghetti & Grimaldi
24 Tunisian Consulate
28 International Communications
29 Monte dei Paschi di Siena
   (Bank & ATM)
31 Telecom Office

32 Record Viaggi (Travel Agency)
35 Netherlands Consulate
36 AVIS Car Rental
38 British Consulate
39 Cathedral
40 Tourist Kiosk
41 Police Station (Questura)
42 Porta Nuova
43 Palazzo dei Normanni;
   Cappella Palatina; Sala
   di Ruggero
44 Chiesa di San Giorgio
   in Kemonia
45 Chiesa di San Giovanni
   degli Eremiti
46 Bus Stop
47 AST Bus Station
48 Ospedale Civico (Hospital)
49 APT Tourist Office
50 Stazione Centrale
   (Train Station)
51 AMAT Bus Station
52 Lo Cascio Pharmacy
53 Telecom Office
55 Intercity Bus Station
56 Segesta Office
57 Botanic Gardens

(English Gardens) and Villa Sperlinga; it's a wide avenue adorned with expensive apartment blocks, outdoor cafes and most of the city's boutiques and designer shops.

INFORMATION
Tourist Offices
The main APT office (☎ 091 58 61 22/38 47) is at Piazza Castelnuovo 35. The staff speak English and you can pick up a map of the city and the free monthly *Tourist Information Magazine*, an excellent bilingual guide to what's going on in the city, with comprehensive listings of all cultural events as well as important addresses and other information. The office is open from 8.30 am to 2 pm and 2.30 to 6 pm Monday to Friday, to 2 pm on Saturday. There is a branch office at the train station (☎ 091 61 65 914), which has the same opening times, and another at Falcone-Borsellino airport (☎ 091 59 16 98), open from 8 am to 10 pm daily. For a free map and cursory information about the city, there's a tourist kiosk at the north-eastern corner of Piazza della Vittoria, close to the cathedral. It is open from 8 am to 8 pm daily.

Money
The exchange office at the train station is open from 8 am to 8 pm daily, and there's another at the airport (Banca di Sicilia). Otherwise, there is no shortage of banks in the city, generally open from 8.30 am to 1.15 pm Monday to Friday. The majority have ATMs, including the Banca Nazionale del Lavoro, Via Roma 297, and the Monte dei Paschi di Siena on Piazza Bagnasco. American Express is represented by Ruggieri & Figli (☎ 091 58 71 44), Via E Amari 40.

Post & Telecommunications
The main post office is at Via Roma 322. It is open from 8.30 am to 7 pm Monday to Friday (to 1.30 pm on Saturday) and has a fax service. There is a Telecom office virtually opposite the train station on Piazza Giulio Cesare. It is open from 8 am to 9.30 pm daily. There is another Telecom office on Piazzale Ungheria.

Email & Internet Access
You can check email or surf the Web at I Candelai (☎ 091 32 71 51), Via Candelai 19, a bar in the historic centre whose five terminals are accessible from 7 pm to 3 am daily except Monday. It costs L10,000 for the first 30 minutes, L5000 for every 30 minutes thereafter. At the time of research, a new Internet cafe was about to open at International Communications (☎ 091 32 63 52), Piazza Bagnasco 27, just off Piazza Castelnuovo. It is open from 9.30 am to 1 pm and 4 to 7.30 pm Monday to Friday (mornings only on Saturday). It costs L5000 for the first 20 minutes and L5000 for every 30 minutes thereafter.

There is a free Internet cafe at Villa Trabia (☎ 091 740 59 41), with its entrance on Via A Salinas; it's open from 9 am to 7 pm daily. Advance booking is required.

Travel Agencies
Sestante CIT (☎ 091 58 63 33), where you can book travel tickets, is at Via della Libertà 12. There is a CTS travel agency (☎ 091 611 07 13) at Via Nicolò Garzilli 28G. Record Viaggi (☎ 091 611 09 10) is at Via Mariano Stabile 168, between Via Ruggero Settimo and Via Roma.

Bookshops
Feltrinelli bookshop (☎ 091 58 77 85), at Via Maqueda 399, has a foreign-language section. Gulliver, on the corner of Via Roma and Piazza San Domenico, also stocks a limited selection of foreign-language books. Libreria Sellerio, founded by Leonardo Sciascia at Corso Vittorio Emanuele 504, is also worth checking out. Generally, bookshops are open from 9 am to 8 pm Monday to Saturday. Several stands around Piazza Verdi sell foreign newspapers.

Laundry
There are only a couple of coin-operated laundrettes in Palermo. Campana is in the university district south-west of the city centre, at Via Cuba 2. Take bus No 309, 339 or 389 from Piazza Indipendenza. A little closer to the centre, Supersecco is at Via Alfieri 25, just off Via della Libertà.

PALERMO

Medical Services

Ospedale Civico (hospital; ☎ 091 666 22 07) is at Via Carmelo Lazzaro. You can call for an ambulance on ☎ 091 30 66 44. There are several pharmacies in the city that stay open until midnight, including Lo Cascio (☎ 091 616 21 17), near the train station at Via Roma 1, and Saladino (☎ 091 58 17 71), Via Principe di Belmonte 110.

Emergency

The central police station (*questura*; ☎ 091 21 01 11), where you should go to report thefts and other crimes, is on Piazza della Vittoria. If your car has been towed away, call ☎ 091 656 97 21 to find out where to collect it.

Dangers & Annoyances

Over the past 30 years Palermo has deservedly earned itself a reputation as a dangerous city – and not just because of the alleged Mafia killings and gangland shootings, which have rarely troubled the foreign visitor. A strong police presence was deemed necessary to counter the widespread scourge of bag-snatchers, pickpockets and other petty-crime merchants who plagued the city. The problem still exists, but it is nowhere near the scale of a decade ago. The effectiveness of the police is largely responsible for the improvement, but renewed efforts to clean up the decay of the historic centre have also played a significant role. Although not problem-free,

---

Palermo & the Mafia

It is an open secret that the Mafia exercised an all-pervasive control over Palermo's affairs for decades. From building contracts to the distribution of EU funds, the Cosa Nostra (an alternative term for the Mafia) ensured that it received the lion's share of the cash. As a political pawnbroker the Mafia has determined the fortunes of city officials of all levels, from the lowliest clerk right up to the mayor's office. In Rome, the powers-that-be postured and made the appropriate noises but did little else to break the Mafia's vice-like grip on the island's affairs.

In the mid-1980s, however, the dogged and courageous determination of the Palermitan magistrature, led by Giovanni Falcone and Paolo Borsellino, began to turn the tide against the bosses. The first maxi-trial took place in Palermo in 1986, when 357 of the 500 accused were convicted and sentenced. The bloodshed that ensued was understood to be the Mafia's vicious reaction to such a body blow, but the magistrates were not to be deterred. In 1990 the current mayor, Leoluca Orlando, for years a luminary of the Sicilian Christian Democrats, was ejected from the party on account of his vocal anti-Mafia stance. Incredibly, Orlando resuscitated his seemingly moribund career and stormed back as the leader of his own political party, La Rete (The Network), and was re-elected mayor in 1991. Although Falcone and Borsellino were tragically eliminated by the unforgiving Mafia, the ever-popular Orlando continues the fight against organised crime (even though his critics claim that he is more interested in his own glory than in defeating the Mafia).

JANE SMITH

Anti-mafia campaigner Giovanni Falcone made a fatal judgement.

Things have changed in Palermo, but the Mafia has not gone away. Behind Mayor Orlando there is a groundswell of popular support, people that is tired of fear and is no longer willing to keep silent. The Cosa Nostra will not be defeated so easily. Palermo's fortunes are too tightly wrapped up with the Mafia for that.

Palermo's trouble areas – in particular the area from the Vucciria market towards the port and the Kalsa quarter to the north-east of the train station – aren't so much the no-go zones they have been in recent decades.

Still, the visitor should remain cautious at all times, remembering that where there is poverty (and parts of Palermo are shamefully blighted) you should avoid being flash. Avoid wearing jewellery or carrying a bag, and keep your valuables in a money belt. Stay away from poorly lit and deserted streets, particularly at night. Women should avoid walking alone in the historic centre at night; the larger the group the better. Watch out for pickpockets around the main inter-city bus station on Via Paolo Balsamo.

THE HEART OF THE OLD CITY
Quattro Canti

The busy intersection of Corso Vittorio Emanuele and Via Maqueda marks the Quattro Canti (Four Corners) of Palermo, the centre of the oldest part of town. Also known as Piazza Vigliena or the Teatro del Sole (Theatre of the Sun), it was originally laid out in 1608 by Giulio Lasso and completed in 1620. In each corner the Spanish baroque facade is decorated with three tiers: in the first, a fountain and a statue of one of the four seasons; in the second, a statue of the Spanish kings Carlos V and Felipe II, III and IV; and in the third, a statue of a patron saints of the city (Christina, Ninfa, Olivia and Agata). In the south-western corner is the baroque **Chiesa di San Giuseppe dei Teatini**, topped by a soaring cupola. The magnificent interior is dripping with marble, lovingly restored after substantial damage suffered during WWII. It is open from 9 am to 6 pm daily; admission is free.

Piazza Pretoria

This square hosts the eye-catching **Fontana Pretoria**, created by Florentine sculptor Francesco Camilliani in 1554–5. At the time of its unveiling, the shocked populace named it the Fountain of Shame because of its nude motifs. Take time to study the numerous figures which decorate every corner. Closing off the eastern side of the square is the

baroque **Chiesa di Santa Caterina** (closed for restoration at the time of research), while the **Palazzo Pretorio** or Muncipio (municipal offices), also known as the Palazzo delle Aquile because of the eagle sculptures that guard each corner of the roof, fronts the southern edge of the square.

La Martorana

Perhaps Palermo's most famous medieval church, La Martorana (☎ 091 616 16 92) is at Piazza Bellini 3, a few steps south of Piazza Pretoria. Its original name was the Chiesa di Santa Maria dell'Ammiraglio (after King Roger II's chief admiral, George of Antioch, who paid for its construction in 1143) but was renamed in 1433 when King Alphonse of Aragon presented it to a Benedictine order founded by Eloisa Martorana. Although the original 12th-century structure has been altered over the centuries, it still retains its Arab-Norman bell tower and the interior is richly decorated with Byzantine mosaics. Totally in keeping with the decoration, the Greek eastern-rite Mass is still celebrated here. Try to time your visit to avoid the many weddings celebrated in the church. It is open from 8 am to 1 pm and 3.30 to 5.30 pm Monday to Saturday and from 8.30 am to 1 pm on Sunday and public holidays. Admission is free.

Chiesa di San Cataldo

Next to La Martorana is this tiny, simple church dating from the period of the Norman domination of Sicily. Its battlements and red domes are another fusion of Arab and Norman styles. You'll need to get the key from the custodian who sits at a small table to the right as you enter La Martorana. It is open the same hours as La Martorana and admission is free.

Chiesa di San Matteo

On the northern side of Corso Vittorio Emanuele, this baroque church has a richly decorated interior. The four statues in the pilasters of the dome represent the Virtues and were carved by Giacomo Serpotta in 1728. The church is open from 8.30 am to 2 pm daily. Admission is free.

PALERMO

Cathedral

Despite its hotchpotch of styles and many alterations, Palermo's cathedral (☎ 091 33 43 76), west of the Quattro Canti along Corso Vittorio Emanuele, is certainly imposing. Construction on a grand scale began in 1184 on the site of an existing basilica at the behest of Palermo's archbishop, Walter of the Mill (Gualtiero Offamiglia), who was eager to challenge the supremacy of the cathedral at Monreale (for more information see the boxed text 'The Battle of the Two Cathedrals').

The cathedral has been an architectural playground many times since, with bits added and removed according to whim. Such lack of aesthetic cohesion has been detrimental to the building, most disastrously between 1781 and 1801 when the architectural harmony of the building was radically affected through the construction of the dome (the brainchild of one Ferdinando Fuga). Not content with messing up the exterior, the delicate basilican plan inside was scrapped in favour of an in-vogue Latin-cross plan, including the addition of side aisles. The only original element is the apse, an impressive example of Norman architectural style. Arab influences in some of the geometric decoration are unmistakable and the graceful Gothic towers distract the eye from the dome.

Despite the architectural mess, the interior is rich in works of art. The **Tombe Imperiali e Reali** (Imperial and Royal Tombs) are to the right of the main entrance are the, four elegant porphyry sarcophagi containing the remains of Roger II (rear left), Frederick II of Hohenstaufen (front left), his mother Constance de Hauteville (rear right) and Henry VI of Hohenstaufen (front right). Also buried here (in the wall) are Duke William and Constance of Aragon. Halfway down the right aisle is a magnificent treasury (unfortunately closed for repairs at the time of research) whose most extraordinary exhibit is a tooth extracted from Santa Rosalia, one of the patron saints of Palermo. Her ashes are also kept here, in a silver urn. The cathedral is open from 7 am to 7 pm Monday to Saturday, and from 8 am to 1.30 pm and 4 to 7 pm on Sunday. Admission to the cathedral is free. Entrance to the treasury (when it is open) costs L1000.

Palazzo dei Normanni

Across the Piazza della Vittoria and the gardens from the cathedral is the Palazzo dei Normanni, also known as the Palazzo Reale (Royal Palace). Built by the Arabs in the 9th century, it was extended by the Normans and restructured by the Hohenstaufens. It is now the seat of Sicily's regional government.

Enter from Piazza Indipendenza to see the **Cappella Palatina**, a magnificent example of Arab-Norman artistic genius, built during the reign of Roger II and decorated with Byzantine mosaics. The chapel is undoubtedly Palermo's most extraordinary treasure, a breathtaking example of art at its

The Battle of the Two Cathedrals

King William II wasn't happy to see his archbishop and former teacher, the Englishman Walter of the Mill, consolidate his position from his basilica in the city centre. Walter was a steadfast ally of Pope Innocent II, who had been feuding with William's family since the pope's capture by Roger II in 1139. To break papal control over his city, William decided to upstage the archbishopric, firstly by endowing a new monastery outside his royal grounds and then, in 1174, by constructing a cathedral so magnificent that it would outshine Walter's new cathedral in the city. William's cathedral at Monreale – built in less than 10 years – quickly became a sight to behold and the enraged Walter decided to stop at nothing to outdo the king. Consequently in 1185 he ordered that the basilica be torn down and a new, infinitely more splendid church be built. As a result of the rivalry Palermo had two outstanding churches, but their construction had very little to do with their founders' piety or love of God. Still, they're not bad results for an ego-trip.

PALERMO

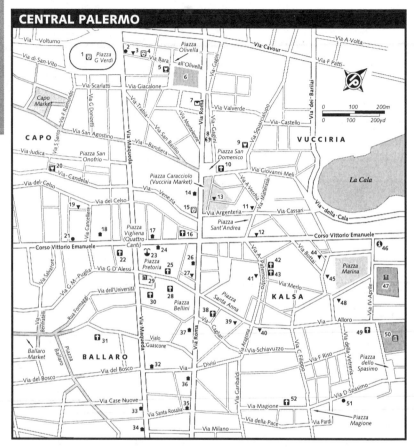

CENTRAL PALERMO

most exalted (the enjoyment of which is only spoilt by the look-and-get-out attitude of some of its guardians – though, in fairness, the place does get pretty packed). The mosaics alone, rivalled only by those of Ravenna and Istanbul, make the chapel an absolute must on any tourist itinerary.

While the mosaics demonstrate the Byzantine influence on Palermitan art, the geometric tile designs are a clear reminder of Arab input. The carved wooden ceiling is a classic example of intricate, Arab-style stalactite design. The chapel is open from 9 am to 12.30 pm and 3 to 5 pm Monday to Friday (mornings only on Saturday). It is also open from midday to 1 pm on Sunday, but forget about it unless you want to suffocate in the crowd of tour groups that cram the place. Admission is free.

The **Sala di Ruggero** (King Roger's Room), the king's former bedroom, is also worth visiting as it is decorated with 12th-century mosaics. It is only possible to visit the room with a guide (free of charge). Go upstairs from the Cappella Palatina.

There are guided tours of the palace itself, but you'll need to book a few days in advance (fax 091 705 47 37). Ask for Mrs

CENTRAL PALERMO

PLACES TO STAY
14 Hotel Moderno
17 Grande Albergo Sole
18 Centrale Palace Hotel
24 Albergo da Luigi
26 Hotel Confort
32 Hotel Sicilia
33 Albergo Orientale
34 Pensione Vittoria
35 Albergo Rosalia
    Conca d'Oro
36 Albergo Piccadilly;
    Albergo Concordia
37 Albergo Corona

PLACES TO EAT
3 Dal Pompiere
11 Sant'Andrea
12 Casa del Brodo
13 Trattoria Shanghai
19 Caffè Arabo
27 Hostaria da Ciccio

39 Trattoria dai Vespri
40 Trattoria Stella
41 Antica Focacceria
    di San Francesco
44 La Cambusa
45 Il Bagatto
48 Trattoria Il Crudo e Il Cotto

OTHER
1 Teatro Massimo
2 Feltrinelli Bookshop
4 Opera dei Pupi (Puppet
    Theatre)
5 Fuso Orario
6 Museo Archeologico
    Regionale
7 Main Post Office
8 Bank & ATM
9 I Grilli Giù
10 Chiesa di San Domenico
15 Teatro Biondo
16 Chiesa di San Matteo

20 I Candelai
21 Libreria Sellerio Bookshop
22 Chiesa di San Giuseppe
    dei Teatini
23 Fontana Pretoria
25 Chiesa di Santa Caterina
28 La Martorana
29 Palazzo Pretorio
30 Chiesa di San Cataldo
31 Chiesa del Gesù
38 Chiesa di Santa Anna
42 Oratorio di San Lorenzo
43 Chiesa di San Francesco
    d'Assisi
46 Tourist Kiosk
47 Palazzo Chiaramonte
49 La Gancia
50 Palazzo Abatellis; Galleria
    Regionale della Sicilia
51 Lo Spasimo; Chiesa di Santa
    Maria dello Spasimo
52 La Magione

Zichichi when you get there. Preference is given to groups and school trips so lone travellers can have difficulty booking, especially when the regional assembly is in session.

Porta Nuova
Next to the palace is the Porta Nuova, built to celebrate the arrival of Carlos V in Palermo in 1535 after a victory over the Tunisians. Designed in the Mannerist style, it was partially destroyed by lightning in 1667 and rebuilt with the addition of the conical top. More than 400 years later, it still serves as a demarcation line between the old and new city.

Chiesa di San Giovanni degli Eremiti
Just south of the Palazzo dei Normanni on Via dei Benedettini, this church (whose name translates as St John of the Hermits) is Palermo's best-known example of the Norman-Arab architectural mix. Built under Roger II, it is topped by five red domes and set in a pretty, tree-filled garden with cloisters that offer temporary respite from the chaos outside. The bare interior of the now deconsecrated church features some badly deteriorated frescoes including, on the left

wall, the 12th-century *Madonna con Gesù Bambino e Santi* (Virgin Mary with Christ Child and Saints). The church (☎ 091 651 50 19) is open from 9 am to 7 pm Monday to Saturday, and 9 am to 12.30 pm on Sunday. Admission costs L4000.

Next door is the 18th-century **Chiesa di San Giorgio in Kemonia**, rebuilt on the site of an older structure. The rococo interior features the paintings of Giuseppe Tresca.

ALONG VIA ROMA
Running north from the train station, Via Roma is one of Palermo's more interesting main streets. Not nearly as elegant as the parallel Via Maqueda, it embodies the mayhem and chaos that is Sicily's capital; the incessant noise of its gridlocked traffic is merely a sideshow to the hubbub of its shops, bars and markets. It is here that you'll find many of Palermo's cheaper clothing outlets, a multitude of basic bars where Palermitans gather to drink coffee and exchange gossip and, in the side streets off the main drag, some of the city's most frequented markets, including the famed but run-down Vucciria. Via Roma is also home to the beautiful Chiesa di San Domenico and the Museo Archeologico Regionale.

euro currency converter L10,000 = €5.16

PALERMO

LA VUCCIRIA

The most renowned of Palermo's four quarters, La Vucciria is a largely off-putting mess of dilapidated buildings and a confusing maze of alleyways. At night the streets are eerily empty and can be quite dangerous: a favourite robber's trick is to throw something from a building to knock over a victim so that they can be robbed more easily. Still, the quarter attracts droves of visitors, most of whom come for its famous market.

Sicilian painter Renato Guttuso's most important work is a painting of the market (unfortunately stashed away in a private collector's hands) and writer Leonardo Sciascia devoted many inches to describing its allure, calling it 'a hungry man's dream'. Every morning except Sunday the stalls are opened in the small Piazza Caracciolo behind the Chiesa di Sant'Antonio and the vendors go to work. In *Midnight in Sicily*, Peter Robb describes the market as 'the belly of Palermo and the heart too.'

As markets go it is still an interesting place but unfortunately La Vucciria is no longer what it was, even up until late in the 1970s when Robb first visited the city. Today it is more of a tourist attraction, with many locals now using markets in other quarters of the historic centre.

To get there, take the steps off Via Roma that run alongside the Chiesa di Sant'Antonio. Remember that the place shuts down during lunchtime.

Museo Archeologico Regionale

A block north of the main post office, at Piazza Olivella 24 (backing on to Via Roma), is the imposing Museo Archeologico Regionale (☎ 091 611 68 05), one of the most important museums of its kind in Europe. Its vast collection includes Greek stone carvings from Selinunte, the Hellenistic *Ariete di Bronzo di Siracus* (Bronze Ram of Syracuse), the largest collection of ancient anchors in the world and finds from archaeological sites throughout the island. The most interesting room is the **Sala di Selinunte**, featuring all of the metopes (stone carvings) from the seven Greek temples uncovered at Selinunte. The best of

these, recovered from Temple E, show Hercules fighting an Amazon, the marriage of Zeus and Hera, and Athena and the Titan. Also worth looking out for is the bronze 5th-century-BC statue of a boy known as the *Efebo di Selinunte* (Youth of Selinunte). Unless you're an avid fan of archaeology you can cruise through the rest of the exhibits, but the museum is definitely worth a visit. It is open from 9 am to 1.30 pm and 3 to 7.30 pm Monday to Friday, and 9 am to 1 pm Saturday and Sunday. Admission costs L8000.

Chiesa di San Domenico

About 200m south of the museum, off Via Roma on Piazza San Domenico, is the eponymous church (☎ 091 32 95 88) that is one of Palermo's most remarkable baroque structures. It was built in 1640 following the design of architect Andrea Cirincione; the facade was added in 1726 after buildings which once occupied the square were demolished to give the church some space. The church serves as the city's pantheon, housing the tombs and cenotaphs of some notable Sicilians including former Italian prime minister Francesco Crispi. The church is open from 9 to 11.30 am daily (also 5 to 7 pm on Saturday and Sunday). Admission is free.

Prigione dell'Ucciardone

Not so much a sight but a landmark, and impossible to visit (unless you're here to visit a 'guest'!), this Bourbon prison overlooking the water is Sicily's most notorious detention centre for the Mafia.

The place is shrouded in myth; it has been suggested that the inmates have a greater say in the running of the place than the authorities, and that Cosa Nostra business is run from here (that is, when they are not eating meals delivered from Palermo's finest restaurants).

After the Falcone-Borsellino murders in 1992 (for more information see the boxed text 'Palermo & the Mafia' earlier in the chapter) the more 'connected' inmates were transferred to prisons on the Italian mainland, but it remains Italy's most Mafia-populated prison.

LA KALSA

Plagued by poverty and decay, La Kalsa – one of the city's original quarters, whose name derives from the Arabic word *khalisa* (meaning 'pure') – was heavily bombed in 1943 and more or less allowed to sink into squalor ever since. This is one of the city's most notorious neighbourhoods and, at least until recently, most visitors were advised to keep away once the sun went down. Thankfully, things are starting to change, albeit slowly, and a number of the quarter's more important attractions are finally being given the attention they deserve after languishing in obscurity for decades. A few restaurants and bars have opened in the hitherto abandoned streets, bringing new life to a moribund quarter. The summer program of free concerts and recitals in the magnificent ruins of the Chiesa di Santa Maria dello Spasimo is one of the city's best attractions (see the Lo Spasimo section later in the chapter). Nevertheless, visitors are advised to exercise caution in the area by keeping away from poorly lit or empty streets and, if possible, not walking alone.

Oratorio di San Lorenzo

Near the old port of La Cala, just south of Corso Vittorio Emanuele on Via Immacolatella, is the Oratorio di San Lorenzo, built in 1569 by the Compagnia di San Francesco, a local Franciscan order. The church is worth visiting for the extraordinary stucco decoration by Giacomo Serpotta, his undoubted masterpiece completed between 1698 and 1710. The work includes ten symbolic statues and a series of panels with details from the lives of St Lawrence and St Francis, the best of which is the *Martirio di San Lorenzo* (Martyrdom of St Lawrence), on the far wall. Even the pews are works of art, laced with mother-of-pearl. A large *Natività* (Nativity) by Caravaggio once hung on the wall behind the altar but it was stolen in 1969 and has never been found.

Opening hours are 9 am to 2 pm Monday to Saturday, but the church keeps closing due to excavations on a site at the back. Admission is free.

Chiesa di San Francesco d'Assisi

Virtually next door to the oratory, this church (☎ 091 616 28 19) was originally built in tribute to St Francis of Assisi between 1255 and 1277 but was substantially altered over the centuries. The side chapels were added in the 14th and 15th centuries; the presbytery was elongated in 1589 and, following an earthquake in 1823, it was restored in neoclassical style. Damaged by Allied bombs in 1943, the restorers went to work on it once again after the war, removing some of the later modifications in an effort to return it to its original appearance. The facade – featuring a fine rose window and a flamboyant Gothic portal – dates from the 19th century and was thankfully left intact. Inside there are sculptures by the Gagini family. The church is open from 7 am to 12.30 pm and 4.30 to 6 pm Monday to Saturday. Admission is free.

Palazzo Chiaramonte

This imposing 14th-century palace near Piazza Marina is also known as the Steri (from the Latin word *hosterium*, meaning 'fortified building') and it is pretty obvious why. Sicily's most powerful baron of the day, Manfredio Chiaramonte, commissioned it in 1307, but it was not completed until 1380. Although it has been extensively altered since then, it still boasts an imposing facade that served as a model for many other buildings in Sicily. The Chiaramonte family, however, didn't have too many years to enjoy their palace: the last member, Andrea, was beheaded in the square in 1396 for his part in a rebellion against King Martino I of Aragon. Following the family's demise, the palace became the seat of the viceroys of Sicily and, in 1601, was made a tribunal of the Holy See, home of the infamous Grand Inquisition. Victims were jailed in the Carcere Filippine, a long area lined with cells; the walls are still decorated with their drawings and poems. At the end of the 18th century it was made the seat of the regular courts and continued in this role until 1960, when the courts were moved to a building in the newer part of the city. Today it serves as the administrative offices of the university and is only open to the public during exhibitions and other events; otherwise phone ☎ 091 33 41 39 to arrange a visit.

Galleria Regionale della Sicilia

Sicily's most important art gallery (☎ 091 623 00 11) is housed in the imposing **Palazzo Abatellis**, building of which began in 1490 by Matteo Carnelivari for the praetor of Palermo, Francesco Abatellis. The Catalan-Gothic building was badly damaged during WWII but underwent restoration by Carlo Scarpa in 1954, the year it opened as the gallery. Today it is home to an impressive collection of work, most notably sculpture and paintings dating from the 14th to 16th centuries but also including work from later years. The ground floor is devoted to sculpture, beginning with a remarkable 12th-century Arabic door frame and a painting of *Madonna con Santi* (Madonna with Saints) by Tommaso de Vigilia (Room 1). Room 2 is the palace's former chapel, and is now home to the *Trionfo della Morte* (Triumph of Death), a magnificent fresco that once hung in the Palazzo Sclafani. It is unclear who the author of the work was, but some experts have attributed it to Pisanello. In the painting, Death is an archer on horseback piercing the wealthy and smug while the miserable (tellingly represented by a painter and his pupil!) pray for release. At the end of the corridor containing Arabic ceramics is Room 4, housing the gallery's most exquisite (and famous) piece, the white marble bust of *Eleonara di Aragona* (Eleonora of Aragon) by Francesco Laurana.

The 2nd floor is devoted primarily to Sicilian art, including Antonello da Messina's well-known panel of the *Assunzione* (Assumption). A number of Flemish paintings are also on show, perhaps to illustrate the influence of the Dutch school on Sicilian art; the most important of these is the *Malvagna* triptych by Jan Gossaert. The gallery, accessed through Via Alloro just off Piazza Abatellis, is open from 9 am to 1.30 pm and 3 to 7.30 pm Tuesday and Thursday, and from 9.30 am to 12.30 pm Saturday and Sunday. Admission costs L8000.

La Gancia

Virtually next door to the gallery at Via Alloro 27 is the 17th-century Chiesa di Santa Maria degli Angeli (☎ 091 616 52 21), better known as La Gancia. Palermo's oldest organ (1620) is over the main doorway (access, however, is through a side door), most probably the work of Raffaele La Valle. Also worth checking out is the pulpit between the fifth and sixth chapels on the right, which is the work of the Gagini school. The church is open from 9 am to 5 pm Monday to Saturday. Admission is free.

Lo Spasimo

South of Piazza Marina, and along Via della Vetreria, this complex of buildings includes the **Chiesa di Santa Maria dello Spasimo** (☎ 091 616 14 86), a typical example of late-Gothic style, although it was actually built during the Renaissance. Building work on the church extended as far as the walls and the soaring apse, but it has stood for centuries without a roof and its interior is host to a couple of tall ailanthus trees. Restored and opened to the public in 1995, the complex is a wonderful venue for concerts, performances and exhibitions, which take place nightly from June to the end of September. It is open from 8 am to midnight daily and admission is free.

At the side of the church is a small building which houses the curator's office; in the foyer is an extraordinary model of historic Palermo. The office is open from 9 am to 1 pm and 4 to 7 pm Monday to Friday; at other times you'll have to content yourself with staring at it through the window.

La Magione

Across Piazza Magione from Lo Spasimo at Via Magione 44 is the Chiesa della Santi Trinità (☎ 091 617 05 96), also known as La Magione. This fine Norman church was founded in 1191 by the Cistercians but was awarded to the Teutonic Knights by the Holy Roman Emperor Henry VI in 1197; they held on to it until 1492, when Pope Innocent VIII expelled them from Sicily. Like most other Palermitan churches it was victim to the fad of redecoration but, in this instance, didn't fare too badly. Inside, the floor contains the marble funereal slabs of a bunch of Teutonic Knights. To the east of the church are the remains of a 12th-century cloister with double-lintel arches set on twin columns adorned by two splendid capitals. They bear a similarity to those in the cloister at Monreale, which is hardly surprising considering they were made by the same artisans. La Magione is open from 8 to 11.30 am and 3 to 6.30 pm Monday to Saturday and from 8 am to 1 pm on Sunday. Admission is free.

THE MODERN CITY
North of Piazza Verdi, Palermo takes on a less worn, more cosmopolitan look. Here, in *la Città del Ottocento* (the 19th-Century City), are some glorious examples from the last golden age in Sicilian architecture. The most obvious examples are Teatro Massimo and the smaller Teatro Politeama-Garibaldi.

Not surprisingly, you will find most of the city's designer boutiques and elegant, outdoor cafes here. Via della Libertà, which strides northwards from Piazza Castelnuovo, is as fancy a street as any you'd see in Rome, Milan or Florence – although the aesthetics of some of the modern apartment blocks leave something to be desired.

Teatro Massimo
Overlooking Piazza Verdi, the proud and haughty 19th-century Teatro Massimo (☎ 091 58 95 75) finally reopened in 1997 following a restoration program that had been in progress for 20 years. Building commenced in 1875 when the original square was levelled to make way for Giovanni Battista Basile's masterpiece, which was eventually completed in 1897 by his son Ernesto. The monumental Corinthian structure was the pride of Sicily when it first opened (with a performance of Verdi's *Falstaff*); it boasted the third-largest stage in the world, after the Opéra Garnier in Paris and Vienna's Staatsoper.

High society and illustrious personages failed to prevent the theatre from falling into disrepair less than 100 years after it opened, and when it closed in 1973 few could have imagined that it would be 24 years before its doors were opened to the public once more. Palermo's current mayor, Leoluca Orlando, made its restoration a priority of his term in office (even though his critics argue that he delayed the opening for political motives) and today it has been returned to its previous lustre. In front of the theatre, two beautiful Art-Nouveau kiosks designed by Ernesto have also been renovated. You can visit the theatre between 9 am and 1 pm Monday to Saturday, except during rehearsals.

Teatro Politeama-Garibaldi
Dominating Piazza Ruggero Settimo, Palermo's second theatre (and the Teatro Massimo's substitute for the length of its closure) was designed in classical form by Giuseppe Damiani Almeyda between 1867 and 1874. It features a particularly striking facade that looks like a triumphal arch topped by bronze chariots. Apart from serving as a theatre (☎ 091 605 33 15 for bookings) it is also home to the **Museo d'Arte Moderna Empedocle Restivo** (☎ 091 588 89 51), installed in 1910 with a fine array of modern and contemporary Italian art. The gallery is open from 8 am to 8 pm Tuesday to Saturday and from 9 am to 1 pm on Sunday. The entrance is at Via Turati 1. Admission costs L5000. The theatre itself is open during performances only.

OUTSIDE THE CITY CENTRE
Catacombe dei Cappuccini
Between the early 17th century and 1881, Sicilians of a certain social standing who didn't want to be forgotten on their death were embalmed by Capuchin monks. The catacombs in the Capuchin convent (☎ 091 21 21 17), on Piazza Cappuccini about 1km west of the city centre, contain one of the city's most bizarre sights – the mummified bodies and skeletons of some 8000 Palermitans. Over the entrance, a sign states that a visit here has three levels of importance: historic, cultural and reflective. Inside, the skeletal remains of the 'lucky' dead line the dimly lit, damp corridors, divided into different categories according to gender and

profession. The most disconcerting sight is the near-perfectly preserved body of Rosalia Lombardo (just follow the signs – in Italian and English – for '*bambina*'/'baby girl'), who died at the tender age of two in 1920. The doctor who embalmed her died soon after, taking a secret formula to the grave which would have been of use to those who struggled with the bodies of Lenin and, later, Chairman Mao. Gory and perturbing, the catacombs are one of the city's premier tourist attractions. They are open from 9 am to noon and 3.30 to 5.30 pm daily. A 'donation' of L3000 is requested. Bus No 327 from Piazza Indipendenza stops right in front of the entrance.

La Zisa

Just north of the catacombs, on Piazza Guglielmo il Buono, is the 12th-century Arab-Norman castle (☎ 091 652 02 69) whose name derives from the Arabic '*el aziz*', which translates as 'the splendid'. The once-magnificent palace was built for William I and completed by William II, who used it as a seasonal residence. After long years of neglect it was purchased by the government who undertook substantial restoration on it. Today it houses a museum of Arabic crafts of which the main features are the superbly crafted screens (called *mush-rabbiya* in Arabic) and a gorgeous 12th-century bronze basin. It is open from 9 am to 7 pm Monday to Saturday and 9 am to 12.30 pm on Sunday. Admission costs L4000. To get there, take bus No 124 from Piazza Ruggero Settimo.

La Cuba

About 1km west of Porta Nuova, at Corso Calatafimi 100, is a marvellous example of Arab-Norman Fatimid architecture known as La Cuba (☎ 091 59 02 99). Built in 1180, the castle was once part of an enormous park, planned by William II, which also incorporated La Zisa. In the 14th century, Giovanni Boccaccio used the castle as the setting for a story of his *Decameron* (Day V, 6); two centuries later it was used as a leper colony before being converted into a cavalry barracks by the Bourbons. Apart from

a model of it in its earlier days, there isn't much to see inside. It is open from 9 am to 1 pm and 3 to 4.30 pm daily (closed Sunday afternoon). Admission costs L4000.

PUBLIC PARKS

Palermo has a number of pleasant parks. The most attractive is Villa Giulia in La Kalsa, reached along Via Abramo Lincoln. This 18th-century landscaped oasis has a bunch of welcome diversions from the city's chaos, including deer and a kid's train. Next door are the **Orto Botanico** (Botanical Gardens). Villa Giulia and the gardens open from 9 am to 6 pm Monday to Friday and 9 am to 1 pm at weekends. To the north of the city centre, skirting along Via della Libertà past Piazza Crispi are the **Giardino Inglese** (English Gardens). Once a pretty little park, in recent decades the gardens have became a seedy hangout for drug addicts, though the city authorities have gone to immense efforts to clean it up in the past couple of years. In the last week of August it hosts the Festa dell'Unità (see the later Special Events section for details).

Farther north (about 3km from the city centre) is Palermo's biggest park, the **Parco della Favorita**. The Bourbon monarch Ferdinand purchased the land in 1799 and he commissioned the original layout; he even lived here in a small palace (now closed) for a couple of years during his exile from Naples. Today, the park is home to Palermo's eponymous soccer stadium – where the city's main team plays – and a brand-new sports centre, as well as public tennis courts.

SPECIAL EVENTS

Palermo's biggest annual festival, a celebration of St Rosalia, takes place between 11–15 July. The saint's relics are brought through the city amid four days of fireworks and partying. It's a great time to be in the city, with all kinds of festivities going on throughout the medieval city, including music, food and fireworks. It's all-round pandemonium actually.

During the last week in August, the Festival of Unity (Festa dell'Unità), a free festival of music, art and food, takes place in the Giardino Inglese. For decades sponsored by the Partito Communista Italiano (PCI; Italian Communist Party), its organisation passed into the hands of the Partito Democratico di Sinistra (PDS; Democratic Party of the Left), the Communists' successors and currently the party at the helm of the national government.

PLACES TO STAY

You should have little trouble finding a room in Palermo at whatever price you choose. The main tourist office will make recommendations, but not bookings.

Head for Via Maqueda or Via Roma, between the train station and the Quattro Canti, for the bulk of the cheap rooms, some of which are in old apartment buildings. Rooms facing onto either street will be noisy. Women on their own should be wary about staying in the area near the train station. The area around Piazza Castelnuovo offers a higher standard of accommodation with fewer budget options (catch bus No 101 or 107 from the train station to Piazza Sturzo).

PLACES TO STAY – BUDGET
Camping

The best camp site is *Trinacria* (☎ 091 53 05 90, Via Barcarello 25) by the sea at Sferracavallo. It costs L9000/9500/5000 per person/tent/car. Catch bus No 616 from Piazzale A de Gasperi (which can be reached by bus No 101 from the train station).

Hostels

Although classified as a hostel, Palermo's only near-equivalent is actually a hotel-cum-dormitory which practises as a B&B. Confused? Well, don't be, because at *Casa Marconi* (☎ 091 657 06 11, Via Monfenera 140) you'll find the best rooms for the cheapest prices in town (L35,000/60,000 for singles/doubles with breakfast thrown in). At the time of research, the hostel was sharing a building with the university hall of residence but plans are afoot to take over the whole building. To get there, take bus No 246 from the train station and get off at the hospital opposite Piazza Montegrappa,

turn left onto Via Monfenera and walk for about 300m. Casa Marconi is on the left.

Hotels

Near the train station, try *Albergo Orientale* (☎ 091 616 57 27, Via Maqueda 26) in an old, and somewhat decayed, building with a once-grand courtyard. Basic singles/doubles with bathroom cost L35,000/55,000. Just around the corner is *Albergo Rosalia Conca d'Oro* (☎ 091 616 45 43, Via Santa Rosalia 7), where ancient but clean single/double/triple rooms with bathroom cost L40,000/60,000/90,000. The cheaper *Pensione Vittoria* (☎ 091 616 24 37, Via Maqueda 8) has still more spartan singles/doubles with shared bathroom for L35,000/55,000.

There are a few hotels in one building at Via Roma 72. *Albergo Piccadilly* (☎ 091 617 03 76) has clean rooms (even if there are holes in the bedspreads). Singles without bath cost L40,000 and doubles with bathroom cost L75,000. *Albergo Concordia* (☎ 091 617 15 14) is also reasonable value at L35,000/55,000; doubles with bathroom cost L65,000.

Albergo Corona (☎ 091 616 23 40, Via Roma 118) has clean, pleasant single rooms for L35,000; doubles with bathroom cost L60,000. *Albergo da Luigi* (☎ 091 58 50 85, Corso Vittorio Emanuele 284) is almost next to the Quattro Canti. It has rooms that cost L30,000/50,000 or L40,000/60,000 with private bathroom, depending on the room – ask for one with a view of Piazza Pretoria and its fountain. Close to Corso Vittorio Emanuele, *Hotel Confort* (☎ 091 33 17 41, Via Roma 188) is an agreeable and clean establishment. Rooms cost L38,000/60,000, or L50,000/80,000 with bathroom.

Hotel Sicilia (☎ 091 616 84 60, Via Divisi 99) has clean, large rooms, although they can be quite noisy. Singles/doubles/triples, all with own bathroom, cost L50,000/75,000/100,000. Near Piazza Castelnuovo, *Hotel Petit* (☎ 091 32 36 16, Via Principe di Belmonte 84) has comfortable rooms. There is only one single (without bathroom) costing L35,000. Doubles/triples with bathroom cost L65,000/90,000.

PLACES TO STAY – MID-RANGE

Almost next door to the train station, *Hotel Elena* (☎ *091 616 20 21, Piazza Giulio Cesare 14*) isn't the best place for the price (L60,000/85,000 for singles/doubles) but its location and the fact that the airport bus stops virtually at its front door make this a good choice for travellers who want to avoid wandering through dodgy streets at night. Farther north, *Hotel Moderno* (☎ *091 58 86 83, Via Roma 276*) offers good but somewhat spartan single/double rooms costing L75,000/105,000, and triples with bathroom for L140,000.

Not too far from Via Roma, occupying the 3rd floor of a corner building on Piazza I Florio, is the best mid-range hotel in town – *Hotel Joli* (☎ *091 611 17 65, Via Michele Amari 11*). The delightful rooms are well-equipped and a bargain at L60,000/90,000 (L10,000 more in the high season). The hotel is within walking distance of most points in the city centre so it can be difficult to get a room – book early. Also recommended is *Hotel Principe di Belmonte* (☎ *091 33 10 65, Via Principe di Belmonte 25*), a clean and well-appointed establishment with rooms costing L50,000/80,000, or L70,000/94,000 with bathroom.

Near Piazza Castelnuovo, *Albergo Libertà* (☎ *091 32 19 11, Via Mariano Stabile 136*) is a good choice; singles/doubles with bathroom cost L55,000/80,000 (L80,000/100,000 in the high season). There are several other hotels in the same building. At *Hotel Tonic* (☎ *091 58 17 54, Via Mariano Stabile 126*), decent singles/doubles with bathroom cost L90,000/120,000. *Hotel Elite* (☎ *091 32 93 18*) has singles/doubles/triples for L80,000/110,000/L140,000, all with private bathroom. *Hotel Boston-Madonia* (☎ *091 58 02 34*) has doubles with bathroom for L98,000, or L70,000 for single occupancy.

PLACES TO STAY – TOP END

Attractive rooms at the *Grande Albergo Sole* (☎ *091 58 18 11, fax 091 611 01 82, Corso Vittorio Emanuele 291*) cost L150,000/200,000, less in the low season. The four-star *Grand Hotel Le Palme* (☎ *091 58 39 33, fax 091 33 15 45, Via Roma 398*), at the Piazza Castelnuovo end of town, is one of the ritziest hotels in Palermo. Its beautiful rooms cost L210,000/300,000, including breakfast. Also four-star, *Centrale Palace Hotel* (☎ *091 33 66 66, fax 091 33 48 81, Corso Vittorio Emanuele 327*) has elegantly furnished singles/doubles/triples that cost L230,000/350,000/435,000 including breakfast.

The best hotel in town, however, is the magnificent *Grand Hotel Villa Igea* (☎ *091 54 37 44, fax 091 54 76 54, Salita Belmonte 43*), 3km north of the city centre in the suburb of Acquasanta. Complete with a private beach and every other luxury, this sumptuous villa designed by Ernesto Basile in 1900 was once the property of the Florio family (of tuna and Marsala-wine fame) and is now a favourite of the moneyed elite. Rooms cost L260,000/400,000, but out of season they fall to a more reasonable L130,000/200,000.

PLACES TO EAT

With more than 300 officially listed restaurants and eateries to choose from in the city and surrounding area, you should have little trouble finding something to suit your taste and budget.

Palermo's cuisine takes advantage of the fresh produce of the sea and the fertile Conca d'Oro valley. One of its most famous dishes is the tasty *pasta con le sarde*, with sardines, fennel, onions, raisins and pine nuts. Swordfish is served here sliced into huge steaks. A reflection of Sicily's proximity to North Africa is the infiltration of couscous, basically a bowl of steamed semolina with a sauce.

Palermitans are late eaters and restaurants rarely open for dinner before 8 pm.

Restaurants

Budget Just up the road from the Opera dei Pupi puppet theatre, *Dal Pompiere* (*Via Bara all'Olivella 107*) has a simple but filling set-menu lunch for L13,000. *Hostaria la Sella* (☎ *091 58 53 21, Via Cavour 97*) also offers a good lunch for L17,000.

If you want to try an age-old Palermo snack – a *panino* (bread roll) with *milza* (veal innards) and ricotta cheese – head for

Antica Focacceria di San Francesco (☎ *091 32 02 64, Via A Paternostro 58)*. It's one of the city's oldest eating-houses and worth seeking out; it also serves pizza slices and similar snacks.

Another Palermitan institution is *Casa del Brodo* (☎ *091 32 16 55, Corso Vittorio Emanuele 175)*. For more than 100 years it has been serving up various broths and boiled meat dishes, all much appreciated by locals. A meal costs around L30,000. *Osteria lo Bianco* (☎ *091 58 58 16, Via E Amari 104)*, off Via Roma at the Castelnuovo end of town, has a menu that changes daily. A full meal will cost around L20,000.

Off Via Roma, past Chiesa di Santa Anna, *Trattoria dai Vespri* (☎ *091 617 16 31, Piazza Santa Croce dei Vespri 8)* has outside tables and excellent food. Around L35,000 will cover a full meal. Meat and seafood are cooked on an outdoor barbecue in summer.

In the heart of La Vucciria, *Trattoria Shanghai* (☎ *091 58 97 02, Vico Mezzano 34)* is a very basic and less-than-clean little place with tables on an atmospheric terrace overlooking the market. Despite its Chinese name, the restaurant serves typical Sicilian food, which is reasonably priced but not the best you can eat in Palermo.

If you feel like a Tunisian night out, with couscous and other typical North African dishes, try *Hostaria Al-Duar 2 (Via Ammiraglio Gravina 31A)* on the first street south of Via E Amari. It has a L18,000 set menu.

If you have a student card you can eat in the subsidised canteen at *Casa Marconi* (see under Hostels in Places to Stay earlier in the chapter); a four-course meal will cost you L10,000. Unlike many other student canteens, the food here is delicious.

Mid-Range Just off Via Roma, *Hostaria da Ciccio* (☎ *091 32 91 43, Via Firenze 6)* is one of Palermo's best-loved cheaper eating places – and the food really is great. A meal will cost from around L30,000.

Trattoria Stella (☎ *091 616 11 36, Via Alloro 104)* is in the courtyard of the old Hotel Patria. In summer, the entire courtyard is filled with tables. A full meal will come to around L40,000.

La Cambusa (☎ *091 58 45 74)* and *Trattoria Il Crudo e Il Cotto* (☎ *091 616 92 61)*, both on Piazza Marina near La Cala, are popular and serve good meals that cost around L30,000. The former (closed on Monday) has a set all-inclusive seafood menu costing L36,000. Also on the square, *Il Bagatto* (☎ *091 611 63 83)* is a great little restaurant with a mouth-watering seafood menu. All mains cost between L12,000 and L16,000.

Sant'Andrea (☎ *091 33 49 99)* is a lovely restaurant on Piazza Sant'Andrea, in the heart of La Kalsa. It serves delicious and imaginative dishes and although it is a little pricier than other places in the area, you can still eat very well for less than L40,000. It is closed on Tuesday.

Top End A Palermo institution, at least with those who can afford it, is *Charleston* (☎ *091 32 13 66)*. Its main establishment is in Palermo at Piazzale Ungheria 30. In summer it generally closes and its Mondello branch takes over, with outdoor eating on Viale Regina Elena (☎ *091 45 01 71)*. Expect to pay around L100,000 per head for a memorable meal.

Most of the posher restaurants are on the outskirts of Palermo or in nearby towns. You'll need your own transport. *I Mandarini* (☎ *091 671 21 99, Via Rosario da Patanna 18)* is at Pallavicino, near Mondello beach. The food is good and a meal will cost at least L45,000. The locals head for Mondello to eat seafood. Try *La Barcaccia* (☎ *091 45 15 19, Via Piano di Gallo 4)*. Again, you will be lucky to eat for under L50,000. A popular but pricey fish restaurant at Sferracavallo is *Al Delfino* (☎ *091 53 02 82, Via Torretta 80)*. Don't expect much change from L100,000.

Cafes

On Via Principe di Belmonte (which is closed to traffic between Via Ruggero Settimo and Via Roma) there are numerous cafes with outdoor tables where you can linger over breakfast or lunch. If you want to spend less, buy a panino in one of the many bars along Via Roma. For an expensive afternoon tea, head for Palermo's best-known cake shop *(pasticceria)*, **Roney** *(Via della Libertà 13)*.

Palermo's trendiest cafe is **Di Martino** *(Via Mazzini 54)*. Its outdoor tables are thronged nightly with the city's hippest go-getters. The sandwiches are superb.

In the historic centre, the atmospheric **Caffè Arabo** *(Piazza Gran Cancelliere 8)* serves North African cuisine; the real treat is to sit on the low-set cushions in the cafe, drink *tè ai pinoli* (pine-nut tea) and imagine yourself in Cairo.

Markets

Palermo's historical ties with the Arab world and its proximity to North Africa are reflected in the noisy street life of the city's ancient centre; nowhere is this more evident than in its markets.

Each of the four historic quarters of Palermo has its own market, La Vucciria being the most famous (see La Vucciria earlier in the chapter). Although it's still popular with tourists, many Palermitans shop elsewhere these days, especially at the Ballaro and Capo markets, which extend through the tangle of lanes and alleyways of their respective quarters. Here you can purchase anything your stomach desires (and several items it may recoil at – slippery tripe and all sorts of fishy things) as well as a host of off-the-back-of-a-truck-style bargains. Markets are open from 7 am to 8 pm Monday to Saturday (until 1 pm on Wednesday). La Vucciria market closes every day at 1 pm. Although great places in which to wander, you should keep an eye on your belongings while walking through the markets: keep your money in a money belt.

For other grocery supplies, try **Standa** *(Via della Libertà 30)*, a run-of-the-mill supermarket.

ENTERTAINMENT

After playing second fiddle to Catania for many years, Palermo is finally re-emerging as Sicily's nightlife and entertainment capital. A bunch of new bars have opened in the historic centre, bringing life to the once moribund quarters. The traditional arts have benefited from a much-needed injection of

funding resulting in the reopening of the Teatro Massimo. The summer program of concerts and recitals at Chiesa di Santa Maria dello Spasimo in La Kalsa is a definite highlight (for more information see Lo Spasimo earlier in the chapter).

Bars

Near the Quattro Canti, Via Candelai is packed with great bars that are doing a roaring trade with the Palermitan youth. The best of them is **I Candelai** at No 19, a converted furniture shop that features live music and a booming sound system. **Fuso Orario** *(Piazza Olivella 2)* is another great spot, with a range of bottled and draught beers to quench every thirst. At No 13 is **Bikers Bar**, which has outdoor tables. Piazza Olivella itself is a great spot to check out, as it is jammed with people virtually every night. Across Via Roma in La Vucciria, **I Grilli Giù** *(Piazza Valverde 9)* is a trendy new spot where you can drink cocktails and listen to a DJ spin the latest sounds.

In the newer city to the north, **Berlin**, at the corner of Via Isidoro and Via Quintino, is an ultra-sleek bar popular with Palermo's gay community (who are a discreet bunch on a largely traditional island). Also worth checking out is **La Cuba** *(Viale F Scaduto)* in the middle of Villa Sperlinga. Not to be confused with the castle of the same name, this is a 19th-century Arabic folly converted into a super-trendy (and pricey) late-night bar. Strictly for the smart set, this is where you can eat sushi and drink fancy cocktails.

Theatre

For opera and ballet, the main venue is the **Teatro Massimo** (☎ 091 58 95 75) on Piazza Verdi, which runs its program from June to October. The **Teatro Politeama-Garibaldi** (☎ 091 605 33 15) on Piazza Ruggero Settimo and the **Teatro Golden** (☎ 091 30 52 17, Via Terrasanta 60) – take bus No 103 from the Politeama-Garibaldi – put on a pretty good year-round program of music and plays. If your Italian is up to it, you can see plays at the **Teatro Biondo** (☎ 091 58 23 64) on Via Roma. The daily paper *Il Giornale di Sicilia* has a listing of what's on.

Something of a Sicilian speciality, the **Opera dei Pupi** (*☎ 091 32 34 00, Via Bara all'Olivella 95*), a puppet theatre just south of Via Cavour, is run by the Cuticchio family and makes for an enchanting experience. It's a good break for young kids, and the elaborate old puppets will endear themselves to adults too. You can generally expect shows to be staged at 5.30 pm at the weekend. Tickets cost L10,000 (children L5000). At No 40 on the same street is one of several artisans who makes and repairs the puppets.

GETTING THERE & AWAY
Air
Falcone-Borsellino airport is at Punta Raisi, 32km west of Palermo. For information on domestic flights, ring Alitalia on ☎ 1478 6 56 41; for European flights ring ☎ 1478 6 56 42. The service is available 24 hours. Alitalia has an office (☎ 091 601 93 33) at Via della Libertà 39. It is usually possible to hunt down charter flights to major European cities such as London between May and October (for more information see under Air in the Getting There & Away chapter).

Bus
The main intercity bus station is on Via Paolo Balsamo, to the east of the train station.

Segesta (☎ 091 616 90 39), Via Paolo Balsamo 26, has a direct daily service to Rome (L65,000 one way). It also runs frequent buses to Trapani (L8500, two hours). SAIS Trasporti (☎ 091 617 11 41), Via Paolo Balsamo 20, runs services to Rome, with a change at Catania (L75,000 one way). It also runs buses twice a day to Cefalù (L11,000). SAIS Autolinee (☎ 091 47 53 20) services Catania (L26,000, more than 15 daily), Enna (L11,000, six daily), Piazza Armerina (L19,400, 11 daily) and Messina (L31,000, every two hours, via Catania). Interbus (☎ 091 616 60 28), Via Paolo Basalmo 16, runs to Syracuse (L34,500, six a day). For Marsala, go to Salemi (☎ 091 617 54 11), Via Rosario Gregorio 44. Cuffaro (☎ 091 616 15 10), Via Paolo Balsamo 13, and Fratelli Camilleri (☎ 091 616 59 14), Via Paolo Basalmo 18, between them operate about 10 buses daily to Agrigento (L21,500).

Away from the main terminal, AST (☎ 091 680 00 11), on the corner between Viale delle Scienze and Via Brasa, runs four daily buses to Ragusa. It also operates services to Corleone, Cefalù, Palazzo Adriano and Montelepre.

Numerous other companies service points throughout Sicily and most have offices in the Via Paolo Balsamo area. Their addresses and telephone numbers, as well as destinations, are listed in the *Tourist Information Magazine*, available at the main APT office.

Train
Regular trains leave for Milazzo, Messina (L25,500, 3½ hours, every 30 minutes), Catania (L26,000, 3 hours 50 minutes, every hour), Syracuse (L29,500, change at Catania) and Agrigento (L24,000, around two hours, every 30 minutes), as well as nearby towns such as Cefalù. There are also Intercity trains to Reggio di Calabria, Naples and Rome. Train timetable information is available in English at the station. There is a Transalpino office inside the station, as well as baggage storage (L8000 per day) and bathing facilities (showers and wash basins).

Car & Motorcycle
Palermo is accessible on the A20 from Messina (only partially completed) and from Catania (A19) via Enna (this route is quicker). Trapani and Marsala are also easily accessible from Palermo by motorway (A29), while Agrigento and Palermo are linked by the SS121, a good state road through the interior of the island.

Rental AVIS (☎ 091 58 69 40) is at Via Principe di Scordia and at the airport (☎ 091 33 38 06). Europcar (☎ 091 32 19 49) has an office at Via Cavour 77A, as well as others at the train station (☎ 091 616 50 50) and the airport (☎ 091 59 12 27). All major rental companies are represented in Palermo.

Boat
Ferries use the ferry terminal (Stazione Marittima) on Molo Vittorio Veneto, off Via Francesco Crispi, for Cagliari (Sardinia),

Naples, Livorno and Genoa (see the Getting There & Away chapter for more details). The Tirrenia office (☎ 1478 9 90 00, 091 602 11 11) is at the port in Palazzina Stella Maris, Calata Marinai d'Italia. Siremar (☎ 091 690 25 55, 091 58 24 03), Via Francesco Crispi 118, runs daily ferries and hydrofoils to Ustica (L16,500 for foot passengers and L40,000 for cars on the ferry; L30,000 on the hydrofoil). SNAV, represented in Palermo by the Pietro Barbaro agency (☎ 091 33 33 33) at Via Principe di Belmonte 55, runs a summer hydrofoil service to the Aeolian Islands. From April to October it also operates a daily ferry service to Naples, departing at 9 am and arriving at 1 pm (going the other way it leaves Naples at 5.30 pm). Tickets cost L96,000 one way (L120,000 during July, August and September).

Grandi Navi Veloci (☎ 091 58 74 04), part of the Grimaldi Group at the port in Calata Marinai d'Italia, runs ferries from Palermo to Genoa (daily) and Livorno (three a week). They have a Web site at www.grimaldi.it.

The baggage deposit facility (L4500) at the ferry terminal is open from 7 am to 8 pm daily.

GETTING AROUND
To/From the Airport
Regular blue buses run by Prestia e Comandé (☎ 091 58 04 57) will take you into town. They leave from outside the train station, in front of Hotel Elena, roughly hourly from 5 am to around 10.45 pm. Buses run from the airport to the train station from 7.30 am to 12.30 am (or until the arrival of the last flight). The timetable is posted at the bus stop outside the train station, to your right as you leave the station. Buses also stop on Piazza Ruggero Settimo, in front of the Teatro Politeama-Garibaldi. The trip takes one hour and costs L6500.

Taxis to the airport cost upwards of L70,000. There is a taxi rank at the airport (☎ 091 59 16 62). Alternatively you could try Autoradio Taxi (☎ 091 51 27 27/ 33 11).

Bus
Palermo's city buses (AMAT) are efficient, and most stop in front of the train station.

Tickets must be purchased before you get on the bus and are available from tobacconists or the booths at the AMAT bus station. They cost L1500 and are valid for one hour. A day pass costs L5000.

Metropolitana
Most visitors will have little cause to use Palermo's metro system, as its 10 stations radiating out from the main train station are a good hike from any destination likely to interest the tourist. There is talk of expanding the system to Falcone-Borsellino airport, which would be useful. A single trip ticket costs L1500.

Car & Motorcycle
Do not drive in Palermo if you can avoid it. The city has a massive problem with gridlock, which makes getting from one side of the city to the other virtually an all-day affair. Also, Palermitans seem to have little respect for the rules of the road, though if you have dealt with Rome or Naples in your own vehicle, Palermo will present no difficulties. Theft of and from vehicles is a problem, however, and you are advised to use one of the attended car parks around town if your hotel has no parking space. You'll be looking at paying between L15,000 and L20,000 for 24 hours. Some hotels have small car parks, but they are often full; check with your hotel proprietor.

Around Palermo

There are beaches north-west of the city at Mondello and Sferracavallo, but if you're really into spending some time by the sea you'd be better off heading farther afield, to Scopello, for example (see that section in the Western Sicily chapter). Mondello is popular with Palermitans, who crowd the beach front, Viale Regina Elena, during their evening strolls. There are numerous seafood restaurants and snack stalls along the avenue. Buses for Mondello and Sferracavallo leave from Piazza A Gasperi.

Between Palermo and Mondello is Mt Pellegrino and the Santuario di Santa Rosalia.

One of Palermo's patron saints, St Rosalia, lived as a hermit in a cave on the mountain, now the site of a 17th-century shrine. The water, which is channelled from the roof of the cave into a large font, is said to have miraculous powers. Whatever your beliefs, this is a fascinating place to visit, but remember that it is a shrine, not a tourist haunt. The sanctuary (☎ 091 54 03 26) is open from 7 am to 7 pm daily. Admission is free. To get there take bus No 812 from Piazza Verdi (L1500, 30 minutes). At the time of research it was not possible to reach the sanctuary by road because of a landslide.

On the northern side of Mt Pellegrino, at Addaura, is the Grotta dell'Addaura, where several cave drawings from the Upper Palaeolithic and Neolithic periods have managed to survive into the 21st century. The cave is open to visitors from 9 am to midday on Friday and Saturday, by prior arrangement through the Soprintendenza Archeologica (☎ 091 696 13 19), next to the Museo Archeologico Regionale in Palermo. To get there head up the road above the beach at Addaura and follow the signposts (the caves are about 400m away).

CATTEDRALE DI MONREALE

The cathedral (☎ 091 640 44 13) at the heart of this unexceptional town on the top of a hill only 8km south-west of Palermo, is one of Europe's premier attractions, and should not be missed on any account. It is easily accessible by frequent city buses.

Considered the finest example of Norman architecture in Sicily, the magnificent 12th-century cathedral in fact incorporates Norman, Arabic, Byzantine and classical elements and, despite renovations over the centuries, remains substantially intact. It was built for William II, whose motivations for ordering its construction were almost entirely political, stemming from his rivalry with the archbishop of Palermo, Walter of the Mill. Eager to curb the growing power of

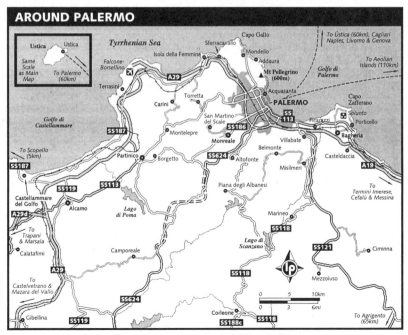

AROUND PALERMO

euro currency converter L10,000 = €5.16

the papacy in Sicily (with whom the archbishop was closely allied), William made Monreale an archbishopric in 1183, thereby devaluing the prestige of Walter's cathedral in Palermo. When William died the cathedral lost much of its political importance; as a work of art, however, it is timeless.

The central doorway has bronze doors by Bonanno Pisano and the northern door is by Barisano di Trani. Although the exterior is both graceful and elegant, nothing can quite prepare you for the dazzling interior, one of the most impressive creations of the Italian Middle Ages and one of the most beautiful to be found anywhere in the world.

The walls of the aisles, sanctuary and apses are entirely covered in magnificent gilded mosaics – a total surface of 6340 sq metres. The artists were local and Venetian mosaicists, but the influence of the Byzantine style is all-pervasive. Completed in 1184 after only ten years' work, the mosaics are the apogee of Norman-Arabic art, an articulate and fitting tribute to the grandeur of Sicilian culture of that time.

In the central apse is the dominating half-figure of Christ *Pantokrator* (all-powerful) giving benediction, and below him the Virgin Mary and child, bearing the legend *Panacrontas* (all-chaste). Beneath them again are the ranks of saints, each identified by name (look out for St Thomas à Becket between Silvester and Laurence; he was canonised in 1173, just before the mosaics were started). The side apses are dedicated to the martyrdoms of St Paul (east) and St Peter (west), whereas the central nave is a pictorial history of the early books of the Bible, beginning with the Creation.

Outside the cathedral is the entrance to the cloisters, which were part of a Benedictine abbey once attached to the church. There are 228 twin columns with polychrome ornamentation. Each of the Romanesque capitals is different, depicting plants, animals and fantastic motifs. The capital of the 19th column on the western aisle depicts William II offering the cathedral to the Virgin Mary.

The cathedral is open from 8 am to midday and 3.30 to 6 pm daily. Visitors are advised to keep L1000 or L1500 in change so they turn on the large electric lights (even though the number of tourists passing through will ensure that the church will not stay dark for long). The cloisters are open from 9 am to 1.30 pm Monday to Saturday (and 3 to 7 pm on Monday, Tuesday and Thursday) and between 9 am and 12.30 pm on Sunday. Admission costs L4000.

There are several frequent bus services from Palermo: bus Nos 603 and 614 both leave from Piazza A Gasperi, Nos 105 and 389 leave from Piazza Indipendenza.

SOLUNTO

About 17km east of Palermo are the remains of the Hellenistic-Roman town of Solunto (☎ 091 90 45 57). Although the ancient city is only partially excavated, it's well worth the trip to see what has been brought to light. Founded in the 4th century BC on the site of an earlier Phoenician settlement, Solunto was built in a particularly panoramic position – on Mt Catalfano, overlooking the sea. Wander along the main street, the Roman *decumanus*, and take detours up the steep, paved sidestreets to explore the ruined houses, some of which still sport their original mosaic floors. Take particular note of the theatre and the **Casa di Leda** (if you can find it), which has an interesting floor mosaic.

The site is open from 9 am to 6 pm Monday to Saturday and from 9 am to 12.30 pm on Sunday. To get there, take the train from Palermo and get off at the Santa Flavia-Solunto-Porticello stop (L2800, 15 minutes, every 30 minutes) and ask for directions. It's about a 30-minute uphill walk. Admission costs L4000.

USTICA
postcode 91100 • pop 1100

Almost 60km north of Palermo lies the lonely island of Ustica. In 1980, a passenger jet crashed near the island in mysterious circumstances, leaving 81 people dead. Investigators suspect the military was involved, and a dozen officers of the Italian airforce officers stand accused of a cover-up.

Ustica is, otherwise, a tranquil place with

BETHUNE CARMICHAEL

BETHUNE CARMICHAEL

Monreale Cathedral: a Norman masterpiece

...the politics have passed but the art remains.

BETHUNE CARMICHAEL

Looking back: view of Palermo from Monreale

Breathtaking inside and out – Monreale Cathedral

Open for opera – Catania's Teatro Bellini

New Year's Day on Piazza 9 Aprile, Taormina

Bella by name, bella by nature – blue skies and clear waters embrace Taormina's tiny island.

PALERMO

barely more than 1000 inhabitants, most living in the mural-bedecked village of the same name. The best months to come are June and September; to visit during August is sheer lunacy. Parts of the rocky coast have been declared a marine reserve, and the limpid waters, kept sparkling clean by an Atlantic current through the Straits of Gibraltar, are ideal for diving and submarine photography.

Information
You'll find an APT tourist office (☎ 091 844 94 56) for the marine reserve on Piazza Umberto I, part of an interlocking series of squares in the centre of the village. It is open from 8 am to 1 pm and 4 to 6 pm Monday to Friday and 8 am to 2 pm on Saturday and Sunday (to 9 pm during summer). The staff can advise on activities around the island – and have a list of the dive centres.

Call the *pronto soccorso* (casualty; ☎ 091 844 92 48) for medical emergencies. For police, call the *carabinieri* (police under the jurisdiction of the Ministry of Defence; ☎ 091 844 90 49).

Activities
Among the most rewarding dive sites are the Secca Colombara, to the north of the island, and the Scoglio del Medico, to the west. Note that Zone A of the marine reserve, taking in a good stretch of the western coast north of Punta dello Spalmatore, is protected. Fishing, diving and even swimming without permission are forbidden in the area. The reserve's information office can organise sea-watch diving excursions into the zone. The only dive hire outlet, Ailara Rosalia (☎ 091 844 91 62), Banchina Barresi, operates during the summer. Otherwise, bring your own gear.

You can also hire a boat and cruise around the island, visiting its many grottoes and tiny beaches. Hotel Ariston (☎ 091 844 90 42), Via della Vittoria 5, is one of several agencies which can organise boat trips, diving and rental motorcycles. You could try Scubaland (☎ 091 844 92 16), Via Petriera 7, to hire a boat or dinghy.

Places to Stay & Eat
There are eight hotels and several *affitta-camere* (rooms for rent) on Ustica. *Pensione Clelia* (☎ 091 844 90 39, ✉ clelia@ telegest.it, Via Magazzino 7) is a decent place with single/double rooms costing L55,000/105,000. In the high season, prices rocket to L89,000 per head for half board. It has a good little restaurant and the town centre offers many other eating options.

Getting There & Around
From April to December there is at least one Siremar hydrofoil a day from Palermo (L30,000). A car ferry runs daily throughout the year (except Sunday during winter); high-season fares are L16,500 for foot passengers and L40,000 for cars. The Siremar office (☎ 091 844 90 02) is on Piazza Capitano V di Bartolo, in the centre of Ustica. During the summer you can also pick up the Trapani-Favignana-Ustica-Naples hydrofoil run by Ustica Lines three days a week. The journey from Naples to Ustica takes four hours and costs L120,000 one way.

Orange minibuses make a round trip of the island, they leave from the village on the hour (L1000, 2½ hours). Alternatively you could hire a moped at the Hotel Ariston (see the earlier Activities section for details).

CORLEONE
postcode 90034 • pop 11,261
• elevation 550m
In the heart of a valley 60km south of Palermo is the farming town of Corleone, unremarkable in every respect but one: since WWII it has been the unofficial capital of the Sicilian Mafia (see the boxed text 'Where Fact and Fiction Meet' on the following page). Centuries of poverty and natural disasters – including a particularly devastating landslide in 1418 – have made it a pretty depressing place, with little to see other than the 14th-century **Chiesa Madre** and the 17th-century **Chiesa di Santa Rosalia**, which is home to a lovely canvas by Giuseppe Velasquez depicting *San Giovanni Battista sull'Isola di Palmos* (St John the Evangelist on the Island of Palmos). Curiously, the town has in recent years

PALERMO

Where Fact and Fiction Meet

Most readers will recognise Corleone as the name given to Mario Puzo's fictional Godfather, Vito Andolini, when he landed at New York's Ellis Island. Puzo's choice was no accident, as this small town has played a pivotal – and grossly disproportionate – role in the bloody affairs of the Cosa Nostra (alternative name for the Mafia) since WWII. The town's importance dates from the American landing in Sicily in 1943. Two returning Corleonesi serving in the US Army, a Captain De Carlo and a 'Mr Vincent', arrived to negotiate the town's surrender to the Americans with the local Mafia boss (and later DC power-broker) Michele Navarra, who happened to be De Carlo's cousin. A bloody struggle between the different players ensued over who would actually control the local *cosca* (family), with De Carlo and Navarra winning out.

The next decade saw the demise of the old feudal Mafia (the sometime employees of the landowners) and the emergence of a new type of illegal profiteer eager to cash in on the blossoming drug trade. Navarra was an old-fashioned don and, although he was one of the six members of the Cupola (a commission set up in 1953 to coordinate the affairs of the new Mafia), he was deemed superfluous to requirements by his greedy young deputy, Luciano Liggio. In 1958 Navarra was ambushed and killed, sparking a five-year war that left hundreds dead. By 1963 Liggio had won the war of succession, but a belated strike by the authorities resulted in the arrest of thousands of Mafiosi, including Liggio and his apprentice, a semi-literate farm boy called Totò Riina. He had proved his loyalty to Liggio by pulling the trigger on Navarra.

In 1968, the newly released Liggio was diagnosed as suffering from Pott's disease and was forced into early retirement. He appointed a killer named Bernardo Provenzano as his heir, but his lack of intelligence ('Shoots like an angel but he's got the brains of a chicken,' Liggio once commented) meant that Riina soon became head of the family, despite being a fugitive from justice, courtesy of a second warrant issued in 1969. This proved to be no more than a minor inconvenience.

Over the next 24 years Riina intimidated and murdered his way to a position of supreme power within the Sicilian Mafia, virtually eliminating the Cupola and making himself the most feared man on the island. His totalitarian control, however, was to have unforeseen consequences: in 1986 Tommaso Buscetta, his life threatened by Riina's Corleonesi, became the first senior Mafioso to turn state's evidence, thus setting off a chain of events that would see hundreds more testify against their own. In 1993 Riina was eventually arrested (his driver told authorities of his whereabouts) but not before he had ordered the brutal killing of Sicily's most heroic magistrates, Giovanni Falcone and Paolo Borsellino, in 1992. In a scene straight out of *The Godfather*, Riina refused to speak during his many trials other than to wish one presiding judge peace, 'but not in this life; in the next one, which is far more important'. Despite Riina's capture, the book on Corleone is far from closed. Opinions differ on who exactly is the current power behind the mob, but one thing is sure: Corleone knows.

become a popular location for Scandinavian weddings, with groups of couples trekking from northern Europe to get hitched.

There is a tourist office (☎ 091 846 11 51) in the town hall, located on Piazza Garibaldi. **Bentivegna** *(Piazza Vittorio Emanuele 1)* is a great pastry shop that creates delicious *cannoli* (cream horns). There are regular buses from Palermo (€500, 1½ hours, four daily).

The Tyrrhenian Coast

The stretch of coast between Palermo to the west and Milazzo to the east is an all-but-uninterrupted line of resorts, beaches and pretty little towns that are almost entirely given over to the tourist industry. Between June and September the well-worn roads carry a steady stream of foreign tourists and Italian holidaymakers to and from the coastline's manifold attractions. The best of these is the pretty town of Cefalù which, although advertising itself as a traditional fishing village, has developed into a resort second only to Taormina in popularity. Just behind Cefalù is the Parco Naturale Regionale delle Madonie (Madonie nature reserve), unlike other parks on the island in that it is dotted with small towns and a ski resort that is becoming increasingly popular. Farther east of Cefalù are the coast's best beaches: clean, unpolluted and relatively uncrowded except at the height of summer. Here you will find some interesting ruins and a couple of hill towns that live in splendid semi-isolation. At the eastern end of the coast is Milazzo, an industrial port that serves as the main point of transit to and from the Aeolian Islands.

Termini Imerese to Cefalù

If you're coming east from Palermo, the first stop of any interest beyond the capital's outer limits is the half-resort, half-industrial centre of Termini Imerese. Not quite the beach resort *par excellence*, the town is surrounded by some pretty grim industrial development that is as bad as it gets until you reach the eastern end of the coast and Milazzo. Out of Termini Imerese the real attractions are inland, past the imposing peak of Mt Calogero (1326m) to the western edge of the Madonie nature reserve (see Parco Naturale Regionale delle Madonie section later in the chapter), where you'll find a couple of hill towns that are worth every effort to visit.

Highlights

- Spend a day in Cefalù: enjoy great swimming, nice walks and a little splendour in the mosaics of the cathedral
- Climb La Rocca: it's tough going, but the views are worth it
- Explore the Parco Regionale Naturale delle Madonie
- Stroll through the hill-top town of Caccamo, topped by an imposing Norman castle
- Admire the Greek ruins at San Marco d'Alunzio, especially the Tempio di Ercole

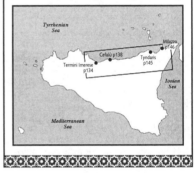

TERMINI IMERESE
postcode 90018 • pop 26,500

The town's origins date from prehistoric times, though its name is derived from the two neighbouring Greek settlements of Thermae and Himera. The latter was destroyed by the Carthaginians in 408 BC and its inhabitants moved to the former, which was then renamed Thermae Himerensis. The town flourished for another 150 years, ruled for a time by local boy Agathocles (who went on to bigger and better things as the first and most ferocious tyrant of Syracuse). It was taken by the Romans in 252 BC and became famous as a thermal spa for the treatment of urological diseases. Among those who came for the cure was the Greek poet Pindar, who

THE TYRRHENIAN COAST

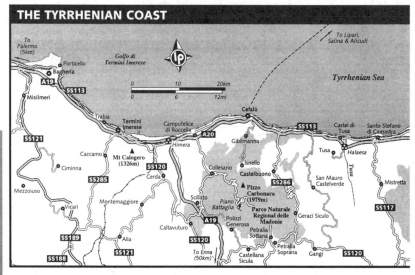

praised the spa's therapeutic values. Traces of the old baths still remain. Until the 19th century Termini Imerese was enclosed within a set of protective walls, but has since spilled out into the outlying countryside. Its growth, however, has been almost singularly industrial, due in large part to the establishment after WWII of a massive power plant and a number of petrochemical factories that have somewhat spoilt the town's overall appearance. Although for a time Termini Imerese experienced some much-needed prosperity, in recent years several plants have closed, causing widespread unemployment.

Orientation & Information

Like so many of Sicily's older settlements, Termini Imerese has an upper and lower town. The upper half is where you'll find all of the sights of interest, whereas the lower half is home to the town's only hotels and most of the town's day-to-day activity. The train station is south-east of the town centre along the coast; all buses arrive and depart just in front of the train station.

The APT office (☎ 091 812 82 53) is in the town hall *(municipio)* on the main square, Piazza del Duomo.

Things to See & Do

At the heart of the upper town is Piazza del Duomo, dominated by the 17th-century **cathedral**; it has been under continuous renovation since the mid-1980s, and the four 16th-century statues that adorned it have been replaced by copies. The facade dates from 1912. Inside the church, the third northern chapel contains sculptures from the Gagini school and the four original statues from the facade. In the fourth southern chapel there is a wonderful relief by Ignazio Marabitti, the *Madonna del Ponte* (Madonna of the Bridge). The cathedral is open from 9 am to 7 pm daily.

To the north of the cathedral, Via Belvedere affords great views of the town and the coast. On Via del Museo, opposite the cathedral, is the **Museo Civico** (☎ 091 812 82 79), established in 1873. It has three different sections devoted to archaeology, art and natural history. It is open from 9 am to 1 pm Tuesday and Friday, and 9 am to 1 pm and 4 to 7 pm Wednesday, Thursday and Saturday. Admission is free, although donations are welcome.

Backed up against the museum is the **Chiesa di Santa Maria della Misericordia**

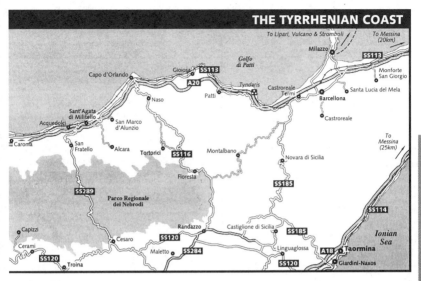

THE TYRRHENIAN COAST

To Lipari, Vulcano & Stromboli
To Messina (20km)
Milazzo
SS113
Golfo di Patti
Monforte San Giorgio
Capo d'Orlando
Gioiosa
SS113
A20
Tyndaris
Santa Lucia del Mela
Naso
Patti
Castroreale Terme
Barcellona
Sant'Agata di Militello
San Marco d'Alunzio
Castroreale
Acquedolci
To Messina (25km)
Caronia
San Fratello
Alcara
Tortorici
SS116
Montalbano
Novara di Sicilia
Floresta
SS185
SS289
Parco Regionale dei Nebrodi
SS114
Capizzi
Randazzo
Castiglione di Sicilia
SS185
Ionian Sea
Cerami
Cesaro
SS120
Maletto
SS284
Linguaglossa
A18
Taormina
SS120
Troina
SS120
Giardini-Naxos

THE TYRRHENIAN COAST

(Church of Our Lady of Mercy). The entrance is off Via Mazzini, west out of Piazza del Duomo. Inside is a marvellous triptych of the *Madonna con Santi Giovanni e Michele* (Madonna with Sts John and Michael; 1453), attributed to Gaspare de Pesaro.

To the north-west of the cathedral, down Via Ianelli, is the **Chiesa di Santa Caterina**, home to a very good fresco of the *Life of St Catherine of Alexandria* by Giacomo Graffeo. The church keeps very irregular hours; check them at the tourist office. From here there are some lovely views of the citrus groves and the sea beyond.

Just beyond the church are the public gardens of **Villa Palmieri**, laid out in 1845. Inside are the remains of a public building known as the **Curia**, which was built sometime during the 2nd century AD, and the faint traces of the town's Roman amphitheatre *(anfiteatro)*.

Special Events

The town celebrates Carnevale with a parade of allegorical floats in the week before the beginning of the Lenten period. For more information call ☎ 091 812 82 53.

Places to Stay & Eat

The nearest camp site is 15km south of town. From the train station, take a bus (L1500) to the *Himera* (☎ 091 814 01 75, *Località Buonfornello),* just beyond the ancient site of the same name. It costs L18,000 per night. The camp site is also equipped with a restaurant, a disco and a number of four-person cabins (L50,000 per night).

The town has only one budget hotel, *Gabbiano* (☎ 091 811 32 62, fax 091 811 42 25, *Via Libertà 221),* which has two room rates: singles/doubles in the annexe cost L40,000/ 60,000 with shared bathroom, while better-equipped rooms with bathroom in the main hotel cost L100,000/130,000. The hotel is about a 15-minute walk south of the train station (just walk parallel to the tracks). Otherwise, the only other option is *Grand Hotel delle Terme* (☎ 091 811 35 57, fax 091 811 31 07, Piazza Terme) in the heart of the upper town. The fancy rooms here cost L160,000/ 220,000 (L120,000/165,000 between October and April) and include free use of the thermal baths which are on the property.

The selection of restaurants in Termini Imerese is surprisingly poor for a resort town. The upper town has a number of bars

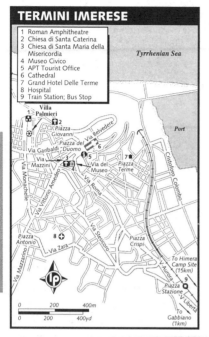

TERMINI IMERESE

1 Roman Amphitheatre
2 Chiesa di Santa Caterina
3 Chiesa di Santa Maria della Misericordia
4 Museo Civico
5 APT Tourist Office
6 Cathedral
7 Grand Hotel Delle Terme
8 Hospital
9 Train Station; Bus Stop

and *paninoteche* (sandwich bars) where you can get a bite to eat.

Getting There & Away

SAIS buses (☎ 091 47 53 20 in Palermo) runs two buses daily from Palermo to the town (L3000, 30 minutes). It also runs one bus daily from Termini Imerese to Cefalù (L3200, 30 minutes).

The best way to get to Termini Imerese is by train, as the town is a stop on the Palermo–Catania and Palermo–Agrigento lines; from 4.50 am to 8.50 pm daily there are departures every 20 minutes or so from the capital's central station (L3200). The trip takes between 20 and 40 minutes, depending on whether you're on a *rapido* (which makes one or two stops only) or the *diretto*, which makes all the stops.

The train station at Termini Imerese also has a left-luggage facility, which is open between 8 am and 8 pm daily and costs L5000 for 12 hours.

HIMERA

elevation 105m

The town of Himera was founded in 648 BC by Greeks from Zankle (now Messina) and was named after the Imera river that flows nearby. It was the first Greek settlement on this part of the island and was a strategic outpost just outside the eastern boundary of the Carthaginian-controlled west. In 480 BC the town was the scene of a decisive battle between the two foes, with the combined armies of Theron of Agrigento and Gelon of Syracuse defeating a sizeable Carthaginian army led by Hamilcar, who lost his life during the fighting. The North Africans had intended to take Himera and then move on to wrest control of the island from Greek hands, but the Greek victory put a temporary end to Carthaginian ambitions and consolidated their own position on the island. As for Himera itself, it paid the price for Carthage's defeat in 409 BC, when Hamilcar's nephew Hannibal completely destroyed the town in revenge for his uncle's death.

Compared with other Greek sites around the island, the remains here are a little disappointing. The only recognisable ruin is the **Tempio della Vittoria** (Temple of Victory), a Doric structure supposedly built to commemorate the defeat of the Carthaginians (although scholars have recently come to doubt that hypothesis). Whatever its origin, Hannibal did a good job of destroying it. To the south of the temple was the town's **necropolis** which is currently being excavated, so apart from a few loose stones and the semblance of a structure there is nothing much to see. The site is open from 9 am until two hours before sunset daily, and admission is free.

Some artefacts recovered from the site are kept in the small **antiquarium** about 100m west of the site's entrance (it's up a small lane off the other side of the main road). Although the more impressive displays are in Palermo's Museo Archeologico Regionale, you can see the well-sculpted lion-head spouts that were used to drain water off the temple's roof. The antiquarium is open from 9 am to 1 pm and 3 to 6 pm Monday to Saturday; admission costs L4000.

The ruins are 8km east of Termini Imerese. Unless you have your own transport you'll have to rely on one of four daily buses that run from in front of the train station in Termini Imerese. The journey takes about 15 minutes and costs L1500.

CACCAMO
postcode 90012 • pop 8600
• elevation 521m

Lorded over by its imposing **castle**, the hilltop town of Caccamo is a popular day trip out of Termini Imerese. A Carthaginian stronghold that served as a constant thorn in Himera's side in the 5th century BC, the official founding of the town wasn't until 1093, when the Normans began building the castle on a rocky spur overlooking a cliff. Most visitors make a beeline for this imposing structure but, while the tour (free, but tips are appreciated) is relatively interesting (if you understand Italian), the castle itself is being slowly converted into a conference centre, which kind of ruins the overall effect. The best parts are the walls and original fortifications, which included some ingenious traps for any intruder who might have breached the outer perimeter.

From the castle there are some great views of the surrounding countryside, including the Rosmarina artificial lake which was created by a controversial dam built in 1993. Submerged within the lake is a stone bridge built in 1307 on the road that once linked the town with Palermo.

Since the 1950s, the town itself has suffered the loss of almost half of its inhabitants to emigration, but you'd never know it wandering through the traffic-filled streets. The attractive 11th-century **cathedral** was remodelled twice, in 1477 and 1614. Inside, the sacristy has some lovely carvings of the *Madonna con Bambino e Angeli* (Madonna and Child with Angels) and *Santi Pietro e Paolo* (Sts Peter and Paul) by Francesco Laurana.

On the left-hand side of the cathedral are two churches: the farthest one away from the cathedral is the **Chiesa dell'Anime del Purgatorio** (dedicated to the Souls of Purgatory) featuring some fine stucco work in the eastern end and an 18th-century organ. Local tour guide Rosario Brancato is almost always on hand to explain the history of the church and guide you downstairs to the musty catacombs, where the skeletons of a number of townspeople lie in niches along the wall, a burial practice that lasted from the 17th century up to 1863.

Places to Stay & Eat
The town's only hotel is *La Spiga d'Oro* (☎/fax 091 814 89 68, Via Margherita 74) whose 14 rooms cost an astonishing L60,000 for a single and L95,000 for a double. The rooms are clean if a little basic, but they're the only show in town. The hotel also has a restaurant, which serves up mains for about L11,000 each.

Getting There & Away
There are 14 buses a day, Monday to Saturday, from in front of the train station in Termini Imerese. The trip costs L3000 and takes 30 minutes.

PARCO NATURALE REGIONALE DELLE MADONIE
This 40,000-hectare park, between Palermo and Cefalù, incorporates the Madonie mountain range and some of the highest mountains in Sicily after Mt Etna (the highest peat is Pizzo Carbonara at 1979m). Instituted in 1989 by the Regione Sicilia, the park also takes in several small towns and villages and plenty of farms and vineyards. It is an area where people live, rather than simply a nature reserve – so you can combine walking with visits to some of the more interesting towns in the park, such as Petralia Soprana and Petralia Sottana. Also worth visiting is the small town of Gibilmanna, where the 17th-century church is the object of pilgrimage.

In summer, Madonie is a popular destination for Palermitans armed with picnic baskets, who tend to make a day of it just wandering or driving through the expanse of the park. In winter it is the only place, other than Etna, where you can go skiing (see the boxed text 'Skiing in the Madonie Mountains' on the following page).

Skiing in the Madonie Mountains

More Swiss than Sicilian, the little ski resort at Piano Battaglia (around Pizzo Carbonara, Sicily's highest peak after Mt Etna) is dotted with chalets that in winter play host to an ever-growing number of Sicilian downhill skiers. At the time of research day passes cost L38,000 (although there was talk of an increase) which entitled you to unlimited runs from 9 am to 5.30 pm. The Rifugio Giuliano Marini (for details see Places to Stay under Parco Naturale Regionale delle Madonie for details) rents out equipment: you should be able to get skis and boots for around L50,000 per day.

THE TYRRHENIAN COAST

Orientation & Information

The best way to visit the park is with your own transport; otherwise you'll have to rely on the limited public transport (see Getting There & Away later in this section). From Termini Imerese head east for 16km along the coastal SS113 to Campofelice di Roccella and then turn off for Collesano, 13km inland. From Cefalù it is even easier: just follow the directions for the Santuario di Gibilmanna (Sanctuary of Gibilmanna), 14km to the south.

There are tourist offices of the Ente Parco delle Madonie (the body responsible for the park) at Petralia Sottana (☎ 0921 68 40 11) and Isnello (☎ 0921 66 27 95) with details about the park and several one-day walks, as well as information about transport and accommodation.

Petralia Soprana & Petralia Sottana

Beautifully positioned at the top of a hill above a tree line of pines, Petralia Soprana is one of the best-preserved little towns in northern Sicily. Unlike in other Sicilian settlements, the stone houses have been left unplastered, thus preserving their medieval appearance. At the heart of the main square, Piazza del Popolo, is a WWI **war memorial** (1929) by Antonio Ugo. The most beautiful church in town is the 18th-century **Chiesa di Santa Maria di Loreto** at the end of Via Loreto, off the main square. Inside is an altarpiece by Gagini and a *Madonna* by Giacomo Mancini. The **cathedral**, off Piazza dei Quattro Cannoli, was consecrated in 1497 and has an elegant 18th-century portico.

Below Petralia Soprana, (hence the name Sottana, from the Italian *sotto* meaning

'under'), the town of Petralia Sottana doesn't have any real sights to speak of, but is a pretty place and nice for a stroll.

Gibilmanna
postcode 90015 ● pop 3100
● elevation 795m

If you're a casual tourist, the main reason for coming here is to appreciate the wonderful view from the belvedere in front of the 17th-century **church**, from where you can see the spread of the Madonie and the peak of Pizzo Carbonara. While here, you will probably mingle with visitors whose intent is a little more serious, as they come in pilgrimage to pray at the elaborately decorated baroque **Santuario di Gibilmanna**, a shrine of the Virgin Mary. During the shrine's coronation on 17 August 1760 (which also marked the official consecration of the church), the Virgin is supposed to have shown signs of life which restored sight to two blind worshippers and speech to a mute. The miracle was confirmed by the Vatican and the church has been one of Sicily's most important shrines ever since.

Places to Stay

Although there are a couple of hotels in the park, the more interesting accommodation is in a choice of *rifugi* (mountain chalets) or *agriturismo* (farmhouses), a welcome change from the usual four walls and a bed.

Rifugi Not quite a youth hostel in the proper sense, *Rifugio Ostello della Gioventù* (☎ 0921 64 99 95, Piano Battaglia, Località Mandria Marcate) caters to all visitors and charges L30,000/70,000 for singles/doubles. Right at Pizzo Carbonara, *Rifugio*

Giuliano Marini (☎ 0921 64 99 94) has chalet-style singles/doubles for L25,000/ 55,000. Approximately halfway between Piano Battaglia and Cefalù, near Isnello, *Luigi Orestano (☎ 0921 66 21 59)* is a little more expensive at L30,000/60,000.

Agriturismo If you're looking for something with a little more character, there are some excellent establishments in the area. *Tenuta Gangivecchio (☎ 0921 68 91 91)* is in a former 14th-century Benedictine convent just out of the town of Gangi, 14km east of Petralia Sottana. Children aged under 10 aren't accommodated at Easter and New Year. Half board costs L100,000 and full board costs L120,000. In Petralia Soprana, *Salaci (☎ 0921 68 72 60)* offers full board for L120,000. Otherwise, singles/doubles cost L60,000/120,000. About 2km outside San Mauro Castelverde on the

road to Cefalù, *Flugy Ravetto (☎ 0921 67 41 28)* offers accommodation in small apartments with kitchens. Half board starts at L80,000 per person.

Hotels In Petralia Sottana, *Madonie (☎ 0921 64 11 06, Corso Paolo Agliata 81)* has singles/doubles for L90,000/130,000. About 3km north of town at Piano Pomieri, *Pomieri (☎ 0921 64 99 98)* is cheaper (but not nearly as nice), with rooms for L55,000/ 95,000. Two kilometres north of Gibilmanna on the road to Cefalù, *Bel Soggiorno (☎ 0921 42 18 36)* charges L45,000/ 80,000. The rooms are very clean and tidy.

Getting There & Away

Transport could be a problem in the Madonie unless you have a car. Gibilmanna is served by local bus (L1500, 20 minutes) from Cefalù's Via Umberto I, and most of the towns

The Targa Florio

Locals have enduring memories of Sicily's famous car race which was run almost every year from 1906 until its demise in 1973. The Targa Florio was created and sponsored by the Marsala wine and tuna-canning family and was contested on the twisting roads of the Madonie mountains, lined with what must have been every inhabitant of the region. In 1970 it was abundantly clear that Sicilian schoolteacher Nino Vaccarella, moonlighting as a Ferrari racing-car driver, was the hometown favourite. V-A-C-C-A-R-E-L-L-A was graffitied across every blank expanse of wall around the 72km length of the circuit and at every corner (and there were over 700 of them!) crowds of Sicilians leaned dangerously out on to the track to watch for the arrival of the local hero.

During its life the Targa Florio was run on a variety of circuits before settling down to the Piccolo Madonie circuit, winding along the coast from the town of Campofelice di Roccella then climbing up into the mountains through Cerda, Caltavuturo, Scillato and Collesano before dropping back down to the coast. Revived after WWII the Targa Florio continued as a major event through the 1950s and into the 1960s and in the last few years became a straight fight between the smaller, more agile Porsches and Alfa Romeos and the powerful Ferraris, of which one in particular was cheered on by the roars of the partisan crowd. In the late 1960s motor racing faced greater demands for increased safety and the prospect of cars capable of over 300kmph (200mph) hurtling along stone-walled straights and into tiny villages, where spectators stood unprotected on the circuit perimeter, became completely intolerable. The Targa Florio was doomed.

Nino Vaccarella never made it in the big leagues of Formula One racing but in Sicily his knowledge of the local roads guaranteed that he would always challenge for the lead. As for the Targa Florio itself, it has been nearly 30 years since a racing V12 Ferrari 512 hurtled through Campofelice, but the memory of the race survives in the Targa Tasmania rally run every year in the Australian island state and with every Porsche 911 Targa to cruise the streets of Los Angeles or London.

Tony Wheeler

are reachable by SAIS and AST bus from Palermo and – to a lesser extent – Cefalù.

CEFALÙ
postcode 90015 • pop 14,000

If Taormina is Sicily's resort town *par excellence*, then Cefalù is its eager younger sibling, desperately trying to catch up. Just over an hour by train or bus from Palermo, this attractive beachside town is now the premier destination on the Tyrrhenian coast. Its popularity is reflected in the number of tour buses that hit town daily during the summer months and the near-exorbitant prices of everything, including restaurants, hotels and even fruit. Still, the town's location on the sea, backed up against the towering mass of a crag known simply as La Rocca (The Rock), plus its relatively unspoilt medieval streets and historic sights, make this a wonderful place to spend a couple of days – just be prepared to feel the pinch!

History

A small Greek settlement existed here from the 5th century BC; its name, Cephaloedium, was derived from the Greek name for 'horse', after the shape of the crag above which (sort of) looks like a horse's head. In 307 BC the town was taken by Agathocles of Syracuse but it only really made its name in the following century when it was captured by the Romans, who used it as a key port in the control of the Tyrrhenian Sea. In AD 857 it was the Arabs' turn, and documentary evidence testifies to the town's importance as an Islamic stronghold. The Normans, however, set about destroying every trace of Eastern influence when they captured Cefalù in 1064. Roger II commissioned the town's impressive cathedral in 1131 and Cefalù became the seat of one of Sicily's most powerful bishoprics. The town's importance, however, began to wane not long after Roger's death, and for the next eight centuries Cefalù was little more than a quaint fishing port with a few elegant buildings and a lovely church.

Information

Tourist Offices The AAST tourist office (☎ 0921 42 10 50), Corso Ruggero 77, is

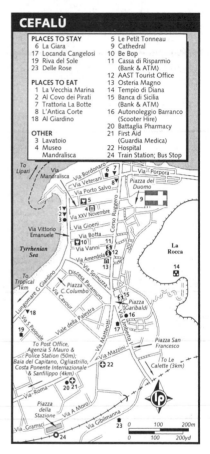

CEFALÙ

PLACES TO STAY
6 La Giara
17 Locanda Cangelosi
19 Riva del Sole
23 Delle Rose

PLACES TO EAT
1 La Vecchia Marina
2 Al Covo dei Pirati
7 Trattoria La Botte
8 L'Antica Corte
18 Al Giardino

OTHER
3 Lavatoio
4 Museo
Mandralisca
5 Le Petit Tonneau
9 Cathedral
10 Be Bop
11 Cassa di Risparmio
(Bank & ATM)
12 AAST Tourist Office
13 Osteria Magno
14 Tempio di Diana
15 Banca di Sicilia
(Bank & ATM)
16 Autonoleggio Barranco
(Scooter Hire)
20 Battaglia Pharmacy
21 First Aid
(Guardia Medica)
22 Hospital
24 Train Station; Bus Stop

open from 8 am to 2 pm and 4 to 7 pm Monday to Friday, to 2pm on Saturday. It has a Web site at www.cefalu-tour.pa.it.

Money The Banco di Sicilia on Piazza Garibaldi has an ATM, as does the Cassa di Risparmio at Corso Ruggero 79. Banks are open from 9 am to 1.20 pm and 2.45 to 3.45 pm Monday to Friday. It's not a good idea to exchange money at any of the *cambi* (exchange) booths around town as they generally charge higher commissions than banks; those that say they don't charge commission make up the difference in the exchange rates. You can, however, change money at the post office, where rates are pretty good.

Post & Communications The unwieldy looking post office is at Via Vazzana 9, off Via Roma. It is open from 8.10 am to 6.30 pm Monday to Saturday. Agenzia S Mauro, across the road from the post office at Via Vazzana 7, serves as the town's telephone exchange.

Medical Services & Emergency The town's hospital (☎ 0921 92 01 11) is on Via A Moro, just off Via Roma. There is a first-aid station (*guardia medica*; ☎ 0921 42 36 23) around the corner from the hospital at Via Roma 15. Battaglia pharmacy next door at No 13 is open from 8 am to 1 pm and 4 to 8 pm Monday to Saturday.

The police station (*questura*) is at Via Vazzana 3, opposite the post office.

Duomo di Cefalù
According to the official version, Roger II ordered that a mighty church be built after he survived a violent storm off the shore of Cefalù. Its origin, however, is more likely the result of Roger's tempestuous relationship with the Palermitan archbishopric, which was busy consolidating its temporal power with the construction of the Cappella Palatina in Palermo's Palazzo dei Normanni (see the Palermo chapter for details). Eager to curb the growing influence of the papacy in Sicily (with whom the archbishopric had close ties), Roger thought that building a mighty church so far from Palermo would prove an effective slap in the face. Built in a time of such hostility, it is hardly surprising that from the outside, the cathedral looks more like a solid fortress than a place of worship, with two massive towers flanking the facade.

The entrance is on the southern side, to the right of the facade. The interior is largely plain until you get to the apse and vault, which are decorated with some of the most beautiful **mosaics** in Sicily – you'll have to go to Monreale or the Cappella Palatina (see the Palermo chapter) to see anything finer.

The mosaics were completed sometime between 1150 and 1160 – some 20 to 30 years before the mosaics of Monreale – and feature (in the central apse) the gigantic figure of Christ *Pantokrator* (all-powerful) holding an open bible bearing a Latin and Greek inscription from John 8:12: 'I am the light of the world; he who follows me shall not walk in darkness.' Underneath is the Virgin Mary flanked by archangels; underneath again, in two rows of six, are the twelve Apostles.

The rest of the church is in the 'stripped-down' stage of perennial restoration. The southern aisle is littered with pieces of stone and mosaic, mostly the dismantled royal and episcopal throne, which once adorned the sides of the altar. There is no definite date for the completion of the cathedral's restoration, a project which is plagued by lack of funding. The little medieval cloister behind the cathedral, itself a wonderful piece of architecture, is also closed.

The cathedral is open from 8 am to noon and 3.30 to 8 pm daily from April to September (until 6 pm the rest of the year). Admission is free though donations are much needed and greatly appreciated.

La Rocca
The massive crag that towers 278m above the town is a popular climb, especially in good weather when the panoramic views of the town and coast are splendid. Steps to the right of the Banco di Sicilia on Piazza Garibaldi mark the start of the clearly signposted, steep path up the cliff. It's a 20-minute climb to the **Tempio di Diana** (Temple of Diana), built sometime during the 4th or 5th century BC. Below it are the straggly remains of a set of **fortified walls** built during the Byzantine period. Apart from a few loose rocks, there is nothing left of the Norman castle that once crowned the rock's peak.

Other Things to See
Off Piazza del Duomo, at Via Mandralisca 13, is the private **Museo Mandralisca** (☎ 0921 42 15 47). Its collection includes Greek ceramics and Arab pottery, as well as paintings, notably the *Ritratto di un Uomo*

THE TYRRHENIAN COAST

Ignoto (Portrait of an Unknown Man; 1465) by Antonello da Messina (1430–79). Unfortunately, the painting is lost within a wide, ugly frame and visitors are kept at a distance by a velvet rope: you're almost better off just buying a postcard. The museum is open from 9 am to 12.30 pm and 3.30 pm to 7.30 pm daily (to midnight during August).

Turn left outside the museum and walk down Via Mandralisca towards the sea. On Via Vittorio Emanuele is the **lavatoio**, a 16th-century wash-house built over a spring which was well known in antiquity.

The town's other main sight is the **Osteria Magno**, on the corner of Corso Ruggero and Via Amendola (across the street from the tourist office). This imposing mansion, built in the 14th-century has been heavily renovated over the centuries and today is only open for temporary art exhibits. If you want to get a look inside at other times, ask for the keys at the tourist office.

Otherwise, the town is a splendid place for a walk. The lovely little port is lined with narrow fishing boats where you might find the occasional fisherman mending his nets (although the demise of the fishing industry makes such an occurrence less and less likely). The boardwalk along the beach is very popular for the evening *passeggiata*, or stroll: in summer the cafes and restaurants that line it are almost always full.

Swimming

Cefalù's crescent-shaped beach is one of the most popular along the whole coast. In summer it is always packed, so be sure to get down early to get a good spot. If you want relief from the blazing sun, you can rent a beach umbrella (L5000) from the bar on the beach. Deckchairs (L5500) are also available. Again, if you want to rent either get here early as they tend to be snapped up pretty quickly.

Places to Stay

Cheap accommodation is like gold dust in Cefalù. Between June and August prices are exorbitant and there is no such thing as value for money. At the height of summer

(mid-July to the end of August) you will have difficulty finding anywhere to stay at any price, so be sure to book early.

The good news is that out of season (between October and April) the hotels that remain open drop their rates substantially, some even by half. Unless otherwise indicated, the accommodation listed below is open year-round.

Camping There are several camp sites in the area, including *Costa Ponente Internazionale* (☎ 0921 42 00 85), about 4km west of town at Contrada Ogliastrillo. It costs L9500/8000/6000 per person/site/car. It is open only from Easter to October. From Cefalù train station catch the bus heading for La Spisa.

Next to Costa Ponente is *Sanfilippo* (☎ 0921 42 01 84) which charges L9000/ 7000 per person/site. It is open from 10 April to 10 September.

Hotels In town, the only really cheap option is *Locanda Cangelosi* (☎ 0921 42 15 91, Via Umberto I 26), with singles/doubles costing L35,000/70,000. There are only four rooms so book in advance.

Uphill from the beach and off Corso Ruggero is *La Giara* (☎ 0921 42 15 62, Via Veterani 40). It has rooms for L52,000/100,000 rising to L74,000/136,000 in August.

A good option is *Delle Rose* (☎ 0921 42 18 85, Via Gibilmanna) which is about a 10-minute walk from the centre on the road to Gibilmanna. It's a very friendly place with doubles for only L90,000 (including breakfast).

Riva del Sole (☎ 0921 42 12 30, fax 0921 42 19 84, Via Lungomare 25) is conveniently near the beach. It has doubles for L140,000.

With only a couple of exceptions, you won't get good value for money in Cefalù's top-range hotels. *Le Calette* (☎ 0921 42 00 03, fax 0921 42 36 88, Via Vincenzo Cavallaro 12, Località Caldura) is on the eastern side of the headland about 2km out of town. It's set in its own grounds, complete with swimming pool, buffet bar and restaurant. Singles/doubles cost L150,000/200,000.

Baia del Capitano (☎ 0921 42 00 05) is in an olive grove near the beach at Mazzaforno, a few kilometres out of town towards Palermo. Its pleasant rooms cost L130,000/210,000.

Places to Eat

Although the town is packed with restaurants, the food can be surprisingly mundane and the tourist menus unimaginative. Still, there are a few spots that stay ahead of the crowd by offering well-prepared dishes at prices that don't make you feel like you're being ripped off, an all-too-common feeling in this tourist-driven town. Most restaurants fill up between 8.30 and 10 pm so, unless you want to find yourself dining at 11.30 pm, book your table in advance (a few hours' notice is sufficient).

A cheap spot for a quick lunch is *Al Covo dei Pirati* (*Via Vittorio Emanuele 59*) which serves excellent sandwiches, a limited number of pasta dishes and an exceptional salad of shaved parmesan, *rucola* (rocket) and *prosciutto* (ham). You should be able to eat your fill for less than L15,000. Ask for a seat on the tiny terrace overlooking the port. It is only open for lunch – at night it turns into a club (see Entertainment later in this section).

Just off Corso Ruggero, *Trattoria La Botte* (☎ 0921 42 43 15, Via Veterani 6) serves full meals for around L30,000. The *pasta con le sarde* (pasta with sardines, anchovies, fennel and onions), a Sicilian speciality found on every menu in town, is particularly good.

L'Antica Corte (☎ 0921 42 32 28, Corso Ruggero 193) is one of the better restaurants in town, and the prices reflect it: expect to pay around L40,000 for a meal.

Similarly priced is *La Vecchia Marina* (☎ 0921 42 03 88, Via Vittorio Emanuele). This is the best fish restaurant in town, serving an array of freshly caught beauties.

Otherwise, there are a few restaurants along the seafront that serve similar menus of fish and meat dishes as well as pastas, all priced around L10,000–15,000 for a main course. The best of the lot is *Al Giardino* (☎ 0921 92 12 90, Lungomare G Giardino).

Entertainment

Bars Cefalù has a number of pretty good bars that are popular in summer. *Le Petit Tonneau* (☎ 0921 42 14 47, Via Mandralisca 66), just down from the Museo Mandralisca, is a French-owned bistro (the name means 'little tuna') that's good for a late-night drink. *Be Bop* (*Via Botta 4*) is another good spot; at the weekend in summer there is live music.

Nightclubs No summer resort is complete without its complement of discotheques, and Cefalù is no different. *Al Covo dei Pirati* (*Via Vittorio Emanuele 59*) is the town's version of an 'alternative' club, with soul, hip hop and beats played by DJs nightly throughout the summer. A more typical summer disco is *Ogliastrillo*, next to the Costa Ponente Internazionale camp site (see Camping under Places to Stay earlier in this section). The outdoor *Tropical* (*Lungomare G Giardino*) is similar. These last two are only open from June to September. Admission costs about L15,000.

Getting There & Away

Buses run to and from outside the train station. SAIS buses leave Palermo for Cefalù twice daily (for details see the Palermo Getting There & Away section). The journey takes about one hour. SAIS also runs a daily bus to and from Termini Imerese (L3200, 30 minutes). Trains are more frequent, usually about two per hour (call ☎ 0921 42 11 69 for details).

The best way of getting here is by train. From Palermo, trains leave every 30 minutes and make the journey in just under an hour (L4600). The line also links Cefalù with virtually every other town on the coast.

You can also get a hydrofoil from Cefalù to the Aeolian Islands from mid-June to September. There are two departures daily for Lipari (L27,000, 2½ hours) that also make a stop at Vulcano.

Getting Around

Cefalù itself is small enough to walk around. If you find yourself heading farther afield, a taxi service (☎ 0921 42 25 54) operates out

THE TYRRHENIAN COAST

of Piazza del Stazione, next to the train station. Rates depend on where you want to go, but a 5km trip, for instance, should cost no more than L5000. Be sure to fix the rate before you leave.

If you are driving, parking can be a problem, but you should be able to find somewhere to stick your vehicle on the roads that run parallel to the long beach southwest of the town centre.

Autonoleggio Barranco (☎ 0921 42 15 25) rents Vespas and other scooters between 50cc and 125cc; typical rates are L40,000 per day for a 50cc Vespa.

East to Milazzo

The 83km stretch of coastline between Cefalù and Capo d'Orlando to the east is dotted with little coves, clean beaches and a couple of small resorts that have become increasingly popular in recent years, including the ceramics centre of Santo Stefano di Camastra and Sant'Agata di Militello. Beyond Capo d'Orlando the coast becomes more developed and industrialised the closer you get to Milazzo, not a great destination in itself but the main point of departure for the Aeolian Islands. The highlights here, however, are the classical remains at Patti and Tyndaris. All places mentioned are on the main Palermo–Messina railways line, which is served by hourly trains throughout the day.

CASTEL DI TUSA
postcode 98079 • pop 480
About 25km east of Cefalù, just inside the province of Messina, is this little resort village that doesn't attract nearly as many tourists as other spots along the coast. Just above the town are the ruins of the **castle** that gave the resort its name. A small road (9km) leads inland to the parent village of **Tusa**, where in the bed of the river of the same name are a number of modern sculptures that have been the subject of much litigation over the years (see the boxed text 'Art in the River'). There's no bus between the two so you'll have to walk if you don't have your own transport.

Between the coastal resort and the village you'll see a signpost for **Halaesa**, a Greek city founded in the 5th century BC. Beautifully positioned on a hill commanding fine views of the surrounding countryside and – on a clear day – the Aeolian Islands, the most conspicuous remains are those of the *agora* (marketplace) and its massive rusticated walls.

Just down the hill are the barely recognisable remains of a small theatre. The site was first excavated in the 1950s and again in 1972, but nothing has been done since then.

Places to Stay
Open between May and October, *Lo Scoglio* (☎ 0921 3 43 45) is a small camp site which costs L12,000 per person. Otherwise, the town's only hotel is *L'Atelier sul Mare* (☎ 0921 33 42 95, Via C Battisti). The name means 'studio on the sea' and indeed each of the 44 rooms is like an artistic installation. The price for sleeping in such an aesthetically conceived room is L90,000/130,000 for a single/double.

Getting There & Away
The town is a 20-minute train ride from Cefalù (L1800) and is served by trains on the Palermo–Messina line hourly throughout the day.

Art in the River

Inaugurated in 1986, *Fiumara d'Arte* (Art in the River Bed) is a controversial project conceived by contemporary artist Pietro Consagra, whose aim was to create art outside of the sterile confines of a gallery's four walls. Placed in the bed of the Tusa River, his pieces generated immediate dismay and opponents rushed to get a court order forcing him to remove them. The courts granted their wish in 1991 and again in 1993, but the work remains and installations by other artists such as Tano Festa, Antonio di Palma and Hidetoschi Nagasawa were set up in other river beds, caves and hills along the coast.

SANTO STEFANO DI CAMASTRA
postcode 98077 • pop 5100

About 8km east of Castel di Tusa, Santo Stefano di Camastra is a popular coach-tour stop on account of its bustling ceramics industry, which ranks alongside that of Caltagirone (see the Central Sicily chapter) as the island's most important. The industry grew up as a result of the presence of numerous clay quarries in the hills above the town. Indeed, until 1693 the town was farther up the hill and was called Santo Stefano di Mistretta; it was destroyed by a landslide in 1692 and a new town was built closer to the coast. The layout of the town resembles a miniature version of the garden at Versailles in France, the streets radiating out from a central square.

Other than ceramics (almost every shop stocks them), the town doesn't offer all that much to the casual visitor. If you're interested in the process behind the manufacturing of ceramics, you can pop your head into the **Museo delle Ceramiche** (Ceramics Museum) in the Palazzo Trabia on Via Palazzo towards the sea. It is open from 9 am to 1 pm and 4 to 8 pm Monday to Friday, June to September only. Admission is free.

The town has a couple of hotels. The cheaper one is the small *Locanda U Cucinu* (☎ *0921 33 11 06, Via Nuova 75)*, where spartan singles/doubles without bathroom cost L10,000/15,000 (a double with bathroom costs L20,000). *La Plaja Blanca* (☎ *0921 33 12 48, Via Fiumara Marina)* is nicer, with doubles only for L85,000. Both hotels have restaurants.

SANT'AGATA DI MILITELLO
postcode 98076 • pop 12,800

This relatively new town (it was founded in the 18th century), 30km east of Santo Stefano di Camastra, is a popular little resort along this stretch of coast, and makes a handy base from which to tour the coastline and the inland Parco Regionale dei Nebrodi (Nebrodi nature reserve; see the Central Sicily chapter). In summer its two hotels are usually crammed with Italian holidaymakers eager to make the most of the nice **beach**. The only sight worth mentioning is the

Chiesa del Carmelo in the centre of town, which has a handsome 18th-century gable.

The cheapest hotel in town is the slightly run-down *Locanda Miramare* (☎ *0941 70 17 73, Via Cosenz 3)* which charges L30,000/50,000 for singles/doubles without bathroom. En-suite doubles cost L10,000 more. In winter the rates are halved. A little fancier is the *Parimar* (☎ *0941 70 18 88, Via Medici 1)* where rooms with a bathroom cost L40,000/80,000. There's also a pretty good restaurant attached.

SAN MARCO D'ALUNZIO
postcode 98076 • pop 2300
• elevation 540m

On the road to Capo d'Orlando from Sant'Agata di Militello, the first turn-off inland (signposted) weaves its way uphill for 5km to this remarkable little town founded by the Greeks in the 5th century BC and later occupied by the Romans, who named it Aluntium.

San Marco d'Alunzio is definitely worth making the effort to visit, at least for a couple of hours. At its entrance is the spectacularly situated **Tempio di Ercole** (Temple of Hercules), with terrific views over the sea. A now roofless Norman church was subsequently built on the temple's red marble base. Virtually all of San Marco's older buildings were constructed using this locally quarried marble, which is named after the town – Aluntium.

From the temple, Via Aluntina leads up to the town proper and a number of interesting churches, the best of which is the **Chiesa di Santa Maria delle Grazie**, where you can find a beautiful statue of the *Madonna con Bambino e San Giovanni* (Madonna and Child with St John), which has been attributed to Domenico Gagini. At the top of the hill are the scant remains of the **castle** built by Robert Guiscard in 1061, the first castle built by the Normans in Sicily.

Buses from Sant'Agata di Militello make the 5km run to San Marco d'Alunzio at least 10 times a day. Departures are from outside the train station and the trip (L800) takes about 10 minutes.

CAPO D'ORLANDO
postcode 98071 • pop 12,000

The busiest resort town on the coast after Cefalù, Capo d'Orlando was founded – at least according to the legend – when one of Charlemagne's generals, a chap called Orlando, stood on the headland and declared it a fine place to build a castle. The ruins of the castle, including traces of the 14th-century masonry and ribbing, are still visible. In 1299 Frederick II of Aragon was defeated here by the rebellious baron Roger of Lauria, backed up by the joint forces of Catalonia and Anjou. Today's rebels are the town's shopkeepers and traders, who have made a name for themselves with their firm stance against the Mafia's demands for the infamous *pizzo* (protection money) – sadly an all-too-rare bit of resistance against a racket that seems ingrained in Sicilian society.

Visitors come here for the **beaches**, both sandy and rocky, that are on either side of town. The best swimming is to the east – the water is that little bit cleaner.

Special Events
On Ferragosto (August 15th) there is a procession of boats along the coast to celebrate the Assumption of the Virgin Mary.

Places to Stay & Eat
The cheapest hotel in Capo d'Orlando is *Nuovo Hotel Faro* (☎ *0941 90 24 66, Via Libertà 7)*, where comfortable singles/doubles with balconies that are overlooking the sea cost L40,000/80,000. *La Meridiana* (☎ *0941 95 77 13, Via Trassari 2)* is an elegant hotel with doubles only for L100,000. The best hotel is *La Tartaruga* (☎ *0941 95 05 12, fax 0941 95 50 56, Lido San Gregorio)*, to the east of town overlooking a wide, sandy beach. The well-appointed rooms here cost L120,000/200,000 with bathroom, L80,000/120,000 without.

There's no shortage of places to get a bite either. *Da Enzo* (☎ *0941 90 17 00, Via Lo Sardo)* is a nice pizzeria with a fine selection of pasta dishes.

Right by the water, *Il Gabbiano (Via Trazzera Marina)* and the adjacent *Gallo d'Oro* are good choices.

Getting There & Away
The best way to get here is by train, from either east or west. From Palermo, it's a two-hour trip (L8600). From Milazzo, it's a 70-minute trip (L6000).

PATTI
postcode 98066 • pop 13,000
• elevation 157m

This fairly nondescript town 26km east of Capo d'Orlando first developed when it was flooded with refugees from nearby Tyndaris (see Tyndaris later in this section) after the latter's destruction by landslide in the 1st century AD.

Patti was a bishopric in Norman times, but was destroyed by Frederick II of Aragon after it sided with the French Anjou family during the revolt of the Sicilian Vespers in the 13th century. In 1554 it was plundered by the pirate Khair-ed-din Barbarossa, or Redbeard. At the top of the hill is the town's 18th-century **cathedral**, built on the site of the Norman church where Roger II buried his mother Adelasia, who died here in 1118. Her remains were later transferred to a fine Renaissance sarcophagus, which you can see in the right transept.

There is an AAPT tourist office (☎ 0941 24 11 36) at Piazza Marconi 11 in the centre of town. Most visitors come here to visit the remains of the **Roman villa** on the eastern outskirts of town beneath the motorway viaduct. Built in the 4th century AD, it was destroyed by an earthquake 100 years later and was not uncovered until 1976. Sadly, the site is badly positioned and poorly maintained, although a plastic roofing was erected to protect the polychrome mosaics from the fumes emanating from the motorway overhead. The museum which was built to house the artefacts found during the excavations has never opened. The site is open from 9 am to one hour before sunset. Admission costs L4000.

TYNDARIS
elevation 230m

About 6km east of Patti, at Capo Tindari, are the ruins of ancient Tyndaris, founded on a rocky promontory by Dionysius the

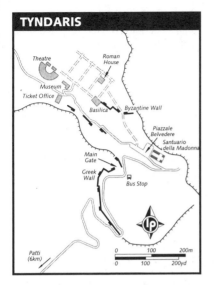

TYNDARIS

Theatre
Roman House
Museum
Ticket Office
Basilica
Byzantine Wall
Piazzale Belvedere
Santuario della Madonna
Main Gate
Greek Wall
Bus Stop

Patti (6km)

0   100   200m
0   100   200yd

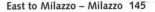

THE TYRRHENIAN COAST

Elder in 396 BC after a victory over the Carthaginians. It remained a close ally of Syracuse until 256 BC when it was taken by the Romans. The town was partially destroyed by a landslide in the 1st century AD, further damaged by an earthquake in AD 365 and finished off by the Arabs in the 10th century. Excavations of the site began in the 19th century, but did not proceed in any cohesive manner until 1949; they have continued ever since.

What was not excavated, but built in the 1960s, is the **Sanctuary of the Madonna**, the first thing you see when you get off the bus from Patti (see Getting There & Away later in this chapter). This enormous church houses the sacred relic that is the *Madonna Nera* (Black Madonna), thought to have been made in Asia Minor. Religious pilgrims flock here in droves to pray at her feet due to the miracles she has allegedly performed: in one particularly brilliant stunt, she concocted a mattress out of thin air and spirited it to the bottom of a cliff where it broke the fall of a young boy. Interestingly, the inscription underneath the icon reads '*Nigra sum, sed hermosa*', which means 'I am black but I am beautiful', perhaps the earliest version of the

famous catchphrase of the 1960s Black Panther movement in the US.

From the sanctuary, a path leads to the site entrance. The majority of the ruins here are of Roman origin, including the **basilica** (to the right of the entrance). In the 1950s the building was the subject of a controversial 'renovation' using modern materials (specifically concrete), which opponents protested were unrepresentative of its original appearance. Just beyond the basilica is a **Roman house** in remarkably good condition. The floor has some fine mosaics. At the far end of the town's main street is the **theatre**, originally a Greek structure but substantially modified by the Romans, who used it as a gladiatorial arena. Part of the theatre was dismantled to build the city's **walls**, which are still in evidence around the perimeter.

To the left of the main entrance is a small **museum** containing finds from the site, including an impressive bust of the emperor Augustus. The site is open from 9 am to one hour before sunset daily and admission costs L4000.

Special Events
In July and August the theatre hosts a festival of Greek drama and modern operas. For information ask at the ticket office at the entrance to the site or at the AAPT tourist office in Patti (see that section for details). Tickets cost around L25,000 for each performance.

Getting There & Away
There are three buses daily (five during July and August) to Tyndaris from Patti's main square, 6km away. Tickets cost L2500. All buses arrive at and depart from a parking lot about 1km from the site itself; you can walk the rest of the way or get one of the shuttle buses which make the run every 10 minutes or so (L1000).

MILAZZO
postcode 98057 • pop 32,000
Hardly Sicily's prettiest town, Milazzo is shrouded in layers of industrial development that can make even the most determined visitor run for the nearest hydrofoil or ferry to the Aeolian Islands. Indeed, the main reason

for ever setting foot in this town is to get off Sicily, as this is the main port for travel to the archipelago. Unless you arrive late in the evening or in the dead of winter, you should be sea-bound within the hour, as departures are very frequent. Still, you could do a lot worse than wander about the surprisingly pleasant streets of the old city, fronted by an elegant promenade lined with palm trees that runs along the water.

Orientation & Information
Everything of interest here is within walking distance of the ferry and hydrofoil port.

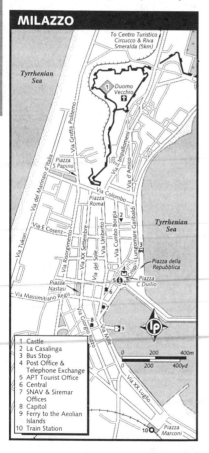

MILAZZO

Tyrrhenian Sea

To Centro Turistico Circucco & Riva Smeralda (5km)

1 Duomo Vecchio

Via Grotta Polifermo

Piazza S Papino

Via del Marmaio d'Italia

Via d'Impallomeni

Via d'Amico

Via Colombo

Piazza Roma

Via Cumbo Borgia

Lungomare Garibaldi

Tyrrhenian Sea

Via E Cosenz

Via Risorgimento

Via XX Settembre

Via Umberto I

Via del Sole

Piazza della Repubblica

Via Tukori

Piazza Nastasi

Piazza C Duilio

Via Massimiliano Regis

Via Giorgio Rizzo

Via G Mila

0   200   400m
0   200   400yd

Via XX Luglio

Piazza Marconi

1 Castle
2 La Casalinga
3 Bus Stop
4 Post Office & Telephone Exchange
5 APT Tourist Office
6 Central
7 SNAV & Siremar Offices
8 Capitol
9 Ferry to the Aeolian Islands
10 Train Station

The train station is on Piazza Marconi, about 1km south of the port along the seafront. Buses between the station and the quayside depart every 20 minutes or so: buy a ticket (L800) at the little kiosk inside the train station.

The APT office (☎ 090 922 28 65), Piazza C Duilio 10, is behind Via Crispi. It is open from 8 am to 2 pm and 4 to 7 pm Monday to Friday (mornings only at the weekend), June to September (closed Sunday the rest of the year). There is a post office next door which also has phones. All of the ticket agencies for travel to the islands are virtually next door to each other on the quayside.

The first-aid station can be called on ☎ 090 928 1158. For the police call ☎ 090 928 1120 and for the *carabinieri* (military police) call ☎ 090 928 6170.

Things to See & Do
Milazzo's **castle** (☎ 090 922 12 91) was originally constructed by Frederick II in 1239 but was enlarged by Charles V of Aragon in the 15th century. The Norman keep is still intact at the centre of the mostly Spanish fortifications. It is open from 10 am to 7 pm Tuesday to Sunday from April to October (until 3.30 pm the rest of the year). Guided tours of the interior run at 11 am, noon and 3, 4 and 5 pm. Admission is free.

Places to Stay & Eat
There are a couple of camp sites at Capo Milazzo, 6km north of the city centre. The huge *Centro Turistico Cirucco* (☎ 090 928 47 46) charges L12,000 per person. *Riva Smeralda* (☎ 090 928 29 80) is smaller and charges L11,000. Both camp sites also rent two-person bungalows for around L100,000 per night. They are open from April to October only.

There are several hotels near the port if you get stuck for the night. *Central* (☎ 090 928 10 43, Via del Sole 8) has basic rooms costing L40,000/75,000. *Capitol* (☎ 090 928 32 89, Via Giorgio Rizzo 91) is close to the hydrofoil dock and has rooms with shared bathroom for L50,000/80,000 (L60,000/L100,000 with private bathroom). Neither hotel accepts credit cards.

For something to eat, you don't need to go far from Lungomare Garibaldi along the seafront. *La Casalinga* *(Via D'Amico)* is particularly good for seafood. Otherwise, there are plenty of other choices in and around the port.

Getting There & Away

Giuntabus (☎ 090 67 37 82) runs an hourly service to and from Messina (L6000, 50 minutes). All intercity buses arrive at and depart from Piazza della Repubblica along the quayside. Milazzo is easy to reach by bus or train from Palermo and Messina. Trains are more frequent, with two departures and arrivals hourly for both Palermo (L13,000, 2½ to 3 hours) and Messina (L4500, 45 minutes). See The Aeolian Islands chapter for details of travel to and from the islands.

The Aeolian Islands

The seven islands of this volcanic archipelago (Isole Eolie) stretching north of Milazzo make up one of the most popular tourist resorts in Sicily. In summer, all but the outlying islands of Alicudi and Filicudi are awash with waves of day-trippers and holidaymakers, tempted by the near-perfect weather that can make a stay here one of the most enjoyable experiences in Sicily. The islands are all different, ranging from the developed tourist resort of Lipari and the understated jet-set haunt of Panarea, to the rugged Vulcano, the spectacular scenery of Stromboli and its fiercely active volcano, the fertile vineyards of Salina, and the solitude of outlying Alicudi and Filicudi. Yet the Aeolian Islands all share one thing in common, at least in summer: the blazing sun warms a limpid, blue sea that laps at the rocky shores and sandy beaches. If you're looking for a day out in the sun, you've come to the right place.

That same limpid sea, however, can turn ferocious, especially in winter, when high waves crash with awesome power against the coast. It is no coincidence that the ancient Greeks believed the islands to be the home of Aeolus (who gave the archipelago its name), the god of the wind (see the boxed text 'The Vulcan Winds' later in the chapter). Although the modern traveller may marvel at the islands' beauty, living here has almost always been a constant struggle. Between the 1930s and 1950s many inhabitants emigrated to Australia (often referred to by locals as the eighth Aeolian Island), leaving the outer islands virtually abandoned and only a small contingent on the others. The advent of tourism has helped avert disaster for five of the islands, but Alicudi and Filicudi still suffer the loss of so many human resources.

As with any popular place, the surge of tourism has its negative side. In July and August Lipari can be mayhem, with accommodation and even a nice spot on the beach that much harder to find. During this period you will need to book accommodation well

Highlights

- Savour your first glimpse of Vulcano from the sea before the rotten smell of sulphurous gases hits you – you know you're in for something special!
- Witness the spectacular eruptions of Stromboli's rumbling crater viewed at dusk
- Visit the archaeological museum in Lipari, home to one of the most fascinating and well-presented collections in Sicily
- Slide down the pumice chutes at Campobianco on Lipari; there's no better way of getting into the water
- Forget about the rest of the world on Alicudi

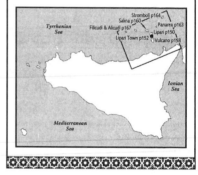

in advance. The best time to come is in May and early June or late September and October, when the weather is still fine and the hordes are either yet to arrive or have been and gone. Ferries and hydrofoils operate year-round, but winter services are much reduced and sometimes cancelled – to the outer islands at any rate – due to heavy seas.

Cinema fans might recognise Salina as the setting for the Oscar-winning *Il Postino* (1995) by Michael Bradford, starring Massimo Troisi in the title role and Philippe Noiret as the Chilean poet Pablo Neruda. Also of local interest is the film *Stromboli* (see Things to See & Do in that section for

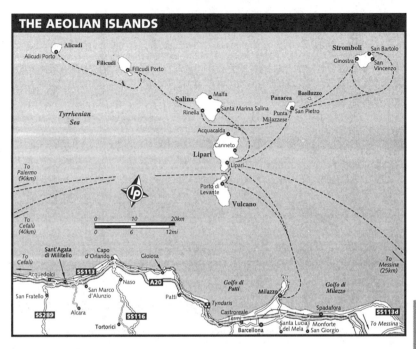

THE AEOLIAN ISLANDS

details) and Nanni Moretti's *Caro Diario* (Dear Diary). Part of this quirky film is set on the islands, and Moretti captures their essence well.

Getting There & Away
Hydrofoil Both SNAV and Siremar (see under Getting There & Away in the Lipari section for contact details) run hydrofoils from Milazzo to Lipari (L19,500, 55 minutes) and on to the other islands. From June to September hydrofoils depart almost hourly to Lipari, and also stop at Vulcano (L18,000, 40 minutes) and either Santa Marina Salina (L24,000, 1½ hours) or Rinella (L24,000, 1 hour 40 minutes) on Salina. Direct services to the other islands are less frequent unless you change in Lipari: there are five departures daily for Panarea (L23,500, two hours) and Stromboli (L30,000, 2¾ hours). There is only one departure for Alicudi (L40,000, three hours) and Filicudi (L40,000, 2 hours 20 minutes).

From October to May the frequency of service is substantially reduced: there are only two departures daily to Vulcano, Lipari and Salina and one daily to Panarea, Stromboli, Filicudi and Alicudi.

Ferry Siremar runs six or seven ferries from Milazzo to Lipari for about half the price of the hydrofoil (L12,500; cars from L32,500 to L46,500, depending on size), but they are slower and less regular. NGI Traghetti (☎ 090 981 1955), Via Tenente M Amendola, also runs a twice-daily car ferry service for around the same rates.

Getting Around
Regular hydrofoil and ferry services operate between the islands, but they can be disrupted, particularly to the outer islands, by heavy seas. Lipari's two ports are separated by the citadel – hydrofoils arrive at and depart from Marina Corta, while Marina Lunga services ferries. Siremar and SNAV

have ticket offices in the same building at Marina Corta. Siremar also has a ticket office at Marina Lunga. Full timetable information is available at all offices. On the other islands, ticket offices are at or close to the docks.

Examples of one-way fares and sailing times from Lipari are:

Alicudi
    L27,000, 1½ hours (hydrofoil)
    L17,500, 3¼ hours (ferry)
Panarea
    L13,000, 30 minutes (hydrofoil)
    L7500, 1 hour (ferry)
Stromboli
    L25,500, 50 minutes (hydrofoil)
    L15,000, 2¾ hours (ferry)

LIPARI
postcode 98050 • pop 11,000
• maximum elevation 602m

The largest of all the islands – it measures 37.6 sq km and is 9.5km long – Lipari is also the most developed and most popular in the archipelago. The main town, of the same name, is typically Mediterranean, with pastel-coloured houses huddled around its two harbours. The island is also home to four other towns – Acquacalda, Canneto, Pianoconte and Quattropani. Most activity begins and ends in Lipari town, although Canneto (only 2km north) does have a couple of restaurants and hotels. A thriving exporter of obsidian in ancient times, it is now a centre for mining pumice stone (another volcanic product) and is the best-equipped base for exploring the archipelago.

History
Lipari has been inhabited since the 4th millennium BC, when it was settled by the Stentillenians, named after the village of Stentinello near Syracuse (where the first traces of this civilisation were found). The island bore the poetic name Meligunis, meaning 'gentle slopes', and its inhabitants were expert miners and traders of obsidian, a hard, glass-like rock that was common all over the island. In 580 BC it was settled by Greeks from Rhodes, who renamed it after the mythical first king of the island, Liparo.

During the Punic Wars Lipari sided with Carthage and in 260 BC the Carthaginians defeated the Romans in a sea battle off the coast. Their control over the islands as a whole, however, only lasted another eight years until they were convincingly defeated by the Romans, who incorporated the entire archipelago into their Sicilian province, where it has remained ever since. They built the nucleus of their city on the ruins of the Greek acropolis, located between the two harbours where the Norman cathedral now stands. Under the Normans in the 12th and 13th centuries Lipari entered a period of growth and prosperity thanks to the extensive mining of sulphur and alum and the excavation of pumice stone. In 1544, however, the town was sacked and as many as 10,000 of its inhabitants were killed or sold into slavery by the pirate Khair-ed-din Barbarossa, or Redbeard, who despite the Arabic name was actually an Italian mercenary with a first name of Ariadeno. The Aragon

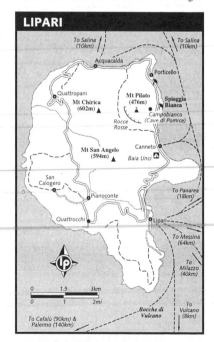

Obsidian For Sale

As far back as 4000 BC, the island's first settlers – the Stentillenians – made up for their lack of metal with their expert working of obsidian. They weren't content to use it domestically, but managed to develop a roaring trade throughout the known world. The crafted stone would be loaded into fast, light boats and shipped to markets in faraway places. Finds at the archaeological site of Pergamum, in present-day Turkey, have revealed fragments of raw and carved Liparese obsidian that was used in the treatment of the ill.

king Charles V succeeded in repopulating the island with Spaniards and Calabrians soon after Barbarossa's death in 1546 and rebuilt the town, adding the solid walls visible today. By virtue of a Fascist decree in 1926 Lipari was declared an open prison for political enemies of the regime; not long after the arrival of the first batch of prisoners – three communist activists – the locals helped them escape by boat to Tunisia.

Orientation

All tourists arrive at one of the two harbours in Lipari town: Marina Lunga and Marina Corta. They are situated either side of the cliff-top citadel (known as the *castello*), which is surrounded by 16th-century walls. Here you'll will find the cathedral, the archaeological museum (Museo Archeologico Eoliano) and a couple of run-down baroque churches. The town centre extends between the two. The main street, Corso Vittorio Emanuele, runs roughly north–south to the west of the castle and is where you'll find banks, bars, offices and restaurants. Hydrofoils dock at Marina Corta, from where you should walk to the right across the square to Via Garibaldi and follow the 'centro' signs for Corso Vittorio Emanuele.

Information

Tourist Offices The AAST office (☎ 090 988 00 95) is on Corso Vittorio Emanuele 202. It is the main tourist office for the archipelago, although offices also open on Stromboli, Vulcano and Salina during the summer. It can assist with accommodation, which is useful in the busy summer months. Pick up a copy of *Ospitalità in Blu* (Italian only), which contains details of accommodation and services on all the islands. The office is open from 8 am to 2 pm and 4 to 7.30 pm (to 6.30 pm between October and April) Monday to Saturday; it is also open from 8 am to 2 pm on Sunday and holidays between May and October.

Money There are several banks in Lipari, including the Banca del Sud on Corso Vittorio Emanuele. You should have no trouble using Visa, MasterCard or Eurocheque cards for cash advances. Outside banking hours, exchange facilities can be found at the post office and several travel agencies.

Note that banking facilities on the other islands are limited.

Post & Communications The post office (☎ 090 981 13 79) is on Corso Vittorio Emanuele 207, near the tourist office, and is open from 8.30 am to 6.30 pm Monday to Friday and to 1 pm on Saturday. Public telephones can be found throughout the town.

If you need to check email or surf the Internet, Netnet (☎ 090 981 24 62) at Via Marte 2 (just off the western end of Marina Corta) is open from 9 am to noon Monday to Saturday and at other times by appointment only. At the time of research charges were L7000 for one hour.

Bookshops La Stampa, Corso Vittorio Emanuele 170, is a bookshop with a selection of foreign language newspapers, usually English, German and French.

Medical Services & Emergency Contact the hospital on ☎ 090 9 88 51 or *pronto soccorso* (casualty) on ☎ 090 988 52 67. Both are on Via Sant'Anna. There are three pharmacies in town. Cincotta (☎ 090 981 14 72) is at Via Garibaldi 60 and Internazionale (☎ 090 981 15 83) is at Corso Vittorio Emanuele 128. Just up the street at No 174 is Sparacino (☎ 090 981 13 92). They are all open from 9 am to 12.30 pm and 3.30 to 8 pm

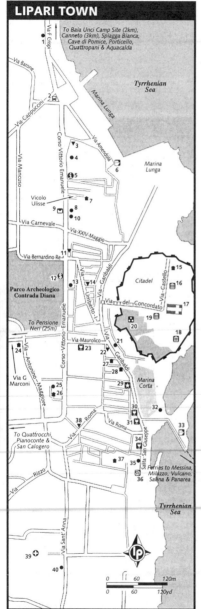

LIPARI TOWN

PLACES TO STAY
7   Lo Nardo Maria
15 HI Youth Hostel
25 Hotel Oriente
27 Diana Brown
28 Casa Vittorio
29 Enzo Il Negro
37 Villa Meligunis

PLACES TO EAT
3   Il Galeone
11 Zum Willi
14 La Trattoria d'Oro
23 Da Bartolo
38 Nenzyna

OTHER
1   Foti Roberto (Boat & Scooter Hire)
2   Bus Stop
4   Supermarket
5   AAST Tourist Office
6   Siremar Ticket Agency (Ferries)
8   Sparacino Pharmacy
9   Post Office
10 La Stampa (Newspapers)
12 Banca del Sud (Bank & ATM)
13 Internazionale Pharmacy
16 Museo Archeologico Eoliano (Classical Section)
17 Cattedrale di San Bartolomeo
18 Museo Archeologico Eoliano (Epigraphic Section)
19 Museo Archeologico Eoliano (Pavilion)
20 Museo Archeologico Eoliano (Archaeological Section)
21 Archaeological Dig
22 Cincotta Pharmacy
24 Kasbah Cafe
26 Viking Office
30 Police Station (Carabinieri)
31 Al Pescatore
32 Il Gabbiano
33 Viking Ticket Booth
34 Siremar & SNAV Ticket Booth (Hydrofoil)
35 Chitarra
36 Netnet Internet Point
39 Hospital
40 First-Aid Centre

Monday to Saturday from May to October (to 7 pm the rest of the year). They take it in turns to be on night-duty; check out the notice board outside each pharmacy for the 'farmacie di turno' timetable.

If you need a doctor in an emergency call ☎ 090 988 52 26. The *carabinieri* (military police; Via Garibaldi) are at ☎ 090 981 13 33.

Citadel (Upper Town)

After Barbarossa's murderous rampage through the town in 1544 the Spaniards rebuilt and fortified Lipari in the area at the top of the small cliff between the two harbours. Although somewhat like closing the barn door after the horse has been captured, tortured and sold into slavery, the citadel's fortifications look impregnable enough and are still relatively intact.

Contained within the walls are substantial reminders of Lipari's troubled past. You enter the area via a set of steps (Via del Concordato) that lead up to the 17th-century **Cattedrale di San Bartolomeo**, built to replace the original Norman cathedral, which was destroyed by Barbarossa. The only element to survive the destruction is the 12th-century Benedictine cloister. The reconstruction (1654) features a handsome baroque facade. The interior is hung with chandeliers and features, in the northern transept, a silver statue of St Bartolomew (1728). The church is open from 9 am to 1 pm daily.

Around the cathedral are the crumbling ruins of a couple of other baroque churches, but the real area of interest is the **archaeological dig** in the southern half of the citadel. Here a rich collection of finds from the Neolithic age to the Roman era have been unearthed, giving archaeologists invaluable clues as to the different civilisations that at one time flourished in the Mediterranean. You won't make much sense of what's here, however, without visiting the town's archaeological museum, Museo Archeologico Eoliano, which is spread about a number of buildings within the citadel.

Museo Archeologico Eoliano If you're at all interested in Mediterranean archaeology and ancient history, this museum (☎ 090 988 01 74) is an absolute must, as it contains a collection of finds that is among the most complete in Europe. The **Archeological Section** (Sezione Archeologica) of the museum is divided into two buildings. Just south of the cathedral, the former Palazzo Vescovile (Bishop's Palace) is devoted to artefacts found on Lipari, beginning with the Neolithic and Bronze Ages upstairs and continuing in chronological order to the Roman age downstairs. Amid the plethora of artefacts – which include all kinds of pottery, flints and a variety of cutting tools – is some finely sculpted obsidian, telling evidence of the relative sophistication of prehistoric civilisation. Prehistoric finds from the other islands are housed in the small pavilion directly in front of the palace.

On the other side of the cathedral is the **Classical Section** (Sezione Classica), which houses finds uncovered from the island's necropolis (11th century BC). These are beautifully displayed, and include a sizeable collection of burial urns as well as a model of a Bronze-Age burial ground and Lipari's necropolis. Upstairs is an impressive array of decorated vases and the museum's most treasured items: the most complete collection of Greek theatrical masks in the world. In the same room are a number of statuettes of dancers and actors – the one of *Andromeda con Bambino* (Andromeda with Child) is particularly beautiful – and some elegant jewellery. The next room contains polychromatic vases decorated by an artist simply known as the 'Il Pittore Liparoto' (the Lipari Painter; 300–270 BC).

JANE SMITH

Masking a turbulent past: Lipari has been home to pirates and prisoners.

The last part of the museum is the **Epigraphic Section** (Sezione Epigrafica), housed in a smaller building behind the Archaeological Section. Here you will find a little garden of engraved stones as well a room of engraved Greek and Roman tombs.

The museum is open from 9 am to 1.30 pm Monday to Friday (to 1 pm on Sunday). The Classical Section is also open from 3 to 6 pm Monday to Saturday. Admission costs L8000.

The Rest of Town

The only worthwhile sight outside the citadel is the **Parco Archeologico Contrada Diana**, west of Corso Vittorio Emanuele, which has revealed part of the original Greek walls (5th and 4th centuries BC) as well a number of Roman houses. At the south-western end of the park is the necropolis, where the tombstones are still visible in the overgrown grass. The park, alas, is rarely open. All of the important finds, however, are housed in the archaeological section of the fascinating Museo Archeologico Eoliano.

Once you've satisfied your cravings for archaeological artefacts, there isn't much left to do save get down to the serious business of ambling around the narrow streets of the town, sitting at a port-side cafe or stretching out on the beach. The main drag is Corso Vittorio Emanuele, and here you'll find an assortment of boutiques, dive shops, grocery shops and restaurants. The best place to write your postcards is in the cafes around the **Marina Corta**, where you can watch the arrival of the hydrofoils, listen in on the animated conversations of the locals or watch the local potter fashion ceramic jars outside of a little shop.

Around Lipari

Although Lipari town is so self-contained that you could easily spend your entire holiday without going farther afield, the rest of the island is worth checking out, especially if you want to find the best swimming spots. Furthermore, it is small enough that a grand tour of the island's perimeter should take no more than 30 minutes by car or bus.

Canneto Only 3km north of Lipari town at the end of a short tunnel, Canneto is a quiet village with nothing much to offer other than to serve as an accommodation spillover when the main town is booked out. There are a couple of bars and shops on the beachfront – a long, pebbled stretch that isn not great for swimming – as well as a couple of hotels.

Just beyond the town (and a popular stop on the bus route) is the **Spiaggia Bianca**, a long sandy beach that is the most popular on the island. Its name means 'White Beach' and derives from the layers of pumice dust that once covered it. These have been slowly washed away by the rough winter seas, leaving it a darker shade of grey. For accommodation, see Places to Stay later in the chapter.

Cave di Pomice Between the Spiaggia Bianca and Porticello lie these pumice quarries at Campobianco, where the pumice that is a mainstay of Liparese industry is extracted for use in a plethora of ways, from toothpaste to construction. This unlikely place is one of the better spots to reach the sea, via one of the pumice chutes that allow you to slide directly into the azure water – a particularly brilliant version of blue due to the deposit of pumice dust – from the hillside above. Locals do it all the time, and the scene features in the Taviani brothers' classic film *Kaos*, based on short stories by Luigi Pirandello.

Above Campobianco looms the ancient crater of Mt Pilato (476m), the source of all of the pumice found in the area. The last eruption occurred in AD 700. All around the crater are fields of solidified obsidian known as the **Rocce Rosse** (Red Rocks) due to the colour of the stone. You can reach the crater via a path from the northern end of Campobianco (about 1.2km).

The bus winds its way northward to the little village of **Porticello**, which has small, stony **beach** and then on to Acquacalda on the northern side of the island. There's nothing much to do here but savour the views of Salina, Alicudi and Filicudi from the rugged cliffs.

West to Quattropani West of Lipari town (and accessible by bus from the Marina Lunga), through some lush vegetation, the road climbs for about 3km to the belvedere known as **Quattrocchi** (Four Eyes), although you'll only need two to appreciate the stunning views of Vulcano to the south. Less than 1km north is the small village of **Pianoconte**; a side road before the village proper veers off to the Roman baths of **San Calogero**, famous in antiquity for the thermal spring that flowed at a constant temperature of 60°C. The last stop on the bus route is at **Quattropani**, from where you can walk the 5km north to **Aquacalda** and catch a bus returning to Lipari.

Diving

Scuba diving is popular on Lipari. For information on courses, contact the Centro Nautico Eoliano (☎ 090 981 26 91), Salita San Giuseppe 8, or the tourist office.

Places to Stay

Lipari provides plenty of options for a comfortable stay, from budget to luxurious. On arrival you will be approached by touts offering you accommodation in a private house where you have your own room (usually a double) with private bathroom and cooking facilities. Don't ignore offers, as they are often ideal considering that there are no hotels in the budget category. In high season you might have to commit to a multi-day stay, sometimes even a week (but usually two nights).

Be warned that prices usually double between July and August and that accommodation can be very difficult to find, so book in advance. If all else fails in peak season, tourist office staff will billet new arrivals in private homes on the island.

To rent an apartment, contact the tourist office for a list of establishments.

Camping The island's camp site, *Baia Unci* (☎ 090 981 19 09), is at Canneto, about 3km out of Lipari town and accessible by bus from the Esso service station at Marina Lunga. Out-of-season prices are reasonable at L14,000 per person (there is no fee for the tent site) or L12,000 per person in a caravan plus L16,000 for the site. In peak season prices rise to L18,000 per person or L14,000 per person in a caravan plus L20,000 for the site.

Hostels The HI *Ostello della Gioventù Lipari* (☎ 090 981 15 40, Via Castello 17) is inside the walls of the citadel. B&B costs L18,500 per person, and L15,000 for a meal – or you can cook your own. It is open between March and October.

Private Homes Off Via Garibaldi near Marina Corta is *Casa Vittorio* (☎ 090 981 15 23, Vico *Sparviero 15)*, where a room costs L50,000 per person (L55,000 with private bathroom). There are also small apartments for L60,000 per person. There are two terraces with views, and use of the kitchen is L5000. You can find the owner (unless he finds you first) at Via Garibaldi 78, on the way from Marina Lunga to the city centre.

Diana Brown (☎ 090 981 25 84, fax 090 981 32 13, Vico Himera 3) is also very close to Marina Corta. It has rooms with bathroom and air-conditioning or apartments for L20,000 per person in the low season and up to L60,000 in August. *Enzo Il Negro* (☎/fax 090 981 31 63, Via Garibaldi 29) has spotless, comfortable digs for up to L60,000 per person in the high season. All rooms have bathroom, air-conditioning, a fridge and balcony, and there is a large terrace. *Lo Nardo Maria* (☎ 090 988 0431, fax 090 981 20 54, Vicolo Ulisse) has pleasant rooms complete with private bath and kitchen overlooking a narrow alleyway; there's a lovely terrace at the top of the house where the owner serves coffee and cold drinks in summer. Rooms (which can sleep up to three) cost L100,000 between May and September and L50,000 the rest of the year.

Hotels Off Corso Vittorio Emanuele, *Pensione Neri* (☎ 090 981 14 13, fax 090 981 36 42, Via G Marconi 43) is in a lovely old, renovated villa. In the low season, a double costs L110,000 and triples/quads L148,000/270,000; in summer, the prices jump to

THE AEOLIAN ISLANDS

L200,000 a double, L270,000 a triple and L340,000 a quad. All rooms have a bathroom and breakfast is included.

Hotel Oriente (☎ *090 981 14 93, fax 090 988 01 98*), next door at No 35, boasts a bar, garden and very comfortable rooms. Low/high season prices start at L55,000/130,000 for a single, L100,000/220,000 for a double and L135,000/280,000 for a triple; quads cost L170,000/340,000. All rooms include a bathroom, air-conditioning and breakfast.

In Canneto, *Hotel Odissea* (☎ *090 981 23 37, fax 090 988 01 98, Via Sauro 12*) has singles/doubles for L120,000/160,000 in the high season.

Lipari's top hotel is *Villa Meligunis* (☎ *090 981 24 26, fax 090 988 01 49, Via Marte 7*), on a hill overlooking Marina Corta. Room rates range from L170,000 to L340,000, depending on the season. The price includes breakfast.

Places to Eat

Try pasta with the island's excellent capers and be prepared to spend big to eat the day's sea catch, particularly swordfish. The waters of the archipelago abound in fish, including tuna, mullet, cuttlefish and sole, all of which end up on restaurant tables at the end of the day. The local wine is the sweet, white Malvasia.

If you have access to a kitchen, you can shop for supplies at the *grocery shops* along Corso Vittorio Emanuele.

Although prices go up in the high season, you can still eat cheaply by sticking to the pizzerie along Corso Vittorio Emanuele. *Il Galeone* (☎ *090 981 16 43, Corso Vittorio Emanuele 222*) has good pizzas for around L10,000 or a set lunch for L22,000. *Zum Willi* (☎ *090 981 14 73*) on the corner of Corso Vittorio Emanuele and Via Umberto I, is basically a bar that serves pizzas for L6000 to L12,000.

For a more complete meal, try *La Trattoria d'Oro* (☎ *090 981 25 91, Via Umberto I 28–32*). For an a-la-carte meal you'll pay around L35,000 and there is a good set menu for L20,000.

Da Bartolo (☎ *090 981 17 00, Via Gari-* *baldi 53*) is one of the island's better *trattorie* (restaurants) and a good choice for seafood. A full meal costs around L35,000. Near Marina Corta, on Via Roma, there are a couple of no-nonsense trattorie, including *Nenzyna* (☎ *090 981 16 60, Via Roma 2*) where you can eat for around L25,000.

Entertainment

Most of the town's nightlife is concentrated in and around the Marina Corta, where there are a handful of bars with outdoor seating. Just off the main square, *Chitarra* *(Salita San Giuseppe)* is a nice little bar where there is live music nightly between June and September. On the square itself, *Al Gabbiano* and *Al Pescatore* have outdoor

---

A Classic Dish

The islands are rightly recognised throughout Sicily for their excellent cuisine, particularly any dish to do with seafood. Here we have included a recipe for a classic, spaghetti with Mediterranean clams, which isn't too hard to make. The dish is for four people.

Spaghetti con le Vongole
400g Mediterranean clams
1 glass of Malvasia dry white wine
3 cloves of garlic (roughly chopped)
1 fresh tomato (diced)
400g of spaghetti
salt and pepper

Thoroughly wash the clams (if you can't get hold of Mediterranean clams other types will do at a pinch). Fry the garlic in a light spread of extra-virgin olive oil. Once browned, add the clams. When they have opened, slowly pour in the wine and wait until it evaporates. Next add the tomato and a pinch of salt and pepper.

During the preparation of the clams have the spaghetti boiling away. The key is to time the preparation of both so that when the clams are ready the spaghetti should be *al dente*, or slightly underdone. When the pasta is ready to go, add it and a ladle of water to the clams in the pan. Saute the whole lot for about one minute and serve.

seating and are very popular with tourists. The only late-night bar in town is **Kasbah Cafe** *(Via Maurolico 25)* which is open until 3 am in summer. Otherwise the town shuts down before midnight.

Getting There & Away
Siremar has two offices in Lipari, at Marina Corta (☎ 090 981 22 00) and on Via Amendola (☎ 090 981 13 12). SNAV (☎ 090 988 02 66) has an office at Marina Corta.

For details of ferry and hydrofoil departures for Milazzo and the other islands, see Getting There & Away and Getting Around at the beginning of this chapter.

Getting Around
Bus Urso buses (☎ 090 981 12 62) run an efficient and frequent service to every point of interest on the island, departing from the Esso service station at Marina Lunga. There are 13 departures for Canneto daily, leaving approximately every hour between 8 am and 9 pm; there is also a regular service to Acquacalda (L2500), Porticello (seven a day) and Quattrocchi (L3000, eight a day). During July and August the service increases to one every 30 minutes to Canneto and one every hour to Porticello and Quattrocchi. The company also offers special round trips of the island. The tourist office has a complete timetable of departures.

Boat Touring the island's waters by boat is the best way to get in some crowd-free swimming, especially in summer. Boats are available for hire at Foti Roberto (☎ 090 981 23 52), Via F Crispi 31, to the right as you leave Marina Lunga. A three-seater motorised rubber dinghy costs L100,000 per day and a 14-seater costs L450,000.

From March to October Viking (☎ 090 981 25 84), Vico Himera 3 (with a ticket booth at Marina Corta), conducts boat tours of all the islands, including one to Stromboli by night for L45,000 to see the Sciara del Fuoco (see Stromboli later in the chapter).

Scooter Foti Roberto also rents out scooters (up to L60,000 per day) and mopeds (L40,000 per day).

VULCANO
postcode 98050 • pop 800
• maximum elevation 500m

Just south of Lipari, and the first port of call for ferries and hydrofoils from Milazzo, Vulcano actually boasts three volcanoes – Vulcano Piano, Vulcanello and Fossa di Vulcano (or Gran Cratere, 'Large Crater'). Only the last of these is still considered active, although it is in its death throes. It constantly emits a thin fumarole, but the most damage it can do is expel an obnoxious stench of sulphurous gases, reminiscent of the smell of rotten eggs. You get a nasty whiff of it as you approach the dock by boat, and though it may put you off disembarking, rest assured that (surprisingly) everyone gets used to it pretty quickly.

Although uninhabited for millenia on account of the volcanic activity, the island today is a favourite playground of the Italian jet-set, with a number of fancy villas and exclusive hotels that cater to those with plenty of credit. Though you may want to give overnighting here a miss on account of the prices, the island is still an excellent destination for a day trip from Lipari. In addition to the volcano, the island also has one of the best beaches in the archipelago. The thermal baths are also renowned for their curative powers, especially for rheumatic pains.

History
To the ancient Greeks, the island of Thermessa, Terasia or Hiera – as Vulcano was variously known – must have inspired a good deal of respect, if not downright fear. Not only did the god of fire and war, Vulcan (Hephaestus to the Greeks), have his workshop here – where he was assisted by the cyclops – but Aeolus, the god of the wind, also swirled about. Still, the island's activity was a source of curiosity to the scientists of antiquity, including Thucydides, Xenofon, Strabo and the Roman writer Pliny, who chronicled the 'birth' of the youngest of the three volcanoes, Vulcanello, in 183 BC. The Romans established a working colony here as they sought to exploit the island's subsoil, rich in alum

euro currency converter L10,000 = €5.16

THE AEOLIAN ISLANDS

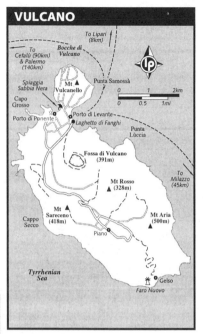

Money The Banco di Sicilia (☎ 090 985 23 35) in the port area has an ATM. It is open from 8.30 am to 1.30 pm and 2.45 to 3.45 pm Monday to Friday between June and September only. You can change money at the Thermessa agency (☎ 090 985 22 30), also in the port area.

Post & Communications The post office (☎ 090 985 30 02) is on Via Piano, which runs off Porto di Levante. There is a public telephone on Via Mercalli.

Medical Services & Emergency From June to September a doctor is on call at ☎ 090 985 22 20. The Bonarrigo pharmacy (☎ 090 985 22 44) is at Via Favoloro 1.

The carabinieri can be reached on ☎ 090 985 2110.

Things to See & Do
Once you've disembarked and settled in (if you plan to stay) you can head over to the **Laghetto di Fanghi,** Vulcano's famed mud baths, adjacent to the dock at the bottom of a 56m-high *faraglione* (stack), a long stone finger jutting up into the sky. The *fanghi* are actually one large mud pit of thick, hot, smelly, sulphurous gloop that has long been considered an excellent treatment for all kinds of rheumatic pains and skin diseases. Rolling around in the mud can be a tantalising experience, even if the smell is absolutely atrocious. If you plan on getting in, be careful to remove all watches and jewellery as the mud will ruin anything it comes in contact with. Also, wear something that you plan on throwing away soon after, because once the smell is in you'll never get rid of it. Experts have advised that prolonged immersion can be bad for you on account of the pit's slight radioactivity; consequently, you should not stay in for more than 10 or 15 minutes and pregnant women should avoid it altogether. Finally, don't let any of the mud get in your eyes as the sulphur can really sting.

When you're done, you can clean off in the nearby sea – a natural Jacuzzi with hot, bubbling water, it's perfect for relaxing in.

Once you're done with the mud baths,

and sulphur. Under the Bourbons the island was used as a working farm populated by convicts from Lipari, but the enterprise collapsed with the decline of the French dynasty. At the beginning of the 19th century a Scot named Stevenson purchased the northern part of the island with a view towards exploiting the island's resources much as the Romans had done, but his plans were shot due to a violent volcanic eruption. The most recent period of serious activity occurred between 1888 and 1890, and vulcanologists have assured us that it was definitely the last.

Information
Tourist Office The tourist office (☎ 090 985 20 28) is little more than a mobile stand in the port area. It is usually open from 8 am to 2 pm Monday to Saturday from June to October. Here you can get a list of accommodation as well as a couple of informative brochures on the island.

The Vulcan Winds

In Homer's *Odyssey* Vulcano is the realm of the wise and benevolent King Aeolus, who had inherited the island by marrying Cyane, the daughter of the island's first king, Liparo.

On their return from the 10-year war against Troy, Ulysses and his crew docked at Vulcano, where Aeolus welcomed them as his guests. On their departure Aeolus presented Ulysses with a present, a bag holding all of the Mediterranean's unfavourable winds that were capable of further delaying Ulysses' epic journey home. Left out of the bag was Zephyr, the only wind that was guaranteed to speed the ship's journey homeward. Aeolus' parting words to Ulysses were to keep the bag closed until he had arrived home. But things were never that easy for the poor voyager. Just as they were within sight of his home island of Ithaca, curiosity got the better of Ulysses' crew, who were convinced that the bag contained a fabulous treasure that their captain was keeping from them. Before Ulysses knew what was happening, the bag was opened and the enraged winds flew out, blowing the ship away from shore and back to Vulcano. Stunned at their greed and stupidity, Aeolus threw his former guests off the island and they once more resumed their journeys. It would be years before they would see Ithaca again.

the island's other main attraction is climbing the **Gran Cratere** (391m). Follow the signs for 'Al Cratere' which take you left (south) out of the port area along Via Provinciale. About 500m farther on a track slopes off to the left (also signposted) which leads up to the crater. It's about one hour's scramble over some pretty tough ground that is totally exposed to the sun, so make sure you wear strong shoes and bring plenty of water. When you've reached the top you can lean over a ledge and look into the main crater, the source of the nasty smell you've had in your nose the whole way up! A handkerchief to cover your mouth and nose wouldn't go amiss. From the top there are some splendid views of all of the other islands.

Swimming

On the far side of the peninsula from Porto di Levante at Porto di Ponente is the **Spiaggia Sabbia Nera** (Black Sand Beach), the only smooth, sandy beach on Vulcano and one of the nicest in the archipelago.

Paddle boats are usually available for hire on the beach (around L15,000 for one hour).

Places to Stay & Eat

Close to the mud baths (and their smell) *Pensione Agostino* (☎ 090 985 23 42, Via Favaloro 1) has doubles with bathroom costing L50,000/100,000 in low/high season. *Pensione La Giara* (☎ 090 985 22 29, Via Provinciale 18) is towards the Gran Cratere. A pleasant spot, its rooms cost around L45,000/90,000 per person, although the management prefers to charge by the week.

Also close to the mud baths, *Sea House Residence* (☎ 090 985 22 19) is a complex of self-contained two-, three-, four- and five-bed apartments in a garden setting. Prices start at L30,000 per person for a double in the low-season and rise to L120,000 in August. It is open from April to October. *Hotel Arcipelago* (☎ 090 9852 002) enjoys a beautiful position on the northern coast of Vulcano. Half board in July costs L185,000 per day or L160,000 if you stay more than six days.

For a decent meal, try *Da Maurizio* or *Da Vincenzino*, both on Via Porto di Levante. Another good option is *Il Caimano* in the Porto di Levante. Count on paying at least L30,000 for a starter and main course (invariably fish-based) at any of these places.

Getting There & Away

Vulcano is an intermediate stop between Milazzo and Lipari and a good number of vessels go both ways throughout the day. See the Getting There & Away section at the beginning of this chapter.

All boats and hydrofoils dock at the Porto di Levante, in the north-west of the island. To your right as you disembark is the small peninsula of Vulcanello.

Getting Around

Pino Marturano (☎ 090 985 24 19), Via Comunale Levante, near the Porto di Levante in

THE AEOLIAN ISLANDS

front of the tobacconist, organises boat trips around the island for L20,000 and to Stromboli for L45,000 (approximately eight hours). The proprietor of Gioielli del Mare (☎ 090 985 21 70) at Porto di Levante organises bus tours (about two hours) around the island for groups of at least 12 people. The price is L20,000 per person. Make a booking and hope a large enough group will form.

Viking (☎ 090 981 25 84) on Lipari offers a boat trip around the island for around L20,000 per person (see under Boat in Lipari's Getting Around section earlier in the chapter).

SALINA
postcode 98050 • pop 850
• maximum elevation 962m

Although it owes its modern name to the *saline* or saltworks of Lingua, Salina is defined and shaped by the two volcanoes that gave it its ancient Greek name of Dydime, meaning 'double'. Although extinct since antiquity, previous eruptions combined with plenty of water have rendered the island the most fertile in all the archipelago. The famous Aeolian capers grow plentiful here, as does the grape used in the production of the renowned Malvasia wine. Only on Salina are you assured of drinking the genuine article, as much of the Malvasia available on other islands is imported directly from the Sicilian mainland and the label slapped on to the bottle.

With the exception of Alicudi and Filicudi, this is the least visited of all the islands, though the number of tourists is growing every year. Consequently, the island isn't geared exclusively to the tourist industry; here you can get a partial impression of what daily life away from the islands' tourist traps is actually like, with most people going about their business – farming and fishing mostly – as they have done for centuries.

History

Salina has been inhabited since the Bronze Age, but the first real settlement dates back to the 4th century BC at Santa Marina Salina. The town was important throughout the Hellenistic and Roman ages as a centre for farming, and it continued to grow up to the 8th century AD, its population swelled by Liparese looking to avoid volcanic activity on Vulcano. Under the Arabs the island

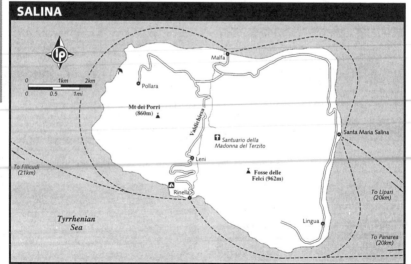

SALINA

Malfa

Pollara

Mt dei Porri
(860m)

Valdichiesa

Santuario della
Madonna del Terzito

Santa Maria Salina

Leni

To Filicudi
(21km)

Fosse delle
Felci (962m)

Rinella

To Lipari
(20km)

Tyrrhenian
Sea

Lingua

To Panarea
(20km)

0   1km   2km
0   0.5   1mi

Dwarfed by Mt Etna, the popular tourist-resort of Taormina is as big and brash as it comes in Sicily.

JUDY WILLOUGHBY

BETHUNE CARMICHAEL

BETHUNE CARMICHAEL

The smell of danger on Mt Etna   The breathtaking backdrop to the Greek Theatre in Taormina

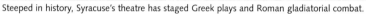

Steeped in history, Syracuse's theatre has staged Greek plays and Roman gladiatorial combat.

Syracuse cathedral is a blend of styles.

Showing the crocodile who's boss, Ragusa Ibla

Still waters belie a turbulent past. Syracuse boasts a rich archaeological and cultural heritage.

was stripped of its wealth and much of the populace was forced to leave; it was only during the 17th century that the island began to thrive once more.

Orientation & Information
Boats dock at Santa Marina Salina, where you will find most accommodation, or at Rinella, a fishing hamlet on the southern coast. The other main villages on the island are Malfa, on the northern coast, and Leni, slightly inland from Rinella.

In summer there are AAST booths in Rinella, Malfa and Santa Marina Salina. The only bank, Banca Agricola Etnea (☎ 090 984 40 62) on the island is in Malfa, at Via Provinciale 2. There is a post office (090 984 30 28) on Via Garibaldi in Santa Marina Salina, where you can also change money. There are a couple of public phones in Bar Rago (☎ 090 980 90 55), Via del Risorgimento 182, also in Santa Marina Salina. For medical assistance, call ☎ 090 984 40 05. For the police (questura), phone ☎ 090 984 30 19.

Things to See & Do
If you are feeling energetic, you could climb the Fosse delle Felci volcano (962m) and visit the nature reserve (riserva naturale). From Santa Marina Salina, head for Lingua, a small village 3km south, from where paths lead up the mountain (follow the signs for Brigantino). Along the way you'll see plenty of colourful flora, including wild violets, asparagus and a plant known locally as cipudazza (Urginea marittima), which was sold to the Calabrians to make soap but used locally as mouse poison! Corn and barley are the main crops around Brigantino, but as soon as you start climbing (take the path to the right) you will see plenty of olive trees which eventually give way to vineyards. A century ago the hilltops were covered in vine, but the local industry has suffered greatly at the hands of competition from the Sicilian mainland, leaving only a few cultivators of the famed Malvasia wine. Once you've reached the top (the last 100m are particularly tough) you have almost unparalleled views of the entire archipelago.

At Valdichiesa, in the valley separating the two volcanoes, is the Santuario della Madonna del Terzito (Sanctuary of the Madonna of Terzito), which is a place of pilgrimage, particularly around the Feast of the Assumption on 15 August.

Rinella is a popular underwater fishing spot. For information, contact the tourist office. Boats are available for rent from June to August at Nautica Levante (☎ 090 984 30 83), Via Lungomare, Santa Marina Salina.

Don't miss a trip to the beach at Pollara, the setting for much of Massimo Troisi's last film, Il Postino. The climb down is a bit tricky but the beach itself with its backdrop of cliffs is absolutely unbeatable.

Places to Stay & Eat
The island's only camp site is Camping Tre Pini (☎ 090 980 91 55), on the beach at Rinella. It costs L12,000/15,000 per person/site. The Pensione Mamma Santina (☎ 090 984 30 54, Via Sanità 40) is in Santa Marina Salina. Head for Via Risorgimento (the narrow main street) and walk north for a few hundred metres. The guesthouse is uphill along a winding lane to your left. Singles/doubles cost L40,000/ 60,000 per person. From June to September half board for up to L140,000 per person is obligatory.

Hotel L'Ariana (☎ 090 980 90 75, Via Rotabile 11) is in a late-19th-century villa overlooking the sea at Rinella. It has terraces and a bar. Half board (with bathroom) ranges from L85,000 in the low season to L150,000 in the high season; full board is from L115,000 to L180,000.

There are several restaurants clustered around the docks at Santa Marina Salina, including Portobello (☎ 090 984 31 25, Via Bianchi 1) – the best restaurant in town. You can eat exceptionally well for around L40,000. For fish dishes, Il Gambero (☎ 090 984 30 49) in Lingua is excellent and charges about the same. The restaurant in the Hotel L'Ariana is also good.

Getting There & Away
Hydrofoils and ferries service Santa Marina Salina and Rinella. There are eight hydrofoil connections between Santa Marina

THE AEOLIAN ISLANDS

Salina and the other islands daily from July to September; service is reduced at other times. There are four hydrofoils daily between Rinella and the other islands. Siremar has ticket booths at the harbours of Santa Marina Salina (☎ 090 984 30 04) and Rinella (☎ 090 980 91 70) as does SNAV (☎ 090 984 30 03 in Santa Marina Salina; ☎ 090 980 92 33 in Rinella). For information on arrivals and departures from Milazzo see the Getting There & Away section at the beginning of the chapter.

Getting Around

Regular buses run from Santa Marina Salina to Malfa and Lingua, and from Malfa to Leni and Rinella. Timetables are posted at the ports. Motorcycles are available for hire from Antonio Bongiorno (☎ 090 984 34 09), Via Risorgimento 240, Santa Marina Salina. A Vespa costs L40,000 a day and a moped L35,000 a day – the rate works out cheaper if you hire for longer periods.

PANAREA

postcode 98050 • pop 320
• maximum elevation 421m

Easily the most picturesque of the Aeolian Islands, tiny Panarea is 3km long and 2km wide. In recent decades it has taken on an air of exclusivity akin to Vulcano, as northern Italians, many of whom have bought summer homes here, descend on the island to make the most of the fabulous swimming and nice rocky beaches. Consequently, finding accommodation can be a nightmare – and grotesquely expensive – in the high season of July and August. Out of season, however, everything quietens down considerably and the prices drop accordingly.

The island's population lives almost exclusively on the eastern side of the island, in one of the three hamlets of Ditella, San Pietro and Drauto, although you'll hardly notice the difference between them as they have all melded into one strip of tangled lanes and pretty seafront houses. Addresses here are approximate as the intimacy of the place makes it unnecessary – everyone knows everyone else by name, history and quirky habits, and even the *forestieri* (out-

siders) who spend their summers here are known by their place of origin ('...oh, you mean that fellow from Turin who owns that fancy villa up past Piero's?..').

All boats dock at San Pietro, where you'll also find most of the accommodation.

In a medical emergency call ☎ 090 98 30 40. There is a pharmacy (☎ 090 98 31 48) on Via Iditella. You can call the carabinieri, between June and September only, on ☎ 090 98 31 81.

Things to See & Do

After wandering around San Pietro (where there's not much to see), head south to **Punta Milazzese**, about a 30-minute walk past a couple of beaches, to see the Bronze-Age village, made up of 23 huts, which was discovered in 1948. It is reckoned that the headland here was inhabited as far back as the 14th century BC, while pottery found at the site shows distinctly Minoan influences, lending credence to the theory that there were ties between the islanders and the Cretans. The artefacts found here are on display in the Museo Archeologico Eoliano at Lipari.

From the Punta Milazzese a set of steps leads down to the **Cala Junca**, a lovely little cove where the swimming is excellent and the water a deep aquamarine. The island's other nice beach is to the north of Ditella, at the end of a track – just follow the signposts for **Spiaggia Fumarola**. The 'Stone Beach' here is isolated and a perfect place for a quiet swim, except in July and August, of course, when the ringing of mobile phones is usually incessant.

Offshore Panarea's own little archipelago consists of six tiny islets off the eastern shore which can only be reached by boat (see Getting Around later in this chapter). The largest island is also the furthest away – **Basiluzzo** – which is given over exclusively to the cultivation of capers. At the back of the island – and visible from land – is the impressive wreck of a Roman ship.

Nearest to Panarea is **Dàttilo**, which has a pretty little beach called **Le Guglie**. Of the three little islands south of Dàttilo, you should make for **Lisca Bianca**, the one far-

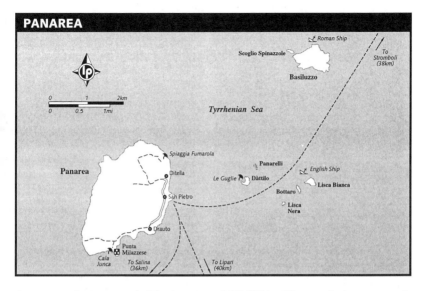

thest away, where you can indulge in your own little spot of wreck-hunting (although you won't find any treasure), if you're equipped with scuba gear. Crossing the narrow channel from the islet of **Bottaro** (actually nothing more than a protruding rock) to Lisca Bianca, you will notice there is a small white beach on Lisca Bianca's southern side. Proceed left past the beach and continue around the sharp point of the island. Here, at a depth of perhaps 40 or 50m, you will find the wreck of an old English ship which sunk in the 19th century.

Places to Stay & Eat

The closest you'll come to a cheap hotel here is the ***Locanda Rodà*** (☎ *090 98 30 23, Via San Pietro*) which is uphill from the port and to the left. Singles/doubles cost L50,000/100,000 and half board costs L110,000 in the low season and L145,000 in the high. It has a pizzeria/trattoria that charges average prices. ***La Sirena*** (☎ *090 98 30 12, Via Drautt 4*) is on the way to the Bronze-Age village and has doubles with bathroom for L120,000 and a pleasant trattoria. In July and August half board at

L160,000 is obligatory. In the same area is ***Trattoria da Pina*** (☎ *090 98 30 32*) with a terrace overlooking the sea. A meal at any of these places should cost no more than L40,000.

Getting There & Away

There are four daily hydrofoils (L23,000) and the occasional ferry (L13,000) daily that link the island with Stromboli to the north and Salina (and on to Lipari and Milazzo) to the south. Both Siremar (090 98 30 07) and SNAV (☎ 090 98 30 09) have offices along the harbour in San Pietro.

Getting Around

Cars are not allowed on Panarea, but you won't need them anyway as the island is small enough to get around on foot. You will, however, need to rent a boat to explore the small islands off its shores and some of the coves and beaches of the main island, which are otherwise inaccessible. Tesoriero (☎ 090 98 30 33) in San Pietro does all kinds of boat rentals, from rubber dinghies to wooden longboats with outboard motors. Expect to pay around L80,000 for four hours.

euro currency converter   L10,000 = €5.16

THE AEOLIAN ISLANDS

STROMBOLI
postcode 98050 • pop 500 • maximum elevation 924m

Stromboli is the most captivating of all the Aeolian Islands, largely because it is the only island to have a permanently active volcano. Experts and amateurs alike are attracted by the island's unique appeal, which combines an overwhelming natural beauty with the threat of the volcano's fiery rage. The Stromboli crater is the youngest in the archipelago – it was formed only 40,000 years ago – and it is still very much awake. It is very explosive, launching periodic showers of incandescent lava accompanied by the more or less violent emissions of sulphurous fumes and small overflows of lava. Technical volcano language, taking this kind of activity as a model, has come to include the term '*attività Stromboliana*' (Strombolian activity).

In recent years, eruptions have been of modest proportions and have occurred within the vicinity of the crater. A major eruption of the crater in 1930 was an additional cause of the emigration to Australia of many of the island's 5000 inhabitants (residents now number around 500). The last substantial eruption was in March 1996 and, although minor, left several people injured (see boxed text 'Facing the Volcano' on the next page). Still, lava flow is largely confined to the Sciara del Fuoco (Trail of Fire) on the volcano's north-western flank, leaving the villages of San Bartolo, San Vincenzo and Scari (which merge into one town) and Ginostra quite safe.

Although remote and farther away than most of the other islands, getting here is not a problem during the summer, when there is a regular ferry and hydrofoil service. In winter or in bad weather, however, the service is often disrupted or cancelled altogether.

Orientation
Boats arrive at Scari/San Vincenzo, downhill from the town. Accommodation is a short walk up the Scalo Scari to Via Roma, or, if you plan to head straight for the crater, follow the road along the waterfront (see Climbing the Volcano later in the chapter for details).

Information
The closest thing the island has to a tourist office is the privately owned Stromboliana information office (☎ 090 98 63 90) under the Ossidiana Hotel. It can help you organise accommodation as well as boat and bike rentals. It is open from 9 am to noon and 3 to 8 pm (9 pm in August) daily between Easter and September. A screen outside the office monitors the volcano's activity via a cable link. You can also try the volcano's own information office, Alpine Guides (☎ 090 98 62 63), just off Piazza San Vincenzo. It's nothing more than a shack and keeps irregular hours but you can get details of the state of the volcano and arrange a guide (see also Climbing the Volcano later in this chapter).

The post office (☎ 090 98 60 27) is on Via Roma. It is open from 8.20 am to 1.20 pm Monday to Saturday. You can exchange travellers cheques and cash. The

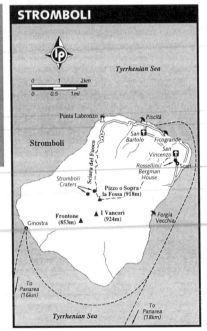

STROMBOLI

Tyrrhenian Sea

0   1   2km

0   0.5   1mi

Punta Labronzo ✴   Piscità

Stromboli   San
                   Bartolo   Ficogrande
                        San
                        Vincenzo
                   Rossellini /   Scari
                   Bergman
                   House
Stromboli
Craters   Pizzo o Sopra
                 la Fossa (918m)

Frontone   ▲ I Vancori   Forgia
(853m) ▲   (924m)   Vecchia
Ginostra

To
Panarea
(16km)

                                  To
                                  Panarea
Tyrrhenian Sea   (18km)

only bank (with ATM) is on Via Nunziante at Ficogrande. It is open only from June to September. Otherwise, exchange facilities are available at the travel agency, Le Isole e Terme d'Italia (☎ 090 98 62 74) on Via Roma near the port.

There is an emergency doctor in Stromboli (☎ 090 98 60 97) and Ginostra (☎ 090 981 2822). The Simone pharmacy (☎ 090 98 60 79) is on Via Roma. The carabinieri can be called on ☎ 090 98 60 21.

Around the Island

There is little to see here other than a couple of churches. Just outside the town (follow Via Roma, which then becomes Via Vittorio Emanuele), the **Chiesa di San Vincenzo** is an unremarkable building, but just a couple of doors down on the right (before the Barbablù hotel) is a **pink house** where Ingrid Bergman and Roberto Rossellini lived during the filming of *Stromboli* in 1949. Film buffs will surely be familiar with the scandal provoked by their liaison – Rossellini was a married man – which was the talk of the film world for a long time thereafter. Aside from a few ashen **beaches** on either side of the dock area (the one north of the dock is a popular spot for naturists), there is little else to do save tackle the ascent to the crater.

Climbing the Volcano

From the port, follow the road along the waterfront, continue straight past the beach at Ficogrande. Once past the village the path heads uphill, deviating after about 20 minutes to a bar/pizzeria and observatory. Alternatively, follow it through a slightly confusing section of reeds until it ascends to the crater. About halfway up is a good view of the **Sciara del Fuoco** (Trail of Fire), although in daylight the glow of the molten lava is imperceptible. The path eventually becomes quite steep and rocky. Note the warning signs at the summit and do not go too close to the edge. The round trip from the village should take about four hours.

The climb is a totally different experience at night, when darkness throws the molten lava of the Sciara del Fuoco and volcanic explosions into dramatic relief.

Facing the Volcano

Do not attempt climbing the crater without an authorised guide. At the point where the normal climb from Punta Labronzo begins, a very visible sign (in English and Italian) warns walkers not to continue unaccompanied, while a recent mayoral ordinance has expressly forbidden it (see Climbing the Volcano). Still, many visitors make the climb without a guide and some even pass the night at the crater, lulled by the rumblings of the eruptions, sheltered within the primitive *fortini* (forts). Many leave the area the following morning without clearing up their litter, an act of irresponsibility that not only ruins the crater's appeal but attracts rats in their dozens; they can be seen scurrying around the crater's edge foraging through the rubbish.

Although the volcano's eruptions rarely trouble the observation posts at the Pizzo or Sopra la Fossa, their power is an uncontrollable variable that must be considered by everyone who attempts the climb. In the unlikely event that you are caught in a hail of incandescent *lapilli* (pumice) or *bombe* (larger masses of molten rock), do not turn your back and try to run, no matter what your instincts say. The best way is to deal with them head on, as they are usually travelling slowly enough to allow you to dodge them easily. If you decide to sleep at the top of the crater, remember that you are at the volcano's mercy: during the 1996 eruptions one unsuspecting visitor was hit in the head while sleeping. He survived, but he didn't need a haircut for quite a while.

Experienced guides can be contacted through the Alpine Guides office (see Information earlier in the chapter). They take groups of 10 people or more to the crater at 4.30 pm daily (depending on weather conditions and if there are enough people to form a group), returning at 11.30 pm (about L30,000 per person). Contact the office around noon to make a booking. For the night climb, you will need heavy shoes and clothing for cold, wet weather, a torch (flashlight), food and a good supply of water. Even during the day, you will need heavy, wet-weather clothing, as conditions are unpredictable.

See Lonely Planet's *Walking in Italy* for more detailed descriptions of walks on Stromboli, both on the volcano and around the island.

Water Sports

La Sirenetta Diving Center (☎ 090 98 60 25), Via Marina 33, at La Sirenetta Park Hotel, offers diving courses. Alternatively, make your way to the beach of rocks and black volcanic sand at Ficogrande to swim and sunbathe.

Places to Stay & Eat

There's nothing much in the budget bracket on Stromboli. One of the cheapest options is the *Casa del Sole (☎ 090 98 60 17, Via Soldato Cincotta)*, off the road to the volcano, before you reach Ficogrande. It is popular with young people, and has single/double rooms costing L25,000/30,000 in the low season, including use of the kitchen. Prices go up by L10,000 in the high season. You will also find a few *affittacamere* (private lodgings), charging from L40,000 per person for a room in the high season. *Locanda Stella (☎ 090 98 60 00, Via Fabio Filzi 14)* has doubles for L85,000 and charges L140,000 for obligatory full board in July/August. *Barbablù (☎ 090 98 61 18, Via Vittorio Emanuele 17)* is a pleasant guesthouse charging from L120,000 to L260,000 for a double with breakfast, depending on the season.

Hotel Villaggio Stromboli (☎ 090 98 60 18, Via Regina Elena) has rooms costing L145,000/250,000 in the high season. It is on the beach front and has a terrace bar/restaurant. *Park Hotel la Sirenetta (☎ 090 98 602 5, fax 090 98 61 24)* is perfectly located on the beach at Ficogrande in front of Strombolicchio, a towering rock rising out of the sea at San Vincenzo. The hotel has a swimming pool, a panoramic terrace with a restaurant and one of the best chefs on the island. Half board in July costs L170,000 per person and L210,000 in August.

For a reasonably priced meal, try *La Trottola* on Via Roma. The *Punta Lena* on the Lungomare, walking away from the northern port towards the volcano, is more expensive and has a terrace overlooking the sea. The pizzeria at the observatory, about 20 minutes walk up the lower slope of the volcano, is also reasonable.

Getting There & Away

There are four hydrofoil and ferry connections between Stromboli and the other islands daily. It takes four hours by ferry to reach the island from Lipari, only two hours by hydrofoil. Ticket offices for SNAV (☎ 090 98 60 03) and Siremar (☎ 090 98 60 18) are at the port. Bear in mind the cost of the trip and the distance if you're considering a day visit – which in any case will rob you of the opportunity of a night climb up the volcano. Heavy seas can cause cancellation of ferry and hydrofoil services.

Getting Around

The Società Navigazione Pippo (☎ 090 98 61 35), Via Roma 47, organises nightly boat trips to view the Sciara del Fuoco from the sea. The boat, named *Pippo*, leaves at 10 pm from the northern port and at 10.10 pm from Ficogrande. The tour costs L25,000 per person and lasts 2½ hours. The same company also runs two daytime trips, leaving at 10 am and 3 pm. Viking offers a similar boat trip, starting in Lipari and departing from the Stromboli ferry port for the Sciara del Fuoco at 8 pm. The same boat also heads out to the Strombolicchio rock, a popular spot for underwater fishing.

FILICUDI & ALICUDI
postcode 98050 • pop 400

The two remotest islands of the Aeolian archipelago are also the least developed, certainly in tourist terms. Battered by winds and rough seas for much of the year, they are also the most difficult to get to, with ferry and hydrofoil services to the islands often cancelled due to bad weather. When the weather is clement, however, these are the islands to visit if you're feeling a strong desire to get away from it all. There is no place in the entire Mediterranean basin with fewer facilities, and the torrent of tourists that

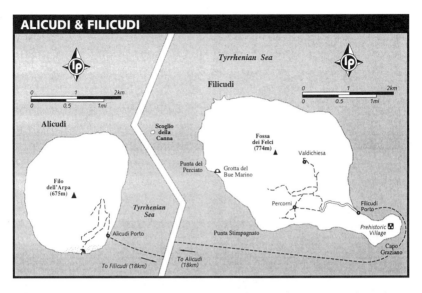

flood the other islands is reduced here to a slow, unsteady trickle. Of the two islands, Filicudi – only an hour by hydrofoil from Lipari – is the more developed. The island has a handful of hotels and an equal number of restaurants, which is more than can be said for its remote sister to the west, a place where electricity is at a premium and a public phone an unheard-of luxury.

Filicudi
maximum elevation 774m
Landing on Filicudi can be a disappointing experience. The port area is a mass of grey concrete houses and one large resort hotel. Once you've moved on the disappointment will fade. The town itself is of no particular interest, but it is where you'll find most of the island's limited facilities, including a small post office (☎ 090 988 90 53) – which is usually open from 9 am to 1 pm Monday to Friday – a public phone and a general store that doubles up as a pharmacy, open from 9.30 to 11.45 am Tuesday, Thursday and Saturday only.

In a medical emergency call the doctor on ☎ 090 988 9961. The carabinieri are on ☎ 090 988 9942.

Things to See & Do The main road goes south-east towards Capo Graziano and the **prehistoric village**, a smattering of Bronze-Age huts that predate Panarea's Punta Milazzese by a few hundred years. The site, discovered in 1952, is always open. From the village you can descend to Filicudi's only real **beach**, a stony affair that offers the easiest swimming on the island – if you want to take a dip elsewhere you'll have to clamber down some jagged rocks or rent a boat.

West of the port via a set of steep steps along the side of the Hotel Phenicusa (see Places to Stay & Eat) is the path to the centre of the island. After about 10 minutes the road forks. You can go north (right) to **Valdichiesa**, a run-down little village on a hillside terrace that has great views. There's little to see here save the seriously dilapidated church – it's nothing short of a miracle that it hasn't collapsed under its own weight (though by the time you read this it may well have done) – it is a pretty unassuming place where you can rest for a few minutes before moving on. Above the village is the peak of the **Fossa dei Felci** (774m), which you can climb – just keep walking in the general direction of the peak.

Alternatively, you can take the path that leads south (left) at the fork and make your way down to the little hamlet of **Pecorini**, nothing more than a cluster of one-storey houses huddled around a church. There are a couple of restaurants here (see Places to Stay & Eat).

The best way of visiting the island, however, is by boat. There's usually someone around the port renting them out for around L30,000 per person for a two hour trip during July and August – less at other times of the year – but if there isn't just ask at any of the shops around the port.

Around the uninhabited western side of the island is the natural arch of the **Punta del Perciato** (Perciato Point) and the nearby **Grotta del Bue Marino** (Cave of the Monk Seal). This cavity is 37m long by 30m wide, and named after the seals that once lived here. You won't see any now, though, as the last one was harpooned about 35 years ago. To the north-east is the **Scoglio della Canna** (Cane Reef), a long, thin stack of rock 71m high that is perhaps the Aeolian's most impressive such feature.

Places to Stay & Eat The island has a handful of places to stay. In the port district, the best of the lot is *La Canna* (☎ *090 988 99 56, Via Rosa 43)*, just uphill from the port, which has doubles costing L80,000 and half board for L115,000 per person in the high season. The food is delicious and the terrace where you dine has wonderful panoramic views. The large imposing hotel that dominates the port is the *Hotel Phenicusa* (☎ *090 988 99 46, Via Porto)*. It has compulsory half board at L90,000 in July and is closed from October to April.

If you don't want to stay in this area, you have two other options. Beyond La Canna at the junction of Via Rosa is *Villa La Rosa* (☎ *090 988 99 65)*, a private residence that rents out doubles/triples for L100,000/135,000 in July and August and L50,000/70,000 at other times of the year. Towards the sea just outside Pecorini, you can try *La Sirena* (☎ *090 988 99 97, Via Pecorini Mare)* which has singles/doubles with bath for L70,000/120,000. Breakfast is included.

For something to eat you can try *Capo Graziano* along the port, or the restaurant in *La Canna*. In Pecorini, *La Sirena* is also a good place for a home-cooked meal.

Alicudi
maximum elevation 675m

When the French novelist Alexandre Dumas visited Alicudi during the 19th century, he wrote to his wife that

'it is hard to find a sadder, more dismal and desolate place than this unfortunate island...a corner of the earth forgotten by creation and which has remained unchanged since the days of chaos.'

The barren nature of the island clearly was not to Mr Dumas' liking, and in some respects he wasn't far wrong in his description.

The island is as isolated a place as you'll find in the entire Mediterranean basin, with minimal facilities (one hotel and restaurant). For a time it served as the Italian equivalent of the French penal colony on Devil's Island off French Guiana, with Mafia prisoners being sent here to serve lengthy prison sentences, but that practice was phased out with the construction of maximum-security prisons on the mainland. Today it is home to a handful of farmers and fishermen who have only recently seen the arrival of electricity and television. The island has no roads to speak of, but it does have a couple of grocery shops – which is convenient considering that you'll need them if you want to eat. There's a post office (☎ 090 988 99 11) by the port that keeps erratic hours; you'll just have to try your luck when you get here.

The doctor is on ☎ 090 988 99 13.

Activities The only thing to do on the island is to climb the central peak of the **Filo dell'Arpa** (String of the Harp; 672m), a hardy, two-hour trek up a pretty rocky path. Be sure to wear sturdy shoes and bring plenty of water as there is absolutely no shade along the way. The only reason for climbing to the top is for the panoramic view. Otherwise, there is nothing else to do save mooch around and find a nice place to sunbathe – the best spots are to the south of the port, where you will have to clamber over some boulders to reach the sea. As you would expect, the waters are crystal clear and there's nothing to disturb you save the occasional hum of a fisherman's boat.

Place to Stay & Eat There is only one hotel and restaurant, the *Ericusa (☎ 090 988 99 02, Via Regina Elena)*. Doubles cost L105,000 and half board is L105,000 per person. It is open only from May to September and it is strongly advised that you book in advance.

Getting There & Away The two islands are the most difficult to reach on account of the intermittent ferry and hydrofoil service, which in winter is virtually non-existent and in summer can be cancelled due to rough seas. In Filicudi, Siremar (☎ 090 988 99 60) and SNAV (☎ 090 988 99 84) both have ticket offices along the port. In Alicudi, both Siremar (☎ 090 988 97 95) and SNAV (☎ 090 988 99 12) are on Via Regina Elena, which runs parallel to the port. At the height of summer both islands are served by three hydrofoils and one ferry daily. See the Getting Around section at the beginning of the chapter for details.

The Eastern Coast

Squeezed in by the long range of the Peloritani mountains to the west and the narrow strait that separates Sicily from Italy to the east, the thin ribbon of coastline that makes up the island's eastern shore is easily Sicily's most popular tourist destination. At its northern end is Messina, the first port of call for travellers crossing the sliver of water that divides the island from the mainland. Although hardly a prime destination in itself, it is surrounded by pleasant seaside towns amid some of the most colourful flora to be found anywhere on the island.

To the south is Catania, point of arrival for many of Sicily's airborne visitors and home to a splendid collection of baroque churches and *palazzi*. The most popular destination, however, lies between the two: the elegant resort of Taormina, a handsome medieval town that was 'discovered' in the 20th century by Europe's elite and adopted as one of their favourite summer playgrounds.

Towering above them all is the mighty peak of Mt Etna (3323m), Europe's largest and most active volcano. It rises west of the Peloritani mountains, where you'll find a couple of splendid hill towns that seem entirely unaffected by the advances of the modern age.

Highlights

- Try a little play-acting in the stunning ruins of Taormina's Greek theatre
- Take a walk near the summit of Mt Etna: you'll rarely see flowing lava this close up
- Enjoy a drink in Savoca's Bar Vitelli, used in Francis Ford Coppola's film *The Godfather* – it's a place so stereotypically Sicillian that it seems almost fictional
- Go for a dip in the Gola del Alcàntara
- Have a night out in Catania after spending the day walking around the city's sumptuous baroque centre

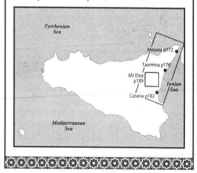

Messina & Around

MESSINA
postcode 98100 • pop 268,000

For many, Messina is their point of arrival in Sicily and you could hardly imagine a less auspicious introduction. From the sea, the wide curve of its beautiful harbour promises much, but once you hit dry land you realise that you left the best behind you. Although prosperous and industrialised, Messina is little more than a transit point for the rest of the island, with little to offer in the way of sights. The city is innocent of all charges, however, as it has been the unfortunate victim of a series of disasters, including two major earthquakes, a few epidemics and a dose of carpet bombing in WWII. Rebuilt after each disaster, Messina is unlike other Sicilian cities to have suffered at the hands of nature and humankind, as the visionary architects and town planners weren't around for the reconstruction. If for any reason you're stuck in Messina, don't despair. The city centre, with its wide avenues, is not a bad place to wander around, and there remain a couple of vestiges of happier days.

History

Founded as a Siculian settlement in 628 BC, Zankle (meaning sickle, on account of the shape of the bay) was conquered by the Greek Dionysius three centuries later, whereupon its name was changed. Strategically located at the heart of the trading routes that linked the four compass points, the city quickly prospered, its role greatly enhanced following the Roman takeover in the 3rd century BC and the construction of two main roads linking the city with Palermo and Catania. Under successive occupants the city continued to grow, and when the Spanish viceroys took charge in the 16th century, Messina was doing a roaring trade in silk, wool and leather. An ambitious building program was undertaken, but much of the new construction came to a sorry end in 1783, when the area was devastated by an earthquake. In the 19th century Messina tried again: a regular ferry service was established across the strait and its links with other Sicilian cities improved with the construction of new roads linking the port with Palermo, Catania and Syracuse. This new-found prosperity was short-lived: no sooner had the city reached the 20th century than disaster struck once more.

The earthquake of 1908 killed over 80,000 people and flattened the city. Deflated, demoralised and understandably panicked, city planners opted for safety over aesthetics and began rebuilding with the one objective of making everything quake-proof. Short, squat and solid were the guidelines of the 'Borzi Plan' (devised in 1911 by chief architect Paolo Borzi), and while this did nothing for the overall appearance of Messina (and generated a huge amount of indignant protest), it sought to allay the fears of those who had survived the terrible devastation.

What nature couldn't destroy, however, the human hand could: in 1943 the Allies carpet bombed the city and once again Messina was forced to rebuild. With such a history of tragedy, it is easy to forgive the unimaginative blandness that characterises the city today. Hardly appealing, but safe as houses.

Orientation

The train station is on Piazza della Repubblica, at the southern end of the long waterfront. FS car and truck ferries arrive just north of here. The main intercity bus station

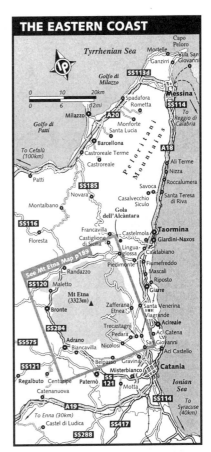

is outside the train station, to the left on the square. To get to the city centre from Piazza della Repubblica, walk either straight across the square and directly ahead along Via I Settembre to the Piazza del Duomo, or turn left into Via Giuseppe La Farina and take the first right into Via Tommaso Cannizzaro to reach Piazza Cairoli.

Those coming by hydrofoil from Reggio di Calabria arrive about 1km north of the train station, on Via Vittorio Emanuele II, while drivers on the private car ferry from Villa San Giovanni land 3km farther on, about 500m north of the trade fair area (Fiera).

THE EASTERN COAST

Information

Tourist Offices There are two tourist offices in Messina that are open year-round. The better-informed, better-equipped provincial AAPIT office (☎ 090 67 42 36) is at Via Calabria 301, 100m to the right as you leave the train station. It is open from 8 am to 2 pm and 3.30 to 7 pm Monday to Saturday, between May and October. The city tourist office (☎ 090 292 32 92) is on the 3rd floor at Piazza Cairoli 45. It keeps the same hours as the AAPIT office. Although ostensibly the main source of information on Messina, at the time of research the city tourist office had a paltry stock and provided little more than a map and an out-of-date list of hotels.

From May to October only there is a third tourist office, the Ufficio Informazioni del Comune (☎ 090 67 29 44), on the corner of Piazza Repubblica and Via Calabria, which deals with the sea of visitors that flows out of the train station in front. It is open from 8.30 am to 1.30 pm and 3 to 6 pm Monday to Friday (mornings only on Saturday). It provides pretty much the same information as the AAPIT office down the road.

Money There are numerous banks in the city centre between Piazza Repubblica and Piazza Cairoli – most with ATMs – and a currency exchange booth at the timetable information office at the train station.

Post & Communications The main post office is on Piazza Antonello on Corso Cavour, near the cathedral. It is open from 8.30 am to 6.30 pm Monday to Saturday. There is a Telecom office on Corso Cavour, near Via Tommaso Cannizzaro.

Travel Agencies The CTS student travel group has an agency (☎ 090 292 67 61) at Via Ugo Bassi 93. Lisciotto Viaggi (☎ 090 71 90 01), at Piazza Cairoli 13, specialises in hard-to-get theatre tickets for performances at such venues as Taormina's Greek theatre (see Taormina later in this chapter).

Medical Services & Emergency The public hospital, the Ospedale Piemonte (☎ 090 22 22 11), is on Viale Europa; at

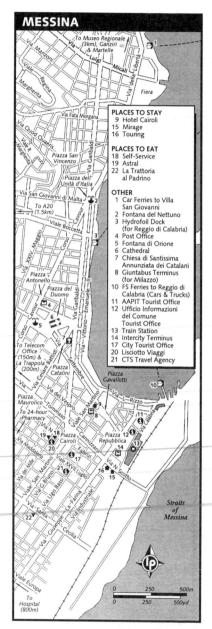

MESSINA

PLACES TO STAY
9 Hotel Cairoli
15 Mirage
16 Touring

PLACES TO EAT
18 Self-Service
19 Astral
22 La Trattoria al Padrino

OTHER
1 Car Ferries to Villa San Giovanni
2 Fontana del Nettuno
3 Hydrofoil Dock (for Reggio di Calabria)
4 Post Office
5 Fontana di Orione
6 Cathedral
7 Chiesa di Santissima Annunziata dei Catalani
8 Giuntabus Terminus (for Milazzo)
10 FS Ferries to Reggio di Calabria (Cars & Trucks)
11 AAPIT Tourist Office
12 Ufficio Informazioni del Comune Tourist Office
13 Train Station
14 Intercity Terminus
17 City Tourist Office
20 Lisciotto Viaggi
21 CTS Travel Agency

night, call ☎ 090 67 50 48. For emergencies, call ☎ 090 222 42 38. There is a 24-hour pharmacy (☎ 090 34 54 22) at the corner of Via Cesare Battisti and Via Camiciotti. A booklet available at the tourist office lists pharmacies open at night on a rotation basis.

The police station (*questura*; ☎ 090 3661) is at Via Plàcida 2. The *carabinieri* (military police) are at Via Monsignor d'Arrigo 5.

Things to See & Do

The Norman **cathedral**, built in the 12th century, was almost completely destroyed by the combined effects of the 1908 earthquake and the bombing in 1943. It was rebuilt virtually from scratch; the fine 15th-century doorway is one of the few original elements. The clock tower houses what is believed to be the world's largest astronomical clock, an intricate bit of machinery that is best appreciated during the noon strike.

In the square facing the cathedral is the **Fontana di Orione** (Orion's Fountain), an elegant 16th-century work by Giovanni Angelo Montorsoli. Built to commemorate the construction of Messina's first aqueduct, the figures that adorn the fountain are intended to represent the Tiber, Nile, Ebro and Camaro rivers, while the verses carved into the stone allude to water-related themes.

Nearby, in Piazza Catalani, off Via Garibaldi, is the 12th-century **Chiesa della Santissima Annunziata dei Catalani**, a jewel of Arab-Norman construction. The statue in front of it is a monument to Don John of Austria, who beat the Turks at the Battle of Lepanto in 1571. Farther north, where Via Garibaldi spills into Piazza dell'Unità d'Italia, is Messina's other great fountain, the 16th-century **Fontana del Nettuno** (Neptune's Fountain).

The **Museo Regionale** (☎ 090 36 12 92), at Viale della Libertà 465 (a bit of a walk from the cathedral or take bus No 8 from the train station), was set up in 1914 to house the works formerly kept in a monastery destroyed by the earthquake of 1908. The gallery's most famous work is the *San Gregorio* (St Gregory) polyptych by local boy Antonello da Messina, born here in 1430. Although in pretty shoddy condition, the five panels of the piece are wonderfully figurative. Other highlights include a *Madonna col Bambino e Santi* (Virgin and Child with Saints) by the same artist and two splendid works by Caravaggio, the *Adorazione dei Pecorai* (Adoration of the Shepherds) and *Risurrezione di Lazzaro* (Resurrection of Lazarus). The museum is open from 9 am to 1.30 pm daily and (oddly) on even days from 4 to 6.30 pm May to October and 3 to 5.30 pm the rest of the year. Admission costs L8000.

Places to Stay & Eat

A couple of hotels are close to the train station. ***Touring*** (☎ 090 293 88 51, Via N Scotto 17) charges L35,000/65,000 for singles/doubles without bathroom and L60,000/ 100,000 with bathroom. A few doors down the street, ***Mirage*** (☎ 090 293 88 44, Via N Scotto 3) has singles/doubles without bathroom for L40,000/70,000 and doubles with bathroom for L98,000. Rates go down substantially out of season. The ***Hotel Cairoli*** (☎ 090 67 37 55, Viale San Martino 63) is of a higher standard and charges L86,000/140,000 for rooms with bathroom and breakfast.

Relaxing by the water on the mid-16th-century Fontana di Orione

THE EASTERN COAST

Cheap eats in Messina are not a problem. *Astral (Via XXVII Luglio 71)*, just off Piazza Cairoli, serves up surprisingly good, if basic, food on plastic plates; expect to pay no more than L10,000 for a main and a drink. *Self-Service (Via dei Mille 12)*, a cafeteria-style lunch spot, is popular with locals in a hurry. *La Trappola (Via dei Verdi 39)* is near the university area. Its good meals are reasonably priced, but not rock-bottom. *La Trattoria al Padrino (Via Santa Cecilia 54)* is a simple place where a meal will cost around L30,000.

Getting There & Away

Bus Interbus (☎ 090 66 17 54) runs a regular service (approximately every hour; last bus leaves at 8 pm) to Taormina (L5000 one way), Catania (L10,500 one way) and Catania's airport. The company's office and bus station are at Piazza della Repubblica 6, to the left as you leave the train station. Segesta has a direct connection to Rome (see Bus in the Getting There & Away chapter). Giuntabus (☎ 090 67 37 82) runs a service to Milazzo (for ferries and hydrofoils to the Aeolian Islands) roughly every hour from Via Terranova 8, on the corner of Viale San Martino.

Train Regular trains connect Messina with Catania, Taormina, Syracuse, Palermo and Milazzo, but buses are generally faster. The train stations for Milazzo and Taormina are inconveniently located some distance from the city centre.

Car & Motorcycle If you arrive in Messina by FS ferry with a vehicle (see also the Getting There & Away chapter), it is simple to make your way out of town. For Palermo (or Milazzo and the Aeolian Islands), turn right as you exit the docks and follow Via L Rizzo (which then becomes Via Vittorio Emanuele II) until you get to Piazza dell'Unità d'Italia. From there, go north along Via Garibaldi. After about 1km, turn left into Viale Boccetta and follow the green *autostrada* (motorway) signs for Palermo. To reach Taormina and Syracuse, turn right onto Via L Rizzo and then take the first left onto Via C Vettoragile, which then becomes Via Giuseppe La Farina, and follow.

If you arrive by private ferry, turn right along Viale della Libertà for Palermo and Milazzo, and left for Taormina and Catania – follow the green autostrada signs. You can also take the SS114 (busy in summer).

Boat Messina is the main point of arrival for ferries and hydrofoils from the Italian mainland, only a 20-minute trip across the narrow straits. For information see Sea in the Getting There & Away chapter. SNAV (☎ 090 36 21 14) hydrofoils link Messina with the Aeolian Islands (Lipari L31,000 one way).

AROUND MESSINA
Ganzirri
postcode 98100 • pop 170
Only 8km north of Messina and accessible via bus Nos 79 and 81 from Piazza della Repubblica, Ganzirri is a pleasant town that on summer evenings plays host to the crowds of youths from the city, who come for the town's bars and restaurants.

Places to Eat Sandwiched as the town is between the sea and a series of brackish ponds that are renowned for their mussels, it's hardly surprising that seafood dominates the menu. Of the many *trattorie* (small, cheap restaurants), *La Terrazza* (☎ 090 39 36 26, Via Lago Grande 57) is pretty good; you should be able to get some change out of L30,000. Otherwise, you could try *Mancuso* (☎ 090 39 21 68, Via Lago Grande 96), which has a tasty tourist menu for L22,000. The more upmarket *Il Gambero Rosso* (☎ 090 39 38 73, Via Pompea 143b) is pricier (around L50,000), but the fish is superb.

Mortelle
postcode 98100 • pop 240
A farther 10km on from Ganzirri (around the tip of the island) is the area's most popular summer resort, *the* place the Messinese go to sunbathe, hang out and eat. On summer evenings, you can hardly walk around for the number of scooters and motorcycles in the place, while during the day you'll have to get down to the beach early if you want to get a good spot.

In July and August, the Arena Green Sky, opposite the Due Palme pizzeria, shows open-air films nightly: screenings are at 8 and 10.45 pm. Tickets cost L8500.

To get here, take bus No 80 from Piazza della Repubblica.

Places to Eat There are plenty of pizzerias and trattorie in town and all serve a similar menu of fish-based dishes. If you fancy a splurge, however, you should go to *Lo Sporting da Alberto* (☎ 090 32 13 90, *Via Nazionale*). Reputed to be the best restaurant in this part of the island, it is frequented by Messina's well-to-do crowd. Not surprisingly, you won't see much change out of L100,000.

Taormina & Around

TAORMINA
postcode 98039 • pop 10,500
• elevation 204m

Sicily's most picturesque town and best-known resort is spectacularly located on a terrace of Mt Tauro, dominating the sea and with views westwards to Mt Etna. A favourite playground of the European jet set, Taormina is given over almost exclusively to the lucrative business of high-end tourism, at least from April through to October. Consequently, *everything* here is expensive and – at least for some travellers – a little glitzy and kitsch. It would be a shame to miss this place, though, as its magnificent setting, Greek theatre and nearby beaches remain as seductive as they were for the likes of Goethe and DH Lawrence.

Travellers should note that in July and August the town is flooded with tourists; it is difficult to find accommodation and even dining can be a problem. A good time to come is at either end of the busy season, when everything quietens down a little bit; perhaps the best time is towards the end of September, when it is still hot but not nearly as crowded.

History
From its foundation by the Siculians, Taormina remained a favourite destination for the long line of conquerors who fol-lowed. Under the Greeks, who moved in after Naxos was destroyed during colonial wars in the 5th century BC, Taormina flour-ished. It later came under Roman dominion and eventually became the capital of Byzantine Sicily, a period of grandeur that ended abruptly in AD 902 when the town was destroyed by Arab invaders. Throughout the subsequent periods of Norman, Spanish and French rules 'Taormina was an important centre of art and trade. Despite the heavy influx of tourism, Taormina today retains much of its medieval character.

Orientation
The train station (Taormina-Giardini) is at the foot of Mt Tauro, and you'll need to get an Interbus bus (L1500) up to the bus station (for local and intercity buses – where you'll arrive anyway if you catch the bus from Messina) in Via Pirandello. A short walk uphill from there brings you to the old city entrance and Corso Umberto I, which traverses the town.

Information
Tourist Offices The well-stocked and friendly AAST office (☎ 0942 2 32 43) is in Palazzo Corvaja, just off Corso Umberto I, near Piazza Santa Caterina. The office also has a useful and informative Web site at www.taormina-ol.it. It is open from 8 am to 2 pm and 4 to 7 pm Monday to Saturday and from 9 am to 1 pm on Sunday.

Money There are several banks in Taormina, mostly along Corso Umberto I. You'll also find currency exchange places along the same street. Check the commissions they charge. Several banks, such as the Monte dei Paschi di Siena on Piazza del Duomo, have user-friendly ATMs. Amex is represented by La Duca Viaggi (☎ 0942 62 52 55), Via Don Bosco 39.

Post & Communications The main post office is on Piazza Sant'Antonio, just outside the Porta Catania, at the far end of Corso Umberto I from the tourist office. There are public telephones in the Avis office (☎ 0942 2 30 41), Via San Pancrazio 7,

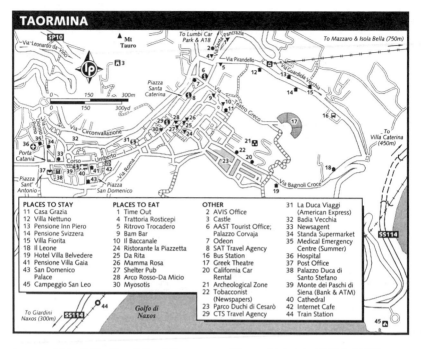

TAORMINA

PLACES TO STAY
11 Casa Grazia
12 Villa Nettuno
13 Pensione Inn Piero
14 Pensione Svizzera
15 Villa Fiorita
18 Il Leone
19 Hotel Villa Belvedere
41 Pensione Villa Gaia
43 San Domenico
     Palace
45 Campeggio San Leo

PLACES TO EAT
1 Time Out
4 Trattoria Rosticepi
5 Ritrovo Trocadero
9 Bam Bar
10 Il Baccanale
24 Ristorante la Piazzetta
25 Da Rita
26 Mamma Rosa
27 Shelter Pub
28 Arco Rosso-Da Micio
30 Myosotis

OTHER
2 AVIS Office
3 Castle
6 AAST Tourist Office;
   Palazzo Corvaja
7 Odeon
8 SAT Travel Agency
16 Bus Station
17 Greek Theatre
20 California Car
   Rental
21 Archeological Zone
22 Tobacconist
   (Newspapers)
23 Parco Duchi di Cesarò
29 CTS Travel Agency

31 La Duca Viaggi
   (American Express)
32 Badia Vecchia
33 Newsagent
34 Standa Supermarket
35 Medical Emergency
   Centre (Summer)
36 Hospital
37 Post Office
38 Palazzo Duca di
   Santo Stefano
39 Monte dei Paschi di
   Siena (Bank & ATM)
40 Cathedral
42 Internet Cafe
44 Train Station

THE EASTERN COAST

to your right off Via Pirandello at the entrance to the old town. For email and Internet access, the Internet Cafe (☎ 0942 62 88 39) is at Corso Umberto I 214. By Sicilian standards it's pricey: L7000 for the first 30 minutes, L8000 for every 30 minutes after that. It's open from 10 am to 10 pm daily.

Newspapers Both the tobacconist at Via Bagnoli Croci 62 and the newsagent at Corso Umberto I 245, just inside the Porta Catania, stock some English-language newspapers, including two-day-old editions of the *Guardian* and the previous day's *International Herald Tribune*.

Medical Services & Emergency There is a free night-time medical service in summer for tourists (☎ 0942 62 54 19), in Piazza San Francesco di Paola. The Ospedale San Vincenzo (☎ 0942 5 37 45) is on Piazza San Vincenzo, just outside the Porta Catania. For an ambulance call the same number.

The carabinieri (☎ 0942 2 31 05) are at Piazza Badia 4.

Things to See & Do

Taormina's most famous sight is undoubtedly the **Greek theatre** (Teatro Greco), at the end of Via Teatro Greco, off Corso Umberto I. Built in the 3rd century BC, it was heavily remodelled in the 1st century AD by the Romans, so what you see is pretty much a Roman structure. The Greeks had originally intended to make the most of the breathtaking views of Mt Etna and the Bay of Schisò, but this view was partially obscured during the rebuilding by a set of arches and columns – luckily these have largely collapsed once again revealing the stunning panorama. Furthermore, the Romans considered the sword mightier than the pen, so the stage and orchestra pit, which once played host to the great tragedies of antiquity, were demolished and converted into a circular arena given over to gladiator fighting. The structure has been much tampered with over the centuries – the family of the Spanish Costanza d'Aragona built its home over part of the theatre (to the right as you face the stage) in the 12th century. However, it remains a most atmospheric place. Film buffs might note that Woody Allen filmed the Greek chorus scenes here for his film *Mighty Aphrodite*. The theatre is open from 9 am to 7 pm from April to October and closes at 4.30 pm the rest of the year. Admission costs L4000. In July and August it hosts a well-respected international arts festival (see Special Events later in the chapter).

Just outside the theatre (to the left as you exit) is a partially excavated **archaeological zone** that is not yet open to the public. Skirting its southern boundary is a set of steps that leads down to the **Parco Duchi di Cesarò**, also known as the Trevelyan Garden, a Victorian folly created for Lady Florence Trevelyan Cacciola (1852–1907). The rich flora includes magnolias, hibiscus, bougainvillaea, cacti and a variety of trees including olive, palm, cypress and cedar. A beehive-shaped aviary, a children's playground and tennis courts complete the picture. Perfect for picnicking on a summer's day, the gardens afford some glorious views over the bay below. Opening hours are the same as for the theatre.

Back in the town centre is the **Odeon**, a small Roman theatre, badly preserved and partly covered by the adjoining Chiesa di Santa Caterina. It was discovered and excavated in the late 19th century and is believed to have been erected on the site of a Greek temple of Apollo. Taormina's **cathedral**, in the Piazza del Duomo along Corso Umberto I, was built in the early 15th century.

There are several mansions in Taormina, including the **Palazzo Corvaja**. Begun by the Arabs as a defence tower in the 11th century, it was extended several times and includes halls dating from the 14th and 15th centuries. Today it is home to the tourist office. The **Palazzo Duca di Santo Stefano**, at the other end of town, is an important example of Sicilian Gothic architecture, with a fanciful mix of Arab and Norman styles.

The nearby **Badia Vecchia** (Old Abbey) is a 14th-century Gothic building, again with Norman-Arab elements.

Just wandering along the main drag, Corso Umberto I, you can see a smattering of stately old buildings, some dating from the 15th century.

The peak of Mt Tauro (884m) is adorned by the lonely, windswept ruins of the town's medieval **castle**, 500m from the town centre along the road to Castelmola (see Around Taormina later in this chapter) or accessible by climbing the linking stairs. The views are great.

You can reach the beaches at **Isola Bella** and **Mazzarò** directly under Taormina by cable car *(funivia)* from Via Pirandello. It costs L5000 return and runs from 8.30 am to 8.15 pm in winter and until 1.30 am in summer. Both beaches are largely taken up by private operators (a space with deck-chairs and umbrella costs up to L20,000 a day), but there is some space for free bathing. Interbus buses also connect the beaches with the upper town.

Organised Tours

CST (☎ 0942 2 33 01), Corso Umberto I 101, runs excursions to various locations. Destinations include Mt Etna (L35,000), Agrigento (L62,000), Syracuse (L55,000) and Lipari (L75,000). Prices exclude entrance to museums and archaeological sites. These are winter prices; expect rises in summer. SAT (☎ 0942 2 46 53, fax 0942 2 11 28), Corso Umberto I 73, also runs tours to Mt Etna.

Special Events

Theatre and music concerts are organised throughout the summer during Taormina Arte, a pretty good international arts festival that runs from July to August. For all information, including what's on and how much it'll cost, and tickets ask at the tourist office. The Reunion of Sicilian Costumes and Carts (Raduno del Costume e del Carretto Siciliano), featuring parades of traditional Sicilian carts and folkloric groups, is usually held in autumn – ask at the tourist office.

THE EASTERN COAST

Places to Stay

Taormina has plenty of accommodation, but in summer you should book in advance as rooms fill rapidly, particularly during August (a good time to stay away). In winter you can sometimes get prices brought down a tad.

Camping You can camp near the beach at *Campeggio San Leo* (☎ *0942 2 46 58, Via Nazionale)*, at Capo Taormina, next to the Grande Albergo. There are no facilities to speak of other than a spot to pitch a tent. The cost is L10,000 per person per night.

Hotels The cheapest option in Taormina is to go for a room in a private house, some of which also include breakfast in the charge. The tourist office has a full list. *Il Leone* (☎ *0942 2 38 78, Via Bagnoli Croci 127)*, near the Trevelyan Gardens, charges L45,000 per person with breakfast; the price drops to L35,000 out of high season. Some rooms have terraces and great views of the sea. *Casa Grazia* (☎ *0942 24 47 76, Via Lallia Bassia 20)* is a no-frills budget option and is also close to the Trevelyan Gardens. Rooms cost L35,000 per person. It is only open from April to October.

There are dozens of hotels in town to suit (virtually) every taste. *Pensione Svizzera* (☎ *0942 2 37 90, Via Pirandello 26,* @ *svizzera@tau.it)*, on the way from the bus station to the town centre, has simple, pleasant singles/doubles with bathroom starting at L50,000/70,000 (prices rise to L80,000/120,000 in the high season), including a buffet breakfast. Farther up the same road, *Pensione Inn Piero* (☎ *0942 2 31 39)*, at No 20, has comfortable singles with bathroom for L72,000/84,000 in the high/low season and doubles for L94,000/120,000. *Pensione Villa Gaia* (☎ *0942 2 31 85, Via Fazzello 34)* is near the cathedral and has rooms for L45,000/95,000, breakfast included. It's closed in winter.

Villa Nettuno (☎ *0942 2 37 97, Via Pirandello 33)*, in front of the cable car station, has singles/doubles with bathroom for L65,000/110,000 and triples for L140,000. A few doors down, *Villa Fiorita* (☎ *0942 2 41 22, Via Pirandello 39)* is one of Taormina's

nicer mid-range hotels. It is well-furnished and comfortable, with a garden, swimming pool, terraces and rooms with sea views. Doubles are priced from L185,000, including breakfast.

If you want to stay near the beach at Mazzarò, try the *Villa Caterina* (☎ *0942 2 47 09, Via Nazionale 155)*, which has pleasant rooms for L60,000 per person.

Hotel Villa Belvedere (☎ *0942 2 37 91, fax 0942 62 58 30, Via Bagnoli Croci 79)* has a swimming pool and garden, and all rooms and terraces face Mt Etna. Singles/doubles with full services cost up to L163,000/257,000. Otherwise, you can bask in the luxury offered by the *San Domenico Palace* (☎ *0942 2 37 01, fax 0942 62 55 06, Piazza San Domenico 5)*, the town's grandest hotel. The views may be unsurpassed but so are the prices: in high season singles/doubles cost L440,000/750,000.

Places to Eat

Those on a tight budget will be limited in their choice of dining spots. There are several gourmet grocery shops along Corso Umberto I, where prices are high. Alternatively, head for the side streets between Via Teatro Greco and the public gardens, where you can buy picnic supplies at several grocery and pastry shops. There is a *Standa supermarket* in Via Apollo Arcageta, just up from the post office. Quite a few restaurants close in winter.

For a quick takeaway, you could do worse than *Myosotis (Corso Umberto I 113)*. It has pizzas, *arancini* (breaded rice balls stuffed with meat sauce and peas then fried – the superior Sicilian version of the Italian *suppli)*, and *panini* (filled bread rolls) for around L5000. For a light meal and pizza try *Shelter Pub (Via Fratelli Bandiera 10)*, off Corso Umberto I. *Time Out (Via San Pancrazio 19)* is a decent little bar and eatery.

For pizza, *Mamma Rosa (Via Naumachia 10)* is a safe bet. Pizzas cost around L10,000 to L12,000. *Ritrovo Trocadero (Via Pirandello 1)* makes exotic-sounding pizzas – with names like Hawaiian and Mexicano – for around L6000 to L14,000.

Trattoria Rosticepi (Via San Pancrazio 10), at the top of Via Pirandello, has good meals for under L25,000 per person. For an excellent meal in lovely surroundings, head for **Ristorante La Piazzetta** *(Via Paladini 5)*, in a tiny piazza downhill from Corso Umberto I. A full meal will cost L30,000 or more. *Il Baccanale (☎ 0942 62 53 90, Piazzetta Filea)*, off Via Giovanni di Giovanni, is a popular restaurant, moderately priced by Taormina standards.

For a quiet drink, head for **Arco Rosso-Da Micio** *(Via Naumachia 7)*, off Corso Umberto I, which serves very good Sicilian wine. Farther down, the busier *Da Rita (Via Calapitrulli 3)* serves excellent salads.

Many of the cafes on Corso Umberto I charge extortionately in the high season. At the pretty *Bam Bar (Via Giovanni di Giovanni 45)*, delicious Sicilian *granite* (drinks made of crushed ice) cost L4000 and large toasted sandwiches are L6000.

Getting There & Away
Bus This is the easiest means of reaching Taormina. Interbus (☎ 0942 62 53 01) services leave for Messina (L5500, 1½ hours) and Catania (about the same) at least hourly from about 6 am to 7 pm.

Train There are also regular trains, but the awkward location of Taormina's station is a strong disincentive. If you arrive this way, catch an Interbus bus up to the town. They run roughly every 30 to 90 minutes (much less frequently on Sunday).

Car & Motorcycle Taormina is on the A18 *autostrada* (motorway) and SS114 between Messina and Catania. Parking can be a problem in Taormina, particularly in summer. The Lumbi car park is open 24 hours daily and there is a shuttle service to the centre from Porta Messina.

Rental California (☎ 0942 2 37 69), Via Bagnoli Croci 86, rents cars and motorcycles at reasonable prices. A small car will cost between L400,000 and L487,000 a week. A Vespa costs L60,000 a day or L370,000 a week.

AROUND TAORMINA
The road south from Messina to Taormina offers little in the way of interesting scenery until you're a good 20km out of town, but then the suburbs recede, the coastline emerges into full view and on a clear day you can see right across the straits to Calabria. The towns on the coast are nothing special, but there are a couple of worthwhile excursions into the foothills of the Peloritani mountains, which trace a parallel course virtually the entire length of the coast between Messina and Taormina. Regular AST buses make the journey, but it is slow and laborious going; you're better off taking a train. If you have your own car, you should avoid the busy and slow state road and stick to the A18 motorway. There's a toll, but it's worth it.

Savoca
postcode 98039 • pop 130
• elevation 980m
Beautifully situated 4km inland from the grey pebble beaches of Santa Teresa di Riva is this lovely village, little more than a cluster of houses, a couple of medieval churches and the ruins of a castle. The road up to the town winds its way through lemon groves and almond stands, and from the top you have a fine view of the coastline stretched out below.

Signs in Savoca show the way to the **Capuchin monastery** located on the outskirts of the village. Inside the monastery, a rickety staircase takes you down to the catacombs, holding the eerie-looking remains of a number of 18th-century nobles and other local bigwigs who paid good money for this kind of 'immortality'. The catacombs are open from 9 am to 1 pm and 4 to 7 pm from April to September; 9 am to midday and 3 to 5 pm the rest of the year. Admission is free, but visitors are expected to make a donation. AST buses run between Savoca and Santa Teresa di Riva.

If the village seems somehow familiar it is because it was used by Francis Ford Coppola in *The Godfather*, as the setting for Michael Corleone's marriage to Apollonia. At the entrance to the town is the *Bar Vitelli*, also used in the film. This is the place to go for virtually everything in town: the keys to

euro currency converter L10,000 = €5.16

THE EASTERN COAST

the churches, directions to the monastery and stories of when the Americans came to make 'that film'.

Castelmola
postcode 98039 • pop 1120
• elevation 529m

Perched above Taormina at the end of a 5km scenic route up the mountain, Castelmola is thought to have been the site of an ancient acropolis called the Tauromenion. The ruins of a medieval castle now stand in its place. There is little to do here other than sample the local *vino alla mandorla* (almond wine), but the views from the tiny town are breathtaking.

Buses make almost hourly runs daily from the terminal at Taormina (L2000).

Giardini-Naxos
postcode 98039 • pop 8600

This small town 5km south of Taormina is a popular alternative to the resort town for accommodation and has one of the nicest beaches on the eastern coast. It is also the site of the first Greek settlement in Sicily. According to legend, the Greeks had stayed well clear of the Sicilian coastline, believing it to be inhabited by monsters and savages. This belief was encouraged by Phoenecians eager to keep the Greeks away from the western Mediterranean, but when the Athenian Theocles was shipwrecked along the eastern shore he found that the stories were untrue. He returned soon after with a group of Chalcidian settlers and the town of Naxos was founded in 735 BC. Allied to Athens, the colony did not survive an attack by the Syracusan tyrant Dionysius in 403 BC.

The ruins are not nearly as impressive as those in other Sicilian excavations. Apart from a 300m-stretch of wall, a small temple and a couple of other structures, the best part of a visit is to simply amble through the lemon groves. A small **museum** has bits and bobs uncovered during the excavation. The park and museum are open from 9 am to one hour before sunset Monday to Saturday. Admission costs L4000. Regular buses leave from the Taormina bus station in Via Pirandello for Giardini-Naxos.

Gola dell'Alcàntara
A relatively short drive up the winding SS185 from Naxos will get you to this series of modest lava gorges on the river of the same name (derived from the Arabic *al cantara*, meaning bridge), a few kilometres short of Francavilla. You could stop off here on your way to Mt Etna. Otherwise, Interbus buses from Taormina depart at 9.30 and 11.30 am Monday to Friday only, returning to Taormina at 2.20 and 3.20 pm; L8500 return.

There is elevator access to the gorges (L4000), and you can hire wading boots (L13,000), which you'll need if you want to do anything more than peer into the gorges; otherwise, take your swimming costume. It is also possible to reach the gorges by the stairs on the main road, 200m uphill from the elevator entrance. It is forbidden to enter the gorges from around November through to May because of the risk of unexpected floods.

Castiglione di Sicilia
postcode 98039 • pop 4500

Ten kilometres farther on from the Gola dell'Alcàntara (take a left at Francavilla di Sicilia and proceed for another 5km) is this medieval hill town that grew up around the **Castel Leone** (Castle of the Lion), which was built by the Normans in the 12th century and is the origin of the town's name. The castle is wedged in a high crevice from where there are commanding views of the surrounding countryside. For the visitor unconcerned with the potential for a frontal attack, the best view is of the town itself and its many bell towers. You'll need your own transport to get here.

Catania

postcode 95100 • pop 376,000

Sicily's second city has long been in the shadow of the capital, Palermo, and for even longer in the shadow of Sicily's most ominous natural presence, Mt Etna. Ignored and overlooked for centuries in favour of the 'other' city as the seat of power on the island, Catania has been the unwelcome focus of Etna's awesome power for thousands of years. Its role as a busy industrial and commercial city, coupled with the chaotic traffic and its reputation as a centre of crime, has hardly done the city any favours and it can appear an uninviting and intimidating place on arrival (the ugly location of the train and bus stations doesn't help), but it does merit the benefit of the doubt. In the best tradition of Sicily, Catania has managed to turn disaster to its advantage, and the reconstruction that followed the devastating earthquake of 1693 heralded the building of an elegant baroque centre using Etna's weapon as a building block: lava. Catania is also well served by hotels and *pensioni* (guesthouses), and the food is good and cheaper than most places on the coast.

HISTORY

According to Thucydides, the Chalcidians founded a settlement here in 729 BC and called it Katane. For 300 years it was engaged in a bitter rivalry with Syracuse over control of the region, before it was sacked by the Romans in 263 BC. Occupied in turn by the Byzantines (AD 535), the Saracens (878) and the Normans (1091), by the mid-17th century Catania was a relatively prosperous urban centre with a sophisticated trading relationship with its surrounding hinterland and the rest of the island. The city had been a victim of Etna's eruptions many times over the previous 2000 years, but the eruption of 1669 covered most of Catania in boiling lava and left the centre a mess of ruined streets and uninhabitable buildings. The countryside, so instrumental in providing food for the city's people, was almost completely destroyed and Catania's citizens were left virtually starving. But worse was to come. The earthquake of 1693 finished off the job begun by Mt Etna and the city was left in ruins. Disease and famine were rampant and the streets were awash with penniless refugees fighting over morsels of bread.

The following year Giuseppe Lanza, duke of Camastra, organised a committee whose brief was to rebuild the city with a view toward minimising the potential damage of another eruption. Under the supervision of architects Giovani Vaccarini and Stefano Ittar, a new street grid was created that allowed for spacious squares and streets of differing widths, all of which would provide escape routes and greater shelter when Etna stirred once more. In keeping with the dominant architectural style of the period, the new city was strictly baroque in appearance. Despite years of neglect that have left many of Catania's elegant palazzi and churches in decay, the modern city is an attractive place to wander, even if the use of the dark lava stone gives it a severe, dour look.

ORIENTATION

The main train station and intercity bus terminal are a 15-minute walk east of the city centre, near the port on Piazza Giovanni XXIII. From the square, Via Vittorio Emanuele runs east–west through the heart of the city, while Via Etnea runs north from Piazza del Duomo. Most sights are concentrated around and west of Piazza del Duomo, while the commercial centre of Catania is farther north, around Via Pacini and Via Umberto I.

INFORMATION
Tourist Offices

The APT office (☎ 095 730 62 22, 095 730 62 23, @ apt@apt-catania.com) is at Via Cimarosa 10–12. It is open from 9 am to 7 pm Monday to Saturday. There are branches at the train station (☎ 095 730 62 55) on platform No 1, open the same hours, and at the airport (☎ 095 730 62 66), open from 8 am to 10 pm daily. There is also a Web site at www.apt-catania.com.

Money

Banks are concentrated along Corso Sicilia, including the Deutsche Bank and Banca Nazionale del Lavoro, both with reliable ATMs, and several have currency exchange offices, open from 8.30 am to 1.30 pm and 2.30 to 4 pm Monday to Friday. There is a currency exchange office at the train station and another one in Piazza Università. Amex is represented by La Duca Viaggi (☎ 095 31 61 55), Via Etnea 63–65. They have another office at Piazza Europa 1.

THE EASTERN COAST

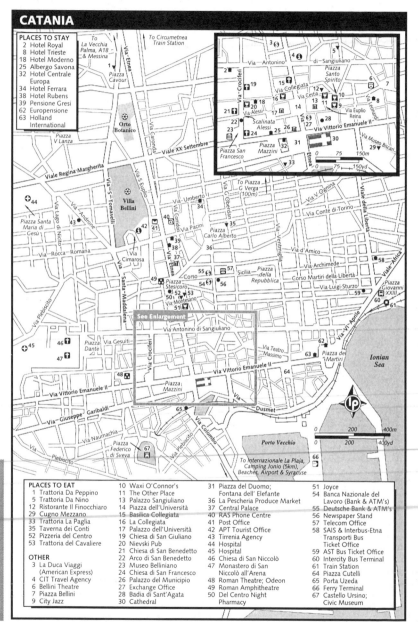

CATANIA

PLACES TO STAY
2 Hotel Royal
8 Hotel Trieste
18 Hotel Moderno
25 Albergo Savona
32 Hotel Centrale
   Europa
34 Hotel Ferrara
38 Hotel Rubens
39 Pensione Gresi
62 Europensione
63 Holland
   International

PLACES TO EAT
1 Trattoria Da Peppino
5 Trattoria Da Nino
12 Ristorante Il Finocchiaro
29 Cugno Mezzano
33 Trattoria La Paglia
35 Taverna dei Conti
52 Pizzeria del Centro
53 Trattoria del Cavaliere

OTHER
3 La Duca Viaggi
   (American Express)
4 CIT Travel Agency
6 Bellini Theatre
7 Piazza Bellini
9 City Jazz

10 Waxi O'Connor's
11 The Other Place
13 Palazzo Sangiuliano
14 Piazza dell'Università
15 Basilica Collegiata
16 La Collegiata
17 Palazzo dell'Università
19 Chiesa di San Giuliano
20 Nievski Pub
21 Chiesa di San Benedetto
22 Arco di San Benedetto
23 Museo Belliniano
26 Chiesa di San Francesco
27 Palazzo del Municipio
28 Badia di Sant'Agata
30 Cathedral

31 Piazza del Duomo;
   Fontana dell' Elefante
36 La Pescheria Produce Market
37 Central Palace
40 RAS Phone Centre
41 Post Office
42 APT Tourist Office
43 Tirrenia Agency
44 Hospital
45 Hospital
46 Chiesa di San Niccolò
47 Monastero di San
   Niccolò all'Arena
48 Roman Theatre; Odeon
49 Roman Amphitheatre
50 Del Centro Night
   Pharmacy

51 Joyce
54 Banca Nazionale del
   Lavoro (Bank & ATM's)
55 Deutsche Bank & ATM's
56 Newspaper Stand
57 Telecom Office
58 SAIS & Interbus-Etna
   Transporti Bus
   Ticket Office
59 AST Bus Ticket Office
60 Intercity Bus Terminal
61 Train Station
65 Piazza Cutelli
66 Ferry Terminal
67 Castello Ursino;
   Civic Museum

Post & Communications

The main post office is at Via Etnea 215, between Via Pacini and Via Umberto I. The Telecom office, Corso Sicilia 67, is open from 9 am to 1 pm and 4 to 7.30 pm Monday to Saturday.

For email and Internet access, RAS Phone Centre (☎ 095 32 64 98), at Via Corridoni 1b, charges L10,000 per hour. It is open from 9 am to 7 pm daily. Nievski Pub (☎ 095 715 12 84), Scalinata Alessi 15–17, has a couple of terminals that you can log on to from 7 pm to 4 am daily (L5000 for 30 minutes).

Travel Agencies

There is a CIT travel agency (☎ 095 715 10 04) at Via Antonino di Sangiuliano 208.

Medical Services & Emergency

In a medical emergency, go to the Ospedale Vittorio Emanuele (☎ 095 743 52 56), Via Plebiscito 268, off Via Vittorio Emanuele II, or try the Ospedale Garibaldi (☎ 095 759 43 71), at Piazza Santa Maria di Gesù 5–7. Del Centro (☎ 095 31 36 85) is an all-night pharmacy at Via Etnea 107 and is open year-round except August. A number of chemists also open at night on a rotational basis – ask at the tourist office for details.

The police station (*questura*; ☎ 095 736 71 11) is on Piazza San Nicolella. The carabinieri (☎ 095 53 78 22) are at Piazza Giovanni Verga 8.

PIAZZA DEL DUOMO & AROUND

Catania's central square was redesigned following the earthquake of 1693, replacing the original square known as the *platea magna* (main square). The city's main thoroughfares – Via Etnea and Via Vittorio Emanuele – converge at Piazza del Duomo, which is also the centre of the Catania's ecclesiastical and political power. At its centre is the remarkable **Fontana del Elefante** (Fountain of the Elephant), designed in 1736 by Vaccarini. This curious piece combines a lava-stone elephant dating from Roman times with an Egyptian obelisk carved with hieroglyphics describing the worship of the goddess Isis. At the top is a sphere bearing the insignia of St Agatha, the city's patron. Vac-

carini successfully mixes pagan and Christian symbolism in an almost humorous whole, a much-needed slice of optimism considering the tragedy that had befallen the city only a few years earlier.

Vaccarini also remodelled the **cathedral**, originally built by Count Roger in the 11th century on the ruins of the Roman baths. It was a case of third time lucky for the church, as it had been destroyed by lava in 1169 and again by the earthquake of 1693. Vaccarini created an ornate baroque facade with two orders of columns taken from the Roman amphitheatre (see Along Via Etnea later in this section). The interior is no less sumptuous and features a number of chapels, including one dedicated to St Agatha which contains all the relics paraded through the city on her feast day (5 February). Inside the main entrance, to the right, is the tomb of the city's native composer, Vincenzo Bellini (1801–35). The cathedral

The Master of Song

In his short life (he died when he was 34) Vincenzo Bellini composed 10 operas, including the trio that made his fame: *La Sonnambula* (The Sleepwalker), *I Puritani* (The Puritans) and *Norma*. Unlike his bel canto contemporaries, Bellini refused to rely on the tried-and-tested seductive melodies that made such hits out of operas like Rossini's *Il Barbiere di Siviglia* (The Barber of Seville) and Donizetti's *Lucia di Lamermoor*. Unperturbed by the ease with which his fellow composers reeled off operas (Rossini wrote an average of one opera every two weeks!), Bellini tried to write works that didn't rely on pretty melodies at the expense of a well-crafted story. Although successful during his short career, Bellini's style fell out of favour after his death and his operas struggled for recognition until the 1950s and the revival of the bel canto style. Wagner, however, had recognised Bellini's genius and wrote that his music was 'strongly felt and intimately wound up with the words', a powerful emotional combination brought to dramatic life by Maria Callas in her 1953 performance in the title role of *Norma*.

THE EASTERN COAST

is open from 8 am to noon and 5 to 7 pm daily.

The northern side of the square is dominated by another Vaccarini creation, the **Palazzo del Municipio** (town hall), with the ubiquitous baroque facade. In keeping with the square's central theme, it is also known as the Palazzo degli Elefanti. Across Via Vittorio Emanuele II from the cathedral is the **Badia di Sant'Agata** (Convent of St Agatha), yet another Vaccarini masterpiece, whose cupola dominates the city centre. The interior was heavily ornamented after Vaccarini's death. It is open from 8 am to 5 pm Monday to Friday.

A few blocks north-east of the cathedral you will stumble into Piazza Bellini. The **theatre** of the same name is an eye-catching example of the city's architectural richness, a richness unfortunately buried beneath deep layers of grime.

West along Via Vittorio Emanuele II, at No 266, is the entrance to the substantial ruins of the **Roman theatre**, built in the 2nd century AD on the site of an earlier Greek theatre (hence its inclusion on some tourist office maps as the 'Teatro Greco'). At one time it could accommodate an audience of 7000. Next door is the smaller **Odeon**, a rehearsal theatre that was used for chorus rehearsals and competitions. Both are open from 9 am to 1 pm and 3 to 7 pm; admission costs L4000.

CASTELLO URSINO

If you walk west from Piazza del Duomo, through the impressive **Porta Uzeda** (built in 1696) and down to Piazza Federico di Sveva, you'll come across the imposing fortifications of this 13th-century castle built by Frederick II. The grim-looking fortress, surrounded by a moat, was once on a cliff top overlooking the sea; following the earthquake of 1693 the whole area to the south was reclaimed and the castle became landlocked. Inside is the **Civic Museum** (☎ 095 34 58 30), which includes finds from the Roman era up to the 18th century. The castle and museum are open from 9 am to 1 pm and 3 to 6 pm Tuesday to Saturday; admission is free.

A word of warning: unless you're travelling in pairs you're best off keeping to the main streets, as this can be a pretty dodgy neighbourhood.

ALONG VIA CROCIFERÌ

The city's most interesting street is probably Via Crociferì, which runs north from Piazza Mazzini (west of Piazza del Duomo) alongside Via Etnea. At the southern end of Via Crociferì, on the western side of the small Piazza San Francesco, is the **Museo Belliniano** (☎ 095 715 05 35), the home of Vincenzo Bellini, now a small museum with a bunch of the composer's memorabilia, including original scores, photographs and his death mask. It is open from 9 am to 1 pm and 3 to 7 pm (6 pm from October to March). Admission is free.

Opposite the museum is the 18th-century **Chiesa di San Francesco**. Just up the street is the **Arco di San Benedetto**, an arch built by the Benedictines in 1704. According to legend, the arch was built in one night as the order sought to defy a city ordnance against its construction on the grounds that it was a seismic liability. On the left past the arch is the imposing **Chiesa di San Benedetto**, built between 1704 and 1713. Inside there is some splendid stucco and marble work.

On the right-hand side about halfway up the street is the **Chiesa di San Giuliano**, designed by Vaccarini and built between 1739 and 1751. The convex central facade makes for an interesting effect. Farther on you will surely notice the notable excavations which have resulted in the whole street being closed off to traffic: here, at the crossroads with Via Antonino di Sangiuliano, a section of the old Roman road and a sizeable floor mosaic have been uncovered and are in the process of being excavated. You can peer over the hoarding to take a look.

CHIESA DI SAN NICOLÒ ALL'ARENA

Directly opposite Chiesa di San Giuliano is the small Via Gesuiti, which leads west to Piazza Dante and Sicily's largest church. Commissioned in 1687, work on the building was interrupted by the earthquake of

1693 and then by problems with its size – it is 105m long, 48m wide and its cupola is 62m high. Consequently, the church was never completed. It has a sombre-looking facade, a stark contrast to the rich embellishments that adorn the city's other baroque structures. The cavernous interior is equally devoid of frills, the long walls interrupted by a series of altars that are almost completely bare. The church is currently undergoing restoration, so you might have to ask to get a peek at the presbytery, which features a splendid organ crafted by Donato del Piano. Unfortunately, it is impossible for the time being to climb up the tambour of the cupola, which provides some of the best views of the surrounding region, including Etna and across the straits to Reggio di Calabria.

Directly behind the church, and part of the same complex, is the old Benedictine **Monastero di San Nicolò all'Arena**, built in 1703 and now part of the city's university. The Benedictines seemed to work on the premise that bigger was better – the monastery was the second largest in Europe after that of Mafra, in Portugal. In pretty poor shape, the monastery is currently under restoration, so you may not be able to get in to take a look at the lovely courtyards.

ALONG VIA ETNEA

The city's main north–south artery runs from Piazza del Duomo right up through the city and into the foothills of Mt Etna, but visitors need only concern themselves with the short stretch between the cathedral to the south and the elegant gardens of Villa Bellini to the north. East off Via Etnea, about 200m north of the cathedral, is Piazza dell'Università. Facing each other on the square are two buildings designed by Vaccarini, the **Palazzo dell'Università** to the west and the **Palazzo Sangiuliano** to the east. The former is the city's university.

A farther 300m north is the large and modern Piazza Stesicoro, whose western side is dominated by the sunken remains of the Roman **amphitheatre**. It doesn't look like much today, but in its heyday (around the 2nd century BC) it could seat up to 16,000 spectators and was second in size

only to the Colosseum in Rome. What you see from the street is only a part of the once massive structure, which extended as far south as Via Penninello. You can explore part of the vaults and get an idea of the true size of the theatre from a diagram. It is open from 9 am to 1 pm and 3 to 7 pm Monday to Saturday; admission costs L4000.

For relief from the madding crowd, continue north along Via Etnea and cut in to the left behind the post office for the lovely gardens of the **Villa Bellini**.

SPECIAL EVENTS

Catania celebrates the feast of its patron saint, Agatha (Festa di Sant'Agata), from 3 to 5 February. During this period, one million Catanians and tourists follow as the *fercolo* (a silver reliquary bust of the saint covered in marvellous jewels) is carried along Via Etnea. There are also spectacular fireworks during the celebrations.

PLACES TO STAY – BUDGET
Camping

Camping facilities are available at *Internazionale La Plaja* (☎ 095 34 83 40, Viale Kennedy 47), with a private sandy beach, on the way out of the city towards Syracuse (take bus No 527 from Piazza Borsellino). *Camping Jonio* (☎ 095 49 11 39, Via Villini a Mare 2), about 5km south of the city, is close to a beautiful rocky beach. Charges are L10,000 per person and L10,000 for a site. To get there, catch bus No 334 from Via Etnea.

Hotels

There are several places with rock-bottom prices, including the *Hotel Trieste* (☎ 095 32 71 05, Via Leonardi 24), near Piazza Bellini, which charges about L25,000 per person for a no-frills room. *Pensione Gresi* (☎ 095 32 27 09, Via Pacini 28) is near Villa Bellini and is considered by many travellers to be the best budget option in town. Out of high season, singles/doubles cost L32,000/46,000; only doubles have a bathroom. Between May and October, however, the prices go up to L60,000/80,000.

On the 2nd floor of a building at the

THE EASTERN COAST

northern end of Piazza dei Martiri, *Europensione* (☎ 095 53 11 52, Piazza dei Martiri 8) offers nothing more than a bed and bed linen for L40,000/60,000. The rooms are large and clean, however. The *Holland International* (☎ 095 53 36 05, Via Vittorio Emanuele II 8) is just off Piazza dei Martiri, near the train station. Located at the back of a huge courtyard, this popular option with budget travellers has singles/doubles without bathroom for L35,000/60,000 and doubles with bathroom for L75,000.

A little more expensive, *Hotel Rubens* (☎ 095 31 70 73, Via Etnea 196) has singles/doubles for L38,000/50,000, or L50,000/72,000 with bathroom. *Hotel Ferrara* (☎ 095 31 60 00, Via Umberto I 66) has rooms for L40,000/63,000, or L58,000/78,000 with bathroom.

PLACES TO STAY – MID-RANGE

The *Hotel Moderno* (☎ 095 32 65 50, Via Alessi 9) is comfortably placed near Via Crociferì and in the heart of the city's nightlife. Singles/doubles cost L60,000/100,000, but out of high season prices drop to a very reasonable L35,000/50,000. The *Albergo Savona* (☎ 095 32 69 82, Via Vittorio Emanuele II 210) has singles/doubles for L41,000/67,000, or L78,000/126,000 with bathroom and breakfast. Close to Piazza del Duomo, this is a clean and tidy hotel that makes a good base for your explorations. Just down the street, at No 167, *Hotel Centrale Europa* (☎ 095 31 13 09) has singles/doubles without bathroom for L45,000/70,000 and doubles with bathroom for L98,000.

PLACES TO STAY – TOP END

The *Hotel Royal* (☎ 095 31 34 48, fax 095 32 56 11, Via Antonino di Sangiuliano 337) is located on the corner with Via Crociferì and has singles/doubles costing L80,000/130,000 including breakfast. *La Vecchia Palma* (☎ 095 43 20 25, fax 095 58 01 03, Via Etnea 668) has nice rooms for L80,000/130,000, also including breakfast. Take bus Nos 1-4 or 1-5 from Piazza Università. If you want to sleep in the lap of luxury, Catania's top hotel is the *Central Palace* (☎ 095

32 53 44, fax 095 715 89 39, Via Etnea 218). Singles/doubles cost L190,000/270,000 and breakfast is included.

PLACES TO EAT

Eating out can be pleasant and inexpensive in Catania. Aside from the usual restaurants, the city has a number of other dining options which involve buying Sicilian snacks and other savoury titbits from stalls or street-facing bar counters. Don't miss the savoury arancini, *cartocciate* (bread stuffed with ham, mozzarella, olives and tomato) or baked onions, available for around L2500 apiece from a *tavola calda* ('hot table', basically a self-service restaurant), found all over town. Stop at a *pasticceria* (pastry shop) to try the mouthwatering Sicilian sweets.

Catania is also well known for its excellent *markets*. Every morning except Sunday, Piazza Carlo Alberto is flooded by the chaos of a produce market known locally as La Fiera. You can pick up supplies of bread, cheese, salami, fresh fruit and all manner of odds and ends. The other major fresh-produce market is *La Pescheria*, off Piazza del Duomo, which sells fresh fish. It is open until 2 pm daily (except Sunday) and is well worth a visit.

Students head for the area around Via Teatro Massimo and to the west of Via Etnea, where there are several sandwich bars and pubs where you can eat a pizza or a filling sandwich. The best of these is the Nievski Pub (see the following Entertainment section).

The central *Pizzeria del Centro* (☎ 095 31 14 29, Via Montesano 11) does great pizzas for between L3500 and L7000. *Trattoria Da Peppino* (☎ 095 43 06 20, Via Empedocle 35) serves good *antipasti* (starters) and pasta. A complete meal costs around L30,000. For a seafood meal, try *Trattoria La Paglia* (☎ 095 34 68 38, Via Pardo 23), just behind Piazza del Duomo. *Taverna dei Conti* (☎ 095 31 00 35, Via G Oberdan 41–3) serves Sicilian antipasti, fish and seafood. *Trattoria del Cavaliere* (☎ 095 31 04 91, Via Paternò 11), downtown, close to Piazza Stesicoro, serves excellent Sicilian food, including grilled fish and horse meat.

THE EASTERN COAST

Trattoria Da Nino (☎ 095 31 13 19, Via Biondi 19) has reasonably priced, good meals. Pricier but very pleasant is the *Ristorante Il Finocchiaro (Via Cestai 8)*.

One of the city's better restaurants is *Cugno Mezzano* (☎ 095 71 58 710, Via Museo Biscari 8), located in the old wine cellar of Palazzo Biscari. Not surprisingly, it is big on wine, but is quite expensive.

ENTERTAINMENT

Not surprisingly for a busy university town, Catania's excellent nightlife is renowned throughout the island. There are dozens of bars, cafes and other nightspots littered throughout the city centre that offer a good mix of music, drinking and fun. Remember that most bars and nightspots are closed on Monday.

One of the city's most popular student hangouts is *La Collegiata (Via della Collegiata 3–7)*, in the basement of a Liberty-style building off Via Etnea. You can eat, drink and listen to live music from 7 pm to 4 am nightly. The *Nievski Pub* (☎ 095 715 12 84, Scalinata Alessi 15–17) is equally popular with Catania's alternative crowd. Revolutionary posters adorn the walls, and the menu (also available at lunchtime) advertises the use of fresh organic produce. At night, this is a great place to hang out and chat with the young crowd, who are both friendly and welcoming. From 7 pm you can also surf the Internet (L5000 for 30 minutes). The place is open from noon to 4 pm (for lunch only) and 7 pm to 2 am Tuesday to Sunday. Virtually a replica of an English pub, *The Other Place (Via Euplio Reina 18–20)* serves pizzas as well as numerous kinds of draught beer. It is open from 9 pm to 2 am.

East of Via Etnea, in and around the lovely Piazza Santo Spirito, there are a few good spots worth checking out. *Joyce (Via Montesano 46)* is an Irish pub where you can enjoy pints of Guinness in a pleasant courtyard. It is closed in July and August. The ridiculously named *Waxi O'Connor's (Piazza Santo Spirito 1)* is the city's other Irish pub, but it manages to stay on the right side of cheesy. The excellent Guinness and the slices of Guinness cake are a great

help. It is open from 9 pm daily. Next door, *City Jazz* is a good spot to listen to – you guessed it – jazz. It is open from 9 pm to 2 am Thursday to Sunday only.

GETTING THERE & AWAY
Air

Catania's airport, Fontanarossa, is 7km south-west of the city centre and services domestic and European flights (the latter all via Rome or Milan). In summer, you may be able to dig up the odd direct charter flight to London or Paris (see the Getting There & Away chapter for more details). To get to the airport, take the special Alibus (L4500) from outside the train station.

Bus

Intercity buses terminate in the area around Piazza Giovanni XXIII, in front of the train station. SAIS (☎ 095 53 62 01), Via d'Amico 181–7, services Syracuse, Palermo (L20,000, two hours 40 minutes via the motorway) and Agrigento. It also has a service to Rome, which leaves at 8 pm. The one-way ticket costs L75,000. AST (☎ 095 72 30 536), Via Luigi Sturzo 232, also services these destinations and many smaller provincial towns around Catania, including Nicolosi and the cable car on Mt Etna. Interbus-Etna Trasporti (☎ 095 53 27 16), at the same address as SAIS, runs buses to Piazza Armerina, Taormina, Messina, Enna, Noto, Ragusa, Gela and Rome.

Train

Frequent trains connect Catania with Messina and Syracuse (both 1½ hours), and there are less-frequent services to Palermo (3¼ hours), Enna (1¾ hours) and Agrigento (an agonisingly slow four hours). The private Circumetnea train line circles Mt Etna, stopping at the towns and villages on the volcano's slopes. See Around Mt Etna later in this chapter.

Car & Motorcycle

Catania is easily reached from Messina on the A18 and from Palermo on the A19. From the A18, signs for the centre of Catania will bring you to Via Etnea.

THE EASTERN COAST

Boat

Tirrenia (☎ 095 31 63 94), Via Androne 43, runs car ferries to Livorno, in Tuscany, four days a week. Gozo Channel, represented by Fratelli Bonanno (☎ 095 31 06 29) at Via Anzalone 7, runs boats to Malta. The ferry terminal is south of the train station along Via VI Aprile.

GETTING AROUND

Many of the more useful AMOUNT city buses terminate in front of the train station. These include: Alibus, station–airport; Nos 1-4 and 1-6, station–Via Etnea; and Nos 4-7 and 4-6, station–Piazza del Duomo. Buy a daily ticket for L3500. In summer, a special service (D) runs to the sandy beaches from Piazza G Verga.

For a taxi call CST (☎ 095 33 09 66) or the 24-hour Taxi Auto Pubblico (☎ 095 33 09 66). There are taxi ranks at the train station and on Piazza del Duomo.

Mt Etna

elevation 3323m

Sicily's most prominent landmark is Europe's largest live volcano and one of the world's most active. At 3323m it literally towers over the eastern coast, dwarfing everything beneath it; its smoking peak is visible from almost everywhere on this side of the island.

Although today the mountain is one of the island's premier tourist attractions, the eastern coast has lived in the shadow of its unpredictable wrath for millennia. Recorded history of the region is littered with eruptions, including major ones in 475 BC, AD 1169, 1329 and 1381, all of which saw molten rock flow right down to the sea. The most devastating eruption occurred in 1669 and lasted 122 days. A massive river of lava poured down its southern slope, engulfing a good part of Catania and reducing the surrounding countryside to a charred mess.

During the 20th century, eruptions occurred frequently, both from the four live craters at the summit (one, the Bocca Nuova, was formed in 1968) and on the slopes of the volcano, which is littered with

Vulcan's Forge

Mt Etna has long been a subject of fear and fascination for Sicily's inhabitants. According to the chronicler Diodonus, who wrote in the 6th century BC, the first Sicanian settlers of the island were forced west due to the volcano's activity, while the Greeks were convinced that 'the big mountain' was in fact the forge of the god Vulcan. Pindar wrote of its devastating power, having witnessed an eruption in 475 BC. But by far the most interesting of antiquity's scholars was Empedocles, the Agrigento-born scientist who saved Selinunte from the scourge of malaria in the 5th century BC. He became convinced that the crater's gases were semi-solid in form and that they were strong enough to support the weight of a human. He spent time up at the summit, making notes and taking samples to test his theory. But Empedocles was a thorough investigator of the facts and in 433 BC decided that the proof was in the proverbial pudding: he threw himself in. Needless to say, Empedocles was wrong and that was the end of him. One question remains, however: wouldn't a sheep have done just as nicely?

crevices and old craters. In modern times, Etna has claimed its fair share of victims, despite the fact that it is monitored by 120 seismic activity stations spread around the mountain and is under constant satellite surveillance. In 1971 an eruption destroyed the observatory at the summit, and another in 1983 finished off the old cable car and tourist centre (you can see where the lava flow stopped on that occasion). Nine people died in an explosion at the south-eastern crater in 1979, and two died and 10 were injured in an explosion at the same crater in 1987. In 1992 a stream of lava pouring from a fissure in the south-eastern slope threatened to engulf the town of Zafferana Etnea. The town was saved when the Italian Air Force dropped a pile of breeze blocks in the lava's path, but not before one family lost their home and others much of their farm land. In September 1999 the mountain roared once more, spitting ash into the skies above and releasing rivulets of molten rock down the northern side. At the time of research, access to the mountain was restricted on account of the renewed activity.

A word of warning: access to the crater's higher slopes is restricted only by a rope (and the semi-vigilance of the guides), but it would be extremely foolish to attempt crossing beyond the safety zone. Not only are you risking your own life, but you are jeopardising the authorities' ability to provide continuous access to the mountain.

ORIENTATION & INFORMATION
The two main approaches to Etna are from the north and from the south. At the time of research, access from the northern side was virtually nil due to the current activity, limiting visitors to a southern ascent. If your time is limited, your best bet is to take the private Circumetnea railway from Catania (see the later Around Mt Etna section), which follows a 114km trail around the base.

On the northern side of the volcano, there is a tourist office in Linguaglossa (☎ 095 64 30 94) at Piazza Annunziata 7. It has information about skiing and excursions to the craters, as well as an exhibition of the flora,

fauna and rocks of the Parco Naturale dell'Etna. It is possible to hire a 4WD and guide to tour the volcano.

On the southern side, there is a local tourist office in Nicolosi (☎ 095 91 15 05), at Via Garibaldi 63. It is open from 8.30 am to 2 pm and 4 to 7.30 pm daily, April to September; mornings only from 9 am the rest of the year. As the northern side looks likely to be inaccessible for some time, your best bet is to start here. An organised excursion to the main craters (maximum ten people) costs L150,000 per group, including jeep and guide. Alternatively, the tourist office in Catania can provide information. NeT Natura e Turismo (☎ 095 33 35 43, @ natetur@tin.it), Via R Quartararo 11, organises tours of the volcano with a volcanologist or expert guide.

TO THE CRATERS
Exploring the area around the summit is an exhilarating experience, even if you miss out on a period of violent activity. Hot lava flows almost constantly from one of the many fissures beneath the main craters, so you'll get to stand within a couple of metres of one of nature's most extraordinary sideshows. Even the smallest, most unthreatening flow is hot – hot enough to melt your shoes and anything in them.

South
With a daily bus link from Catania via Nicolosi, the southern side of the volcano presents the easier option for an ascent towards the craters. The bus drops you off at the **Rifugio Sapienza**, from where a cable car (SITAS, ☎ 095 91 41 41) climbs to 2600m year-round from 9 am to 3.30 pm (L34,000 return). From here you have a choice. In summer, 4WD vehicles (actually minibuses with big wheels) then take you through the eerie lava-scape close to the 3000m level. The all-in price for cable car, 4WD and guide is L65,000 return (L58,500 from October to April). In winter, you are expected to ski back down (snow permitting) – there is no transport beyond the cable car. A one-day ski pass costs L35,000.

Some tourists make the long climb from

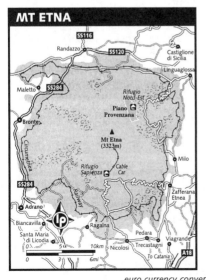

MT ETNA

SS116
Randazzo
Castiglione di Sicilia
SS120
Linguaglossa
Maletto
SS284
Rifugio Nord-Est
Piano Provenzana
Bronte
Mt Etna (3323m)
Milo
Circumetnea
Rifugio Sapienza
Cable Car
SS284
Zafferana Etnea
Railway
Adrano
Biancavilla
Ragalna
Pedara
Viagrande
Santa Maria di Licodia
Nicolosi
Trecastagni
To Catania
A18
0   5   10km
0   3   6mi

THE EASTERN COAST

the Rifugio Sapienza to the top (3½ to four hours on a track winding up under the cable car and then following the same road used by the minibuses). Alternatively, take the cable car and then walk up to the top – be sure to buy a ticket only for the cable car if this is the option you take.

North

Several ski lifts operate at Piano Provenzana, snow permitting (a one-day ski pass costs up to L25,000). From the lifts, you're looking at about an hour's walk to come close to the top – a difficult proposition on snow. Inquire about hiring a guide and the feasibility of the walk in winter at the Linguaglossa tourist office.

In summer, the lifts don't operate, but 4WDs make the same journey. Again, consider a guide for the hour's scramble from where the vehicles stop. At Piano Provenzana, Le Betulle/S.T.A.R. (☎ 095 64 34 30) charges L60,000 for the three-hour round trip to 3100m with a 4WD and guide.

PLACES TO STAY

Accommodation around Etna is scant and for the most part you're better off staying in Catania, where you get better value for money. If you do plan to stay around the mountain, be sure to book in advance as rooms are at a premium, especially in summer. All prices quoted are summer rates; these tumble outside the busy season.

South

Camping The *Etna* camp site (☎ 095 91 43 09, Via Goethe), in Nicolosi, charges L29,000 per two-person tent.

Hotels The *Hotel Corsaro* (☎ 095 91 41 22), 200m from the cable car at the Rifugio Sapienza, has singles/doubles for L90,000/130,000. In Nicolosi, the cheapest place to stay is the *Monte Rossi* (☎ 095 791 43 93, Via Etnea 177), on the main road in town. Threadbare but clean singles/doubles cost L40,000/60,000. More expensive but better quality is the *Gemmellaro* (☎ 095 91 13 73, fax 095 91 10 71, Via Etnea 160), just down the street. Rooms cost L90,000/140,000.

If you have your own transport, you could stay in the nearby town of Pedara, only 5km east of Nicolosi. On the western edge of town is the elegant *Bonaccorsi* (☎ 095 91 53 37, fax 095 91 51 36, Via Luigi Pirandello 2), which charges L65,000/100,000 for well-appointed singles/doubles.

North

Camping In Lingualossa, the *Clan dei Ragazzi* (☎ 095 64 36 11, Strada Marraneve 47) is a small camp site charging L25,000 per night for a two-person tent.

Hotels At Piano Provenzana, the *Rifugio Nord-Est* (☎ 095 64 79 22) has beds for L40,000 a night and half-board for L65,000.

In Lingualossa, you could try *La Provenzana* (☎ 095 64 33 00), which has singles/doubles for L50,000/80,000. *Le Betulle* (☎ 095 64 34 30) charges L90,000/150,000.

GETTING THERE & AWAY

Having your own transport will make life much easier around Mt Etna, but there are some public transport options. The easier approach is from the south.

South

An AST bus (☎ 095 53 17 56) for Rifugio Sapienza leaves from the car park in front of the main train station in Catania at 8.15 am, travelling via Nicolosi. It returns from the Rifugio Sapienza at 4.30 pm. The return ticket costs L7000. The AST office in Nicolosi (☎ 095 91 15 05) is at Via Etnea 32 and is open from 8 am to 2 pm Monday to Saturday. You can also drive this route (take Via Etnea north out of Catania and follow the signs for Nicolosi and Etna).

North

SAIS and FCE buses connect Linguaglossa with Fiumefreddo, on the coast (from where other SAIS buses run north to Taormina and Messina and south to Catania). Unless the FCE puts on a winter ski-season or summer bus to Piano Provenzana, your only chance from Linguaglossa is your thumb. If driving, follow the signs for Piano Provenzana out of Linguaglossa.

AROUND MT ETNA

Another option is to circle Mt Etna on the private Circumetnea train line. It starts in Catania from the train station at Corso delle Province 13, opposite Corso Italia. Go to the ticket office (☎ 095 37 48 42) at the Circumetnea station for information. Catch bus Nos 401, 448 or 628 from the main train station to Corso delle Province.

The line runs around the mountain from Catania to the coastal town of Riposto, passing through numerous towns and villages on its slopes, including Linguaglossa. You can reach Riposto (or neighbouring Giarre) from Taormina by train or bus if you want to make the trip from that end.

Catania–Riposto is about a 3½-hour trip, but you needn't go that far. If leaving from Catania, consider finishing the trip at Randazzo (two hours), a small medieval town noted for the fact that it has consistently escaped destruction despite its proximity to the summit. Randazzo itself is mildly interesting, with a couple of churches to punctuate a brief stroll along a few quiet streets, some lined with Aragonese apartments. A good example of lava architecture are the walls of the Norman **Cattedrale di Santa Maria**, while the **Chiesa di Santa Maria della Volta** preserves a squat 14th-century bell tower.

An FS branch railway line connects Randazzo with Taormina/Giardini-Naxos, but services are subject to cancellation. The infrequent SAIS buses are more reliable.

Syracuse & the South-East

The history of Sicily's south-eastern corner is really the tale of two glorious epochs and one disastrous event. Settled by the Greeks, the region flourished and for nearly 500 years was considered a centre of culture, learning and political power. Nearly 2000 years later the south-east blossomed again as the birthplace of an ornate and much-lauded architectural style known as Sicilian baroque. The region's renaissance, however, was only made possible by a devastating earthquake which flattened many towns and villages on 11 January 1693. Although separated by nearly two millenia, these three episodes have virtually defined the character and appearance of the south-east, no less so than in the region's largest and most visited city, Syracuse (Siracusa). By almost universal consent the most beautiful city on the island, Syracuse has successfully combined the glory of its ancient past with the architectural splendour of the 18th century in a unified, aesthetic whole that has few rivals in all of Italy.

Although it is tempting to devote all of your time to exploring the city only, the rest of the region deserves more than just a cursory glance. In Noto and Ragusa you will find the apogee of the Sicilian baroque, while the traditional mountainous interior is not just a convincing journey into a pastoral past but a field trip to some of Sicily's best-preserved and interesting archaeological digs.

Syracuse (Siracusa)

postcode 96100 • pop 125,900

The cradle of Greek civilisation in Italy and at one time a rival to Athens as the most important city in the Western world, Syracuse is one of the most impressive and rewarding highlights of a visit to Sicily. Although now no more than a peripheral player in Sicilian affairs, this tidy and compact provincial capital is an unmissable repository of

Highlights

- Sip on a cappuccino in Syracuse's Piazza del Duomo, one of the most beautiful squares in all of Italy
- Take a stroll around Ortygia, where ancient Greek and 18th-century baroque live side by side in near-perfect symmetry
- Visit Syracuse's Greek theatre in the Neapolis Parco Archaeologico
- Relax on a boat trip on the Cyane river, where papyrus grows wild
- Have a wander through the town of Noto: the most perfect example of baroque genius in Sicily

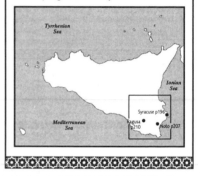

archaeological and architectural treasures dating back some 2700 years. Its glorious classical past now confined to ancient history, Syracuse has changed its identity many times since, no less so than in the 17th and 18th centuries, when virtually the entire city was rebuilt following the earthquake of 1693. Today it offers an intoxicating mix of antiquity and the baroque, with a fair amount of Byzantine and Spanish thrown in for good measure. Although it languished in the provincial backwaters for over 1000 years, the 20th century was relatively kind to Syracuse and today the city is one of Sicily's most flourishing and prosperous urban centres.

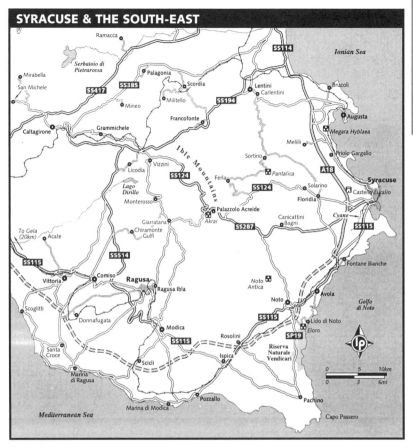

SYRACUSE & THE SOUTH-EAST

HISTORY

Syracuse's origins date to the 13th century BC, when the island of Ortygia was settled by Sicilian tribes who prospered through trading with other settlements in the Mediterranean basin. In 734 BC the island was seized by a group of Corinthian colonists under the leadership of Archia. Four years later, the colonists expanded onto the mainland with a second town called Acradina (in the area of the Syracusan Forum). The two settlements were linked by an earth causeway and later a bridge behind the modern-day main post of-fice. The growing city of Syracoussai de-rived its name from a torrential stream called the Syrakò which flowed nearby.

Protected on all sides and with a plentiful supply of water, Syracuse grew increasingly powerful and eventually broke its colonial relationship with Corinth and began trading in its own right, a new rival to the Mediterranean powers of Athens and Carthage. In 485 BC the 'tyrant of Gela', Gelon (540–478 BC), seized the city and ordered that the populations of all other Sicilian colonies transfer to Syracuse, triggering a sharp increase in the city's population and size. Two new quarters were created: Tyche (after the Greek goddess of Fortune) in the north-east and Neapolis (meaning 'new city') in the north-west, in the area now occupied by the archaeological park. With the help of Akragas (now Agrigento) and Gela, Syracuse inflicted a heavy defeat on the Carthaginians in 480 BC, paving the way for the city's gradual domination of the Mediterranean basin. This steady expansion was in large part due to the city's rigid political structure, which saw a series of sometimes capable but often brutal tyrant-kings maintain a totalitarian grip on the reins of power.

Threatened by this new rival to the west, in 415 BC Athens dispatched one of the largest fleets ever put together to deliver Syracuse into Athenian hands. Athenian muscle proved no match for Syracusan strategy and the fleet was almost completely destroyed. Syracuse's revenge was unmerciful: those prisoners who escaped execution were incarcerated for seven years in the city's notorious quarries, a move that drew condemnation from the Hellenistic world. Their temporary isolation from other Mediterranean powers merely spurred Syracuse to cement its dominance.

Cruel and vicious though they often were, the Syracusan tyrants were clever and vain enough to actively pursue a modicum of cultural respectability. As well as order an impressive program of public works that saw the construction of mighty temples and other monuments to the gods (and put their personal stamp on the city), Syracuse's kings went to great lengths to attract the finest minds of their time to the city. Pindar and Aeschylus were invited by Hieron I, who ruled from 478 to 466 BC; it is probable that Aeschylus' masterpieces *Prometheus Bound* and *Prometheus Released* were first shown in the city's amphitheatre *(anfiteatro)*. Successive kings continued to promote Syracuse as a capital of arts and sciences; Dionysius II (who reigned from 367–343 BC) was greatly taken with the 'philosopher-king' theories expounded by his tutor Plato, although when the philosopher objected to the king's more outlandish behaviour he was forced to flee lest he meet a premature end.

Following Dionysius' death the city entered an unsteady stream of alliances aimed at preserving the status quo in the face of antiquity's newest emerging power: Rome. The tyrants became more conciliatory, and the city even underwent a short experiment in democracy. It was, however, the beginning of the end for the city's independence, and not even the ingenious defences devised by the city's most famous son, Archimedes, were enough to stave off the ransack of the city by Roman troops in 211 BC.

Under Roman rule Syracuse remained the

The Man who Cried 'Eureka!'

Arguably the classical world's greatest scientific mind, Archimedes, was born in Syracuse in 287 BC. Following his studies in Alexandria, he returned to his native city where he proceeded to astound the scientific world with his theories on geometry, algebra and calculus. King Hieron II was eager to put Archimedes' fine mind to use, and the story goes that he asked him to find a precise way of measuring the mass of gold. Archimedes pondered the question for a long time but could find no working solution. The scientist's wife, noting his tension and frustration, advised him to relax and take a bath. Archimedes duly did so, but no sooner had he got into the water than he jumped out and cried 'Eureka! I have found it!' Thanks to his wife, Archimedes had stumbled upon the principle of measuring mass through the displacement of water.

Beloved of his fellow citizens, no less for devising a brilliant system of refractory mirrors that used sunlight to burn the Roman fleet in 212 BC, Archimedes played a key role in the defence of his city but not even his genius was enough to stop the Roman onslaught. Out of respect the Roman consul Marcus Marcellus gave a direct order that his life be spared, but an unknowing centurion burst into his house and before he had time to identify his victim he pulled out a sword and hacked him to death.

capital of Sicily and was the seat of the praetors, but the city was in decline. It was briefly the capital of the Byzantine empire in 663 when Constans set up court here, but was sacked by the Saracens in 878 and reduced to little more than a fortified provincial town. The population fell drastically, and the next 800 years were marked by famine, plague and earthquakes. The Val di Noto earthquake in 1693, however, marked the beginning of Syracuse's renewal. Urban planners took advantage of the damage to the city to undertake a massive program of reconstructing and restoring old buildings in the baroque style of the day. Following the unification of 1865 Syracuse was made a provincial capital and the city began to grow once more. In the 20th century, prosperity came at the price of some rather ugly urban developments and the growth of heavy industry, but the heart of the city remains unsullied.

ORIENTATION
Tidy and compact, Syracuse is a very manageable city to visit. The main sights are in two areas: on the island of Ortygia and 2km across town in the Neapolis Parco Archeologico (Neapolis Archaeological Park). Most accommodation is in the newer part of town, to the west (although Ortygia has some lovely, if more expensive, hotels). The best dining spots are in Ortygia.

INFORMATION
Tourist Offices
The main APT office (☎ 0931 6 77 10), Via San Sebastiano 45, opens from 8.30 am to 1.30 pm Monday to Saturday. There's also a branch office at the archaeological park in Neapolis. The AAT (☎ 0931 46 42 55) on Ortygia, Via Maestranza 33, deals specifically with Syracuse and is probably the most convenient office at which to pick up a map and hotel list. It is open from 9 am to 1 pm and 4.30 to 8.30 pm Monday to Friday and mornings only on Saturday.

Money
Numerous banks line Corso Umberto, including the Banca Nazionale del Lavoro at No 29, which has ATMs. There are others on Corso Gelone. The rates at the train station exchange booth are generally poor.

Post & Communications
The post office is on Piazza della Posta, to your left as you cross the bridge to Ortygia. It is open from 8.30 am to 6.30 pm Monday to Friday (to 1 pm on Saturday).

The Telecom office, Viale Teracati 42, is open from 8.30 am to 7.30 pm Monday to Saturday. Night-time callers can use the phones at the Bar Bel Caffè, Piazzale Marconi 18, which is open until the wee hours.

Internet Services
Libreria Gabò, on Corso Matteotti 38 on Ortygia, has one terminal and charges L5000 per 30 minutes. It is open from 9 am to 1 pm and 4.30 to 8.30 pm Monday to Friday, 9 am to 1 pm and 4.30 to midnight on Saturday and 6.30 to 8.30 pm on Sunday.

Medical Services & Emergency
The public hospital is at Via Testaferrata 1 (☎ 0931 46 10 42). For medical emergencies, ring ☎ 0931 6 85 55.

The police station (questura; ☎ 0931 40 21 11) is at Via San Sebastiano 12.

ORTYGIA
The island of Ortygia is the spiritual and physical heart of the city. It is a living museum of a succession of epochs – Greek, Norman, Aragon and baroque – purposefully combined in a harmonious symmetry to impress even the most cynical visitor. Pride of place goes to the simple but elegant Piazza del Duomo, one of the most beautiful baroque squares in all of Europe, but be sure to allow plenty of time to wander in and out of the tangled maze of streets and alleyways; virtually every house is worth a look. Centuries of neglect have certainly taken some of the lustre off Ortygia's beauty, but in recent years city authorities have made concerted efforts to reverse the decay. Ignore the occasional scaffold!

Piazza Archimede & Around
This elegant square is virtually in the middle of the island. Its centrepiece is the

SYRACUSE & THE SOUTH-EAST

SYRACUSE (SIRACUSA)

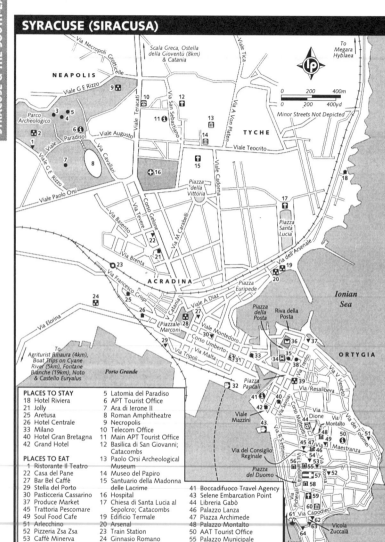

PLACES TO STAY
18 Hotel Riviera
21 Jolly
25 Aretusa
26 Hotel Centrale
33 Milano
40 Hotel Gran Bretagna
42 Grand Hotel

PLACES TO EAT
1 Ristorante Il Teatro
22 Casa del Pane
27 Bar Bel Caffè
29 Stella del Porto
30 Pasticceria Cassarino
37 Produce Market
45 Trattoria Pescomare
49 Soul Food Cafe
51 Arlecchino
52 Pizzeria Zsa Zsa
53 Caffè Minerva
54 Il Cenacolo
62 Trattoria la Foglia
63 Ristorante Osteria
   da Mariano
64 La Medusa

OTHER
2 Greek Theatre
3 Orecchio di Dionisio
4 Grotta dei Cordari

5 Latomia del Paradiso
6 APT Tourist Office
7 Ara di Ierone II
8 Roman Amphitheatre
9 Necropolis
10 Telecom Office
11 Main APT Tourist Office
12 Basilica di San Giovanni;
   Catacombs
13 Paolo Orsi Archeological
   Museum
14 Museo del Papiro
15 Santuario della Madonna
   delle Lacrime
16 Hospital
17 Chiesa di Santa Lucia al
   Sepolcro; Catacombs
19 Edificio Termale
20 Arsenal
23 Train Station
24 Ginnasio Romano
28 Syracusan Forum
31 Banca Nazionale del
   Lavoror (Bank & ATM)
32 Ferry Terminal
34 Intercity & Urban
   Bus Station
35 AST Bus Ticket Office
36 Post Office
38 Interbus Bus Ticket Office
39 Tempio di Apollo

41 Boccadifuoco Travel Agency
43 Selene Embarcation Point
44 Libreria Gabò
46 Palazzo Lanza
47 Piazza Archimede
48 Palazzo Montalto
50 AAT Tourist Office
55 Palazzo Municipale
56 Palazzo Beneventano
   del Bosco
57 Cathedral
58 Palazzo Arcivescovile
59 Chiesa di Santa Lucia alla
   Badia
60 Museo Regionale d'Arte
   Medioevale e Moderna
61 Fontana Aretusa
65 Castello Maniace

20th-century **fountain** (by Giulio Moschetti) depicting Artemis the Huntress surrounded by handmaidens and sirens. The square is Syracuse's 'drawing room', where locals sit around and drink coffee at the cafes that circle the square. Above them are a number of Catalan-Gothic *palazzi* (mansions), including **Palazzo Lanza** with its elegant twin-lighted mullioned windows and the **Palazzo Platamone**, now home to the Banca d'Italia. If you can, take a peek at the Palazzo's courtyard, where there is a gorgeous 15th-century staircase.

To the north-east, Via Montalto gives its name to perhaps the most handsome of all of Syracuse's palazzi, **Palazzo Mergulese-Montalto**. Built in 1397, it was presented to the Montalto family by Constance of Aragon, and is a clear sign of the wealth and elegance of 14th-century Syracuse. Its main features are the exquisitely crafted twin- and triple-lighted mullioned windows. Unfortunately, the building is not open to the public.

Piazza del Duomo

Syracusans seem to delight in amazing their visitors. Just as they have finished admiring the graceful elegance of Piazza Archimede, the unsuspecting stumble across Piazza del Duomo, one of the most wonderful public spaces in Italy. In this semi-elliptical, elongated square the baroque is king, surrounded as it is on all sides by a series of palazzi built after the earthquake of 1693. The square – which occupies the highest part of the island – is where the ancient acropolis of the Greek city once stood, giving it religious importance across 2700 years of history.

Directly north of the cathedral is the **Palazzo Municipale** or Palazzo Senatoriale, built in 1629 by the Spanish architect Juan Vermexio, nicknamed 'Il Lucertolone' or the lizard. On the left corner of the cornice is the architect's signature: a small lizard carved into a stone. Recent excavations beneath the building have uncovered the unfinished remains of an Ionic temple to Artemis. The palazzo now serves as city hall. To see the temple's remains, just ask at the gate. Attached to the cathedral's south-

ern side is the elegant, 17th-century **Palazzo Arcivescovile** (Archbishop's Palace), which is home to a library of rare manuscripts, including a number of letters by Schopenhauer. Visits are by appointment only; call ☎ 0931 6 79 68.

In the north-western corner of the square is the **Palazzo Beneventano del Bosco**, which has a pretty 18th-century facade, while at its southern end is the **Chiesa di Santa Lucia alla Badia**, dedicated to St Lucy, the city's patron saint, who was martyred at Syracuse during the reign of the Roman emperor Diocletian. The church's baroque facade is decorated with a wrought-iron balustrade. At the time of research it was closed for restoration.

The Cathedral There is no better example of Syracuse's long and distinguished mix of architectural styles than the city's cathedral *(duomo)*. Inside, traces remain of a Doric temple dedicated to Athena which date from the early decades of the 5th century BC. Below them is an even more extraordinary sight, an altar *(ara)* built by the Siculi three centuries earlier, the only surviving evidence of the island's first settlers.

The original Greek temple was renowned throughout the Mediterranean, in no small part thanks to Cicero, who visited Ortygia in the 1st century BC. The doors were adorned in gold and ivory, while the interior was lined with magnificent paintings of Agathocles fighting the Carthaginians. The roof was crowned by a golden statue of Athena which served as a beacon to sailors at sea. The temple was 'Christianised' in the 7th century and a number of alterations were made. The 36 columns which ran along the length of the interior were walled off (though 24 are still visible in the masonry) and the central nave was split into three aisles. The towers on the left side of the church's exterior were built by the Saracens, who used the building as a mosque. During the 12th century the church was adorned with mosaics, but these were destroyed during the earthquakes of 1545 and 1693, the second of which also resulted in the collapse of the facade. The great stylist of the Sicilian baroque, Andrea Palma, drew up plans for the cathedral's restoration and a new, more impressive facade was built with statues by Marabitti.

Fontana Aretusa

On the waterfront south of Piazza del Duomo along Via Picherali is the Fontana Aretusa, a 1000-year-old natural freshwater spring. Legend has it that the goddess Artemis transformed her beautiful hand-maiden Aretusa into the spring to protect her from the unwelcome attention of the river god Alpheus. Undeterred and unwilling to be apart from her, Alpheus jumped into the pool. Now populated by ducks, grey mullets and papyrus plants, the fountain is a popular spot for Syracusans during their evening stroll.

Museo Regionale d'Arte Medioevale e Moderna

Housed in the former monastery of St Benedict, itself located in the 13th-century Palazzo Bellomo, this gallery of medieval and modern art has a sizeable collection of sculpture and painting dating from the high Middle Ages right up to the 20th century. The gallery's most important pieces are an *Annunciazione* (Annunciation) by Antonello da Messina (1474) and *La Sepoltura di Santa Lucia* (The Burial of St Lucy) by Caravaggio (1609). The gallery also has a number of statues by the Gagini school and a lovely collection of the applied arts such as silver- and goldsmithery, ceramics and terracotta. The gallery (☎ 0931 6 96 17) is at Via Capodieci 14, and is open from 9 am to 2 pm Monday to Saturday (also 3 to 7 pm Wednesday and Friday) and 9 am to 1 pm on Sunday. Admission costs L8000.

Other Sights

At the entrance to Ortygia, on Piazza Pancali, lies the **Tempio di Apollo** (Temple of Apollo), one of the first Greek structures built here. Little remains of the 6th-century BC Doric structure, apart from the bases of a few columns. The Byzantines used it as a church, the Saracens as a mosque and the Spaniards converted it into a barracks in the 16th century.

At the southern tip of the island is the 13th-century **Castello Maniace**, built by Frederick II as part of a massive program of construction that more or less turned Ortygia into an island fortress. The castle is still used as a barracks and as such is off limits.

THE MAINLAND

Although not nearly as picturesque as Ortygia, you should still devote at least a day to exploring the mainland quarters of Syracuse. The Acradina quarter, directly across the bridge from Ortygia, is the modern city, built on the site of the ancient settlement of the same name. To the north-east in the Tyche quarter are the city's extensive catacombs and the renowned Archaeological Museum. To see the real thing, go west to Neapolis and the archaeological park.

Acradina

The most developed and modern part of the city, Acradina has only a couple of interesting sights. Bombed twice during WWII (by

---

Syracuse & the Mafia

Although not particularly noted for its Mafia links, like all Sicilian cities Syracuse too has had to contend with the nefarious influence of organised crime. In the summer of 1999, one of Sicily's most distinguished sons, the filmmaker Giuseppe Tornatore (of *Cinema Paradiso* fame), was forced to shut down the filming of his latest work, *Malena*, which was being shot on location in Syracuse. Some important equipment had 'disappeared' from the store rooms and it emerged that the Mafia were holding it in lieu of payment of the notorious *pizzo* or protection money. Local newspapers cried foul and expressed their disgust that one so respected as Tornatore should be a victim of this particularly Sicilian form of blackmail. A couple of days later, however, filming resumed and the story faded from the front pages. What happened is unclear, and the question remains: was the pizzo paid or was the equipment returned out of shame? In Sicily, one never knows.

the Allies in 1943 and then by the Luftwaffe in 1944), most of the quarter bears the unmistakable stamp of the post-war aesthetic: functional and not too pleasing on the eye. On Piazzale Marconi the old **Syracusan Forum** (Foro Siracusano), once the site of the marketplaces *(agora)*, is now bisected by a number of busy streets and the few remains have been overshadowed by a hideous Fascist war memorial and church built in 1936.

A few hundred yards west of the forum along Via Elorina, however, is a sight well worth visiting (though few ever seem to): the ruins of the **Ginnasio Romano** (Roman Gymnasium), built in the 1st century. Despite the name, this was actually a small theatre at the heart of a building that also contained a large atrium and a theatre directly behind the stage. Illustrations help create a visual impression of what it looked like at the time. Unfortunately, part of the complex was flooded in 1998 and remains under water. The site is open from 9 am to 1 pm Monday to Saturday. Admission is free.

Along the water to the east of the forum (take Via dell'Arsenale) are the fenced-off remains of the ancient **arsenal**, once a set of rectangular pits into which ships would be pulled for re-provisioning. Adjacent are the ruins of the **Edificio Termale** (Thermal Building), a Byzantine bathhouse where it is claimed the Emperor Constans was assassinated using a soap dish in 668.

North of the arsenal is one of the city's loveliest squares, **Piazza Santa Lucia**, whose northern end is dominated by the **Chiesa di Santa Lucia al Sepolcro**. The 17th-century church is built on the spot where the city's patron saint, Lucy, an aristocratic girl who devoted herself to saintliness after being blessed by St Agatha, was martyred in 304. Unfortunately, most of the treasures have been removed from the building, so it isn't nearly as interesting as it used to be, but the square itself is worth visiting, if only to admire the rows of trees than line three sides of it.

Underneath the church is a network of **catacombs** that are the largest in Italy after those in Rome. These remain closed, however, as authorities continue to bolster the walls in order to make them safe for visitors.

Catacombs of Tyche

According to Roman law, Christians were not allowed to bury their dead within city limits (which during the Roman occupation did not extend beyond Ortygia). Forced to go elsewhere, Christians conducted their burials in the outlying district of Tyche and its underground aqueducts, unused since Greek times. New tunnels were carved out and the result was a labyrinthine network of burial chambers, most of which are inaccessible except the ones underneath the **Basilica di San Giovanni**, directly opposite the tourist office on Via San Sebastiano. The church itself has been abandoned since the end of the 17th century and its interior is overgrown, but it once served as the city's cathedral. The first bishop of Syracuse, St Marcian, was flogged to death in 254 while tied to a pillar at the bottom of a set of steps.

The catacombs are, for the most part, dank and a little eerie. Thousands of little niches line the walls and tunnels lead off from the main chamber *(decumanus maximus)* into *rotonde*, round chambers used by the faithful for praying. All of the treasures that accompanied the dead on their spiritual journey fell victim to tomb robbers over the centuries except one: a sarcophagus unearthed in 1872 and now on exhibit in the Paolo Orsi Archaeological Museum.

The church and catacombs are open from 9 am to 12.30 pm and 2 to 5.30 pm daily except Tuesday; admission to the church is free, the catacombs cost L4000.

Paolo Orsi Archaeological Museum

At the top of Via Cadorna (which runs north from Piazza Euripede) is Sicily's most extensive archeological museum (☎ 0931 46 40 22). Located in the grounds of the Villa Landolina, the museum (named after the archaeologist Paolo Orsi, who arrived in Syracuse in 1886 and devoted the next 45 years to uncovering its ancient treasures) contains an extremely well-organised and extensive collection. At the centre of the building is a large atrium that serves as a reference point for the three sections of the museum as well as containing a wealth of information on virtually every exhibit included here.

To the left as you enter is Sector A, which begins with a geological overview of Sicily and then moves on to cover all of the artefacts that date from the Palaeolithic period to the early Greek settlements. Sector B, at the far end of the atrium from the entrance, deals with the history of Greek settlement in Sicily, with a particular emphasis on Megara Hyblaea and Syracuse. Of note are a number of sculptures uncovered at the former, including one of the physician Sambrotidas and one of a woman nursing twins, both sculpted in the 6th century BC. Of the Syracusan finds, the most famous is the splendid copy of *Venere Uscendo dall'Acqua* (Venus Emerging from the Sea), also known as the 'Landolina Venus' (named after Saverio Landolina, who found it in 1806). Sector C, to the right of the entrance, concentrates on the Syracusan outposts of Eloro, Akrai, Kasmenai and Kamarina. There is also an interesting selection of material found in the major Doric colonies of Gela and Agrigento.

The museum is open from 9 am to 1 pm and 3.30 to 6.30 pm daily except Monday. Admission costs L8000.

Museo del Papiro

This small museum (☎ 0931 6 16 16) at Viale Teocrito 66 has exhibits including papyrus documents and products. The plant grows in abundance around the Cyane river, near Syracuse, and was used to make paper in the 18th century. The museum is open from 9 am to 2 pm Tuesday to Sunday. Admission is free.

Santuario della Madonna delle Lacrime

Syracuse's most recent noteworthy building (it opened in 1994), the vast and cavernous Sanctuary of Our Lady of the Tears was commissioned to house a statue of the Virgin that allegedly wept for five days in 1953. If you stand on the opposite side of the street and look up you can just about make out that the church is in the shape of a giant teardrop; religious fervour in Sicily does not lend itself easily to subtlety. Next

door, an extensive network of houses and streets from the Greek and Roman periods has been discovered. The church is open from 7 am to 12.30 pm and 4 to 7 pm daily.

Neapolis Parco Archeologico

About 500m west of the museum off Viale Teocrito is the extensive Neapolis Parco Archeologico (Neapolis Archaeological Park), Syracuse's most visited site. Indeed, the trappings of mass tourism are everywhere, from the countless beverage stands and souvenir stalls to the rows of tour buses lined up in the car park, not forgetting the hordes of visitors that in summer overrun the place. Still, the park should be on your 'not-to-be-missed' list as it contains some of the most impressive classical ruins in Sicily. The park is open from 9 am to two hours before sunset (usually 6.30 pm from May to October and 3 pm the rest of the year). Admission costs L4000. There is an APT tourist kiosk just before the entrance to the park. To get to the park, take bus No 1, 4, 5, 6, 8, 11, 12 or 15 from Piazza della Posta to Corso Gelone/Viale Teocrito.

Greek Theatre For the classicist, Syracuse is summed up in one image – that of the sparkling white, 3rd-century BC Greek theatre (Teatro Greco), completely hewn out of the living rock. A masterpiece of classical architecture, the ancient theatre was commissioned by Hieron II and was built on the site of an older theatre erected 200 years earlier. Old records show that Aeschylus staged some of his later plays here, which would have been watched (most likely) by a capacity crowd of 16,000 people. When the Romans took Syracuse they made alterations to the theatre, mostly so that they could stage gladiatorial combats.

Other Ruins Near the theatre is the **Latomia del Paradiso** (Garden of Paradise), which was a limestone quarry run by the Greeks along the lines of a concentration camp, where prisoners cut blocks of limestone in subterranean tunnels for building projects. It was here that the Athenians captured after the great sea battle of 413 BC were imprisoned and held for seven years in inhumane conditions. Most of the area remained covered by a 'roof' of earth, which collapsed during the 1693 earthquake. After this, the garden of citrus and magnolia trees was created.

A renowned curiosity at the heart of the garden is the ear-shaped grotto known as the **Orecchio di Dionisio** (Ear of Dionysius). According to Caravaggio, who visited it in the 17th century, the tyrant-king Dionysius must have had it built so that he could listen in on the conversations of the prisoners, but it is most likely that the grotto, 23m high and 65m deep, was dug out as a rock quarry and later used as a sounding board for the theatre performances nearby.

Next to it is the now-closed **Grotta dei Cordari** (Cordmarkers' Cave), a grotto, supported by pillars, once used in the manufacture of rope; in antiquity, humidity was an essential ingredient in rope's manufacture and the cave had plenty of it.

In the north-eastern tip of the park is a **necropolis** used during Roman times. Two tombs stand out, each fronted by Doric semi-columns: one of them is thought to contain the remains of Archimedes.

The Greatest Show on Earth?

Performances in Syracuse's theatre were pretty intense affairs, particularly during the six-day Feast of Dionysus, god of wine and merriment (not to be confused with the tyrant-king Dionysius). Daily performances of a tetracycle (three tragedies and a satirical work thrown in for good measure) and no less than five comedies kept audiences glued to their seats from dawn till dusk. As the festival was essentially a hedonistic religious ceremony, the high point of the day's performance (usually during the third tragedy) saw the audience whipped into a frenzy of delirium described by Aristotle as 'catharsis', after which they were made to laugh for a few more hours and then sent home. After nearly 20 centuries without a festival, 1914 saw the start of a new series of productions performed every even year. See Special Events for details.

Back outside this area and opposite the APT tourist office you'll find the entrance to the 2nd-century AD **Roman amphitheatre**, the third-largest in Italy after the Colosseum and the amphitheatre in Verona. The structure was used for gladiator-fights and horse races. Roman punters used to park their chariots in the area between the amphitheatre and Viale Paolo Orsi. The Spaniards, little interested in archaeology, largely destroyed the site in the 16th century, using it as a quarry to build the city walls on Ortygia. West of the amphitheatre is the 3rd-century BC **Ara di Ierone II** (Altar of Hieron II). The monolithic sacrificial altar was a kind of giant abattoir where 450 oxen could be killed at one time.

BOAT TRIPS

Between April and October, the *Selene* takes passengers around Ortygia in a 45-minute ride that offers splendid views of the city (truly the best way to appreciate it). The boat departs the dock in front of the Grand Hotel from 10 am onward daily: specific departure times depend on demand. Sandwiches and music are thrown into the very reasonable price of L22,000 per person. A real treat is to go after dark, on the so-called 'Syracuse by Night' trip. For bookings, go to the dock or call ☎ 0368 66 67 21; ask for Signor Castagnino.

SPECIAL EVENTS
Greek Classical Drama

Since 1914, in every even-numbered year, Syracuse has hosted a festival of Greek classical drama during May and June. Performances are given in the Greek theatre and prices range from around L40,000 on weekdays to L70,000 at the weekend. Two tragedies run on alternate days for the duration of the festival; also thrown in is the occasional classical comedy. The performances have attracted some of Italy's finest actors to its stage, including Marcello Mastroianni and Vittorio Gassman. All the performances are in Italian. Tickets are available from the APT office or at a booth at the entrance to the theatre. You can telephone for information on ☎ 0931 6 74 15. At the time of research the authorities were in a quandary about the festival's prohibitive costs and were considering alternating the plays with some opera: check with the tourist office for details.

Festa di Santa Lucia
On 13 December a characteristic festival to commemorate the city's patron saint begins on Piazza del Duomo, with a procession carrying a silver statue of the saint through the streets. The route winds its way through Ortygia and on to the mainland until it reaches Piazza Santa Lucia. The whole festival is accompanied by plenty of colour and fireworks which more than make up for the sombre disposition of its participants.

PLACES TO STAY
Camping
There are camping facilities at *Agriturist Rinaura* (☎ 0931 72 12 24), 4km west of the city on SS115; catch bus No 21, 22 or 24 from Corso Umberto. It costs L8000/19,000 per person/site (including electricity and car space). *Fontane Bianche* (☎ 0931 79 03 33) is 19km south-west of Syracuse, at the beach of the same name. It is slightly more expensive than Agriturist Rinaura and is open from April to October. Catch bus No 21 or 22.

Hostels
The non-HI *Ostello della Gioventù* (☎ 0931 71 11 18, Viale Epipoli 45) is 8km west of Syracuse; catch bus No 11 or 25 from Piazzale Marconi. Beds cost L25,000; full board is L42,000.

Hotels – Budget
Close to the train station, *Hotel Centrale* (☎ 0931 6 05 28, Corso Umberto 141) has small, basic singles/doubles costing L35,000/50,000. *Milano* (☎ 0931 6 69 81, Corso Umberto 10), near Ortygia, has no-frills rooms for L30,000/55,000 or L50,000/80,000 with a bathroom.

The two-star *Aretusa* (☎/fax 0931 2 42 11, Via Francesco Crispi 75) is close to the train station and has comfortable singles/doubles for L45,000/70,000. With a bathroom, you're looking at L50,000/80,000. *Hotel Gran Bretagna* (☎ 0931 6 87 65, Via Savoia 21) is

pleasant and has rooms for L53,000/87,000 or L63,000/99,000 with bathroom.

Hotels – Mid-Range
The *Scala Greca* (☎ 0931 75 39 22, fax 0931 75 37 78, Via Avola 7) is north of the archaeological park and has singles/doubles with a bathroom for L75,000/98,000. It is, like several other better hotels, quite a distance from the centre. With stunning views from a 1st-floor terrace, the *Hotel Riviera* (☎ 0931 6 70 50) is a good choice. The rooms are large and elegant, if a little spartan. Singles/doubles cost L70,000/110,000.

Hotels – Top End
Near both the station and the archeological park, *Jolly* (☎ 0931 46 11, fax 0931 46 11 26, Corso Gelone 45) is a very good choice. Fully serviced, sound-proofed rooms cost up to L215,000/270,000. The newly restored *Grand Hotel* (☎ 0931 46 46 00, fax 0931 46 46 11, Viale Mazzini 12) on Ortygia has top-class, fully appointed rooms for L240,000/350,000.

PLACES TO EAT
Ortygia
There is no shortage of places to eat on the island. For tasty and filling sandwiches and salads, the *Soul Food Cafe* (Via Maestranze 17), set at the back of a lovely courtyard, is an excellent choice. One of the cheapest restaurants on the island is *Il Cenacolo* (☎ 0931 6 50 99, Via del Consiglio Reginale 10), down a tiny lane off Via Roma. You can eat well here for around L20,000. Near the cathedral, the *Trattoria Pescomare* (Via Landolina 6) serves up a good selection of local fish dishes and a wide range of pizzas. All mains cost about L10,000. At *Trattoria la Foglia* (☎ 0931 6 62 33, Via Capodieci 21), off Largo Aretusa, the eccentric owner/chef and her vegetarian husband serve whatever seafood and vegetables are fresh on the day, and bake their own bread. A full meal can cost around L40,000. *Arlecchino* (☎ 0931 6 63 86, Via dei Tolomei 5) is near the waterfront. It is one of the city's better restaurants and you'd be lucky to get away with paying less than L45,000 per head.

If you're looking for something other than fish, the exceptional **Ristorante Osteria da Mariano** (☎ 0931 6 74 44, Vicolo Zuccalà 8) serves very good traditional inland Sicilian fare, including a particularly delicious pasta with pine nuts (*pinoli*). It is a small place and fills up quickly, so be sure to book ahead, especially at the weekend. **Pizzeria Trattoria Zsa Zsa** (Via Roma 73) serves 65 different kinds of pizzas, antipasti and pasta. A meat-based tourist menu is L17,000; another with fish costs L19,000. **La Medusa** (☎ 0931 6 14 03, Via Santa Teresa 23) specialises in Tunisian cuisine.

Caffè Minerva (Via Roma 58) is a pleasant cafe that does typical Sicilian dessert treats and a nice, frothy cappuccino. It is also a great spot for people-watching.

In the streets near the post office, there's a produce **market** until 1 pm daily except Sunday.

The Mainland

The selection of restaurants isn't as good on the mainland. For snacks, try the excellent takeaway pizza and *focaccia* (flat bread) at **Casa del Pane** (Corso Gelone 65). In the new part of town, the **Stella del Porto** (☎ 0931 6 05 82, Via Tripoli 40), off Via Malta, is a simple restaurant with a small menu concentrating on seafood. Try the spaghetti with swordfish (*pesce spada*). A full meal will cost about L25,000.

In the archaeological park, close to the Greek theatre, **Ristorante Il Teatro** (☎ 0931 2 13 21, Via Agnello 8) has a good tourist menu for L22,000. It is a popular weekend spot for Syracusans, but it is difficult to get to unless you have your own transport. For good Sicilian sweets such as *cannolo di ricotta* (ricotta cheese pastry horn) and *cassata* (cream, fruit and chocolate sponge) go to **Pasticceria Cassarino** (☎ 0931 6 80 46, Corso Umberto 86).

There are several **grocery shops** and **supermarkets** along Corso Gelone.

GETTING THERE & AWAY
Bus

Unless you're coming from Catania or Messina, you'll find buses faster and more convenient than trains. Interbus buses (☎ 0931 6 67 10) leave from Riva della Posta or near the Interbus office at Via Trieste 28, a block in. They connect with Catania and its airport, Palermo (L20,000, four hours), Enna and surrounding small towns, including Noto. Interbus also has a daily service to Rome, leaving Syracuse at 7.45 am and connecting with the Rome bus at Catania. A single ticket costs L67,000 or L57,000 for under 26s and over 60s.

AST buses leave for Catania, Piazza Armerina, Noto, Modica and Ragusa from their office (☎ 0931 46 48 20) at Riva della Posta 9–11.

Train

More than a dozen trains depart daily bound for Messina (three hours) via Catania (1½ hours). Some go on to Rome, Turin, Milan and other long-distance destinations. There is only one direct connection to Palermo, leaving at 6.40 am and taking five hours. If you insist on using trains and miss this one, you'll have to go to Catania and wait there for a connection. There are several slow trains from Syracuse to Modica and Ragusa.

Car & Motorcycle

By car, if arriving from the north, you will enter Syracuse on Via Scala Greca. To reach the centre of the city, turn left at Viale Teracati and follow it around to the south; it eventually becomes Corso Gelone. There is ongoing confusion over the road connection between Catania, Syracuse and towns such as Noto further along the coast. A motorway is supposed to connect the towns but it starts and ends virtually in the middle of nowhere some kilometres out of Syracuse. You will need to follow the signs to get there.

Boat

There are a number of catamaran services to Malta during the summer months (June to September). Tickets cost around L180,000 return. For information check with the Boccadifuoco travel agency (☎ 0931 46 38 66), Viale Mazzini 8.

GETTING AROUND

If you arrive by bus, you'll be dropped on or near Piazza della Posta in Ortygia. Only a few kilometres separate the archaeological park and Ortygia, about a 20-minute walk. Otherwise, bus Nos 1 and 2 make the trip from Piazza della Posta. All city buses cost L1500 for one hour, irrespective of the number of buses you take.

AROUND SYRACUSE
Castello Eurialo

Seven kilometres west of the city in the outlying quarter of Epipolae is the castle that was the stronghold of Syracuse's Greek defensive works. Built during the reign of Hieron II, Castello Euriolo (Euryalus Castle) was adapted and fortified by Archimedes and was considered impregnable. Unfortunately for Syracuse, the castle was taken by the Romans without a fight. The castle is open from 9 am to one hour before sunset daily; admission is free. To get there, take bus No 9, 11 or 12 from the archaeological park.

The Cyane River & The Olympeion

A popular diversion between May and September is a 5km longboat trip on the Cyane river, only 5km west of the city along Via Elorina. The two-hour trip brings you from the mouth of the river right up to the source pool, said to have been formed by the tears of the nymph Cyane when her mistress Persephone (Proserpine in Roman mythology) was abducted by Hades (Pluto). This is the only place outside North Africa where

papyrus grows wild; the plants were originally a gift to Hieron II by Ptolemy (see the boxed text 'From Papyrus to Paper'). Along the way, you can check out the ruins of the **Olympeion**, a temple from the 6th century BC. Boat rentals cost L70,000 per boat, so the bigger the group the better (maximum 15 people). For bookings and information, call ☎ 0931 6 90 76. To get there, take bus No 21, 22 or 23 from Piazza della Posta on Ortygia.

Megara Hyblaea

The area north from Syracuse is a largely unattractive sprawl of refineries and heavy industry, but right in the middle of it are the ruins of the ancient settlement of Megara Hyblaea, founded in 728 BC by Greeks from Megara. Its history is largely unfortunate: razed to the ground and all its inhabitants evicted in 483 BC by the tyrant of Gela, Gelon, it was rebuilt on the same spot by Timoleon in 340 BC but only survived until 213 BC when it was destroyed for the second time by the Roman general Marcellus, who then went on to take Syracuse. A small population continued to live there until the 6th century, but it has been abandoned ever since. You'll need your own car to get there (25 minutes north of Syracuse on SS114); otherwise, infrequent trains stop at Megara Giannalea (L3000) from where you'll have to walk 1km northwards.

The South-East

THE SYRACUSAN INTERIOR

The mountainous interior of the province lacks the popular appeal of the coastline and is difficult to explore unless you have your own transport. The high limestone cliffs, cut through by deep gorges and valleys and topped by arid plateaux, have always served as a natural fortress against the attentions of unwelcome intruders, be it the ancient Greeks or the modern industrialists. Amidst the drystone walls and scattered villages, however, there are a couple of interesting sights that make a journey inland more than worthwhile, not least the extensive necropolis of Pantalica and the baroque town of Palazzolo Acreide.

From Papyrus to Paper

The Syracuse region has long been renowned for its manufacture of papyrus, the only place in Europe where it grows wild. The slender stalk is split into long strips, which are soaked in a special vegetal solution. Once softened, they are spread out and arranged in a woven crosshatch, first vertically and then horizontally. The crosshatch is then rolled and glued together with an adhesive also derived from the papyrus stalk. And, *voilà*, paper is born!

Pantalica

Forty kilometres west of Syracuse lies Sicily's most important necropolis, with more than 5000 tombs of various shapes and sizes honeycombed along the cliffs that surround the barren plateau of Pantalica, settled by the Siculi in 1270 BC. The town – called Hybla – thrived until the 8th century BC and the Greek founding of Akrai (see the Palazzolo Acreide section later in the chapter) in 664 BC, after which Hybla disappeared and many of the tombs were converted into cave dwellings. These were used in later centuries by Christians escaping from a wave of barbarian invasions. Of the town itself very little survives other than the **Anaktron** or prince's palace.

Getting There & Away The site is a difficult place to reach unless you have your own transport. If you don't, your best bet is to take a bus (L5500) from Syracuse to the town of Sortino, 5km north-east of the site. The first bus departs Syracuse at 7.15 am, the last leaves Sortino at 6.30 pm and the journey takes about an hour. Once in Sortino, signposts lead the way. Remember to stock up on food and – most importantly – liquids before you leave Sortino; there's nowhere else to buy anything along the road, which can be very hot in summer.

Alternatively, the Zuccalà travel agency (☎ 0931 74 07 32, Viale Pipoli 136) in Syracuse does one-day coach excursions to the site leaving at 9 am and returning at 4.30 pm from Monday to Saturday, May to October; prices start at L42,000 per person and include a basic lunch.

Palazzo Acreide

postcode 96010 • pop 9100
• elevation 670m

The archetypal baroque answer to the earthquake of 1693, Palazzolo Acreide was built in the shadow of the ancient Greek settlement of Akrai, founded in 664 BC as a strategic fortress to command the Syracusan hinterland.

The handsome baroque town is centred on the elegant Piazza del Popolo, itself dominated by the massive bulk of the 18th-century **Chiesa di San Sebastiano** and the **Palazzo Municipale**, built in 1908. The building is also home to a small tourist office (☎ 0931 88 20 00) which is open from 9.30 am to 1 pm and 3.30 to 6.30 pm Monday to Saturday. North of the square, at the end of a tight lane, is Piazza Moro (after Aldo Moro, the Italian prime minister assassinated by the Red Brigades in 1979) and two other exquisite baroque churches: on the northern side of the square the **Chiesa Madre** and on the southern side the **Chiesa di San Paolo**. At the top of Via Annunziata (the main road leading right out of Piazza Moro) is the fourth of the town's baroque treasures, the **Chiesa dell'Annunziata**, with a richly adorned portal.

Off Piazza del Popolo, at Via Machiavelli 19, is the **Casa-Museo di Antonino Uccello**, formerly the home of the poet and scholar (1922–79) and since 1984 a museum with an important collection of Sicilian folk art. Uccello devoted himself to preserving what he feared was disappearing from Sicilian life, so here's the place to go if you want to see what 18th-century farmers would have worn or how exactly they ground olives to make oil. The museum is open from 9 am to 1 pm daily and admission is free.

Akrai Although the baroque town is definitely worth exploring, most visitors head straight for the ruins of the archaeological zone covering the site of Akrai, a 20-minute walk south-west of the modern town along Corso Vittorio Emanuele. Syracuse's first inland colony was key to defending the overland trading route to other Greek settlements such as Akragas, and reached its apogee under the reign of Hieron II (265–215 BC). It was less important under Roman rule, and apart from a brief role as an early Christian centre it continued to decline and was eventually destroyed by the Saracens in the 9th century. The archaeological zone is open from 9 am to 7 pm daily; admission costs L4000.

The most impressive ruin is that of the **Greek theatre**, built at the end of the 3rd century BC and subsequently altered by the Romans, who used it for sittings of the local senate. This perfect semicircle once had an audience capacity of 600 divided into three separate sections. Behind the theatre are two quarries *(latomie)*, from which stone to build the city was removed by prisoners. The quarries were later converted into Christian burial chambers. The larger of the two, the **Intagliata**, has catacombs and altars cut into its sides, while the narrower one, the **Intagliatella**, has a wonderful relief of a large banquet cut into the rock face; it is thought to date from the 1st century BC. Other remains worth noting are the hardly recognisable **Tempio di Afrodite** (Temple of Aphrodite, Venus in Roman), south of the Intagliata, and the **Tempio di Persefone** (Temple of Persephone, Proserpine in Roman), off to the west of the theatre.

You can also follow a trail south of the archaeological zone which brings you to the remarkable stone sculptures which are known as the **Santoni** (Holy Men), 12 statues set in rock and devoted to the goddess Cybele, herself depicted on a seat. The largest figurative complex devoted to this particular goddess was created sometime during the 3rd century BC. It's a 15-minute walk down to the statues.

Places to Stay & Eat There is only one hotel in town, the fairly modern *Senatore* (☎ *0931 88 34 43, fax 0931 88 34 44, Largo Senatore Italia)*, which has comfortable singles/doubles for L50,000/70,000 with a bathroom, L10,000 less without.

There are a handful of good restaurants in town. Recommended is *Alfredo (☎ 0931 88 32 66, Via Duca d'Aosta 27)*, just off Piazza del Popolo. The focus is on Sicilian meat dishes; most mains cost around L10,000. It is closed Wednesday. Alternatively, *Da Nunzio (☎ 0931 88 22 86, Corso Vittorio Emanuele 7)* is a tasty fish restaurant. Prices are marginally more expensive than Alfredo's, and it is closed Monday.

Getting There & Away Unless you have your own transport, the only way to get here is by AST bus from Syracuse. The one-hour journey costs L8000. Buses depart every couple of hours from 7.15 am onwards from Piazza della Posta. The last bus for Syracuse leaves Piazza del Popolo (you can buy tickets in Bar Canguro, next to the church) at 8 pm.

NOTO
postcode 96017 • pop 23,000
• elevation 152m
Although a town called Noto or Netum has existed here for many centuries, the 'modern', 17th-century town of Noto dates its existence to 18 January 1693, one week after the flattening of the original Noto by earthquake. On this day the architect Giuseppe Lanza, duke of Camastra, was given the biggest commission of his life: build a town from scratch. He set about his task with a stubborn single-mindedness and a blatant disregard for the wishes of the now homeless townspeople, who were horrified when they heard that the new town was to be 15km away. Lanza was undaunted and, funded by the wealthy nobles of the area, his town was to be the highest expression of Sicilian baroque. It is also a wonderful example of organised and coherent town planning.

Lanza's true genius, however, was in his choice of collaborators. With the help of the Flemish military engineer Carlos de Grunemberg, the master craftsman Rosario Gagliardi and the architects Vincenzo Sinatra (an ancestor of the great crooner perhaps?) and Paolo Labisi, the new Noto put into practice a revolutionary idea based on the creation of two quarters, one for political and religious administration, the other a residential area. Both quarters were built with a careful emphasis on symmetry and visual harmony; indeed, the warm gold and rose hues of the local stone tone soften the heavily embellished palazzi and churches, making the town very picturesque.

However, many of Noto's most important buildings are in a state of extreme disrepair – the result of decades of neglect and plenty of minor earth tremors. The town was shocked in early 1996 when the dome and roof of its splendid baroque cathedral collapsed. Apparently local authorities knew that the dome was cracked beforehand, but

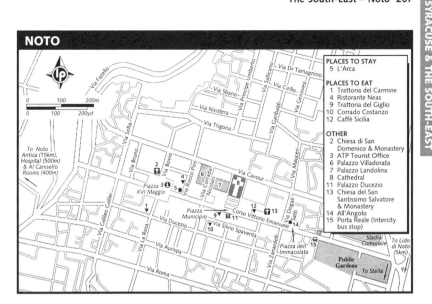

NOTO

To Noto
Antica (15km),
Hospital (500m)
& Al Canisello
Rooms (400m)

PLACES TO STAY
5 L'Arca

PLACES TO EAT
1 Trattoria del Carmine
4 Ristorante Neas
9 Trattoria del Giglio
10 Corrado Costanzo
12 Caffè Sicilia

OTHER
2 Chiesa di San
   Domenico & Monastery
3 ATP Tourist Office
6 Palazzo Villadorata
7 Palazzo Landolina
8 Cathedral
11 Palazzo Ducezio
13 Chiesa del San
    Santissimo Salvatore
    & Monastery
14 All'Angolo
15 Porta Reale (Intercity
    bus stop)

nothing was done to repair it. Fortunately, no-one was in the church at the time, but the absence of the dome has dramatically altered the town's skyscape.

Noto is also good for your tastebuds and particularly known for its cakes and pastries. Be aware that accommodation can be a problem as there aren't many places to stay.

Orientation & Information

Intercity buses drop you at the Porta Reale, at the beginning of Corso Vittorio Emanuele, the town's main street. You can get a map at the APT tourist office (☎ 0931 57 37 79), along the street on Piazza XVI Maggio (open 8 am to 2 pm and 3.30 to 7 pm Monday to Saturday).

In a medical emergency call ☎ 0931 57 12 25. The public hospital is on Via dei Mille, on the way out of town towards Noto Antica.

The *carabinieri* (military police) are at ☎ 0931 83 52 02.

Things to See & Do

The collapse of the cathedral dome revealed that most previous restoration work done on the city's monuments had been very super-

ficial – a significant problem, since the local white tufa stone is very soft and, as a building material, requires constant maintenance. The situation is so bad that several buildings remain standing only because they're held up by wooden supports. Lots of money has been allocated in the past, only to remain unspent, or to evaporate into the ether. However, it seems that this time the authorities are serious and numerous projects are under way to restore the cathedral and other important buildings in the city centre. There has also been a move to have Noto added to UNESCO's World Heritage List, which would guarantee substantial international funding for its restoration and maintenance.

Most of the important monuments line Corso Vittorio Emanuele. Overlooking Piazza XVI Maggio are the **Chiesa di San Domenico** and the adjacent **Dominican monastery**, both designed by Rosario Gagliardi. Back towards the Porta Reale is the **Palazzo Villadorata** (also known as Palazzo Nicolaci), on Via Corrado Nicolaci. Each of the palazzo's richly sculpted balconies is different, sporting a veritable menagerie of centaurs, horses, lions, sirens and tragic masks. Once the home of the princes of Villadorata (a baronial family during the Spanish occupation), it is now partly used as municipal offices and some rooms are open to the public.

The **cathedral** stands at the top of a sweeping staircase overlooking Piazza Municipio. The facade is imposing, but less extravagant than most of Noto's other baroque monuments. Next to the cathedral is the **Palazzo Landolina**, now abandoned, but belonging to the Sant'Alfano, Noto's oldest noble family. Across the square is the **Palazzo Ducezio**, Noto's town hall, which has been buried in scaffolding for years.

Further along the street are the **Chiesa del Santissimo Salvatore** and an adjoining **nunnery**. The church's interior is the most impressive in Noto. The nunnery was reserved for the daughters of local nobility. The fountain suspended on a wall next to the nunnery remained after Noto's streets were lowered in 1840 to facilitate the movement of carriages.

If you are interested in taking home a few pieces of Sicilian **ceramics**, All'Angolo, on the corner of Piazza dell'Immacolata and Corso Vittorio Emanuele has an excellent selection of pieces from Caltagirone and Santo Stefano di Camastra.

If you fancy a swim, there's a pleasant **beach** at Noto Marina, 15 minutes away by car or bus (although the latter only run between May and September).

Special Events
Noto's wonderfully colourful flower festival, Infioraci, takes place on the third Sunday in March. Artists line the length of Via Nicolai with artwork made entirely of flower petals, a pretty cool way to greet the arrival of spring.

Places to Stay
There are only a handful of hotels in Noto. *Stella* (☎ 0931 83 56 95, Via F Maiore 44), near the public gardens, has singles/doubles for L35,000/60,000. *L'Arca* (☎ 0931 89 42 02, Via Rocco Pirri 14), close to Corso Vittorio Emanuele, has singles/doubles for L70,000/95,000. See its Web site at www .polosud.it/arca. At the end of Corso Vittorio Emanuele, *Al Canisello Rooms* (☎ 0931 83

57 93, Via Pavese 1) is a quiet farmhouse with singles/doubles for L80,000/100,000.

The only other alternative is at Noto Marina, 5km away on the coast. Hotels include *Albergo Korsal* (☎ 0931 81 21 19), which has rooms for L60,000/95,000, and *President* (☎ 0931 81 25 43), with a higher standard of rooms for L105,000/170,000.

Places to Eat
The people of Noto are serious about their food, so take time to enjoy a meal and follow it up with a visit to one of the town's excellent pastry shops, where *gelati* (ice cream) and *dolci* (cakes) are divine. *Caffè Sicilia* (☎ 0931 83 50 13, Corso Vittorio Emanuele 125) and *Corrado Costanzo* (☎ 0931 83 52 43), round the corner at Via Silvio Spaventa 9, are neck and neck when it comes to the best ice cream and cakes in Noto. Both make superb *dolci di mandorle* (almond cakes and sweets), real cassata cake and *torrone* (nougat), as well as heavenly *granite* – try the one made with *fragolini* (tiny wild strawberries).

Trattoria del Carmine (☎ 0931 83 87 05, Via Ducezio 9) serves excellent home-style meals for about L23,000/27,000 per head (try the *coniglio alla stimpirata*, rabbit in local sauces), as does *Trattoria del Giglio (Piazza Municipio 8–10). Ristorante Neas* (☎ 0931 57 35 38, Via Rocco Pirri 30), close to Corso Vittorio Emanuele, serves typical Sicilian fare.

Getting There & Away
Noto is easily accessible by AST and Interbus buses from Catania (L4500, 40 minutes) and Syracuse (see Getting There & Away under Syracuse). From June to August only, buses run frequently between Noto and Noto Marina (in winter there is a school bus service).

AROUND NOTO
Noto Antica
Fifteen kilometres north-west of Noto but only accessible by car are the hardly inspiring remains of the original town of Noto, or Noto Antica, flattened by the earthquake of 1693. The only recognisable structure among

the weed-infested ruins is the gate of the castle, which once served to defend the town against attackers but is now about the only highlight of a thoroughly depressing and frankly uninteresting site.

Eloro

On the sea 9km south-east of Noto are the ruins of the ancient Syracusan colony of Helorus, or Eloro. The town, founded in the 7th century BC, is in the early stages of being excavated, but so far a portion of the city walls, a small temple dedicated to Demeter (Ceres in Roman mythology) and a theatre have been uncovered. The site is open from 8 am to one hour before sunset Monday to Saturday and admission is free. When it is closed you can still get a look at the place through the fence. You'll need your own transport to get here.

On either side of the hill where the sparse ruins lie are long, sandy beaches comparatively free of the usual crowds. Unfortunately, a storm-water drain spills into the sea at the beach to the south.

Riserva Naturale Vendicari

Less than 1km south of Eloro is the northern boundary of the protected Vendicari Nature Reserve, made up of three separate marshes and a splendid sandy beach that is popular in summer but rarely overcrowded. The reserve is replete with all manner of water birds, including black-winged stilts, slender-billed gulls and Audoin's gulls; bird watchers are well catered for by special observatories. At the centre of the reserve is an abandoned Hohenstaufen tower. The reserve is open from 9 am to 6 pm daily (to 5 pm from November to March). Admission is free. It is possible to reach the park by the SAIS bus connecting Noto and Pachino or by the Interbus (☎ 0931 83 50 23) from Largo Pantheon behind the public gardens.

RAGUSA & RAGUSA IBLA
postcode 97100 • pop 68,000
• elevation 502m

Next to Noto, the best example of the Sicilian baroque is to be found in Ragusa, the capital of the province that shares its name.

Like Noto, the old town of Ragusa Ibla was flattened by the earthquake of 1693 and rebuilt in the baroque style on a highland above the site of the original settlement. Unlike Noto, however, the old town was also rebuilt, with the result being a curious cocktail of medieval and baroque. A rivalry developed between Ragusa Ibla and the 'new' town of Ragusa which lasted until 1926, when the Fascist authorities merged the two towns into one. Unification proved disastrous for Ragusa Ibla, whose population abandoned it for the more prosperous and commercially oriented upper town.

City bus Nos 1 and 3 run from Piazza del Popolo in the upper town to Piazza Pola and the Giardino Ibleo in the lower town of Ragusa Ibla.

Orientation & Information

The lower town, Ibla, has most of the sights, but transport and accommodation are in the newer upper town. The train station is on Piazza del Popolo and the intercity bus station is on the adjacent Piazza Gramsci. From the train station, turn left and head along Viale Tenente Lena, across the bridge (Ponte Nuovo) and straight ahead along Via Roma to reach Corso Italia, the upper town's main street. Turn right on Corso Italia and follow it to the stairs to Ibla, or follow the winding road to the lower town.

The tourist office (☎ 0932 62 14 21) is at Via Capitano Bocchieri 33 in Palazzo La Rocca. It is open from 9 am to 1.30 pm Monday to Saturday. The main post office is at the corner on Via Ecce Homo, on the corner with Via Rapisardi. The public hospital, the Ospedale Civile (☎ 0932 62 39 46 for the Guardia Medica), is across Piazza del Popolo from the train station. For an ambulance, call ☎ 0932 62 14 10. For police attendance, ring ☎ 113.

Ragusa Ibla

Despite the general look of decay and abandonment that pervades the lower town, it is by far the more interesting of the two. Aside from the churches mentioned below, the best thing about the town is simply to wander through its narrow streets checking out the

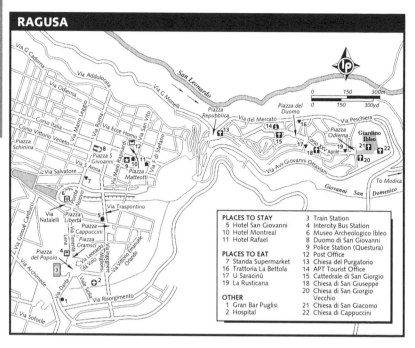

RAGUSA

PLACES TO STAY
5 Hotel San Giovanni
10 Hotel Montreal
11 Hotel Rafael

PLACES TO EAT
7 Standa Supermarket
16 Trattoria La Bettola
17 U Saracinù
19 La Rusticana

OTHER
1 Gran Bar Puglisi
2 Hospital

3 Train Station
4 Intercity Bus Station
6 Museo Archeologico Ibleo
8 Duomo di San Giovanni
9 Police Station (Questura)
12 Post Office
13 Chiesa del Purgatorio
14 APT Tourist Office
15 Cattedrale di San Giorgio
18 Chiesa di San Giuseppe
20 Chiesa di San Giorgio Vecchio
21 Chiesa di San Giacomo
22 Chiesa di Cappuccini

abandoned baroque palazzi that seem to cry out for some interested developer to take a restoring hand to them. The old town is best accessed via the *salita commendatore*, a winding pass made up of stairs and narrow archways that bring you right down to Piazza della Repubblica and the **Chiesa del Purgatorio**, whose main altar features a depiction of *Anime in Purgatorio* (Souls in Purgatory) by Francesco Manno. If you continue east along Via del Mercato (which has great views of the valley below) you'll get your first side view of Piazza del Duomo, whose western end is dominated by the wonderful **Cattedrale di San Giorgio**, one of the best examples of the Sicilian baroque. The brainchild of Rosario Gagliardi (of Noto fame), the church's facade is an elegant wedding-cake structure divided into three tiers, each level supported by gradually narrowing Corinthian columns and punctuated by jutting cornices. Don't hold your breath for the interior, however, as apart from 13 20th-century polychrome stained glass windows depicting the martyrdom of St George there isn't much else to see.

The genius of Gagliardi is also evident in the facade of the **Chiesa di San Giuseppe** on Piazza Pola, east of Piazza del Duomo on Corso Aprile. Like San Giorgio, it is divided into three tiers with Corinthian columns and statues. The elliptical interior is topped by a cupola decorated with a fresco of the *Gloria di San Benedetto* (Glory of St Benedict; 1793) by Sebastiano Lo Monaco.

At the eastern end of the old town is the **Giardino Ibleo**, a pleasant public garden laid out in the 19th century that is perfect for a picnic lunch or a lie-down. In its grounds are the remains of three medieval churches – San Giacomo, San Domenico and Cappuccini – as well as the Catalonian-Gothic portal of what was once the large **Chiesa di San Giorgio Vecchio**. In the lunette there is an interesting bas-relief of St George killing the dragon.

The Upper Town

The upper town is crowned by the **Duomo di San Giovanni** dedicated to John the Baptist, built between 1706 and 1760 as a lasting symbol of Ragusa's urban renewal. An elegant square fronts the ornate facade, made asymmetrical by a stout bell tower on its western flank. South of the cathedral on Via Natalelli, off Via Roma, is the **Museo Archeologico Ibleo** (☎ 0932 62 29 63), an important archaeological museum housing the finds from the Greek site at Camarina on the coast. Also of interest are ceramics from the caravan centre of Scornavacche, including a reconstructed kiln. The museum is open from 9 am to 1.30 pm and 3 to 7.30 pm daily; admission costs L4000.

Places to Stay

All of Ragusa's accommodation is in the upper town and there are no budget hotels. *Hotel San Giovanni (☎ 0932 62 10 13, Via Traspontino 3)* has singles/doubles for L40,000/60,000, or L60,000/96,000 with a bathroom. To get there from Piazza del Popolo, head down Viale Leonardo da Vinci, turn left at Via Ingegnere Migliorisi and follow it to the footbridge.

At Corso Italia 40 is *Hotel Rafael (☎ 0932 65 40 80)*, a pleasant establishment with singles/doubles with a bathroom costing L80,000/120,000. Nearby, on Corso Italia 70, is *Hotel Montreal (☎ 0932 62 11 33)*, with good singles/doubles with a bathroom and breakfast for L90,000/125,000.

Places to Eat

There is a *Standa supermarket* at Via Roma 187, near the bridge. *Trattoria la Bettola (☎ 0932 65 33 77, Largo Camerina 7)*, downhill to the left off Piazza del Duomo, is pleasant, and meals are priced at around L30,000. *La Rusticana (☎ 0932 22 79 81, Via XXV Aprile 68)* is another reasonable little place. *U Saracinù (☎ 0932 24 69 76, Via del Convento 9)*, off Piazza del Duomo, has a L25,000 tourist menu; otherwise a full meal will come to around L40,000.

Getting There & Away

Ragusa is accessible by 11 trains daily from Syracuse (L6500) and nine daily from Noto (L3500) and Agrigento (L8000). Interbus-Etna Trasporti (☎ 0932 62 34 40), a subsidiary of SAIS (information and tickets at Gran Bar Puglisi, Via Dante 94), runs eight buses daily to Catania.

AST (☎ 0932 68 18 18) serves Palermo (four buses a day) and runs more regularly to Noto and Syracuse (seven a day). An AST timetable is posted on Piazza Gramsci where AST and SAIS buses stop.

MODICA
postcode 97015 • pop 50,500
• elevation 296m

About 20km east of Ragusa, Modica seems to be a close cousin. It has the same sun-bleached colour and is also divided into two sections: Modica Alta (High Modica) and, you guessed it, Modica Bassa (Low Modica).

The highlight is the **Chiesa di San Giorgio** in the upper part of town (local buses run by from the lower end), easily one of the most extraordinary baroque churches in the province. A majestic stairway sweeps up to a daringly tall facade, erected by Rosario Gagliardi in the early 18th century – it looks as if it was meant to be a tower. There are regular AST buses from Ragusa to Modica.

Central Sicily

Highlights

- Visit the Roman villa at Casale; no Sicilian holiday is complete without seeing its breathtaking polychrome mosaics
- Gaze at the spectacular view from Enna's Castello di Lombardia
- Join a jeep tour through the heart of the Parco Regionale dei Nebrodi
- Take a trip back in time as you wander through the maze of streets in Calascibetta
- Admire the hand-painted ceramics that decorate the Scalinata di Santa Maria del Monte in Caltagirone.

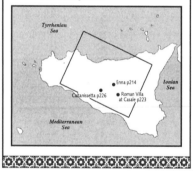

Away from the tourist trails that extend their way around much of Sicily's coastline, the vast expanse of the mountainous interior is more representative of traditional Sicilian life than any other area on the island. With only a few exceptions – and despite the presence of the A19 motorway, which cuts a swathe through most of the interior between Palermo and Catania – the centre is isolated and forbidding. On an island whose considerable natural beauty has been substantially damaged by overdevelopment, this is, however, a key element of its allure. Here, hilltop towns survive in splendid semi-isolation, particularly in the eastern interior. In the western half the isolation is less splendid and more desperate, as tiny

villages struggle to survive in a landscape ravaged by poverty, emigration and the nefarious influence of the Mafia. While the eastern half has Piazza Armerina, Caltagirone, the Roman villa (Villa Romana) at Casale and even Enna proudly displayed across its tourist itineraries, in the west the towns of Prizzi (made famous by the film *Prizzi's Honour* starring Jack Nicholson and Kathleen Turner), Lercara Friddi and Corleone (see the Palermo chapter for details) are known only for their Mafia ties.

For over a decade tour operators and the Sicilian tourist authorities have been touting the areas away from the sea as the next big tourist destinations but so far nothing substantial has come of it, with most visitors still preferring the coastal cities and resorts to the mountainous inland. The problem is not the lack of interesting sights or splendid natural settings, but the deficit of tourist infrastructure, particularly accommodation options. Transportation is also more problematic than on the coast, and you'll be better off with your own vehicle outside the bigger towns.

Enna

postcode 94100 • pop 29,000
• elevation 931m

Situated high on a commanding ridge in the sun-scorched centre of Sicily, Enna towers above the surrounding countryside in an enviable position that has earned it two nicknames: it is known as the *belvedere* (panoramic viewpoint) or the *ombelico* (umbilicus) of Sicily. It makes a good base for exploring the surrounding region, especially if you combine it with a visit to the region's eminent tourist attraction, the extraordinary mosaics of the Roman villa at Casale (see Villa Romana later in the chapter). For centuries an almost impregnable fortress town, Enna has preserved much of its medieval centre in remarkably good order, which is pretty impressive when you consider that it is the capital of

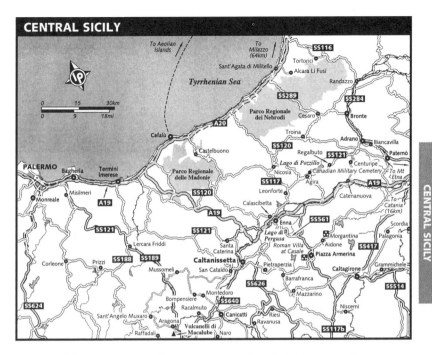

CENTRAL SICILY

one of the island's poorest provinces. The beautiful approach to the town has been somewhat spoilt by some ugly modern construction, particularly on its southern slope, but there is enough to see within its core to warrant at least a one-day visit. One of the most pleasant sights in town is when locals flood onto the traffic-free Via Roma for the traditional *passeggiata* (evening stroll).

HISTORY

The colony of Henna was founded on this high plateau in 664 BC by colonists from Gela eager to exploit the area's agricultural resources. In 397 BC the town fell to Dionysius of Syracuse, and it remained in Syracusan hands until the 3rd century BC when it entered the orbit of Roman power. The First Servile War broke out here in 135 BC under the command of the slave Eunus (a later rebellion made the name of the hero-slave Spartacus); the Romans eventually recaptured the town after a two-

year siege. In AD 859 it was the turn of the Saracens, who had to sneak in one by one through a sewer to breach the town's hardy defences. They renamed it 'Kasr Janna' (from the Latin 'Castrum Hennae', Garrison Town of Henna) and held on until the Normans arrived in 1087. The name was corrupted into Castrogiovanni, by which it was known until 1927, when it was changed back to Enna (the original 'h' being dropped entirely). Today the town retains its importance as an agricultural centre.

INFORMATION

The APT office (☎ 0935 52 82 28) is at Via Roma 413. The staff are helpful and you can pick up a map and information on the city and province. The office is open from 9 am to 1 pm and 3 to 7 pm Monday to Saturday. The AAST office (☎ 0935 50 08 75), next to the Grande Albergo Sicilia at Piazza Colaianni 6, has information mainly on the city itself and is open from 8 am to 2 pm daily.

The post office is at Via Volta 1, just off Piazza Garibaldi. Public telephones are scattered about the town, or you can try at the Grande Albergo Sicilia (see under Places to Stay & Eat later in the section), which also has a public phone.

There are several banks around the city centre, including the Banco di Sicilia at Via Roma 367 and the Cassa Centrale di Risparmio at Piazza Vittorio Emanuele 18. Both have ATMs.

For medical assistance, go to the Ospedale Civile Umberto I (hospital) on Via Trieste, or ring ☎ 0935 4 51 11. At night, call ☎ 0935 50 08 96 for medical emergencies. The police station (questura; ☎ 0935 52 21 11) is at Via San Giuseppe 2.

CASTELLO DI LOMBARDIA
Enna's most visible monument dominates the eastern side of town. The original castle was built by the Saracens and later reinforced by the Normans; Frederick III of Aragon or-dered that a powerful curtain wall be built with towers on every side. The wall is still in-tact but only six of the original 20 towers re-main. Within the walls is a complex structure of courtyards that were opened in sequence; the closest one to the entrance (Cortile di San Martino; Courtyard of St Martin) is used in summer as an outdoor theatre (see Special Events later in the section). From the same courtyard you can climb up one of the towers (the Torre Pisana) from where the view is simply breathtaking, at least when the fog – an enduring element of Enna's weather – has lifted. Across the valley is the town of Calas-cibetta (see that section later in the chapter) and to the distant north-east you can just about make out the towering peak of Mt Etna. The castle is open from 9 am to 1 pm and 3 to 5 pm daily. Admission is free.

ROCCA DI CERERE
To the north of the castle a small road leads down to the remains of the temple of the

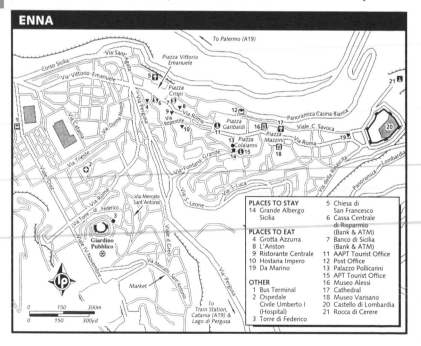

ENNA

PLACES TO STAY
14 Grande Albergo Sicilia

PLACES TO EAT
4   Grotta Azzurra
8   L'Ariston
9   Ristorante Centrale
10 Hostaria Impero
19 Da Marino

OTHER
1   Bus Terminal
2   Ospedale Civile Umberto I (Hospital)
3   Torre di Federico
5   Chiesa di San Francesco
6   Cassa Centrale di Risparmio (Bank & ATM)
7   Banco di Sicilia (Bank & ATM)
11 AAPT Tourist Office
12 Post Office
13 Palazzo Pollicarini
15 APT Tourist Office
16 Museo Alessi
17 Cathedral
18 Museo Varisano
20 Castello di Lombardia
21 Rocca di Cerere

goddess of agriculture, Ceres (the Greek Demeter). Enna was the centre of an important cult of Ceres, and the temple was supposedly erected in 480 BC by the tyrant Gelon, who was eager to gain favour with the goddess lest his plans for the capture of Syracuse be foiled by a couple of bad harvests (for details see the Syracuse & the South-East chapter). Ceres' daughter was Proserpine, whose removal to Hades is the subject of one of the most enduring of all Roman myths; the action is supposed to have taken place 9km south of town at Lago di Pergusa (see under the South from Enna section later in the chapter). The temple's remains are not enclosed.

ALONG VIA ROMA

Back in town, Enna's main artery is Via Roma, which extends westwards from the castle and is lined with most of the town's more important sights. Coming from the castle, the first of these is the **cathedral**. Founded in 1307 by Eleonora, the wife of Frederick III, the Gothic structure was destroyed by fire in 1446 and slowly rebuilt over the next 200 years in early baroque style. The curious facade (complete with 17th-century bell tower) covers its Gothic predecessor, while the rich interior is almost entirely 17th century in design. The dark-grey basalt columns are worth looking at for their highly ornamented bases, which are carved with a series of grotesques, such as snakes with human heads. The five paintings (1613) in the presbytery are by Filippo Paladino and feature scenes from the New Testament. Also worth checking out are the altarpieces by Guglielmo Borremans on the southern side of the church; of particular interest is the splendid painting of *Sante Lucilla e Giacinto* (St Lucy and Hyacinth). The cathedral is open from 9 am to 1 pm and 4 to 7 pm daily.

Next door is the **Museo Alessi**, which houses the contents of the cathedral's treasury. Originally the property of Canon Giuseppe Alessi (1774–1837), who left the collection to his brother with the intention that he then donate it to the Church. Eager to turn a tidy profit, Alessi's brother then

entered into lengthy negotiations with the clerical authorities who eventually bought the collection in 1860 and first displayed it in 1862. A good thing, too, because some of the pieces are stunning, including a fabulous pelican-shaped jewel and a gold crown encrusted with jewels and enamels (1653) by Leonardo and Giuseppe Montalbano. The museum is open from 9 am to 1.30 pm and 4 to 6 pm (closed Monday); admission costs L2000.

On the far side of Piazza Mazzini from the cathedral is the **Museo Archeologico Varisano,** which has a good (if small) collection of artefacts excavated throughout the region. Of particular interest is the Attic style red-and-black *krater* (drinking vessel) found in the town itself. The museum is open from 9 am to 1.30 pm and 3 to 7.30 pm daily; admission costs L4000.

About 100m farther down Via Roma, on the south-western side of Piazza Colaianni next to the Grande Albergo Sicilia, is the Catalan-Gothic **Palazzo Pollicarini**, one of Enna's most handsome buildings. Although it has been converted into private apartments, you can still nip in to take a peak at the medieval staircase in the central courtyard.

TOWERS

On Piazza Vittorio Emanuele, the most impressive element of the **Chiesa di San Francesco** is its 15th-century bell tower *(campanile)*, adorned with fine Gothic windows. The tower once formed part of the city's defence system. From the square head over to the chunky **Torre di Federico** (Tower of Frederick II) in the public gardens (Villa Comunale) in the new part of town, also part of the old defences. The octagonal tower, standing 24m high, was once linked by a secret passage to the Castello di Lombardia. At the time of writing it was closed for restoration.

SPECIAL EVENTS

During Holy Week at Easter, Enna is the setting for colourful, traditional celebrations. On Good Friday, thousands of people wearing hoods and capes of different colours participate in a solemn procession to the cathedral.

CENTRAL SICILY

The Feast of the Virgin of the Visitation (Festa di Maria Santissima della Visitazione), Enna's patron saint, is celebrated on 2 July. Traditionally, the saint's icon was dragged through town on a cart (called La Nave Dorata, the Golden Ship) by farmers wearing nothing but a white band over their hips; today the band has been replaced by a long, embroidered sheet. The feast is accompanied by a salvo of fireworks.

During June and July the Castello di Lombardia hosts a series of nightly plays and performances, all with a medieval theme. At the time of research prices and specific dates were unavailable: contact the APT office for more information.

The Palio dei Normanni on 13 and 14 August is a medieval pageant celebrating Count Roger's capture of the town from the Moors in 1087. On 14 August, amid parades in traditional costume and other assorted festivities, there is an actual joust, complete with armour, lances and horses. Check with the tourist office for specific details of the festival.

PLACES TO STAY & EAT

There is no cheap accommodation in Enna, so be warned. Enna itself has only one hotel, **Grande Albergo Sicilia** (☎ 0935 50 08 54, Piazza Colaianni 7). Singles/doubles cost L90,000/155,000 with breakfast. For other accommodation, you'll have to catch city bus No 5 from Piazza Vittorio Emanuele to Lago di Pergusa (for details see that section under South of Enna later in the chapter).

Dining is not a problem, however. Unlike the coast, the main staple here is meat and, while you will find an assortment of fish dishes, the local specialities usually involve some cut of mutton or beef. There is a **market** every morning from Monday to Saturday on Via Mercato Sant'Antonio where you can find basics such as fresh fruit, bread and cheese. Near the castle, **Da Marino** (☎ 0935 2 52 22, Viale C Savoca 62) is a no-fuss pizzeria where you can also get pasta dishes. Mains cost about L9000, and pizzas range from L7500 to L11,000. It is closed on Monday.

Hostaria Impero (☎ 0935 2 60 18, Via Ree Pentite 17), off Via Roma, is slightly more expensive but it's worth it. Similarly priced is **Grotta Azzurra** (☎ 0935 2 43 28, Via Colaianni 1). It is closed Saturday.

L'Ariston (☎ 0935 2 60 38, Via Roma 353) is one of the better restaurants in town. Expect to pay around L50,000 including wine. Slightly cheaper is **Ristorante Centrale** (☎ 0935 50 09 63, Piazza VI Dicembre 9). The menu of Sicilian specialities changes daily. You'll pay around L40,000 for a full meal.

GETTING THERE & AWAY

Buses arrive at and leave from the bus terminal (☎ 0935 50 09 05) on Viale Diaz. SAIS buses (☎ 0935 50 09 02) connect Enna with Catania (L8500, 1½–two hours, eight daily) and Palermo (L14,000, 11 daily). It is possible to reach Agrigento via Caltanissetta (L4000, 13 daily). Regular SAIS buses also run to Piazza Armerina (L4600, 45 minutes).

The train station is 5km south of the town centre, and though local buses (L1000) make the steep run hourly to town (except Sunday, when you might have to wait a couple of hours between buses), you're best off not bothering with the train at all. If you don't want to wait for the bus, you can call for a taxi on ☎ 0935 50 09 05.

North from Enna

The winding SS121 makes its way out of Calascibetta in a north-easterly direction through some of the most splendid inland scenery on the island before it eventually reaches Catania. There are a couple of towns worth taking time to stop in, if only to get a sense of what Sicilian life is like away from the tourist trail. All of the towns mentioned are reachable by bus from Enna (eight daily); check at the tourist office or the bus terminal for departure details and prices, which vary between L1000 and L8000, depending on how far you go. The best way to explore this area, however, is with your own transport.

CALASCIBETTA
postcode 94010 • pop 5000
• elevation 681m

Just 2km north of Enna across a valley and the A19 motorway lies this hilltop town where Count Roger I camped during his siege of Enna in 1087. Seemingly ambivalent to the influence of modernism, Calascibetta is a densely packed maze of little streets above an enormous drop (on its eastern side). The 14th-century **cathedral** (dedicated to St Peter) is worth popping your head into, if only for the good collection of liturgical objects. It is open from 9 am to 1 pm and 3 to 7 pm daily. Admission is free.

Only 1km or so north-west of town is the well-signposted **Necropoli di Realmese** where some 300 rock tombs dating from 850 to 730 BC have been found. The site is unenclosed and open at all times.

The town is within easy access from Enna by bus (L1000) from the main bus terminal; buses depart every 45 minutes or so between 8 am and 9.30 pm daily.

LEONFORTE
postcode 94013 • pop 4500
• elevation 603m

A further 18km north-east along the SS121 is this attractive baroque town, founded in 1610 and once renowned for its horse breeding. The town's most imposing building (visible from the road) is the **Palazzo Baronale**, which has a pretty, ornate facade. The town's **cathedral** houses some good wooden sculptures, but the real sight of interest is the **Granfonte**. Built in 1651 by Nicolò Branciforte, it is an ornate fountain made up of 24 separate jets against a sculpted facade. The fountain is about 300m down a small road from the cathedral (follow the signpost).

If you are driving, you can continue northwards along the SS117; from Nicosia take the SS120 on to the Parco Regionale dei Nebrodi (Nebrodi nature reserve; see that section later in the chapter) or continue along the SS121 towards Mt Etna.

There are 11 buses daily between Enna and Leonforte: the journey takes just over one hour and costs L3800.

AGIRA
postcode 94011 • pop 2800
• elevation 670m

From a distance, Agira rises up in an almost perfect cone with the ruins of its medieval castle at the top. The town was colonised by Timoleon in 339 BC and was later captured by the Romans, who added substantially to the existing Greek settlement. The Augustan historian Diodorus Siculus was born here and declared that the amphitheatre *(anfiteatro)* was matched in beauty only by that of Syracuse. Apart from a few unremarkable traces, there is little that remains of its distinguished past, and even the town's 16th-century church is closed. Still, this is a popular stop if only because it has the only hotel in the area, the *Aurora* (☎ 0935 69 14 16, Via Annunziata 6). The rooms are bare but clean; singles/doubles with bathroom cost L40,000/65,000.

From Enna, there are eight SAIS buses daily except Sunday (when there are four); the trip takes about 1 hour and 45 minutes and costs L5000. There are also three SAIS buses daily between Agira and Troina (see East from Nicosia later in the chapter).

THE SS121 TO REGALBUTO
The road to Regalbuto (about 14km northeast of Agira) is more interesting than the town at the end of it. A couple of kilometres out of Agira (signposted to your left), atop a little hill, is a well-tended **Canadian Military Cemetery** where lie the bodies of 480 soldiers killed in July 1943. Farther on, still to your left, is a large artificial lake known as the **Lago di Pozzillo**. This is a great spot for a picnic, amid the almond trees and prickly pears. Under no circumstances try to pick one of these pears without gloves: although they look harmless enough, they are covered in tiny needles that are very difficult to remove from your skin!

CENTURIPE
postcode 94010 • pop 3000
• elevation 719m

About 13km past Regalbuto on the road to Adrano and Mt Etna is a turn-off south for this little town, known as the Balcone di

CENTRAL SICILY

Sicilia (Balcony of Sicily) on account of its commanding position on a ridge in front of the volcano. The approach from the turn-off (you will need your own transport) brings you through 7km of lovely citrus groves and then uphill into the town, which has been fought over many times due to its strategic importance. The last battle occurred in 1943; with the town's capture by the Allies the Germans realised that their foothold in Sicily had slipped and they retreated back to the Italian mainland. The town centre was partially destroyed by Allied bombs and much of it is now a collection of uninspired modern buildings, with the sole exception of the 17th-century pink-and-white **cathedral**.

From here you have a couple of options. You can double back up to the SS121 and keep moving north along the SS575 until you hit the SS120, or you can continue south to Catenanuova and the A19 motorway, which will take you directly to Catania.

NICOSIA
postcode 94014 • pop 15,000
• elevation 724m

This sizeable town is a good base from which to begin your exploration of the region. Although it was originally a Byzantine settlement (which was later captured by the Saracens), Nicosia's salad days were during the Norman era, when it was the most important settlement of a series of fortified towns that stretched in a line from Palermo to Messina. Although in an alarming state of decay, the private residences that line the town's streets are a good indication of its former prosperity, when wealthy Franco-German landowners competed with each other to build the most sumptuous house.

At the centre of town is the busy Piazza Garibaldi, dominated by the 19th-century **cathedral** which was built to replace a smaller, 14th-century church, but incorporating the original portal and bell tower. Of particular interest inside is a baptismal font by Domenico Gagini and a wooden crucifix by Fra Umile di Petralia, which is carried through the town on Good Friday.

At the top of the hill is the 19th-century **Chiesa di Santa Maria Maggiore**; this is another reconstruction as the original 13th-century church was destroyed by a landslide in 1757. In 1968 the bell tower was demolished by an earthquake and its bells rehung on a low iron bracket – the chime you hear is electric. Inside is a lovely marble polyptych by Gagini.

Places to Stay & Eat

Like so much of the island's interior, accommodation is in short supply and the little that exists is hardly inspiring. The only hotel in the town centre is *Hotel Patria (☎ 0935 64 61 03, Via Vittorio Emanuele 11)* which is near Piazza Marconi at the bottom of the hill. Bland singles/doubles cost an exorbitant L60,000/95,000. If you have your own transport, you're much better off staying at one of two hotels on the outskirts of town: *Pineta (☎ 0935 64 70 02)* – a couple of kilometres south of town – and *Vigneta (☎ 0935 64 60 74)*, a little farther afield, about 5km south of the Pineta. The latter charges L45,000/60,000 for singles/doubles; the Pineta is more expensive at L60,000/100,000 but they're both clean and pretty comfortable.

There is a *restaurant* in Hotel Patria and a couple of *bars* on Piazza Garibaldi that can rustle up a sandwich and even a hot plate at lunch. The best place to eat, however, is the cavernous *La Cirata (☎ 0935 64 05 61)* which is 5km south of town on the SS117. In summer the place is a popular stop for bus tours, the occupants of which come for the solid rustic cuisine. Expect to pay about L9000 for a main course.

Getting There & Away

Nicosia is well-served by SAIS buses from Leonforte and Enna (11 daily; L3100 and L5500 respectively). From Enna the trip takes about 1½ hours; from Leonforte only 40 minutes. Buses arrive and depart from Piazza Marconi. You can buy your tickets in the bar by the bus stop.

EAST FROM NICOSIA

From Nicosia the SS120 skirts the southern border of the wide expanse of the Parco Regionale dei Nebrodi, across some of the most beautiful scenery on the whole island. Before the construction of the A20 (incomplete) motorway along the northern Tyrrhenian coast, this was the main route between Messina and Palermo. Thankfully this is no longer the case, as the kilometre-long queues of cargo-laden lorries snaking their way through the mountains not only made travelling a slow and laborious process but ruined the air of tranquillity that now prevails.

The road is not well-served by public transport, but has a couple of places worth checking out if you have your own wheels. About 34km along the road is the village of **Troina**, standing over 1000m high on a narrow perch. It was one of the first towns taken by the Normans from the Arabs. Count Roger I nearly suffered a humiliating defeat here in 1064; had he been defeated, it would have resulted in a withdrawal from Sicily by his troops. To commemorate his victory, Roger founded a **convent** (San Basilio) which is now in ruins.

If you are dependant on public transport and absolutely must get here, you can take an SAIS bus in Agira (L3800, one hour) that winds its way up the narrow road from the south.

PARCO REGIONALE DEI NEBRODI

In the heart of the Nebrodi mountains, which span from the Peloritani range in the east to the Madonie range just east of Palermo, this nature reserve was set up in 1993 and constitutes the single largest forested area on the island. Cutting through the heart of the park is the SS289 which links Cesarò in the interior with Sant'Agata di Militello on the Tyrrhenian coast. Along the way you'll come across a wide variety of trees, including oak, elm, ash, beech, cork, maple and yew, as well as a variety of landscapes that cater to different breeds of animals. In the uplands you will find farm animals grazing on the holly bushes, while lower down you can catch sight of the San Fratello breed of horses, unique to this area and recognisable by their odd-shaped noses.

Although ostensibly a protected area, hunters roam the woodlands looking for game, a problem that is largely due to the convoluted bureaucracy that made the park the responsibility of four different agencies. Although they all claim to protect the park's delicate flora and fauna, in-fighting and disagreements have resulted in the absence of a coordinated policy; furthermore, local groups object to the strict laws governing the park and flaunt them openly, hence the presence of hunters and the like.

Between May and September all-day jeep tours of the park are available out of the small town of Alcara Li Fusi, just off the park's northern boundary (signposted along a tiny road off the SS289). At the time of research the tours cost L60,000 and lasted 3½ hours. Call ☎ 0941 79 32 13 for details. You'll need to book in advance. Otherwise, you'll need your own transport to get around the park.

South from Enna

Although the natural scenery is not nearly as spectacular as it is to the north of Enna, the southern part of the province has been enriched by human hand. The 17th-century town of Piazza Armerina, perhaps the most attractive of all of the interior's towns, is worth devoting a day to, while lovers of all things beautiful will revel in the exquisite ceramics produced in Caltagirone. The remains of the Greek city of Morgantina, just east of Aidone, are considerable and worth more than the trickle of visitors they receive. The real highlight, however, is just outside Piazza Armerina at Casale, the site of one of the most extraordinary finds from antiquity and a 'must-see' attraction on any Sicilian itinerary: a sumptuous Roman villa that lay buried in mud for over 700 years until it was discovered in 1950.

LAGO DI PERGUSA

Sicily's only natural lake lies 9km south of Enna along the SS561 (the road to Piazza Armerina). Its popularity as a tourist resort since the 1950s has been its ruin: the lake is surrounded by a motor racing track and much of the vegetation on its shores has long since disappeared, along with most of the birdlife. The brackish water laps against the sandy beaches that in summer are crammed with tourists escaping from Enna. It is difficult to imagine, but the lake plays a central role in one of Greek mythology's most enduring and romantic tales – the removal of Proserpine from earth by Hades (see the boxed text 'A Devil's Bargain' below).

To get there, take bus No 5 from Piazza Vittorio Emanuele in Enna (L1000, every 30 minutes from 7 am to 9.30 pm daily).

Places to Stay

The area around the lake has a few hotels that are a popular alternative to staying in Enna.

Cheapest is *Miralago* (☎ *0935 54 12 72, Via Naz-ionale, Contrada Staglio)* with single/double rooms costing L50,000/ 70,000. It is the first place you pass on the right before entering the town proper along Via Nazionale. About 500m farther on is *Park Hotel La*

Giarra (☎ 0935 54 16 87, fax 0935 54 12 67, Via Nazionale 125), with better-appointed singles/doubles costing L75,000/95,000.

PIAZZA ARMERINA
postcode 94015 • pop 22,300
• elevation 697m

Set amid some of the most fertile territory on the island, this town (called simply Piazza until the 18th century) takes its name from one of the three hills on which it is built, the Colle Armerino. It is actually two towns in one: the original Piazza was founded by the Saracens in the 10th century on the slope of the Colle Armerino, while a 15th-century expansion to the south-east was redefined by an urban grid established in the 17th century.

Orientation & Information

The AAST tourist office (☎ 0935 68 02 01) is at Via Cavour 15, in the town centre, up-

A Devil's Bargain

According to myth, the god of the underworld, Pluto, had fallen in love with Ceres' beautiful daughter Proserpine, but she wasn't falling for his wily charms. After much persistence Pluto agreed to leave her alone on the condition that she did not eat. One day, while picking flowers on the banks of a lake, she found a pomegranate from which she picked 12 seeds. She must have been pretty hungry because she forgot her deal with Pluto and ate six of them. Pluto, of course, being a god, hadn't forgotten. A chasm appeared in the lake and up popped Pluto, who then promptly disappeared into the lake with Proserpine in tow. A devastated Ceres began searching for her beloved daughter, ignoring her duties as goddess of agriculture and causing the corn to stop growing. Sensing disaster, Jupiter decided to intervene to settle the matter. Pluto argued his case well, but Ceres would not back down. Finally, Jupiter found the solution: as Proserpine had only eaten six of the seeds, she would only have to spend six months of the year in the underworld; for the rest of the year she lived as a god on earth. Ceres was satisfied and the corn began to grow once more. The story makes an appearance in Milton's *Paradise Lost*:

> Not that faire field
> of Enna, where Proserpin gathring flours
> Her self a fairer Floure by gloomie Dis
> was gather'd, which cost Ceres all that pain
> To seek her through the World.'

JANE SMITH

Pluto purloins Proserpine.

hill along Via Umberto I or Via Garibaldi from the intercity bus stops. It is open from 8 am to 2 pm Monday to Saturday. You can pick up a copy of the brochure covering the Roman villa from here (often unavailable at the site itself); it explains the layout of the ruins and the mosaics.

Things to See

The town itself is a collection of slightly run-down but still-handsome *palazzi* (mansions) and churches. At the heart of the old town is Piazza Garibaldi, on which you will find the elegant **Palazzo di Città** and the **Chiesa di San Rocco** (also known as the Fundrò); the latter has an impressive doorway carved out of tufa stone. In between the two buildings is Via Cavour, which leads up the hill to the **cathedral**, founded in 1627. The facade dates from 1719 and the dome was added in 1768. The airy blue-and-white interior contains an altar, behind which is a copy of a Byzantine painting called the *Madonna delle Vittorie* (Virgin of Victories), the original of which was supposedly presented to Count Roger I by Pope Nicholas II. The 15th-century bell tower (part of an earlier church) complements the baroque cathedral although it was built in the Catalan-Gothic style (look at the windows). Opposite the cathedral on the square is the baronial **Palazzo Trigona**, whose facade has recently been restored. The statue in the middle of the square is of Baron Marco Trigona, who financed the cathedral's construction.

From the square, there are a couple of roads you might wander down. To the side of Palazzo Trigona, Via Floresta leads down to the ruins of a 14th-century **castle** past four beautiful baroque residences, each in a extreme state of disrepair. From the castle you can continue walking and end up back in Piazza Garibaldi. The medieval city's most important thoroughfare was Via Monte, which descends west from Piazza del Duomo through the town's most picturesque quarter.

Places to Stay & Eat

If you want to stay in Piazza Armerina, about the cheapest accommodation is the *Villa Romana* (☎ 0935 68 29 11, Via A De Gasperi 18) which has singles/doubles at L80,000/130,000 including breakfast. *Hotel Mosaici da Battiato* (☎ 0935 68 54 53, Contrada Paratore 11) is 3km out of town on the way to the Roman villa. It has rooms costing L60,000/80,000. *Azienda Agriturista Savoca* (☎ 0337 88 90 52, fax 0935 68 30 78) is also about 3km out of Piazza Armerina, on the road to Mirabella. It has pleasant doubles costing L80,000, with bathroom and breakfast included. Ask for a room in the older building, in preference to the newer rooms under the swimming pool.

Totò (☎ 0935 68 01 53, Via Mazzini 29) is a typical Sicilian restaurant and serves a good meal for L25,000. *Del Teatro* (☎ 0935 8 56 62, Via Teatro 1) is just off the eastern end of Via Garibaldi and is similarly priced. Otherwise, you can try the restaurant in the *Hotel Mosaici da Battiato* which serves traditional inland cuisine and is popular with tour groups. Main meals cost between L8000 and L12,000.

Getting There & Away

There are about 10 SAIS buses which connect Enna and Piazza Armerina (L4600, 45 minutes). There is also a daily AST bus from Syracuse (L11,000, two hours).

VILLA ROMANA

The extraordinary Romana villa at Casale is easily the most important ruin of the Roman era in Sicily. It was the property of a Roman dignitary of some standing and wealth, possibly even Maximian (Maximianus Herculeus), co-emperor during the reign of Diocletian (AD 286–305) – hence its other name, the Villa Imperiale. Although other surviving villas testify to the magnificent lifestyles enjoyed by wealthy Romans – for example Hadrian's villa at Tivoli and Diocletian's getaway retreat in Split, Croatia – the Casale country residence stands out for its sheer size coupled with the breathtaking extent of its polychrome floor mosaics.

The villa is made up of four connected groups of buildings which date from the early 4th century and were built on the site of a more modest 2nd-century home (possibly a

CENTRAL SICILY

JANE SMITH

Detail from the Great Hunting Scene in the Villa Romana

hunting lodge). Scholars believe that the buildings were maintained until about the year 1000, after which they were abandoned to local squatters and then partially destroyed. In the 12th century the entire area was covered by a landslide which left the villa under 10m of mud. The ruins were only noticed again in 1761, but it wasn't until 1881 that the first attempts at excavation were made; these were resumed in 1929 and again between 1935 and 1939. Finally, in 1950, the main structure was finally exposed, as a result of a properly financed excavation. The work continues today and large parts of the estate – including the extensive slave quarters and outbuildings – remain covered. The fact that the mosaics have been concealed by mud for so long has proven to be a blessing in disguise; in 1991 they were badly damaged by a flood which suggests that had they not been covered they would hardly have survived nearly 2000 years of inclement weather and petty vandalism.

Much of the villa has been covered with a protective structure and raised walkways carry visitors through the house's many rooms in a particular sequence. The description below follows the order of that sequence.

The **main entrance** leads through the remnants of a triumphal arch into an elegant **atrium** (forecourt). To the west are the substantial **thermae** (baths), all-important in a Roman house. The small **latrine** is a good indication of the house's elegance, adorned with a brick drain, a marble wash basin and rich mosaics. From the latrine area you access the villa proper, walking around the western side of the massive **peristyle**, or central courtyard, where in Roman times guests would be received by the host. The paths around the courtyard are decorated with mosaics depicting animal heads draped in laurel leaves. To your left you can look down into the **palaestra** (gymnasium), with a splendid mosaic depicting a scene from the Circus Maximus in Rome (the room is also known as the Salone del Circo or Circus Room). Of the rooms on the northern side of the peristyle, the most interesting is the second-last one, depicting a hunting scene in great detail. But this is merely an appetiser for what follows.

A small staircase brings you to the eastern side of the peristyle and the **Ambulacro della Scena della Grande Caccia** (Ambulacrum of the Great Hunting Scene), a long corridor (64m) where the mosaics are considered to be among the finest ever found. The first figure is resplendent in a Byzantine cape and is flanked by two soldiers, most likely Maximian himself and two members of his personal legion, the Herculiani. They are overseeing an extraordinary scene which shows all kinds of animals – tigers, leopards, elephants, antelopes, ostriches and a rhino – being herded onto ships. The detail is breathtaking.

At the far end of the corridor, steps lead south around the peristyle and the **Sala delle Dieci Ragazze** (Room of the Ten Girls), home of probably the most famous of all the villa's mosaics. The mosaic depicts ten girls, all sporting bikinis (!), and dates from the end of the 4th century. In the far left-hand corner you can see that the mosaic is laid over an earlier representation.

ROMAN VILLA AT CASALE

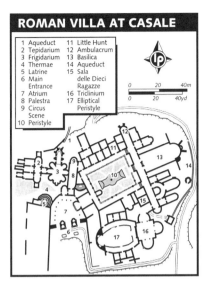

1 Aqueduct
2 Tepidarium
3 Frigidarium
4 Thermae
5 Latrine
6 Main Entrance
7 Atrium
8 Palestra
9 Circus Scene
10 Peristyle
11 Little Hunt
12 Ambulacrum
13 Basilica
14 Aqueduct
15 Sala delle Dieci Ragazze
16 Triclinium
17 Elliptical Peristyle

The walkways then lead through the rest of the house. On the other side of the long corridor is a series of apartments, whose floor illustrations reproduce scenes from Homer, as well as mythical subjects such as Arion playing the lyre on a dolphin's back, and Cupid and Faunus wrestling. Of particular interest is the **triclinium** (dining room), with a splendid depiction of *I Labori di Ercole* (The Labours of Hercules).

The villa is open from 9 am to one hour before sunset daily. Get here early if you want to avoid the large tourist groups which start arriving at around 9.30 am and tend to block up the narrow passageways. Admission costs L4000.

Getting There & Away

From May to September ATAN buses (☎ 0935 68 22 72) depart for the villa from Piazza Senatore Marescalchi in Piazza Armerina, at 9, 10 and 11 am, and 4, 5 and 6 pm, returning 30 minutes later. The trip costs L2000. You will need your own transport if you visit between October and April (head south along the SS117; the villa is clearly signposted). You will be charged L2000 to park your vehicle outside the entrance.

MORGANTINA

About 16km north-east of Piazza Armerina and about 4km beyond the town of Aidone are the noteworthy remains of this sizeable Greek colony, spread across two hills and the valley between. Morgeti, an early Sicilian settlement, was founded in 850 BC on Cittadella hill, but this town was destroyed by Ducetius in 459 BC and a new town built on the second hill, the Serra Orlando. It reached its apogee during the reign of the Syracusan tyrant Hieron II (269–215 BC), but in 211 BC took the losing Carthaginian side during the Second Punic War and was delivered by the Romans into the unmerciful hands of a Spanish mercenary called Moericus, who promptly stripped it of its wealth. By the reign of Emperor Augustus the town had lost all importance and was eventually abandoned. In 1955 archaeologists funded by Princeton University identified the site and began its excavation, which continues to this day.

The centre of the town is the **agora** (meeting place), spread over two levels. A trapezoidal stairway linking the two was also used as seating during public meetings. The upper level had a **market**; you can still see the walls that divided one shop from the next. The lower level was the site of the **theatre** which has been preserved in excellent condition.

To the north-east are the **residential quarters** of the city, made up of the remains of what must have been houses for the town's wealthiest class, as testified by the ornate wall decorations and handsome mosaics in the inner rooms. Another residential quarter has been found behind the theatre, and its considerable ruins are well worth checking out.

Morgantina is an easy detour if you have your own transport, but a difficult proposition without. It doesn't really feature on most people's itinerary and consequently there is no way of getting there by public transport. It is open from 9 am to one hour before sunset daily. Admission costs L4000.

CALTAGIRONE

postcode 95041 • pop 36,900
• elevation 608m

The elegant baroque town of Caltagirone is renowned throughout Sicily for the high quality of its ceramics, which have been produced here for over 1000 years. Although the town's earliest settlers were engaged in terracotta work, it was only with the arrival of the Arabs in the 10th century that the industry really took off. Not only did they give the town its name (from the Arabic *kalat* and *gerun* meaning 'castle' and 'cave') but they introduced the wide array of glazed polychromatic colours – particularly yellow and blue – that have distinguished local ceramics since then. The town (and most of the ceramic workshops) was destroyed in the earthquake of 1693 and rebuilt in the ubiquitous baroque style – most of the town's buildings date from the 18th-century reconstruction. The ceramics industry flourished once again in the 19th century and continues to do so today.

Orientation & Information

Caltagirone is divided into an upper and lower town. All buses stop on Piazza Municipio in the upper town, where most of the town's sights are located. AST buses depart from in front of the Metropol Cinema on Viale Principe Umberto in the lower town, but stop at Piazza Municipio on the way. The train station is in the lower town, at the western end of Viale Principe Umberto, along with Caltagirone's only accommodation. If you are travelling by bus and just planning a quick visit, you can go right up to Piazza Municipio, but if you plan on overnighting here you should get off in the lower town.

The small Pro Loco tourist office (☎ 0933 5 38 09) is at Via Volta Libertini 3, a little alley off Piazza Umberto in the upper town. It is usually open from 9 am to 12.30 pm and 4 to 7.30 pm Monday to Saturday between April and September. The public hospital (☎ 0933 5 79 02) is on Via Porto Salvo in the lower town.

Things to See

Caltagirone's pleasant upper town is a bustling centre of activity amid some gorgeous baroque buildings and churches. The most evocative sight in town is a set of steps, the **Scalinata di Santa Maria del Monte**, which rises up from Piazza Municipio to the

Chiesa di Santa Maria del Monte, at the top of the town. Each of the 142 steps is decorated with hand-painted ceramics, and no two are the same. On either side of the steps are rows of ceramic workshops where you can watch local artisans and admire their handiwork (as well as buy some). The steps are the focus of the Festa di San Giacamo (Feast of St James), the town's patron saint (see the Special Events section for details).

In the south of the upper town, on Via Roma (which leads into the lower town), is the **Ceramic Museum** (☎ 0933 2 16 80) where you can trace the history of ceramics from prehistoric times to the present day. The museum is open from 8 am to 6pm Tuesday to Sunday; admission costs L8000.

Special Events

During the Feast of St James (24–25 July), the Scalinata di Santa Maria del Monte is lit up by more than 4000 oil lamps for the religious procession that goes from Chiesa di Santa Maria del Monte down through the town and back again. Between 6 December and Christmas the town plays host to an exhibition of terracotta cribs; contact the tourist office for details.

Places to Stay & Eat

There are only a couple of hotels in Caltagirone, both located in hard-to-get-to spots in the lower town. The best option is to rent a room at the B&B *La Scala 2* (☎ 0933 5 15 52, fax 0933 5 77 81, Piazza Umberto) which is a residence in the centre of the upper town. The rooms are dingy and small, but cheap at L40,000 for a double. In summer be sure to make an advance booking. The *Monteverde* (☎ 0933 5 36 82, fax 0933 5 35 33, Via delle Industrie 11) is on the southern outskirts of town. Walk south along Via Roma and take the first fork to the right (past the public gardens) onto Via Santa Maria di Gesù; Via delle Industrie is about 800m on, to the right. Singles/doubles cost L45,000/70,000. If you don't have your own transport it's a bit of a walk.

Eating is less of a problem. The upper town has plenty of small, cheap restaurants where you can get a good meal. *Iudeca &*

Once you're immersed in the emptiness of Central Sicily, bustling coastal towns seem a world away.

Abandoned farmhouses in the island's interior tell a story of isolation and emigration.

Dramatic against a stormy sky, the dome of Piazza Armerina's cathedral dominates the horizon.

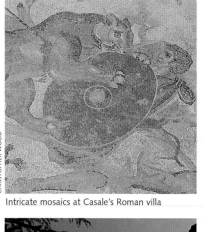

Intricate mosaics at Casale's Roman villa

Defending Enna – the Torre di Federico

Snapshot of the Valley of the Temples, Agrigento

Trieste (Discesa Collegio) off Piazza Municipio is particularly good. You can eat well for around L25,000.

Getting There & Away

Caltagirone is well-served by AST buses from Enna (L6500, eight daily) and Syracuse (L9000, six daily, via Ragusa). The town is also served by trains from Gela (L4500, 10 daily) and Catania (L7000, nine daily).

The Western Interior

The western interior is the traditional heartland of Sicily, an area of rolling hills dotted with small villages and towns that receives fewer visitors than any other spot on the island. This is in part due to the dearth of public transport that makes getting around almost impossible unless you have your own wheels, but the main reason for the area's almost insular seclusion is that it has been ravaged by poverty for centuries (see the boxed text 'A Region Blighted'). The tourist authorities have done their optimistic best to promote the area for its wild and natural beauty, but without a tourist infrastructure of any kind it is difficult to imagine anything changing for a long time. Even the interior's biggest city, Caltanissetta, is a victim: largely unattractive and industrial, it holds little appeal for the casual visitor.

CALTANISSETTA

postcode 93100 • pop 61,300
• elevation 568m

Sitting atop a hill that gently slopes downwards into the valley, Caltanissetta was originally a Saracen settlement but was captured by the Normans in 1086. A charter was granted to the town in accordance with Count Roger's vast plan for the urbanisation of Sicily, and the urban plan that is still in evidence today was laid out. Caltanissetta is the hub of public transport in the area, and makes a good base for planning your explorations, but beyond that there is little to see and do in town.

Orientation & Information

The town is well-served by buses and trains coming from all corners of the island. If you arrive by train and plan on going on to Enna, you're better off getting off here and switching to a bus as the train station in Enna is inconveniently located outside town. Calanisetta's train station is in the west of town, on Piazza Roma. The bus station is also to the west but slightly farther

A Region Blighted

You'll get no clearer sense of the effect of poverty in Sicily than when travelling through the interior west of Caltanissetta. Unlike other parts of the island, this area has never known prosperity and has been largely ignored by Sicily's conquerors and city-builders. For centuries the rolling hills and bleached landscapes were divided into large *latifundi*, or landed estates, that were the property of absentee landlords who cared little for the fate of the peasants trying to eke out a meagre living from the difficult soil. By the end of the 19th century an avenue of escape was opened up through emigration to the United States: in 1900 Sicily was officially the chief area of emigration in the world, with nearly 1.5 million Sicilians desperate to try their luck elsewhere. Although an island-wide problem, the effect of depopulation was greatest here, as villages were left to those too old to make the long journey across the sea. Emigration continued into the 20th century, with new destinations opening up: Argentina, Australia and, after WWII, the industrial centres of northern Italy, Switzerland and Germany attracting Sicilians in their tens of thousands.

It is difficult to imagine that anything substantial will be done to reverse the trend of poverty in the area. The few development projects that have been launched to much fanfare over the years have yielded few tangible benefits for the local population. A combination of mismanagement, indifference and misappropriation have ensured that the only ones who gain are the all-pervading Mafia – strongly represented here – and the bankers with whom they keep their accounts.

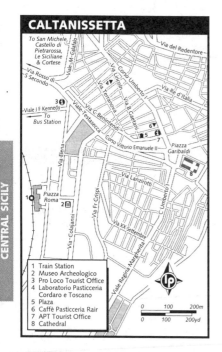

CALTANISSETTA

To San Michele,
Castello di
Pietrarossa,
Le Siciliane
& Cortese

Via Rosso di
S Secondo

Via del Redentore

Via M. Caldato

Corso Umberto I

Via Lincoln

Via Terranova

Via Re d'Italia

Via Testasecca

Viale J F Kennedy
— To
Bus Station

Via C Beninterdi

Via G Gaetani

Viale Testasecca

Corso Vittorio Emanuele II

Piazza
Garibaldi

Via Elena

Via Lanzirotti

Via Fr Crispi

Piazza
Roma

Umberto I

Via XX Settembre

Via Colajanni

Via Regina Margherita

Viale Sicilia

1 Train Station
2 Museo Archeologico
3 Pro Loco Tourist Office
4 Laboratorio Pasticceria
  Cordaro e Toscano
5 Plaza
6 Caffè Pasticceria Rair
7 APT Tourist Office
8 Cathedral

0   100   200m
0   100   200yd

19th century have ruined the overall effect. Inside are frescoes by Guglielmo Borremans that are worth admiring. The most interesting sight in town is the **Museo Archeologico** (☎ 0934 2 59 36), at Via Colajanni 3, about 100m east of the train station. The displays are mostly from prehistoric times and include finds from digs conducted in the 1950s, including vases and tools from the Bronze Age and early Sicilian ceramics. Also of interest are finds from a number of necropoli spread about Caltanissetta's hinterland. One such necropolis was known by the Arabs as Gibil Habil, meaning 'mountain of death'. The museum is open from 9 am to 1.30 pm and 3.30 to 7.30 pm Monday to Saturday (closed the first Monday of the month). Admission costs L4000.

To the west of town, but within easy walking distance of Piazza Garibaldi, are the ruins of the **Castello di Pietrarossa**, precariously balanced on a rocky outcrop. There isn't much left of the castle, but the walk and the views from the rock are pleasant enough.

Places to Stay & Eat

The town's only affordable hotel is *Plaza* (*☎/fax 0934 58 38 77, Via B Gaetani 5*). Airy singles/doubles cost L35,000/70,000. A more expensive option is the five-star *San Michele* (*☎ 0934 55 37 50, fax 0934 59 87 91, Via Fasci Siciliani*) which is north-west of town. Singles/doubles cost L80,000/120,000.

For food, locals recommend *Le Siciliane* (*☎ 0934 53 42 97, Piazza Trento 12*), off Via Rosso di S Secondo (take the second right). A little further along is *Cortese* (*☎ 0934 59 16 86, Viale Sicilia 166*) which is an excellent restaurant serving local specialities such as *pasta con frutti di mare e funghi* (pasta with seafood and mushrooms). You shoul not spend more than L30,000 in either place. Otherwise, there are a couple of great *pasticcerie* (cake shops) where you can eat some fabulous *cannoli* (cream horns). At *Caffè Pasticceria Rair* (*Corso Umberto I 163*) you should try the *cannolicchi alla ricotta*, smaller versions of cannoli filled with ricotta and dusted with cinnamon, ground hazelnuts and almonds. *Laboratorio Pasticceria Cordaro e Toscano* (*Via dei Mille 42*)

afield, about 1km from the Pro Loco tourist office on Viale Testasecca. To get there walk up Viale Kennedy, turn right at Piazza Sturzo and left at Via Salemi, which then becomes Via Turati. At the end of the road is Piazza Repubblica and the bus station.

There are two tourist offices in town. The main APT tourist office (☎ 0934 2 95 32) is on Corso Umberto I, just west of Piazza Garibaldi. The smaller Pro Loco tourist office (☎ 0934 42 10 89) is about 300m north of the train station at the corner of Viale Testasecca and Viale Kennedy. Both offices are open from 9 am to 1 pm and 3 to 6 pm Monday to Saturday (until 7.30 pm between June and September).

Things to See

Sights in Caltanissetta are pretty thin on the ground. The 17th-century **cathedral's** late-Renaissance appearance breaks the baroque mould that is so common in this part of this island, but substantial alterations made in the is an authentic pastry shop that is open on Sunday only.

Getting There & Away

There are AST buses to Agrigento 10 times daily Monday to Saturday, seven on Sunday (L5500, 1¼ hours); two daily to Caltagirone (L9000, two hours); nine daily to Catania (L8500, 1½ hours); four to Enna Monday to Saturday (L3000, 40 minutes); and one daily for Piazza Armerina (L8000, 1½ hours). If you plan on travelling into the western province from Caltanissetta, you're better off having your own transport. There are nine trains daily to/from Agrigento via Gela (L8500, 1 hour 20 minutes). There are also 11 trains daily to/from Enna (L6000, one hour), but you're better off getting the bus.

WEST OF CALTANISSETTA
Along the SS640

This road heads south-west alongside the railroad tracks that link Caltanissetta with Agrigento. About halfway between the two cities is **Canicattì**, a little market town that is the Italian Timbuktu, at least in terms of remoteness. Its name is also comically mispronounced by Italian children as 'Canigattì' or 'Cats & Dogs'. Other than that, there is nothing to see in town. Still, your Italian friends will chuckle if they receive a postcard with the town's postmark.

If you're driving you can get to **Mussomeli**, 22km north-west of Canicattì along a thin secondary road (follow the signs for Montedoro and then Bompensiere). On the far side of this little village is the imposing, 14th-century **Castello Manfredonico**, built by the Chiaramonte family.

RACALMUTO

postcode 92021 • pop 10,700
• elevation 445m

About 13km east of Aragona off the SS189 is the signposted town of Racalmuto, an important centre for sulphur mining until the beginning of the 20th century. Since then it has survived on agriculture and rock-salt mining. Its only claim to fame is as the birthplace of Leonardo Sciascia (1921–89), widely regarded as one of the best Italian writers of the 20th century. See the boxed text 'A Sicilian Iconoclast' in the Facts about Sicily chapter.

ARAGONA & THE VULCANELLI DI MACALUBE

postcode 92021 • pop 10,400
• elevation 400m

The small farming town of Aragona is 14km north of Agrigento on the SS189 (take the signposted fork to the left about 12km along). The town itself is unremarkable with the exception of the interior of the 17th-century **Chiesa Madre**, which contains some fine stucco work by Giacomo Serpotta and an expertly crafted 18th-century wooden creche. The most interesting sight, the **Vulcanelli di Macalube**, is 3km south of town in the middle of a field.

Take the last left south out of Aragona (signposted) and follow the road for about 1km. At the first fork, take a left down a dirt road. When the road forks again, take a right and keep going until you reach a chain barring the way and a sign saying '*Proprietà Privata*' (private property). Dump your car here and walk 300m or so up the path. On your right is an elevated field that is fenced off against the intrusion of cows. As you approach, you will notice that the field is in fact a greyish expanse of clay which looks like the surface of the moon. This is caused by a rare geographical phenomenon known as sedimentary vulcanism. Throughout the field are little mini-volcanoes formed by the pressure of methane gas and sulphur pushing up through the surface. The crust is constantly bubbling and little lakes of whitish liquid are formed at the top of each 'volcano'.

Although this is private property, visitors (who are few and far between) are welcome if they stick to the path and the Vulcanelli. If you see someone on the property, it's polite to ask for permission (which is always given). Try '*Le dispiace se visito i Vulcanelli?*' (Do you mind if I visit the Vulcanelli?)

LERCARA FRIDDI

If you keep going north past Mussomeli for about 12km you'll hit the main SS189 which links Agrigento and Palermo. About

A Very Lucky Man

Mafia boss Salvatore 'Lucky' Luciano was born Salvatore Lucania in Lercara Friddi in 1897. When he was a child, his family joined the countless others on the emigrant trail to New York. In a story more than slightly reminiscent of *The Godfather II*, the young Salvatore became involved with the local Mafia and quickly rose through the ranks until he became the undisputed *Capo di tutti i Capi* (Boss of all Bosses). In 1936 his spectacular career came to an abrupt halt when he was sentenced to 30 years imprisonment for 62 counts of 'voluntary prostitution'. What saved him, however, was WWII. He was released from prison in 1943 on condition that he help the US forces during their landing in Sicily. One story tells that the troops wore yellow scarves with 'L' for 'Lucky' emblazoned on them so that the local Mafia, eager to rid the island of the Fascists, would be able to recognise them. Whatever the truth of it, Luciano's help was instrumental in allowing the Americans to take the whole island in just 39 days. His reward was extradition back to Italy, where he helped negotiate a deal between the Sicilian and American mobs that led to the creation of an international narcotics syndicate still in operation today. Luciano died, peacefully, in Naples in 1962.

24km north of the turn is the small town of Lercara Friddi, renowned for only one reason: it is the birthplace of Salvatore 'Lucky' Luciano, one of the most notorious and important figures in Mafia history (see the boxed text 'A Very Lucky Man').

SANT'ANGELO MUXARO

This tiny town is famous for the prehistoric **rock tombs** *(tholos)* that litter the hillside on its southern side. They date from the 11th to the 5th century BC and resemble stone beehives. The largest one is known as the **Tomba del Principe** (Tomb of the Prince). Whatever treasures they once contained have long since disappeared into the display cases of Europe's museums or into private hands. The tombs are always accessible.

To get here, take the SS188 west out of Lercara Friddi and turn south (towards Agrigento): Sant'Angelo Muxaro is about 50km down the road. From Agrigento, Lattuca Bus does a day tour of the area, leaving from in front of the Astor Cinema on Piazza Vittorio Emanuele at 9 am and returning at 4 pm; the trip costs L15,000.

The Southern Coast

The stretch of land between Sciacca to the west and Gela to the east, commonly referred to as the Agrigentino after the region's most important town, is the least populated of all of Sicily's coastlines. The site of three important Greek colonies in ancient times – at Eraclea Minoa, Akragas (now Agrigento) and Gela – the southern coast today shifts between wonderful natural landscapes that bear a striking resemblance to the North African coastline and heavy industrial development, not least at the eastern end. The main attraction here is the magnificent Valley of the Temples (Valle dei Templi) at Agrigento, one of the most important archaeological sites in Europe, but not to be ignored are the pleasant town of Sciacca and the stunning beaches below the remains of Eraclea Minoa, to the west. At the eastern end is Gela, a pretty ugly industrial centre but home to a fascinating museum which boasts a stunning collection of ancient vases. Also worth visiting are the remote Pelagic Islands, a tiny archipelago 240km off the southern coast that is accessible by boat from Agrigento. Closer to Africa than Sicily, these sun-scorched, windswept islands make a good weekend getaway.

GELA
postcode 93012 • pop 72,500
There is really only one reason for coming to Gela – to visit the archaeological museum. The town itself is a horrible mess of tangled steel and industrial mayhem. A huge petrochemical plant is responsible for the faint smell of chemicals that seems to hang in the air, and although there are beaches along the coast the water is less than clean.

It was not always so, however. Founded in 689 BC by colonists from Rhodes, Gela quickly became one of the most important Greek cities on the island, rivalling even Syracuse as a centre of learning. According to legend, the playwright Aeschylus met an unfortunate end here when an eagle dropped a tortoise on his head, mistaking his bald pate for a stone!

Highlights

- Marvel at the formidable ruins of the Valley of the Temples in Agrigento

- Enjoy the fine view from Piazza Scandaliato in Sciacca

- Wander around the extraordinary sculpted figures in the garden of the Castello Incantato outside Sciacca, all created by one lonely man

- Admire the view of the coastline from Eraclea Minoa

- Visit the magnificent collection of red- and black-clay *kraters* in Gela's archaeological museum

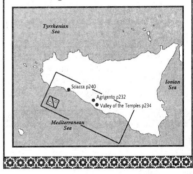

Gela was completely destroyed by Carthage in 405 BC, was refounded in 338 BC and destroyed again in 282 BC, this time by an army led by the tyrant Finzia of Agrigento. The area lay in ruins until 1230, when Frederick II ordered that a new town called Terranova be built on the site of the ancient city. The name was changed back to Gela in 1927, but that is the only resemblance between the modern city and the colony of old.

The **archaeological museum** (☎ 0933 91 26 26) lies at the eastern end of Gela's main drag, Corso Vittorio Emanuele. On the ground floor are finds from the ancient city's acropolis. These mostly date from

THE SOUTHERN COAST

prehistoric times up to the 5th century BC, but also include artefacts from the 4th and 3rd centuries BC, when the acropolis was converted into an artisans' district.

The best part of the museum, however, is upstairs. Here you'll find the world's largest collection of red- and black-figure vases, Gela's speciality between the 7th and 4th centuries BC. Although there are some examples of these in archaeological museums throughout Europe, the collection here is simply staggering. Also on display is part of an important collection of ancient coins minted in Agrigento, Gela, Syracuse, Messina and Athens. At one time the collection numbered over 1000 coins, but it was stolen in 1976 and only about half of it was recovered.

The museum is open from 9 am to 12.30 pm and 4 to 7 pm daily (except the last Monday of the month). Admission costs L4000.

The only other worthwhile sight in Gela is at the other end of Corso Vittorio Emanuele (turn left on Via Manzoni and follow the road to the sea; it's about a 4km walk), where you will find the remains of the ancient **Greek fortifications**. They are in a remarkable state of preservation, most likely due to the fact that they were covered by sand dunes for thousands of years until they were discovered in 1948. The wind used to blow huge amounts of sand onto the town, which was dealt with in antiquity by building 8m-high protective walls. Today many of the walls are in ruins and the authorities have planted trees to act as a buffer against the encroaching sand. The site is open from 9 am to one hour before sunset daily. Admission costs L4000.

Getting There & Away

Gela is easily reached by train and bus from every town on the southern coast. There are at least 14 trains daily from Agrigento to Gela (L7400). All buses arrive at and depart from the front of the train station (ask at the Autolinee office across the street for a timetable). The journey between Agrigento and Gela takes about an 1¼ hours (L5500).

AGRIGENTO
postcode 92100 • **pop 55,200**
• **elevation 230m**

At first glance, this sizeable town appears nothing more than an expanse of unremarkable modern development strewn across a

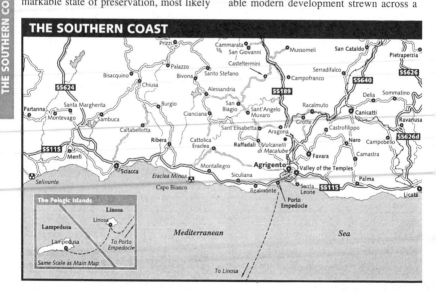

THE SOUTHERN COAST

hill. Obscured by the aesthetic myopia of the 1960s and '70s, however, is a lovely and compact medieval town that is deserving of more than just a cursory glance on the way to the area's main draw, the spectacular Valley of the Temples, spread out below the modern city towards the sea. Although the ruins should be on every traveller's itinerary, too many tour buses head straight there and give the town a miss altogether, which is a shame considering that interspersed among the narrow, climbing streets are a couple of sights worth checking out.

On a negative note, Agrigento tops the list of a number of dreadful statistics. It is one of the poorest towns in Italy (although you'd never know by strolling past the elegant boutiques on Via Atenea) and an important centre of Mafia activity. It is reputed that Agrigento's crime families are key players in the multi-billion-dollar narcotics industry and that in the surrounding countryside are located a number of secret heroin refineries.

History

The area has been inhabited since prehistoric times but, despite claims that Agrigento was first founded by Daedalus, father of Icarus

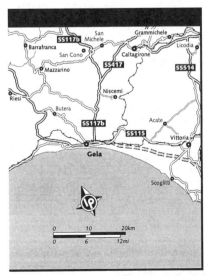

(he of flying-too-close-to-the-sun fame), the first organised settlement here dates from 581 BC, when a colony from Gela united with settlers from Greece to found Akragas, one of the last Greek colonies in Sicily. Strategically located halfway between Gela and Selinunte, the new town was conceived as a lookout post over the Mediterranean to monitor potential Carthaginian invasions. This threat was temporarily eliminated following the Battle of Himera in 480 BC, and the town grew substantially in size and population. Most of the temples that you see today date from this period, a time when it was reckoned that tyrant-ruled Akragas was home to 200,000 citizens. The Greek poet Pindar described the city as 'the most beautiful of those inhabited by mortals'.

Its good fortune came to an abrupt end in 406 BC when the old enemy Carthage finally overcame Greek resistance, but it was reclaimed in 338 BC by the Corinthian general Timoleon, who instituted a liberal and democratic regime, and Akragas more or less picked up where it had left off before the Carthaginian interlude. In 210 BC it was the Romans' turn to take the city. They renamed it Agrigentum and encouraged the farming and trading sectors, thus laying the foundations for the city's future as an important centre of commerce under the Byzantines.

In the 7th century the bulk of the city's inhabitants moved up the hill to the site of the modern city, virtually abandoning the old town. Although experts are still at a loss as to why exactly such a shift occurred, it has been suggested that it was to fend off the island's latest conquerors from North Africa, the Saracens. Despite its best efforts, Agrigento fell to the Saracens at the start of the 9th century, and for the next 200 years took on the shape of a typical Arab town, complete with elegant courtyards and narrow, twisting streets. Today the Arabic influence can also be seen in some of the town's street names, such as Via Bac Bac and Piazza Bibbiria. Under the Normans, at the end of the 11th century, the town continued as before, trading with North Africa and the rest of the island.

Agrigento did not change much until the 19th century, when the western half of the

THE SOUTHERN COAST

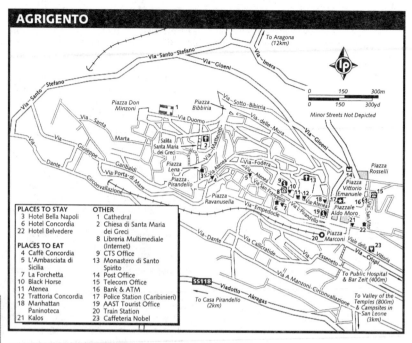

AGRIGENTO

To Aragona (12km)

0   150   300m
0   150   300yd

Minor Streets Not Depicted

PLACES TO STAY
3   Hotel Bella Napoli
6   Hotel Concordia
22 Hotel Belvedere

PLACES TO EAT
4   Caffè Concordia
5   L'Ambasciata di Sicilia
7   La Forchetta
10 Black Horse
11 Atenea
12 Trattoria Concordia
18 Manhattan Paninoteca
21 Kalos

OTHER
1   Cathedral
2   Chiesa di Santa Maria dei Greci
8   Libreria Multimediale (Internet)
9   CTS Office
13 Monastero di Santo Spirito
14 Post Office
15 Telecom Office
16 Bank & ATM
17 Police Station (Caribinieri)
19 AAST Tourist Office
20 Train Station
23 Caffeteria Nobel

SS118
To Casa Pirandello (2km)

To Public Hospital & Bar Zeit (400m)

To Valley of the Temples (800m) & Campsites in San Leone (3km)

city was built. In the 20th century the urban sprawl flowed down the hill and into the valley that was hitherto the preserve of the ancient city, now crumbled away. The period following WWII was particularly ruinous for the Valley of the Temples as a furious spate of wildcat construction gravely affected the valley's appearance, leading to accusations that Agrigento's cultural and environmental heritage was being destroyed. So far little has been done to arrest the development, but signs are that a change is on the way (see the boxed text 'The Construction Scourge' later in this section).

Orientation

All public transport arrives at and departs from the centre of town. Intercity buses arrive in Piazza Rosselli, just off the northern side of Piazza Vittorio Emanuele. The train station is about 300m south, on Piazza Marconi. Lying between the two is the green oasis of Piazzale Aldo Moro, at the eastern end of Via

Atenea, the main street of the medieval town. Frequent city buses run to the Valley of the Temples below the town. For details, see Getting Around later in this section.

Information

Tourist Office The AAST office (☎ 0922 2 04 54) is at Via Cesare Battisti 15, just off the eastern end of Via Atenea. It is open from 8.30 am to 1.30 pm and 4.30 to 7 pm Monday to Friday and from 8.30 am to 1 pm on Saturday.

Money Banks are generally open from 8.30 am to 1.30 pm (larger banks also open from 3 to 4 pm), and the Monte dei Paschi di Siena at Piazza Vittorio Emanuele 1 has an ATM. Out of hours, there's an exchange office at the post office and another at the train station – watch the rates.

Post & Communications The post office, on Piazza Vittorio Emanuele, is open from

8.30 am to 6.30 pm Monday to Friday (to 12.30 pm on Saturday).

There is a Telecom office at Via A de Gasperi 25, open from 9 am to 7 pm Monday to Friday.

You can check email and surf the Internet at the Libreria Multimediale, Via Celauro 7. It is open from 9 am to 1 pm and 4.30 to 8 pm Monday to Saturday. Rates start at L2500 for 15 minutes, L5000 for 30 minutes and L9000 for one hour.

Newspapers & Magazines You can buy foreign newspapers and magazines at a stand next to the bar in the car park for the Valley of the Temples.

Medical Services & Emergency The public hospital, the Azienda Ospedaliera San Giovanni di Dio (☎ 0922 49 21 11), is at Via Rupe Atenea 1. For an ambulance, call ☎ 0922 40 13 44.

The *carabinieri* (military police; ☎ 0922 59 63 22) are at Piazzale Aldo Moro 2.

Valley of the Temples

One of Sicily's premier attractions, the complex of temples and old city walls that remain from the ancient city of Akragas are reason enough to warrant a visit to the southern coast of the island. After visiting the area, Goethe waxed that 'we shall never in our lives be able to rejoice again, after seeing such a stupendous view in this splendid valley'. While some modern construction and an enormous flyway detract from the overall picture, he wasn't far wrong. Still, earthquakes and vandalism have done their fair share of damage, and the temples in the valley (actually a ridge) are in various states of ruin.

The archaeological park is divided into eastern and western zones by the main SS118 road (Via dei Templi) that leads to the temples from town. By the entrances to the two zones is the car park, where you will also find a bar/restaurant, a newspaper kiosk and the usual assortment of souvenir stands.

The Eastern Zone The temples that stand unfettered and unenclosed in the eastern zone are the most spectacular of all. The first

of these is the **Temple of Hercules** (Tempio di Ercole), immediately inside the entrance to the right. Its origin is uncertain, but it is believed to be the oldest of the lot, dating from the end of the 6th century BC. Eight of its 38 columns have been raised and you can wander around the remains of the rest.

Moving east past the remains of the ancient walls, the next temple along the path is the **Temple of Concord** (Tempio della Concordia), the only one to survive the unforgiving hands of time and history relatively intact. It was built around 430 BC and was converted into a Christian basilica in the 6th century AD; the new tenants reinforced the main structure, giving it a better chance of surviving an earthquake. In 1748 the temple was restored to its original form. The architect in charge of the restoration, Tommaso Fazello, gave the temple its name, but it is thought that it was originally dedicated to either Castor or Pollux. Today it is undergoing another restoration and is fenced off, with one end entirely covered by scaffolding.

At the eastern end of the ridge, a farther 400m on, is the **Temple of Juno** (Tempio di Giunone), partially destroyed by an earthquake in the Middle Ages. Just behind the eastern end is a long altar originally used for sacrifices; the traces of red are the result of fire damage, most likely during the Carthaginian invasion of 406 BC.

The eastern zone is open from first light to 9 pm (8 pm from September to April). You're better off getting here early in the morning to avoid the crowds (and to avoid having a gawping tour group in all your photos!).

The Western Zone Across Via dei Templi is the entrance to the western zone, the main feature of which is the crumbled remains of the **Temple of Jupiter** (Tempio di Giove). Covering an area measuring 112m by 56m, with columns 20m high, it would have been the largest Doric temple ever built had its construction not been interrupted by the Carthaginian sack of Akragas. (The historical irony is that the foundations for the temple had been laid by Carthaginian prisoners captured after the Battle of Himera nearly 100 years previously.) The

THE SOUTHERN COAST

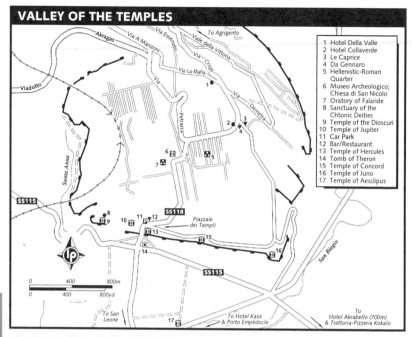

VALLEY OF THE TEMPLES

1 Hotel Della Valle
2 Hotel Collaverde
3 Le Caprice
4 Da Gennaro
5 Hellenistic-Roman Quarter
6 Museo Archeologico; Chiesa di San Nicolo
7 Oratory of Falaride
8 Sanctuary of the Chtonic Deities
9 Temple of the Dioscuri
10 Temple of Jupiter
11 Car Park
12 Bar/Restaurant
13 Temple of Hercules
14 Tomb of Theron
15 Temple of Concord
16 Temple of Juno
17 Temple of Aesclipus

incomplete temple was later destroyed by an earthquake. Lying flat on his back amid the rubble is a telamon, a sculpted figure of a man with arms raised, intended to support the temple's weight. One of several planned for the temple, the figure is 8m long.

Across the path from the ruins is a little temple set on a high base, known as the **Tomb of Theron** (Tomba di Therone), the Greek tyrant of Agrigento. In fact, the structure dates from around 75 BC, during the Roman occupation, nearly 500 years after the tyrant's death.

About 50m farther on is the smaller **Temple of the Dioscuri** (Tempio dei Dioscuri), also known as the Temple of Castor and Pollux. It was built towards the end of the 5th century, but was destroyed by the Carthaginians, later restored in Hellenistic style and then destroyed again by an earthquake. What you see today dates from 1832, when it was rebuilt using materials from other temples.

Just behind the temple is a complex of altars and small buildings believed to be part of the **Sanctuary of the Chtonic Deities** (Santuario delle Divine Chtoniche or, more commonly, Santuario di Demetra e Kore), which dates from the early 6th century BC.

Back at the crossroads just inside the entrance to the zone, the path south leads to the **Temple of Aesclipus** (Tempio di Esculapio), off the second fork to the left. The smallest of all the temples, it is distinguished by having solid walls instead of a colonnade.

This area is open daily from 9 am to one hour before sunset; admission costs L4000. In the evenings, the temples are bathed in a hue of amber light. They are lit up between 9.30 and 11.30 pm from May to October, and between 8 and 10 pm the rest of the year.

Museo Archeologico About halfway up the road towards town from the temples is this interesting museum (☎ 0922 49 72 21) housing a large collection of artefacts from the excavated site. Room (sala) 1 contains an archaeological plan of ancient Akragas, helpful if you want to get a sense of the scale of the old city, which covered 1400 hectares. Room 3 features a rich collection of ceramics in both black and red dating from the 6th to the 3rd centuries BC. Of particular note is the *krater*, a red ceramic chalice from 490 BC. In Room 6 is a telamon standing 7.75m high, as well as the heads of three others. Room 9 features a fine *Ephebus* – a statue of a young boy – which was sculpted in 470 BC. The last rooms hold artefacts from around the province – be sure to check out the wonderful ceramic bowls.

In the grounds of the museum is the 13th-century Cistercian **Chiesa di San Nicola**, with a fine Gothic doorway. Inside is a Roman sarcophagus (second chapel on the right) which bears a wonderful relief of the myth of Phaedra. On the church's esplanade is an ancient odeon called the Ekklesiasterion, built in the 3rd century BC for public meetings. Alongside it is the **Oratory of Phalaris** (Oratorio di Falaride), a temple dating from the 1st century BC that was converted into an oratory during the Middle Ages.

The Construction Scourge

Although unplanned and unlicensed construction is a problem throughout the Mezzogiorno (virtually all of the regions south of Rome), Agrigento is a particularly galling example of the scourge of irresponsible and illegal construction (widely reported as a convenient way for the Mafia to launder drug profits). The Valley of the Temples has been scarred by such construction – the products of which is known in Italian as *case abusive* (literally, abusive houses) – which has provoked the consternation and condemnation of conservationists, environmentalists and lovers of Sicily's rich cultural heritage alike. The government in Rome has been making noises about the problem since the late 1960s, but it was only in October 1999 that officials finally decided to make a decisive stand: they announced that all unlicensed houses would be demolished. At the time of research the bulldozers had yet to start their engines, but hopefully it's just a matter of time.

The museum and grounds are open from 8 am to 1 pm daily. They are also open from 2 to 5 pm Wednesday to Saturday. Admission costs L8000.

Hellenistic-Roman Quarter Directly opposite the museum is the Hellenistic-Roman Quarter (Quartiere Ellenistico-Romano), featuring a well-preserved street layout that constituted part of urban Akragas (and later, under the Romans, Agrigentum). The regular grid is made up of main streets *(plateiai)* intersected at right angles by secondary streets *(stenopoi)*, all of which were laid out towards the end of the 4th century BC. The Romans didn't alter the layout, but added their own embellishments, including mosaic floors and stucco work. They were also responsible for adding water and heating pipes, and introduced drainage facilities for rainwater and sewage. The site keeps the same hours as the western zone. Admission is free.

The Medieval Town

Next to Akragas, Agrigento is comparatively modern, even though the area west of Piazzale Aldo Moro is strictly medieval. The town's main artery is Via Atenea, lined with elegant shops and a popular street for a stroll with locals and visitors alike. Off Via Atenea, however, everything is quieter, more run down and – at night – a little intimidating. Still, it is fun to wander in and out of the narrow, climbing streets, where you can catch a glimpse of the lovely Arabic courtyards and get a real feel for the medieval town.

At the top of a set of winding steps north off Via Atenea is the Cistercian **Monastero di Santo Spirito** (Monastery of the Holy Spirit), founded around 1290. A handsome Gothic portal leads inside, where there is some fine stucco work by Giacomo Serpotta and his school and a statue of the *Madonna Incoronata* (Virgin Enthroned) by Domenico Gagini. Upstairs is a small anthropological and ethnographical museum (☎ 0922 59 03 71), where the miscellany of objects is not very well labelled. It is open from 9 am to 1 pm and 4 to 7 pm Monday to Saturday; admission is free. The church is usually open during these times, but if it

THE SOUTHERN COAST

Shh! We're in a Church!

By virtue of a remarkable acoustic phenomenon, even the faintest sound carries in Agrigento's cathedral. Two people are needed to try this little experiment: the first stands in the presbytery, while the second stands at the entrance. If the first person so much as whispers, the sound is carried right through the church to the entrance, fully 85m away!

isn't ring the bell next door (No 2), where you can also buy cakes and pastries baked on the premises by the resident nuns (see Places to Eat later in this section).

At the western end of Via Atenea is the small **Chiesa di Santa Maria dei Greci**, accessed through a lovely garden with palm trees and cypresses. It was built in the 11th century on the site of a 5th-century Doric temple dedicated to Athena. Inside are some badly damaged Byzantine frescoes and the remains of the original Norman ceiling. Opening hours are from 8 am to 12 pm and 3 pm till dusk Monday to Saturday, but they are not strictly adhered to. If you find it closed, check with the custodian at Salita Santa Maria dei Greci 1 (to the right as you face the church), who will expect a tip to open the doors.

About 300m west of the church (take a left and then a right onto Via Duomo) is Agrigento's fragile-looking **cathedral**, built in the year 1000. It is dedicated to the town's first archbishop, the Norman San Gerlando (St Gerland). It was radically restructured over the centuries, and adjoining it is an unfinished 15th-century bell tower *(campanile)*. Inside is the saint's tomb, set in the right wing of the transept.

Casa Natale di Pirandello

South-west of Agrigento, about halfway along the busy road to Porto Empedocle in the suburb of Caos, is the birthplace of one of the great heavyweights of Sicilian literature, Luigi Pirandello (1867–1936). His early career was taken up with the writing of short stories and novels (including *Il Fu Mattia Pascal*, The Late Mattia Pascal, pub-

lished in 1904), but he concentrated on writing for the theatre after WWI. Considered some of the most important plays written in the Italian language, his works include such masterpieces as *Sei Personaggi in Ricerca di un Autore* (Six Characters in Search of an Author) and *Enrico IV* (Henry IV). In 1934 he was awarded the Nobel Prize for Literature.

The central themes of his work are loneliness, disillusionment and the falling away of idealism, hardly surprising considering that his private life was marked by sadness and tragedy (see the boxed text 'Nietta Pirandello'). Nevertheless, Pirandello's legacy is a rich one. His explorations into the world of the absurd and his heavy use of irony set the tone for later playwrights such as Eugene Ionesco (author of the absurdist classic *Rinoceronte*, or Rhinoceros) and Jean-Paul Sartre, while his insightful observations into the arcane ways of his fellow Sicilians did much to inspire his two great successors, Giuseppe di Lampedusa (author of *Il Gattopardo*, The Leopard) and Leonardo Sciascia (see the boxed text 'A Sicilian Iconoclast' in the Facts about Sicily chapter).

Pirandello's ashes are kept in an urn buried at the foot of a pine tree, which in recent years has been stripped of all its branches. Even the magnificent view of the sea has been spoilt by the industrial landscape. The villa in which Pirandello was born and spent most of his summers has been converted into a museum (☎ 0922 51 11 02) containing a lot of memorabilia. It is currently undergoing renovation and will not reopen to the public until the end of 2001.

Special Events

The city's big annual shindig is the Festival of the Almond Blossom (Sagra del Mandorlo in Fiore), a folk festival held on the first Sunday in February in the Valley of the Temples. The Feast of St Calogero (Festa di San Calogero) is the second big party in Agrigento, lasting a whole week from the first Sunday in July. For information on both festivals check with the tourist office or call ☎ 0922 2 03 91.

Places to Stay

Camping The nearest camp sites are in the small coastal town of San Leone, 6km south of Agrigento. *Internazionale San Leone* (☎ 0922 41 61 21) charges L7000 per person and L8000 per two-person tent. To get there, take bus No 2 (L1000) from in front of the train station in Agrigento; you'll have to walk about 1km east along the beach at San Leone. Alternatively, drive down Via dei Templi, continue along Viale Emporium towards the sea and turn left at Lungomare Akragas. About 400m farther on is *Camping Nettuno* (☎ 0922 41 62 68) which costs the same but isn't as comfortable.

Hotels – Agrigento There's a handful of cheap hotels around the medieval town. They tend to get full pretty quickly, so book early if you can. *Hotel Bella Napoli* (☎ 0922 2 04 35, fax 0922 2 04 35, Piazza Lena 6) is uphill off Via Bac Bac. It has clean, basic singles/doubles for L25,000/55,000 without bathroom or L44,000/75,000 with bathroom. The showers are a bit dodgy, and you might have to ask for soap at the reception. The

Hotel Belvedere (☎ 0922 2 00 51, fax 0922 2 00 51, Via San Vito 20) is in the newer part of town, uphill from Piazza Vittorio Emanuele. It has singles from L50,000 to L68,000 and doubles with bathroom from L70,000 to L98,000, depending on the season. *Hotel Concordia* (☎ 0922 59 62 66, Piazza San Francesco 11) is in a small square just off Via Atenea, where the daily produce market is held. It has somewhat noisy single/double rooms for L30,000/60,000 without bathroom or L45,000/70,000 with bathroom.

Hotels – Valley of the Temples Most of Agrigento's better hotels are out of town, around the Valley of the Temples or near the sea. *Hotel Akrabello* (☎ 0922 60 62 77, fax 0922 60 61 86) is in the Parco Angeli area, east of the temples. It is modern and comfortable and has single/double rooms for up to L130,000/180,000, including breakfast. *Collaverde Park* (☎ 0922 2 95 55, fax 0922 2 90 12, Passeggiata Archeologica) is well located close to the temples. Singles/doubles cost L100,000/150,000 (L160,000/240,000 with bathroom).

Nietta Pirandello

Overshadowed by the literary achievements of her husband, the life of Maria Antonietta Portulano, wife of Luigi Pirandello, is a particularly Sicilian tragedy. Known affectionately as Nietta, she was betrothed to Pirandello in 1894 in an arranged marriage (their fathers were business associates). The early years of their union were apparently happy and they produced three children: Stefano (who later became the writer Stefano Landi), Lietta (who moved to Chile and married writer Manuel Aguirre) and Fausto (who became a painter). After Fausto's birth in 1899, however, Nietta began to suffer anxiety attacks and fits of depression, which doctors tried to treat with prolonged periods of 'rest'. In 1903 a landslide destroyed the sulphur mine that was Nietta's dowry and the only real source of income for the Pirandellos, and Nietta's attacks became more violent, resulting in paralysis and paranoid obsessiveness. The onset of WWI worsened her condition and in 1919 she was committed to an asylum, where she remained for the rest of her life.

To a Sicilian woman of the 19th century, the dowry, known as *la roba*, was not simply an accumulation of her material wealth but a symbol of her status and importance in the world. Nietta's husband was hardly wealthy, but he was a Sicilian male who was defined by his ability to write. Nietta, on the other hand, was a woman in a strictly patriarchal society and, as such, could only maintain her independence through her possessions, which in this case were made up of a considerable income from the mine. The loss of the mine was really a loss of identity, a loss made all the more damaging by the fact that she was an active, intelligent woman who saw her marriage to her husband as one based on equality. As for Pirandello, he was devastated by his wife's illness and consoled himself through writing. Apart from a dalliance with an actress called Maria Abba, he lived alone for the rest of his life.

THE SOUTHERN COAST

Hotel Della Valle (☎ *0922 2 69 66, fax 0922 2 69 66, Via dei Templi*) has lovely rooms with full services, a pool and gardens. Rooms cost up to L150,000/220,000 for a single/double. *Hotel Kaos* (☎ *0922 59 86 22, fax 0922 40 21 80*) is by the sea, about 2km from the temples. It is a large resort complex in a restored villa. Rooms cost up to L200,000/280,000.

Places to Eat
Eating well is not a problem in Agrigento, and you can do so without spending a fortune either. One of the best meals in town can be at *La Forchetta* (*Piazza San Francesco 9*), next door to Hotel Concordia (see the previous Places to Stay section). The cramped dining room is popular with locals who come for the ever-changing daily specials; the *spaghetti al pesce di spada* (spaghetti with swordfish) is an excellent choice at L8000. It is closed on Sunday. A good choice for a light lunch is the *Manhattan Paninoteca*, up Salita M Angeli from Via Atenea.

Just off Via Atenea, the *Black Horse* (☎ *0922 2 32 23, Via Celauro 8*) serves tasty, reasonably priced meals; the L13,000 set menu is particularly good value. Another fine choice with a similar menu is the *Atenea* (☎ *0922 2 57 61, Via Ficani 12*). The recently renovated *L'Ambasciata di Sicilia* (☎ *0922 2 05 26, Via Giambertoni 2*) offers typical Sicilian fare, and an enjoyable meal will cost under L30,000. If you can, get a table on the small outdoor terrace, which has splendid views of the town and the temples.

Another good restaurant for traditional Sicilian food is *Kalos* (☎ *0922 2 63 89, Via Salita Filino 1*). A full meal costs around L50,000. If it's fish you're after, try the *Trattoria Concordia* (☎ *0922 22 26 68, Via Porcello 8*).

If you have a car, head for *Trattoria-Pizzeria Kokalo* (☎ *0922 60 64 27, Viale C Magazzeni 3*), east of the temples, where they dish up the area's best pizza.

One of Agrigento's better restaurants is *Le Caprice* (☎ *0922 2 26 46*), between the town and temples. A full meal will cost between L40,000 and L50,000. Take any bus heading for the temples and get off at the Hotel

Colleverde, from where it's a short sign-posted walk. *Da Gennaro* (*Via Petrarca*) is nearby and also serves excellent cuisine. A full meal will cost around L70,000.

A good breakfast option is *Caffè Concordia* (*Via Atenea 349*), virtually unchanged since the 1950s (check out the retro decor). You can drink a cappuccino and eat a bun in the company of the locals who flock here daily.

The nuns at the *Monastero di Santo Spirito* (see The Medieval Town, earlier) bake heavenly pastries and cakes, including *dolci di mandorla* (almond cakes), pistachio couscous and *bucellati* (rolled sweet dough with figs). They are expensive, but it's worth it for the taste and the experience. Press the doorbell, say '*Vorrei comprare qualche dolce*' (I'd like to buy a few cakes), and see how you go.

Entertainment
Agrigento goes to bed pretty early. With only a few exceptions, you won't find much going on after 10 pm. *Caffeteria Nobel* (*Viale della Vittoria 40*) stays open till 1 am and is a good place to go for a quiet drink or a late-night coffee. The basement bar *Bier Zeit* (*Viale della Vittoria 127*) is the Sicilian version of a German *bierkeller*. Loud music and a selection of German draught beers are the norm; during summer months this is a popular spot for visitors. It is open from 8 pm until 2 am daily.

Getting There & Away
Bus For most destinations, bus is the easiest way to get to and from Agrigento. The intercity bus station is on Piazza Rosselli, just off Piazza Vittorio Emanuele, and timetables for most services are posted in Bar Sprint on the square. Autoservizi Cuffaro (☎ 0922 41 82 31) and Camilleri & Argento (☎ 0922 47 27 98) both run about six buses daily to Palermo (L19,500). Lumia (☎ 0922 2 04 14) has 12 departures daily (except Sunday) to Trapani (L18,000). SAIS (☎ 0922 59 52 60) buses serve Catania (L18,500, eight daily) and Caltanissetta (L11,200, 14 daily). For more information about SAIS buses, go to Via Ragazzi del '99 12.

Train There are plenty of trains daily to and from Palermo and Catania. To Palermo, the journey takes two hours (L24,000); to Catania, 3½ hours (L29,500). Although trains serve other destinations as well, you're better off taking the bus. The train station has a good left-luggage office, which is open from 8 am to 9 pm (L5500 per item).

Car & Motorcycle Agrigento is easily accessible by road from all of Sicily's main towns. The SS189 links the town with Palermo, while the SS115 runs along the coast, west towards Sciacca and east for Gela and eventually Syracuse. For Enna, take the SS640 via Caltanissetta.

There is plenty of parking at Piazza Vittorio Emanuele, in the centre.

Getting Around

City buses run down to the Valley of the Temples from in front of the train station. Take bus Nos 1, 1/, 2, 2/ or 3 (every 30 minutes) and get off at either the museum or farther downhill at the Piazzale dei Templi. The Linea Verde (Green Line) bus runs every hour from the train station to the cathedral, for those who prefer not to make the uphill walk. Tickets cost L1000 and are valid for 1½ hours.

SCIACCA
postcode 92019 • pop 40,000
One of the prettiest towns on the southern coast, Sciacca is definitely worth a flying stop, if only to check out the wonderful views of the Mediterranean from the elegant square at the centre of the old town. Although many of the older churches and buildings are in an alarming state of disrepair, there is still enough within the walls that enclose the town to warrant a bit of sightseeing. The best time to visit is in February, as the town celebrates the Lenten period with a spectacular carnival.

History
Founded in the 5th century BC by the Greeks as a thermal spa for Selinunte, whose citizens came here to bath in the sulphurous springs of Mt Cronio, which rises up behind the town, Sciacca itself owes its origins to the Saracens, who settled here in the 9th century. Although the origins of the town's name have been much debated, it is thought to have come from the Arabic word *xacca*, meaning 'water'. The Saracens built the original walls and laid out the street grid, which was later expanded by the Normans. Throughout much of the Middle Ages, the town was at the centre of a bloody feud between rival baronial families and, as is often the case, it was the citizenry that bore the brunt of the fighting: in less than 100 years over half the population was killed by one side or the other.

In the 15th and 16th centuries the town's medieval buildings were torn down to make way for grander, and sturdier, *palazzi* (mansions) and the walls were rebuilt. In the 18th century a spate of construction gave it the baroque look it has today.

Orientation
Sciacca still retains much of its medieval layout, which divided the town into quarters, each laid out on a strip of rock descending towards the sea. To the north of Via G Licata is Terravecchia, a maze of streets and alleyways, still largely intact, that wind their way up to the northern walls. Between Via G Licata and the town's central artery, Corso Vittorio Emanuele, is a narrow strip containing most of the town's fine buildings and churches. Below the terrace of Piazza Scandaliato (in the middle of Corso Vittorio Emanuele) is the traditional quarter of fishermen, ceramists and potters, which descends right down to the jetty.

All buses arrive at the Villa Comunale (public gardens) on Via Figuli. The town is not served by trains.

Information
The helpful and informative tourist office (☎ 0925 8 62 47) is on Corso Vittorio Emanuele 94, right on Piazza Scandaliato. It is open from 9 am to 1 pm and 3 to 7.30 pm Monday to Saturday. There is also an APT office (☎ 0925 2 11 82) down the street at No 84 which gives out free maps of the town.

The Banca Commerciale Italiana at Corso Vittorio Emanuele 106 has an ATM. The post

euro currency converter L10,000 = €5.16

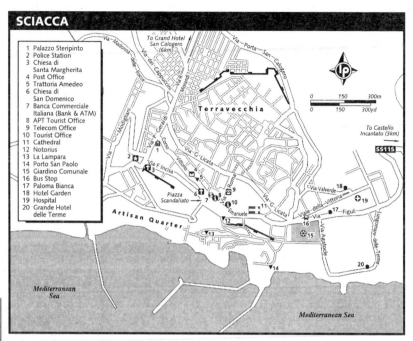

SCIACCA

1 Palazzo Steripinto
2 Police Station
3 Chiesa di
   Santa Margherita
4 Post Office
5 Trattoria Amedeo
6 Chiesa di
   San Domenico
7 Banca Commerciale
   Italiana (Bank & ATM)
8 APT Tourist Office
9 Telecom Office
10 Tourist Office
11 Cathedral
12 Notorius
13 La Lampara
14 Porto San Paolo
15 Giardino Comunale
16 Bus Stop
17 Paloma Bianca
18 Hotel Garden
19 Hospital
20 Grande Hotel
   delle Terme

office is next door to the APT tourist office, at Corso Vittorio Emanuele 104. There is a Telecom office about 50m north of Piazza Scandaliato, at Via Roma 36. The hospital (☎ 0922 9 43 76) is on Viale della Vittoria, next to the public gardens. The police station (*questura*) is at Piazza Luigi Sturzi 2, just outside the eastern gate to the old city.

Things to See & Do

At the heart of the town is the terraced **Piazza Scandaliato**, a central meeting place for locals, which has a splendid view of the sea below. At the square's western end is the **Chiesa di San Domenico**, an 18th-century reconstruction of a church built in the 16th century. To the north-east off the square is the town's **cathedral**, first erected in 1108 and rebuilt in 1656. Only the three apses survive from the original Norman structure. The unfinished baroque facade features a set of marble statues by Gagini.

At the western end of the old city, off

Corso Vittorio Emanuele on Via F Incisa, is the small, 14th-century **Chiesa di Santa Margherita**, of which the superb Gothic portal is the only surviving original feature. To the north is the imposing **Palazzo Steripinto**, recognisable by its diamond-point rustication and twin-mullioned windows. It was built in the Catalonian-Sicilian style at the beginning of the 16th century.

Although it doesn't look like much, the **artisan quarter** below the old town is worth checking out. The traditional artisans – mostly ceramists – live side by side with Sciacca's fishing community. The risers on the steps leading down to the port have been adorned with locally produced ceramic tiles; not one is the same as the other. Although there is nothing specific to see down here, it's worth wandering around the docks, cluttered with fishing vessels and little bars.

About 3km east of the city (take bus Nos 1 or 4 from the public gardens) is the **Castello Incantato** (Enchanted Castle), actually a large park with thousands of heads sculpted in wood and stone. The *auteur* of this bizarre collection was a local farmer-sculptor called Filippo Bentivegna, whose story is beset by woe. While living in America, he was ditched by his fiancee and later beaten up so badly that he was thought dead. He returned to his home town in 1917 and devoted the rest of his life (he died in 1967) to exorcising the memories of his American experiences through sculpture; each head supposedly represents one of his enemies. He was undoubtedly deranged, as he liked to be treated like a king, going so far as to demand that people addressed him as '*Eccellenza*' (Your Excellency). The park is open from 10 am to noon and 4 to 8 pm Tuesday to Saturday. Admission is free.

Special Events

Sciacca's big festival is Carnevale, celebrated during the week before the beginning of Lent (February). The highlight of the festivities is the parade of bizarre figures mounted on floats, famous throughout Italy for their gaudy expressions. The whole town lends a hand in the celebrations, which involve plenty of eating and drinking.

Places to Stay & Eat

On the eastern side of town, *Paloma Blanca* (☎ 0925 2 51 30, Via Figuli 5) has singles/doubles for L50,000/80,000, while *Hotel Garden* (☎ 0925 2 62 99, Via Valverde 2) has singles/doubles for L45,000/75,000. The only other inexpensive option is the *Grand Hotel San Calogero* (☎ 0925 2 10 05), which is 6km north of town in the foothills of Mt Cronio. Not quite 'grand', the fairly ordinary singles/doubles cost L48,000/80,000. You'll need your own transport to get there.

If you can afford it, you could treat yourself to a fancy room and a thermal cure at the *Grand Hotel Delle Terme* (☎ 0925 2 31 33, fax 0925 8 70 02, Via delle Nuove Terme) set on a cliff just east of the public gardens. The rates are surprisingly affordable: singles/doubles cost L83,000/140,000 out of season and L122,000/217,000 between June and September.

The best places to eat are in and around

the port, where relatively inexpensive *trattorie* (small restaurants) serve up abundant menus of (mostly) seafood dishes. *La Lampara* (☎ 0925 8 50 85, Vicolo Caricatore 33) is particularly good and you can eat well for around L25,000. *Porto San Paolo* (☎ 0925 2 79 82, Largo San Paolo 1) has a nice terrace overlooking the sea. A full meal will set you back about L35,000.

In the upper town, *Trattoria Amedeo* (☎ 0925 2 32 03, Corso Vittorio Emanuele 86) serves good pizzas and a variety of fish dishes for around L11,000 each. It is closed on Wednesday. Next to Piazza Scandaliato, *Notorius (Piazza Matteotti 6)* does tasty sandwiches and other bar food. The views from the terrace are terrific.

Getting There & Away

There are 11 Lumia buses daily between Sciacca and Agrigento (L8500). They stop at virtually every town along the way, however, so the journey takes about two hours. Buses leave from Via Agatocle. Direct buses also serve Palermo (L13,000, two hours, four times daily). You can buy your tickets at Viale della Vittoria 22.

ERACLEA MINOA

A colony within a colony, Eraclea Minoa lies about halfway between Sciacca and Agrigento, atop a wild bluff overlooking a splendid, sandy beach and the magnificent Capo Bianco cliff. Founded by Selinunte in the 6th century BC, the original colony stood on one of the most beautiful headlands in Sicily, with breathtaking views of the sea and the surrounding countryside. The **ruins** themselves are comparatively scanty and the seating in the 4th-century **theatre** has been covered in moulded plastic to protect the crumbling remains. The site is open from 9 am to one hour before sunset daily; admission costs L4000.

Apart from the ruins, the main reason to come here is for the **beach**, a crescent-shaped length of golden sand that is one of the best on the whole island. Just behind it is a self-contained tourist village complete with a supermarket, a couple of bars and various places to stay.

euro currency converter L10,000 = €5.16

THE SOUTHERN COAST

Places to Stay

Accommodation is only available between 15 June and 15 September; through the rest of the year the place is deserted. The **Eraclea Minoa Village** (☎ 0922 84 73 10) is a well-equipped camp site just behind the beach that charges L15,300 per person and a two-person tent. Two-bedroom cabins are also available for around L480,000 a week per cabin.

Getting There & Away

Buses running between Sciacca and Agrigento (L4500) will drop you at the turn-off for Eraclea Minoa, from where it's a 3.5km walk. In summer, buses go from Cattolica Eraclea (which can be reached from Agrigento and Sciacca) to the site.

The Pelagic Islands

Some 240km south of Agrigento, this tiny archipelago (Isole Pelagie) lies farther from mainland Sicily than Malta, and in many respects has more in common with nearby Tunisia or Libya than Italy. Indeed, of the three islands, only Linosa is part of the Sicilian continental shelf; the other two are part of the submerged African land mass.

In July and August the archipelago's most popular island, Lampedusa, is overrun with visitors. If you want a little peace and tranquillity, you might consider skipping across the water to the small volcanic island of Linosa, where the black beaches are usually empty and the swimming is great. Tiny Lampione is little more than an uninhabited pimple and isn't even on the ferry route.

HISTORY

The Pelagic Islands (from the Greek *pelagos*, meaning 'sea') have always been largely neglected and only ever had a few inhabitants. In 1661 Lampedusa was awarded to the Tomasi family (hence Giuseppe Tomasi di Lampedusa, of *The Leopard* fame). In 1839 they tried to sell it to the British, but King Ferdinand II of Naples jumped in and forked out 12 million ducats to stop the British gaining yet another strategic foothold in the Mediterranean. The islands were

bombed in 1943 by the Allies, and the Americans later set up a military base here, which itself was the target of a bomb attack in 1986, when Libya's Colonel Gaddafi launched a couple of wobbly missiles in retaliation for the US bombing of his country. The missiles missed their target and landed out to sea.

During Fascist times, Lampedusa was used as a place of exile for political enemies of the regime (they were called *confinati*, from *confine*, meaning 'border'). In later years, Mafia prisoners were sent here while awaiting trial, but the Italian government yielded to pressure from the islanders and stopped the practice on account of the fact that it was damaging tourism.

LAMPEDUSA
postcode 92010 • pop 5400

Lampedusa, a rocky, sparsely covered and, in winter, wind-whipped place, is becoming increasingly popular with Italians looking for an early tan, and the water is enticingly warm. There is no site of any interest in the town itself and most people make a beeline straight for the sea and the sand.

Orientation

Whether by ferry or by plane, all visitors arrive on Lampedusa, in the town of the same name. If you arrive by ferry, it's a 10-minute walk up to the old town or a 15-minute walk west to the harbour at Porto Nuovo, where you'll find many of the hotels. The airport is not much farther away on the south-eastern edge of town. The bus station, handy if you want to visit beaches around the island, is on Piazza Brignone in the centre of town.

Information

The archipelago's only tourist office (☎ 0922 97 14 77) is at Via Roma 155. It is only open from April to October and the hours are very erratic even then. If it is closed, try the travel agency 35° Parallelo (☎ 0922 97 19 06), at Via Anfossi 4.

The Banco di Sicilia at Via Roma 129 has an ATM, as does the Banca Popolare S Angelo, just down the street at No 50.

The post office (which also doubles up as a Telecom office) is on Piazza Piave. It is open from 8.30 am to 1 pm and 4 to 7 pm Monday to Saturday.

In an emergency, dial the *guardia medica* (first-aid station) on ☎ 0922 97 06 04. There is a pharmacy at Via Roma 26. The police station (*questura*; ☎ 0922 97 00 01) is at Via Roma 37.

Beaches
Of the several beaches on the southern side of the 11km-long island, the best known is the **Isola dei Conigli** (Rabbit Island), 7km west of town. It's an easy swim away (you can even walk to it if the tide is out) and has a small nature reserve, unique in Italy in that it is the only place where Caretta-Caretta turtles lay their eggs, between July and August. You will be lucky to see one, though, as these timid creatures generally only come in when no-one's about.

Other good swimming spots on the island include the **Cala Croce**, the first bay west of the town.

Diving
The waters of Lampedusa are crystal clear and brimming with different kinds of fish. Consequently, diving is very popular. Lo Verde Diving (☎ 0922 97 19 86), at Via Roma 118, and Mediterranee Immersioni (☎ 0922 97 15 26), on the harbour-front, organise gear rental and diving trips around the island. Expect to pay around L85,000 per day for a complete set of equipment.

Places to Stay & Eat
Cheap accommodation can be hard to find and, if you do find a place, you may be obliged to stay for a minimum of three nights. The small guesthouses are often full in summer and closed in winter. The tourist office has full lists of all hotels and room rentals.

There are two official camp sites on the island. *La Roccia* (☎ 0922 93 38 22), at Cala Greca, 3km west of town past the Guitgia beach, charges L12,000 per person. *Lampedusa* (☎ 0922 93 38 22), at Cala Francese, about 2.5km east of town past the airport, charges L11,000 per person.

You could try *Albergo Le Pelagie* (☎ 0922 97 02 11, Via Bonfiglio 11), off Via Roma, a

30-minute walk west along the waterfront from the port (alternatively, ring when you get to the port and staff will come and pick you up). It has singles/doubles for L90,000/ 180,000, but, like most places, makes at least half board compulsory in summer.

You'll have no problem finding somewhere to eat, even though prices tend to be more expensive than on the mainland. At night during summer, Via Roma's cafes and restaurants are chock-a-block with tourists tucking into a plethora of fish dishes and the ubiquitous couscous. *Al Gallo d'Oro (Via Vittorio Emanuele 45)* is a cheap and cheerful place, with a good tourist menu for L18,000.

LINOSA
postcode 92010 • pop 160
Linosa is essentially the summit of a dormant volcano that has been extinct for nearly 2000 years. Its black beaches and rocky coves don't attract nearly as many visitors as Lampedusa, but they are worth checking out if you fancy getting away from the crowds that flock to the larger island. In recent years Linosa has been slowly building up its own tourist trade and today is an increasingly popular day trip from Lampedusa.

There is only one hotel on the island, the *Linosa* (☎ 0922 97 20 60), which charges L55,000/90,000 for singles/doubles with bathroom. In July and August, however, the rate skyrockets to L100,000/160,000. Be sure to book in advance.

GETTING THERE & AWAY
Air
You can fly directly to Lampedusa from Palermo. Air Sicilia (☎ 091 625 05 66) and Alitalia operate the one-hour, twice-daily flights for about L180,000 one way. You can buy tickets at the airport at Palermo or contact a travel agency, who might scout around for a good deal.

Boat
The easiest way to get to the islands is by ferry from Porto Empedocle, 7km southwest of Agrigento. Buses (L2500) depart from in front of Agrigento's train station every 30 minutes from 8 am to 8.30 pm,

euro currency converter L10,000 = €5.16

which is inconvenient considering the ferry departure times (see later in this section). The 10-minute journey brings you to Piazza Italia, about 100m north of the ferry dock, along Via Quattro Novembre. Alternatively you can get a taxi from Piazzale Aldo Moro (about L8000).

You can buy ferry tickets from the Siremar ticket office (☎ 0922 63 66 83) on the quayside, which is open from 9 am to 1 pm, 4 to 7 pm and 9 pm to midnight daily. Walk-on passengers for Lampedusa pay L65,000 one way and L130,000 return. Although you can take your car (L89,000 one way), you're best advised to leave it on the mainland; you can rent vehicles pretty cheaply on Lampedusa should you need to. Although most passengers go to Lampedusa, you can also get off at Linosa (L53,000/106,000).

The ferry leaves Porto Empedocle at midnight and gets to Lampedusa at 8 am (Linosa at 6 am). From June to September there are daily departures, but the rest of the year there is no ferry on Friday. From Lampedusa, the ferry departs at 10.15 am (12.15 pm from Linosa) and arrives in Porto Empedocle at 6.15 pm daily. In the low season there is no return ferry on Saturday. For the outward, night-time journey you should consider reserving a couchette (a fold-out bed) for L25,000 or a reclining seat (L6000). For the return, you can get in some quality sunbathing on the deck.

GETTING AROUND

Lampedusa is surprisingly well organised on the getting around front. From June to September, orange minibuses (L2000) run hourly from Piazza Brignone to the different beaches around the island. Although moving about on foot isn't too much of a problem, if you're pushed for time you might be better off renting a bike, scooter or even a car from one of the many rental outlets dotted around town.

To/From the Airport

You can walk into town from the airport. Most hotels and camp sites, however, arrange courtesy buses that transport passengers from the airport to their accommodation. You can also get a taxi, which shouldn't cost more than L5000.

Car & Motorcycle

There are plenty of places to rent scooters or cars on Lampedusa. Licciardi Autonoleggi (☎ 0922 97 07 68), on Via Siracusa (a few steps from the docks at Porto Vecchio), rents scooters for about L25,000 a day and cars for about L50,000. You can also rent bicycles for about L10,000.

Boat

Ústica Lines runs a hydrofoil between Lampedusa and Linosa from June to September. The trip takes one hour and costs L29,000 return. The hydrofoil departs Lampedusa at 9.30 am daily and returns at 6.45 pm. You can buy your ticket at the Agenzia Marittima Strazera (☎ 0922 97 00 03), at Via F Riso 1.

Western Sicily

Poor Western Sicily. For decades it was written off most tourist itineraries as a remote and uninteresting corner of the island, with little to recommend it save a couple of Greek ruins and – for those fascinated by the macabre – its reputation as a hotspot of seismic instability and Mafia activity. Consequently, the area never developed the sophisticated tourist industry that attracts visitors to other Sicilian holiday centres such as Taormina and Syracuse.

But if you ignore the west, you risk missing out. Not only does it have some of the most beautiful stretches of coastline on the entire island, and a number of towns and cities to hold your keen attention, but it is also a virtual repository of Sicilian history, a region defined and shaped by the multiculturalism that has influenced the island from prehistory to the modern day. Furthermore, here it is possible to gain a meaningful insight into Sicilian life away from the larger cities and chic tourist resorts.

Although most of the action is concentrated along the south-western coast, there are good reasons for not staying on the A29 as it winds its way from Palermo through the mountains of Gibellina, south to Mazara del Vallo. East of Trapani lie the splendid ruins of Segesta, including a temple that remains virtually intact after 2500 years. Farther south are another set of ruins of an altogether more chilling nature: the ruins at Gibellina date from 1968 when the entire town was levelled by a powerful earthquake.

GETTING AROUND

Western Sicily is relatively compact and easy to get around. There are regular train connections between all the towns along the coast as well as with the inland towns of Castelvetrano and Salemi-Gibellina. The Autoservizi Tarantola (AST) bus service is excellent, linking the entire province. If you're travelling by car, the A29 motorway between Palermo and Mazara del Vallo travels southward in an arc through the in-

Highlights

• Take a stroll around the cliff-top Greek ruins of Selinunte

• Visit the Greek theatre at Segesta, an incomparable combination of architectural elegance and wonderful natural setting

• Wander through Mazara del Vallo's Casbah, an intricate maze of narrow alleys and backstreets that are more African than European

• Witness the mattanza on Favignana, a bloody ritual that must be seen to be believed

• Marvel at the incredible scenes that accompany Trapani's Easter Procession of I Misteri

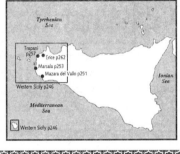

terior, with an offshoot going to Trapani and Birgi airport. The coastal route SS115 and the secondary road SP21 link Trapani with Marsala and Mazara del Vallo.

The coastline between Castellammare del Golfo and Mt Cofano (659m) is perhaps the most beautiful in all of Sicily, a promontory jutting out into the sea, distinguished by coves and rocky beaches washed by the clearest and cleanest of waters. At its heart is the Riserva Naturale dello Zingaro, Sicily's first nature reserve, stretching north for 7km from Scopello to the foot of Mt Cofano. Although none of the towns along this

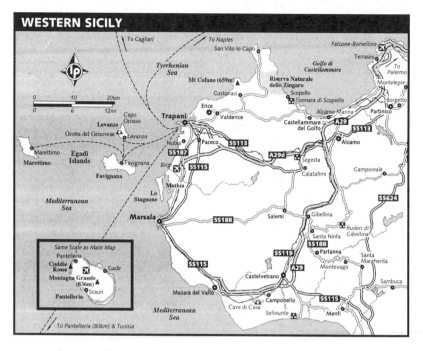

coast can boast any fine museums or particularly beautiful churches, they are worth stopping in nonetheless, particularly the tiny medieval hamlet of Scopello and the seaside town of San Vito lo Capo, home of the best fish couscous in Sicily.

The South-Western Coast

One of the least-explored areas of Sicily, the coastline south of Marsala is both diverse and rich in landscapes and sites of historical interest. Here, the vine is king – hardly surprising considering that Marsala, 30km south of the provincial capital, is home of the popular dessert wine (see the boxed text 'How Sweet It Is' later in this section). At the water's edge outside Marsala are more saltpans and the island ruins of Mothia (Mozia), a Phoenician settlement. Farther

south is the pleasant port town of Mazara del Vallo, where Norman baroque meets Tunisian casbah. Pride of place, however, goes to Selinunte, east along the coast, one of Sicily's most important sites of antiquity.

RUDERI DI GIBELLINA

Twenty-three kilometres south-east of Segesta (see under Around Trapani later in this chapter), and only accessible by car along the winding SS118, which leads off the A29 as it heads towards the south-west coast, are the disconcerting ruins (*ruderi*) of the town of Gibellina, completely flattened by an earthquake during the night of 14 January 1968. All that's left of the town are a few semi-destroyed houses and a large slab of white concrete known as **Il Cretto**. Designed by architect Alberto Burri, the concrete covers what remains of the town. Walking through the channels in the concrete (which follow the town's original street plan) is an eerie and disturbing experience, considering that no more than 30 years ago this was a busy farming town. Now silence prevails.

The second tragedy of Gibellina occurred during the resettlement of the survivors (of a population of 5000, only 541 were killed). For nearly 15 years most were kept in temporary accommodation while the authorities dallied over what to do. Eventually, the inhabitants were moved 18km west to **Gibellina Nuova**, one of the strangest towns in all of Sicily. Following a thoroughly modern (at least in the late 1970s!) urban design, the town is dotted with sculptures by renowned Sicilian and other Italian artists, intended to capture the town's suffering and survival. Despite the best intentions, however, it resembles a lifeless American suburb.

Since 1981, the ruins of the original town have been host to annual classical performances known as the **Orestiadi**, which take place in August. For information on dates call the Museo Civico in Castelvetrano (see the following Castelvetrano section for details).

CASTELVETRANO
postcode 91027 • pop 30,200
• elevation 187m

On the road to Selinunte, 30km south of Gibellina, Castelvetrano is of limited interest save for the small **Museo Civico** (Civic Museum; ☎ 0924 6 74 28), on Via Garibaldi, home of the remarkable *Efebo di Selinunte*, the bronze statue of a young man from the 5th century BC. The museum is open from 9 am to 1 pm and 3.30 to 7.30 pm daily; admission is free. Up the street, on Piazza Garibaldi, is the 19th-century **Teatro Selinus**, built by Giovanni Battista Basile as a smaller-scale model of his Palermo masterpiece, the Teatro Massimo. It is built on the site of a hotel where Goethe stayed in 1787. The large curtain protecting the stage shows the philosopher Empedocles being thanked by the citizens of Selinunte for saving them from malaria. The theatre opens the same hours as the Museo Civico and admission is also free here.

Those familiar with the story of the bandit Salvatore Giuliano (see under Post-War Sicily in the History section of the Facts about Sicily chapter) might want to check out the completely unremarkable courtyard where his body was found in 1950, at Via Mannone 94–100.

There are regular bus services to Castelvetrano from various places in the region, including Agrigento (L8500, two hours, five services daily from Monday to Saturday), Selinunte (L2500, 20 minutes, seven services daily from Monday to Saturday), Marsala (L3500, 40 minutes, eight daily) and Trapani (L5600, 1½ hours, nine services daily).

SELINUNTE

Selinunte is one of the more captivating ancient sites in Italy, atop a cliff overlooking the sea. At its peak, the city had 165,000 inhabitants and was the most advanced point of the Greek expansion into the western Mediterranean. Today, it's a huge archaeological site.

History

The area was first colonised by Greek settlers from Megara Hyblaea in 628 BC (according to the Greek historian Thucydides). They named their settlement Selinus, from the Greek word for parsley *(selinon)*, which grows in abundance here and consequently became the symbol of the city, appearing on all its coins.

Originally allied with Carthage, it switched allegiance after the Carthaginian defeat by Gelon of Syracuse at Himera in 480 BC, and under Syracusan protection it grew in power and prestige. The city's growth resulted in a litany of territorial disputes with its northern neighbour, Segesta, which ended abruptly in 409 BC when the latter called for Carthaginian help. Selinunte's jilted former ally happily obliged and arrived to take revenge.

Troops commanded by Hannibal utterly destroyed the city after a nine-day siege, leaving as survivors only those who had taken shelter in the temples; these were spared not out of a sense of humanity but because of the fear that they might set fire to the temples and prevent their looting. In a famous retort to the Agrigentan ambassadors who sought to negotiate for the survivors' lives, Hannibal replied that as they hadn't been able to defend their freedom, they deserved to be slaves. One year later, Hermocrates of Syracuse took over the city and initiated its recovery. In

250 BC, with the Romans about to conquer the city, its citizens were relocated to Lilybaeum (Marsala), the Carthaginian capital in Sicily, but not before they destroyed as much as they could. What they left standing, mainly temples, was finished off by an earthquake in the Middle Ages.

The city was forgotten until the middle of the 16th century when a Dominican monk identified its location. Excavations began in 1823 courtesy of two English archaeologists, William Harris and Samuel Angell, who uncovered the first metopes.

Information

The archaeological site is divided into four zones – the acropolis, the ancient city, the eastern temples and the Sanctuary of Malophorus – spread out over a vast area dominated by the hill of Manuzza, site of the ancient city proper. You can access the site via two entrances: one leads to the eastern temples, while the other requires a 15-minute hike across the depression known as the Gorgo di Cottone (once the city's harbour).

There is a pretty helpful tourist kiosk in the car park outside the main entrance to the site. It is open from 9 am to noon and 3 to 6 pm Monday to Saturday. The site itself is open from 9 am until one hour before dusk daily. Admission costs L4000 (free for people aged under 18 or over 60).

The Acropolis

The acropolis, the heart of Selinunte's political and social life, occupies a slanted plateau overlooking the now-filled-in harbour. It is crossed by two thoroughfares – one running north–south, the other east–west, dividing the acropolis into four separate sections. Huddled in the south-eastern part are five temples (A to D and O). The northernmost is **Temple D**, built towards the end of the 6th century BC and dedicated to either Neptune or Venus. Virtually the symbol of Selinunte, **Temple C** is also the oldest temple on the site, built in the middle of the 6th century BC. The stunning metopes found by Harris and Angell were once a part of this formidable structure, as was the enormous Gorgon's mask that once adorned the pediment (both of these can be viewed in the Museo Archeologico Regionale in Palermo; see that chapter for details). Experts believe that the temple was dedicated to Apollo.

Adjacent is the smaller **Temple B**, which

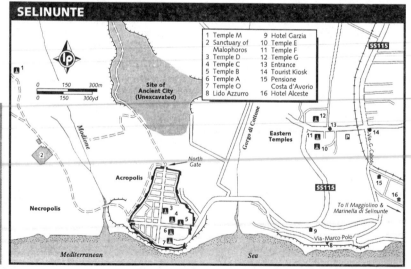

SELINUNTE

1 Temple M	9 Hotel Garzia
2 Sanctuary of Malophoros	10 Temple E
3 Temple D	11 Temple F
4 Temple C	12 Temple G
5 Temple B	13 Entrance
6 Temple A	14 Tourist Kiosk
7 Temple O	15 Pensione Costa d'Avorio
8 Lido Azzurro	16 Hotel Alceste

WESTERN SICILY

dates from the Hellenistic period and could have been dedicated to the Agrigentan scientist and philosopher Empedocles, whose water-drainage scheme saved the city from the scourge of malaria (a bitter irony for William Harris, who contracted the disease during the initial excavations and died soon after). The two other temples, **A** and **O**, closest to the sea, are the most recent, built between 490 and 480 BC. They are virtually identical in both style and size, and it's been suggested that they might have been dedicated to the twins Castor and Pollux. In front of Temple O, an area has been excavated that is believed to be a sacred spot dating from the period after the destruction of the city.

The Ancient City

Occupying the hill of Manuzza, to the north of the acropolis, the ancient city where most of Selinunte's inhabitants lived is the least excavated of all the sites. Exploration of the area has only begun in recent years, and evidence suggests that survivors of the destruction of 409 BC may have used the city as a necropolis. Finds also suggest that the city stretched beyond the original wall to the north-west, but you can't verify this for yourself for another few years at least as the area remains a closed dig.

The Sanctuary of Malophorus

Walk west from the acropolis across the Modione river (formerly the Selinon) and up the dirt path to the hardly impressive ruins of the temple dedicated to Demeter, the goddess of fertility and harvests. The temple, renowned in antiquity, survived the Carthaginian siege and was used in later times for both Christian and Byzantine worship. Amid the debris, two altars can be made out; the larger of the two was used for sacrifices. Despite the lack of visual appeal, these are perhaps the most important finds of the whole site, as they provide a fascinating and detailed insight into the social history of Selinunte. Archaeologists remain perplexed by the votive offerings found in the area, which include steles crowned with human heads, compelling evidence that another, non-Greek, civilisation inhabited the area at the same time.

The Eastern Temples

South of the main door in the admission hall is the most visually stunning of all Selinunte's ruins, crowned by the majestic **Temple E**. Reconstructed in 1958 amid much criticism, it stands out due to its recently acquired completeness. Built in the 5th century BC, it is the first of the three temples at the eastern end of the site, close to the ticket office. The more outstanding metopes in Palermo's Museo Archeologico Regionale (see the Palermo chapter for details) came from this temple and Temple C. **Temple G**, the northernmost temple, was built in the 6th century BC and, although never completed, was one of the largest in the Greek world. Today it is a massive pile of rubble, but evocative nonetheless.

Places to Stay & Eat

The nearest town to the ruins is Marinella di Selinunte, where you can find accommodation and a couple of reasonably priced restaurants. *Il Maggiolino* (☎ 0924 4 60 44), 1.5km north of Marinella di Selinunte, is one of a couple of camp sites; it costs L8000/5000/5000 per person/tent/car. Just outside the archaeological site, *Pensione Costa d'Avorio* (☎ 0924 4 62 07, Via Stazione 10) has singles/doubles for L35,000/50,000 without bathroom, or L40,000/80,000 with bathroom. It also has a *trattoria* (cheap restaurant). *Hotel Alceste* (☎ 0924 4 61 84, Via Alceste 23) has more upmarket rooms with bathroom costing L90,000/120,000. *Hotel Garzia* (☎ 0924 4 66 60, Via Pigafetta 8), has nice rooms on the seafront for L80,000/130,000 including breakfast.

There are some pleasant little restaurants along the beachfront. Try *Lido Azzurro*, also known as Baffo's, where you can eat good pizzas, pasta and fresh seafood virtually beside the water's edge, all for around L10,000.

Getting There & Away

AST buses link Marinella di Selinunte to Castelvetrano, which can be reached by Lumia buses from Agrigento, Mazara del Vallo, Marsala and Trapani. If travelling by car, take the Castelvetrano exit off the A29 and follow the brown signposts for about 6km.

WESTERN SICILY

CAVE DI CUSA

18km north-west of Selinunte is the **Cave di Cusa**, the stone quarry used for the building of the city. Virtually untouched since Selinunte's destruction in 409 BC, the quarry is hardly spectacular, but fascinating nonetheless, offering clues as to exactly how the massive stones used in the building of the temples were cut out of the rock. About 400m in from the gate are two carved columns ready for extraction. Around each is a gap of 50cm to allow the stonemason access to the column. When removed, the columns would have been transported to Selinunte across wooden logs by oxen or slaves. Archaeology aside, the site is an oasis of peace and quiet and is perfect for a picnic or a stroll.

The site is easily reached if you have your own transport. If you don't and you really must get here, get an AST or Lumia bus to nearby Campobello di Mazara; it's a 3.5km walk south-west of town (follow the signposts).

MAZARA DEL VALLO
postcode 91026 • pop 48,000

The African influence is most strongly felt in this charmingly dishevelled port town, one of the key cities of Saracen Sicily and the landing point for the thousands of Tunisian immigrants that arrive annually in Sicily. Many work on Mazara's fishing fleet, currently Italy's largest, and live within the labyrinth of streets informally known as the Casbah. Towering over them are the baroque churches and fortified homes of the Norman conquest, which makes for an interesting and often elegant contrast.

History

The city, formerly Selinunte's trading port, was the site of the first Saracen landing in Sicily, in AD 827. It was made capital of one of the three administrative districts (*walis*, or *valli* in Latin) into which they divided Sicily, hence the city's name today. In 1087 Mazara was taken by Count Roger, who ensured its continuing prosperity by declaring it an episcopal see. In 1098 the first Norman parliament sat here. Mazara's role as an important administrative and trading centre lasted another seven centuries until 1817, when it relinquished its role as provincial capital to Trapani. Today, aside from fishing and agriculture, little remains of Mazara's former glory.

Orientation

Mazara's main street, Corso Umberto I, runs north–south from Piazza Matteotti down to Piazza Mokarta, on the waterfront. The Casbah is in the old city, north-west of Piazza Mokarta; the best eateries are by the water. The train station is east of Corso Umberto I, and is also where all AST buses arrive and depart from.

Information

The tourist office (☎ 0923 94 17 27) is on Piazza S Veneranda. It's open from 8 am to 1.30 pm Monday to Saturday (and 3 to 6 pm Monday and Wednesday). There are two banks with ATMs on Piazza Mokarta. The post office is on Via Garibaldi, behind the cathedral.

Things to See

For a city with such a rich history, the sights are surprisingly few and badly maintained. On Piazza Mokarta, the ruins of Count Roger's Norman **castle** don't look much during the day, but they make for a much more pleasant sight at night, when they are bathed in light. Mazara's **cathedral**, on Piazza Repubblica, was founded in 1093 but was completely rebuilt between 1690 and 1694, hence its baroque features. Over the portal is a telling relief of Count Roger trampling a Saracen. Inside, the heavily ornamented altar features the *Trasfigurazione* (Transfiguration), a group of seven statues, dating from 1537 and sculpted by Antonello Gagini, surrounded by stuccoes by the Ferraro family.

Other buildings on the square include the elegant, two-storey **Seminario dei Chierici** (1710), which houses the Diocesan Museum, whose library contains a number of 18th-century texts. It is open from 10 am to noon at weekends only. Admission is free. Facing it, on the square's northern side, is the 16th-century **Palazzo Vescovile** (Bishop's Palace), remodelled in the 18th century.

From the square, Via XX Settembre leads

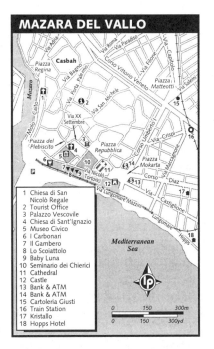

MAZARA DEL VALLO

1 Chiesa di San
   Nicolò Regale
2 Tourist Office
3 Palazzo Vescovile
4 Chiesa di Sant'Ignazio
5 Museo Civico
6 I Carbonari
7 Il Gambero
8 Lo Scoiattolo
9 Baby Luna
10 Seminario dei Chierici
11 Cathedral
12 Castle
13 Bank & ATM
14 Bank & ATM
15 Cartoleria Giusti
16 Train Station
17 Kristallo
18 Hopps Hotel

west to Piazza del Plebiscito and the **Museo Civico** (Civic Museum), housed in a former Jesuit college. The museum contains Roman artefacts and a series of medieval Muslim sculptures. It's open from 9 am to 2 pm Monday to Saturday; admission is free. Flanking it is the baroque **Chiesa di Sant'Ignazio**.

To the north-west is the **Casbah** quarter – a maze of tiny streets and alleyways that were once the heart of the Saracen city, the most important of which was **Via Bagno**, the old city's main thoroughfare. Today, the area is pretty run down but still interesting, if only because it retains a strong Arabic connection through the thousands of Tunisians that live here. As you wander through the quarter you will hear Arabic mixed with Sicilian dialect and strains of North African music pouring out from the windows above. There are few sights of interest here, however, save a couple of baroque churches that loom above the quarter, most notable of which is the small **Chiesa di San Nicolò Regale**, at the

area's western edge. Originally built in 1124, it was heavily influenced by the Saracen style. Unfortunately, it has been closed for years for renovation.

Places to Stay & Eat

There are only two hotels in the town. The cheaper is **Kristallo** (☎ 0923 93 26 88, Via Valeria 36), a short walk from the train station. Here you'll get a pretty clean single/double room for L40,000/70,000. Your only other option is the luxurious **Hopps Hotel** (☎ 0923 94 61 33, fax 0923 94 60 75, Via G Hopps 29), at the eastern end of the Lungomare Mazzini. The well-appointed rooms cost L100,000/140,000.

Eating well here isn't much of a problem. Flanking the public gardens on Via Nicolò Tortorici are three similarly priced restaurants, all with terraces overlooking the water: **Il Gambero** (closed Tuesday), **Lo Scoiattolo** (closed Thursday) and **Baby Luna** (closed Sunday) all serve pretty much the same menu of local specialities and pizza at around the L10,000 mark. Alternatively, you can get a pretty good lunch at **La Bèttola** (Corso Diaz 20), in front of the train station. Expect to pay no more than L25,000 for a filling meal.

If you fancy an after-dinner beer, the best place to go is **I Carbonari** (Lungomare Mazzini), just down the street from Il Gambero. It's got loud chart music and is plenty of fun.

Getting There & Away

AST has four buses daily to/from Trapani (L7000, 1½ hours), Marsala (L4000, 25 minutes) and Castelvetrano (L4000, 20 minutes). The terminus is beside the train station; you can buy a ticket on the bus. Lumia has two buses daily (9.15 am and 4.20 pm) serving Marsala (L4000) and Trapani (L7500), and four daily to Castelvetrano (L4000), leaving from Piazza Matteotti. Buy your tickets in the Cartoleria Giusti on the square; it's open from 8 am to 12.45 pm and 3.30 to 7 pm Monday to Saturday (mornings only on Sunday).

There are train connections every hour or so with Trapani (L6000, 50 minutes), Marsala (L4000, 20 minutes) and Castelvetrano (L4000, 20 minutes). Coming from Palermo, you must change at Alcamo Diramazione,

WESTERN SICILY

from where there are 10 trains daily (L6000) to Mazara del Vallo.

MARSALA
postcode 90125 • pop 80,000
Best known for its sweet dessert wines and often omitted from tourist itineraries, Marsala is a surprisingly pleasant town with an interesting historic quarter. Its tidy streets and well-preserved old centre bear testimony to the town's administration, considered the most progressive in Western Sicily. If you have a car, it's a good alternative to Trapani as a base for exploring the region, although your lodging options are far more limited than those available farther north.

History
Founded as Lilybaeon on Cape Lilibeo by Carthaginians who had fled nearby Mothia after its destruction by Syracuse, the city was so heavily fortified (with walls 7m thick!) that it was the last Punic base to fall to the Romans. In AD 830 it was conquered by the Arabs, who renamed it Marsa Alí (Port of Ali, the Prophet Mohammed's son-in-law) or Marsa Allah (Port of God), and established it as the main port of entry for Africans landing in Sicily.

Under the Normans the city was Christianised through the construction of numerous churches and monasteries. It continued to grow and prosper until 1575, when the port was blocked in to protect it from pirate raids, after which it declined in importance until the turn of the 19th century, when a group of English traders 'discovered' the local wine and began trading it as an alternative to port and Madeira. On 11 May 1860, Garibaldi and his One Thousand landed at Marsala (under the unofficial protection of a couple of English frigates), thus beginning his struggle for Italian independence.

Orientation
Marsala hugs a small promontory looking out onto the Mediterranean Sea. The old city is clustered around the tip, separated from the sea by Via Lungomare Boeo. The main entrance to the old city is through the Porta Nuova (New Gate) at the end of Viale

Vittorio Veneto, which runs south-east from Via Lungomare Boeo. Alternatively, from Piazza Piemonte e Lombardo, walk north along the Viale dei Mille and go through the older Porta Garibaldi. Piazza della Repubblica is at the top of Via Garibaldi. The train station is south-east of the old city.

Information
Marsala's APT office (☎ 0923 71 40 97) is at Via XI Maggio 100, just off Piazza della Repubblica, in the centre of town. It is open from 8 am to 2 pm and 3 to 8 pm Monday to Saturday. An APT information kiosk beside the entrance to the Museo Nazionale Lilibeo, on Via Lungomare Boeo, is open from 9 am to 2 pm and 4 to 8 pm Tuesday to Sunday (mornings only on Monday), June to mid-September. There are banks with ATMs all over town.

The post office is on Via Garibaldi, just south-east of Piazza della Repubblica. There is a good bookshop, Pellegrino, just inside the Porta Nuova, at Via XI Maggio 36. It stocks a couple of English-language cookbooks on Sicilian specialities.

The public hospital (*ospedale*; ☎ 0923 71 60 31) is in Piazza San Francesco, just north of the city centre. In a medical emergency, call ☎ 0923 95 14 10. The local police station (*questura*; ☎ 0923 92 43 71) is at Via San Giovanno Bosco 26.

Piazza della Repubblica
Most of Marsala's historical sights are in and around the central Piazza della Repubblica, the heart of the city. The elegant square is fronted on one side by the imposing **cathedral**, dedicated to St Thomas of Canterbury. Although started in 1628, the church's facade wasn't completed until 1956, courtesy of a cash donation by a returning emigrant. The cavernous interior, divided into three aisles highlighted by tall columns, contains a number of sculptures by the Gagini brothers but little else.

On the eastern side of the square is the **Palazzo Comunale**, or town hall, formerly known as the Palazzo Senatorio (Senatorial Palace). The top floor still has its original lamps. At the time of writing it was swathed

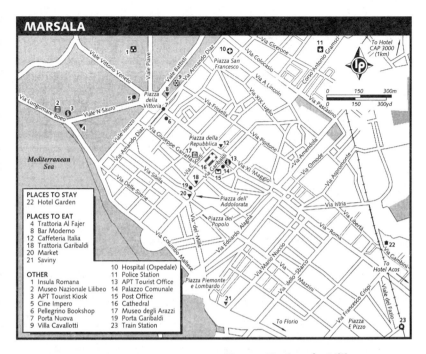

MARSALA

PLACES TO STAY
22 Hotel Garden

PLACES TO EAT
4 Trattoria Al Fajer
8 Bar Moderno
12 Caffeteria Italia
18 Trattoria Garibaldi
20 Market
21 Saviny

OTHER
1 Insula Romana
2 Museo Nazionale Lilibeo
3 APT Tourist Kiosk
5 Cine Impero
6 Pellegrino Bookshop
7 Porta Nuova
9 Villa Cavallotti
10 Hospital (Ospedale)
11 Police Station
13 APT Tourist Office
14 Palazzo Comunale
15 Post Office
16 Cathedral
17 Museo degli Arazzi
19 Porta Garibaldi
23 Train Station

in a massive tarpaulin, due to a restoration of the facade. At Via XI Maggio 89, Garibaldi fans can see where the man himself spent his first night after landing; the building now houses a bank.

Museo degli Arazzi

The most interesting museum in Marsala (☎ 0923 71 29 03), at Via Garraffa 57, is just behind the cathedral. It is home to eight magnificent Flemish tapestries made in Brussels between 1530 and 1550. The Marsala-born archbishop of Messina, Antonio Lombardo (1523–95), who also happened to be ambassador to the Spanish court, had received them as a gift from Felipe II and, in 1589, he presented them to the cathedral. Representing the capture of Jerusalem from the Saracens, the tapestries have been carefully restored and are now on display across three dimly lit floors. The museum is open from 9 am to 1 pm and 4 to 6 pm daily; admission costs L2000.

Museo Nazionale Lilibeo

On the promontory, along Via Lungomare Boeo, is Marsala's most popular museum (☎ 0923 95 25 35), housed in the Baglio Anselmi, a typical manor house from Saracen times. Naval enthusiasts and classicists will savour the prospect of seeing the world's only recovered Punic *liburna*, or warship, discovered in 1971 by the marine archaeologist Honor Frost in the Stagnone lagoon near Mothia. It's actually only part of the original ship, carefully reconstructed to give an impression of what it would have looked like. Manned by 68 oarsmen, the 35m-long warship is thought to have been part of a Carthaginian fleet attacked by the Romans in 241 BC at the Battle of Egadi. The find is extremely important, mainly because it has provided a valuable insight into Punic shipbuilding techniques: one of the more intriguing puzzles is how the metal nails did not rust after nearly 1800 years underwater.

The exhibit also includes objects found on

WESTERN SICILY

board: ropes, ceramic fragments, corks from amphorae, a brush and a sailor's wooden button. In an adjacent room are two beautiful mosaics from the 3rd and 5th centuries, as well as other bits and bobs recovered from the nearby dig of the **Insula Romana**, a 3rd-century Roman villa. The museum is open from 9 am to 2 pm and 4 to 8 pm Tuesday to Sunday (mornings only on Monday); admission costs L4000. Access to the archaeological dig is north of the museum along Viale Vittorio Veneto: it's open from 9 am to 1 pm and 3 to 7 pm daily; admission costs L4000.

Other Things to See & Do

On the western edge of Piazza della Vittoria (at the top of Viale Vittorio Veneto) is the **Cine Impero** (Empire Cinema), a marvellous example of Italian futurist architecture popular during the Fascist era. Built at the start of the 20th century, it was remodelled in the 1930s and served as a cinema until the 1970s. Today it is a cultural centre. Directly opposite is the **Porta Nuova**, the most recent of Marsala's gates, built in 1790 in classical Renaissance style.

If you're travelling with small children, they might enjoy a break in the **Villa Cavallotti**, a large park just outside the Porta Nuova that has a playground and acres of space for a relaxing walk.

Special Events

Marsala's most important annual religious event is the Processione del Giovedì Santo (Holy Thursday Procession). A centuries-old tradition, the procession of actors depicts the events leading up to Christ's crucifixion. Many children participate in the procession, dressed in colourful costume as saints.

Places to Stay

Accommodation in Marsala is surprisingly thin on the ground. The cheapest is *Hotel Garden* (☎ 0923 98 23 20, Via Gambini 36), near the train station, to the south-east of town. Its very basic single/double rooms cost L55,000/85,000. *Hotel CAP 3000* (☎ 0923 98 90 55, Via Trapani 161) is outside the old centre, on the SS115 to Trapani. It has rooms with bathroom, phone and TV for L90,000/

130,000. *Hotel Acos* (☎ 0923 99 91 66, Via Mazara 14) is even farther away from town, south-east of the train station, but its rooms are better equipped and cheaper at L85,000/110,000.

A far more interesting option if you have your own transport is *Baglio Vajarassa* (☎ 0923 96 86 28, Contrada Spagnola 176), a traditional manor house 6km north of Marsala, near Mothia. Rooms cost L50,000/80,000 and a hearty lunch of local dishes is included.

Places to Eat

A full meal at *Trattoria Garibaldi* (☎ 0923 95 30 06, Piazza dell'Addolorata 5) will come to about L35,000. It specialises in fish dishes. You can also eat well, and for a bit less, at *Trattoria Al Fajer* (☎ 0923 71 30 30, Via Lungomare Boeo 38). Otherwise, the central and popular *Saviny* (Via Mario Nuccio 2) is good for a quick lunch; in the evening it is a popular bar. For some lovely pastries you won't beat *Caffeteria Italia* (Via XI Maggio 2), directly facing the cathedral. Sandwiches and other snacks are also available at *Bar Moderno* (Piazza della Vittoria), just next to the Porta Nuova. In the evening, Marsala's young crowd gather here and in the square to chat and while away the hours.

Marsala's open-air fresh produce *market* is held every morning except Sunday on a square off Piazza dell'Addolorata, next to the municipal offices *(comune)*. In this small, lively marketplace, you're likely to be serenaded by a fruit vendor.

Shopping

Tipplers should head to **Florio** (☎ 0923 78 11 11), on Lungomare Florio (bus No 16 from Piazza del Popolo) – this is the place to buy the cream of Marsala's wines. Florio opens its doors to visitors to explain the process of making Marsala wine, and to give you a taste of the goods, from 9 am to noon and 2.30 to 5 pm Monday to Thursday (morning only on Friday), June to September; guided tours run at 3.30 pm sharp between October and May. For free tasting try the wine shops *(enotecas)* Luminario or La Ruota, both at Via Lungomare Boeo 36.

How Sweet It Is

Marsala wine was 'discovered' by Englishman John Woodhouse, who, after landing in the city in 1773 and tasting the local product, decided it should be marketed all over Europe. His first competitor was Benjamin Ingham, who established his own factory in the town and began exporting the wine to the USA and Australia.

One particularly interesting figure in the Marsala-making trade was Ingham's nephew, Joseph Whitaker, who bought the island of San Pantaleo, where the ancient city of Mothia was based (see the following section), and built a villa there (it is still in his family today). Whitaker was responsible for renewing interest in the archaeological site of Mothia and for the few excavations carried out. His former villa is now the museum of Mothia, which houses finds from the ancient city, including the statue the *Giovinetto di Mozia* (The Youth of Mothia). The museum is open from 9 am to 1 pm daily and from 4 to 7 pm on Wednesday, Saturday and Sunday. Admission is free.

Getting There & Away

Buses head for Marsala from Trapani (AST or Lumia, L4500, 55 minutes, eight daily), Agrigento (Lumia, L17,500, 3½ hours, four daily) and Palermo (Salemi, L12,900, 2½ hours). Palermo buses arrive at Piazza del Popolo, off Via Mazzini, in the centre of town. All other buses stop in Piazza E Pizzo, in front of the train station. The Agrigento buses generally stop at Castelvetrano, from where you can take another bus to Selinunte.

Regular trains serve Marsala from Trapani (L5000, approximately one hour) and Palermo (L13,000, although from the latter you have to change at Alcamo Diramazione.

From June through September, Sandokan (☎ 0923 71 20 60, 0923 95 34 34) runs a boat service from Molo Dogana to the Egadi Islands (L14,000).

MOTHIA & LO STAGNONE
postcode 91025
Best reached from Marsala, the Phoenician ruins of Mothia (also spelled Mozia or Motya) are on the small island of San Pantaleo, in the Stagnone lagoon, about 5km north of Marsala. Mothia was one of the most important Phoenician settlements in the Mediterranean, coveted for its strategic position and eventually destroyed by Dionysius the Elder, tyrant of Syracuse, in 379 BC. Today, it is the island's picturesque position in the saltpans that attracts visitors. Very little remains of the city that once covered it, but it is interesting to follow the path around the island and visit the various excavations, including the ancient port and dry dock, as well as some ruins. Note the submerged road at the port, which connects the island to the mainland. The island is home to the **Whitaker Museum** (☎ 0923 71 25 98); its main treasure is the *Giovinetto di Mozia*, a Phoenician statue of a young boy dating from the 5th century BC and considered by experts to be the best example of Phoenician sculpture ever found in Sicily. Admission costs L5000.

The island and lagoon form part of the **Riserva Naturale dello Stagnone** (Stagnone Nature Reserve), a noted humid zone which has a large population of water birds. Swimming here is permitted but hardly encouraged: the word *stagnone* actually means large swamp! There are plans to develop better facilities for tourists in the area of the saltpans, such as cycling and walking tracks, but for now you'll have to settle for the extraordinary sunsets that prevail in the area. The Riserva Naturale dello Stagnone organises guided nature tours costing around L2000 per person (depending on the size of the group). The tours last for approximately one hour and are available from 9 am to 6 pm.

At the end of the pier is the small **Museo Saline Inferza**, a salt museum similar to that up the coast at Nubia (see Saline di Trapani in the later Around Trapani section). It has a pretty good video explaining the whole process of extracting salt (in Italian only), and also rents canoes (L9000 per hour; summer only) so that you can weave your way in and out of the saltpans. It is open from 9 am to 8 pm daily; admission costs L5000.

WESTERN SICILY

Getting There & Away

Arini e Pugliese runs a boat to the island (L5000 return) from 9 am to 1 pm and 3 to around 6 or 7 pm (mornings only in winter). The ticket includes admission to the museum. Ettore Inferza runs traditional-style boats to and from the island between 9 am and 6 pm daily (L5000 return). To get to the ferry landing from Marsala, take local bus No 4 from Piazza del Popolo (L8000, daily except Sunday); the trip takes around 25 minutes.

Trapani

postcode 91100 • pop 72,500

The administrative capital of the province of the same name (which encompasses virtually all of Western Sicily), Trapani is a largely inconspicuous, modern city with little to hint that it was, until relatively recently, a powerful and strategic trading port. The only clue to its past lies in the jumbled maze of streets that makes up the historic centre, at the tip of the thin peninsula on which the city is built. There is little here to keep you for more than a day or so, except at Easter, when the city is given over to the extraordinary celebrations known as I Misteri (The Mysteries; see the boxed text of the same name later in this section). On a negative note, Trapani has long been burdened with the reputation of being one of the main centres of Mafia activity.

Still, the city is the best base for visiting the region, within easy striking distance of all the major points of interest in the west and with regular connections to the Egadi Islands.

HISTORY

Originally a Phoenician post, Trapani (or Drepanon, as it was called) was the key port in the Carthaginian defence of Sicily during the Punic Wars. After the sack of Erice (Eryx) in 260 BC by Hamilcar, part of the population was moved down the hill and the port was raised to the status of a city; however, in 241 BC it was captured by the Romans and the nascent city went into decline. Subsequent conquests by the Saracens in the 9th century and the Normans 300 years later led to the rebuilding of the city and its re-establishment as a major link in the trading route that joined Tunis, Anjou and Aragon. Edward I of England stopped off here in 1272 on his return from a crusade, whereupon he learnt of his accession to the throne. Peter of Aragon landed here in 1282 to begin the Aragonese occupation of Sicily that followed the overthrow of the Angevin kings (the famous Sicilian Vespers; see under History in the Facts about Sicily chapter). In recent times, Trapani thrived on the salt and wine trades, while today it is largely a city devoted to service industries. Extensive bombing during WWII led to the construction of some fairly ugly modern blocks which, unfortunately, dominate the city today.

ORIENTATION

Trapani is narrow and relatively compact, bordered on either side by the sea. The main street, Via GB Fardella, runs east–west, splitting the modern city into two neat halves. On either side a chessboard street-grid dominates as far as the historic centre, which is a confusing maze of small streets, many of which do not have signposts. All of the sights of interest are concentrated in this area, from where there is also access to the ferry terminal. The main bus station is on Piazza Montalto, in the new town, with the train station around the corner on Piazza Umberto I. The cheaper hotels are in the heart of the historic centre, about 500m to the west.

INFORMATION
Tourist Offices

The helpful and informative APT office (☎ 0923 54 55 11, @ appt@mail.cinet.it) is at Piazzetta Saturno 1/2, at the eastern edge of the historic centre. It is open from 8 am to 8 pm Monday to Saturday, 9 am to 12 pm on Sunday, year-round. There is also an APT office (☎ 0923 2 90 00) at Via S Francesco d'Assisi 27, which has detailed information on the whole province. For

CHRISTOPHER WOOD

With views like this, who wants a roof? This Doric temple at Segesta has stood the test of time.

BETHUNE CARMICHAEL

Detail of a rather uninviting doorway, Trapani

BETHUNE CARMICHAEL

Scenic and salt-crushing: windmills at Mothia

BETHUNE CARMICHAEL

From the Sicilian vine comes a fine wine, Marsala

Mounds of salt drying under a Sicilian sun – stick around to watch it set on this strange landscape.

Ruins of an illustrious past, Selinunte

Not the only fruit, but a popular crop in the west

Cobbled streets in the medieval hill town of Erice

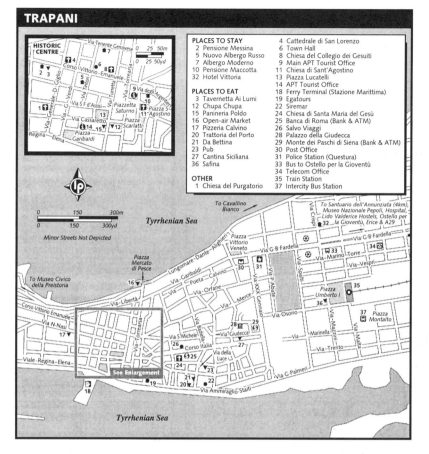

TRAPANI

HISTORIC CENTRE

Via Tenente Genovese

PLACES TO STAY
2 Pensione Messina
5 Nuovo Albergo Russo
7 Albergo Moderno
10 Pensione Maccotta
32 Hotel Vittoria

PLACES TO EAT
3 Tavernetta Ai Lumi
12 Chupa Chupa
15 Panineria Poldo
16 Open-air Market
17 Pizzeria Calvino
20 Trattoria del Porto
21 Da Bettina
23 Pub
27 Cantina Siciliana
36 Safina

OTHER
1 Chiesa del Purgatorio

4 Cattedrale di San Lorenzo
6 Town Hall
8 Chiesa del Collegio dei Gesuiti
9 Main APT Tourist Office
11 Chiesa di Sant'Agostino
13 Piazza Lucatelli
14 APT Tourist Office
18 Ferry Terminal (Stazione Marittima)
19 Egatours
22 Siremar
24 Chiesa di Santa Maria del Gesù
25 Banca di Roma (Bank & ATM)
26 Salvo Viaggi
28 Palazzo della Giudecca
29 Monte dei Paschi di Siena (Bank & ATM)
30 Post Office
31 Police Station (Questura)
33 Bus to Ostello per la Gioventù
34 Telecom Office
35 Train Station
37 Intercity Bus Station

Tyrrhenian Sea

Minor Streets Not Depicted

To Cavallino Bianco

To Santuario dell'Annunziata (4km), Museo Nazionale Pepoli, Hospital, Lido Valderice Hostels, Ostello per la Gioventù, Erice & A29

To Museo Civico della Preistoria

Tyrrhenian Sea

See Enlargement

further information, see the Web site at www.cinet.it/apt.

Money

There is no shortage of banks in Trapani. Among others, the Banca di Roma, at Corso Italia 38, and the Monte dei Paschi di Siena, at Via XXX Gennaio 80, have ATMs that take Visa and MasterCard, as well as exchange facilities.

Post & Communications

The main post office is on Piazza Vittorio Veneto and is open between 8.20 am and

7 pm Monday to Saturday. The Telecom office at Via Agostino Pepoli 82 is open from 9 am to 12.30 pm and 4.30 to 8 pm daily.

Medical Services & Emergency

The public hospital, Ospedale Sant'Antonio Abate (☎ 0923 80 91 11), is on Via Cosenza, some distance from the centre of town. Dial the same number for an ambulance. For *pron-to soccorso* (casualty) dial ☎ 0923 80 94 50. For the *guardia medica* (first-aid station), Piazza Generale Scio 1, phone ☎ 0923 2 96 29.The police station (*questura;* ☎ 0923 59 81 11) is on Via Virgilio.

WESTERN SICILY

euro currency converter L10,000 = €5.16

THINGS TO SEE

The 16th-century **Palazzo della Giudecca**, at Via Giudecca 43, with its distinctive facade, stands out among the general decay of the old and run-down Jewish quarter. Built in the Spanish Plateresque style by the aristocratic Ciambra family, it has been extensively renovated and very little survives of the original plan, save an embossed tower and (facing the street) a series of windows adorned with lavish cornices and pillars.

Cross Corso Italia and head west to reach the **Chiesa di Santa Maria del Gesù**, on Via San Pietro, whose exterior has both Gothic and Renaissance features. Dating from the first half of the 16th century, its ground plan is similar to that of the cathedral at Monreale (see the Cattedrale di Monreale section in the Palermo chapter). Inside, the chapel contains the exquisite *Madonna degli Angeli* (Madonna with the Angels), a glazed terracotta statue by Andrea della Robbia. Unfortunately, at the time of research the church was undergoing renovations and was not open to visitors. On Piazzetta Saturno, near the APT office, the 14th-century **Chiesa di Sant'Agostino** is worth a look for its fine Gothic rose window and portal. It is open from 8 am to 1 pm daily.

Head west along Corso Vittorio Emanuele, noting the **Chiesa del Collegio dei Gesuiti** (whose main feature is the lovely *Immacolata* [Immaculate], carved in white marble by Ignazio Marabitti), open from 8 am to 4 pm daily, and the 17th-century **town hall** (not open to the public), before reaching the **Cattedrale di San Lorenzo**, also open from 8 am to 4 pm daily. Built in 1635 on the site of an already existing church, the cathedral boasts an elegant baroque facade and, inside, the *Crocifissione* (Crucifixion), the work of local artist Giacomo Lo Verde but often erroneously attributed to Van Dyck. Off Corso Vittorio Emanuele, on Via Generale D Giglio, the **Chiesa del Purgatorio** houses the Misteri, 20 18th-century, life-sized wooden figures depicting Christ's Passion. On Good Friday they are carried in procession (see the boxed text 'I Misteri').

At the tip of the promontory, to the west of the historic centre, is the Torre di Ligny,

I Misteri

Sicily's most venerated Easter procession is a four-day festival of extraordinary religious fervour. Since the 17th century, the ordinary citizens of Trapani – represented by 20 traditional *maestranze*, or guilds – have begun the celebration of the Passion of Christ on the Tuesday before Easter Sunday with the first procession of a remarkable, life-sized wooden statue of the Virgin Mary. Over the course of the next three days, nightly processions make their way through the old quarter and port to a specially erected chapel in Piazza Lucatelli, where the icons are stored overnight. Each procession is accompanied by barefooted women following the men (who carry the statues on their shoulders) and a local band, which plays dirges to the slow, steady beat of a drum.

The high point of the celebration is on Friday afternoon, when the 20 guilds emerge from the Chiesa del Purgatorio and descend the steps of the church (in Sicilian dialect the *scinnuta*, or descent) carrying each of the statues to begin the 1km-long procession up to Via GB Fardella and back to the church the following morning. The massive crowds that gather to witness the slow march often reach a peak of delirious fervour that is matched only by that which accompanies the Easter *pasos* celebration in Seville, Spain. If you're not around for Easter, you can always see the figures in Chiesa del Purgatorio, where they are stored throughout the year. A guardian is usually on hand to explain the origins of each one.

built in 1671 as a fortress by the Spanish viceroy. Today it is home to the **Museo Civico della Preistoria**, an excellent collection of prehistoric artefacts. It is open from 9.30 am to 12.30 pm and 4 to 7 pm daily; admission costs L2000.

Trapani's most important sight, however, is some distance east of the city centre. The **Santuario dell'Annunziata**, on Via A Pepoli, was built between 1315 and 1332. It was radically remodelled in baroque style in 1760, when the original three aisles were made into one single nave. The only elements left from the original building are the Gothic rose window and the doorway. Behind the altar is the actual sanctuary of the church, the Cappella della Madonna, built in 1530. The large marble arch contains wonderful reliefs by Antonino and Giacomo Gagini, as well as the venerated *Madonna di Trapani* (also known as Madonna and Child), carved, it is thought, by Nino Pisano. The church is open from 7 am to noon and 4 to 8 pm daily, between June and September; 7.30 am to noon and 4 to 7 pm daily, between October and May. Admission is free. To get here, take bus Nos 24, 25 or 30 from Corso Vittorio Emanuele or Via Garibaldi and get off at Villa Pepoli.

The adjacent **Museo Nazionale Pepoli** (☎ 0923 55 32 69), housed in a former Carmelite monastery, has an archaeological collection, statues and coral carvings. Highlights are Titian's *San Francesco con Stigmata* (St Francis with Stigmata) and the *Pietà* by Roberto di Oderiso. It is open from 9 am to 1.30 pm Monday to Saturday (to 12.30 pm on Sunday) and also from 3 to 6.30 pm on Tuesday and Thursday. Admission costs L8000.

SPECIAL EVENTS
Trapani is famous throughout Italy for its Easter celebrations, the Procession of the *Misteri*, which begins on the Tuesday before Easter and reaches its climax on the night between Holy Thursday and Good Friday (see the boxed text opposite).

PLACES TO STAY
Camping
The nearest camp site is *Lido Valderice* (☎ 0923 57 30 86, Cortiglione), 7km north of the city, on the road to Erice. It's open June to September only and costs L12,500 to pitch a two-person tent. There are six buses daily that head for Erice from the bus station.

Hostels
Ostello per la Gioventù (☎ 0923 55 29 64, Raganzili) is 3km north of town on the Erice road. B&B in a dorm costs L19,000 (L47,000 for full board). It's a 15-minute bus ride on the No 23 from Via GB Fardella to the Ospedale Villa dei Gerani. From there, turn right and then take the second right and walk about 500m uphill. The hostel opens at 6 pm daily.

Hotels
Trapani has the best choice of hotels in the region, and even then the choice isn't spectacular. The cheapest – and most central – hotel in town is *Pensione Messina* (☎ 0923 2 11 98, Corso Vittorio Emanuele 71), a fairly run-down spot on the 3rd floor of a 17th-century building at the back of a courtyard, with singles/doubles for L20,000/40,000. There are only nine rooms, so try to book early. From June to September, prices go up by L5000 per person. *Pensione Maccotta* (☎ 0923 2 84 18, Via degli Argentieri 4), off Piazza Sant'Agostino, has higher-standard singles/doubles costing L30,000/50,000, or L40,000/70,000 with bathroom.

The not-so-modern *Albergo Moderno* (☎ 0923 2 12 47, Via Tenente Genovese 20), has simple rooms with bathroom costing L45,000/70,000 (slightly less off-season). *Nuovo Albergo Russo* (☎ 0923 2 21 66, fax 0923 2 66 23, Via Tintori 4), off Corso Vittorio Emanuele, has rooms, some of them classics of the 1950s, that cost L38,000/65,000, or L65,000/110,000 with bathroom.

More expensive, but offering a better standard, is *Cavallino Bianco* (☎ 0923 2 15 49, fax 0923 2 66 23, Lungomare Dante Alighieri), 1km to the north-east of the city centre, overlooking the sea. Rooms in this modern hotel start at L60,000/135,000 (L90,000/150,000 from June until August). Closer to the centre, *Hotel Vittoria* (☎ 0923 87 30 44, fax 0923 2 98 70, Via Crispi 4) has singles/doubles costing L85,000/140,000.

PLACES TO EAT
Sicily's Arab heritage and Trapani's unique position on the sea route to Tunisia has made couscous (or cuscus, as they spell it here) something of a speciality, particularly when served with a fish sauce that includes tomatoes, garlic and parsley.

Pizzeria Calvino (Via N Nasi 77), towards the port, is the town's favourite takeaway pizza and pasta place. A meal costs between L6000 and L10,000. You can eat a set lunch at the self-service *Pub* (Via della Luce 8) for L16,000. The best-value meal in town is at *Safina* (Piazza Umberto I 35), directly across from the train station, where you can eat your

WESTERN SICILY

fill for less than L20,000. It is closed on Sunday. One of the city's most popular restaurants is **Cantina Siciliana** *(Via Giudecca 52)*, opposite the Palazzo della Giudecca, where you'll eat extremely well for under L30,000. **Trattoria del Porto** *(Via Ammiraglio Staiti 45)*, also known as Da Felice, is more up-market, but it has excellent set meals costing around L35,000. Similarly priced is **Da Bettina** *(Via San Cristoforo 5)*, around the corner; it's closed Wednesday.

If you fancy eating something other than fish, try **Tavernetta Ai Lumi** *(Corso Vittorio Emanuele 75)*, which specialises in rustic cuisine from the interior of the island. It is closed on Sunday and from late August to mid-September.

The area around Piazza Lucatelli is a pleasant place for a sandwich and a coffee. **Panineria Poldo** serves good sandwiches. For a decent ice cream, try **Chupa Chupa**, also on the square. An open-air **market** is held every morning from Monday to Saturday on Piazza Mercato di Pesce, on the northern waterfront.

GETTING THERE & AWAY
Air
Trapani's small national airport (☎ 0923 84 12 22, 0923 84 11 24), is 16km south of town at Birgi. AST buses connect Trapani bus station and the airport (L5000, 20 minutes).

Bus
All intercity buses arrive and depart from the bus station on Piazza Montalto. Tickets can be bought from kiosks in the station. Segesta runs a service from Trapani to Palermo (L8500, two hours); Lumia (☎ 0923 2 17 54) serves Agrigento (18,000, 3½ hours, four daily). AST buses serve Erice (L6000, 40 minutes, nine daily), Castellammare del Golfo (L10,000, one hour, four daily), Castelvetrano (L17,000, 1½ hours, seven daily) – from where you can connect to Selinunte – Marsala (eight daily), Mazara del Vallo (L8500/14,500, four daily) and San Vito lo Capo (L5500/9000, 1¼ hours, six daily). AST also runs a bus service to Segesta (two hours) and Calatafimi. The frequency decreases dramatically off-season, so check at the bus station for off-peak departures.

Train
For general train information call ☎ 0923 54 04 16. Trapani is linked to Palermo (L12,500, two hours, 10 to 12 daily), Castelvetrano (L7500, one hour 10 minutes, 12 daily) and Marsala (L4200, 35 minutes, 10 to 15 daily). For Segesta, you can either get off at Segesta Tempio (L4000, 25 minutes, one daily), from where you'll have to walk 3km to the temple, or Calatafimi (L4500, 30 minutes, one daily), on the Palermo line. The stations are roughly equidistant from the ancient Greek site.

Boat
Siremar (☎ 0923 54 54 55, @ siremar@gestelnet.it), Via Ammiraglio Staiti 61, runs a night ferry to Pantelleria. There is no service at weekends except in summer. The high-season fare for the six-hour trip is L42,000; with booking it goes up to L59,000. The boat departs from Trapani at midnight and leaves Pantelleria at 11 am (weather permitting), returning to Trapani at 5 pm.

Ustica Lines (☎ 0923 2 22 00) operates a hydrofoil service from Naples to Trapani (L151,000), June to September only, via Ustica (L117,00) and the Egadi Islands (L141,000). It also has a ferry to Pantelleria (L60,000). In Trapani, get tickets at Egatours, Via Ammiraglio Staiti 13, or directly at the Ustica Lines embarkation point.

Tirrenia runs weekly ferries to Tunisia from Trapani, departing at 9 am on Monday. Tickets for the eight-hour trip cost L92,000 for an airline-type seat and L116,000 for a bed in a 2nd-class cabin during the high season. The return boat leaves Tunisia at 8 pm. There is also a weekly Tirrenia service to Cagliari (Sardinia), departing at 9 pm on Tuesday. Tickets cost L67,000 for an airline-style seat and L92,000 for a bed in a 2nd-class cabin. Tickets can be purchased at Salvo Viaggi (☎ 0923 54 54 11), Corso Italia 48, or directly from the ferry terminal (Stazione Marittima; ☎ 0923 54 54 33).

GETTING AROUND
To/From the Airport
AST buses (L3500/5000 one way/return) leave from Piazza Montalto to coincide with flights. Segesta (☎ 0923 2 00 66) runs

a daily bus to the main Falcone-Borsellino airport at Punta Raisi. Its timetable changes regularly, so check with the APT office.

Taxis
There are taxi ranks on Piazza Umberto (☎ 0923 2 28 08) and at the ferry terminal (☎ 0923 2 32 33).

Around Trapani

Trapani makes a good base for exploring the city's hinterland, a far more rewarding and diverse excursion altogether. From the fascinating saltpans south of the city to the hilltop town of Erice, the area surrounding the provincial capital is well worth exploring.

SALINE DI TRAPANI
The coastline between Trapani and Marsala has long been known for its salt production, and travelling down the secondary road that runs west of the larger SS115 you will see the famous *saline* (saltpans). The most extraordinary features are the large mounds of salt left to dry in the sun and the Dutch-style windmills, some of them still in working order. Salt production became big business during the Norman occupation and continued during the Aragonese reign; at the end of the 19th century there were as many as 40 salt works along the coast. In recent decades production has fallen off enormously, but they are still a unique and impressive sight.

At Nubia, 5km south of Trapani, is the **Museo delle Saline** (Salt Museum), housed in a 17th-century salt mill. Exhibits demonstrate how the salt is extracted: water is pumped into the saltpan via a windmill and then left to evaporate in the summer sun. The salt is then removed and piled up on the pier, where it is covered in terracotta tiles to protect it from humidity. The museum is open from 9 am to 1 pm and 3 to 7 pm, and admission is free. To get to the museum, take the AST bus for Marsala from Piazza Montalto in Trapani (see the earlier Trapani section for details) and get off at Nubia; the well-signposted museum is about 1km to the west, at the water's edge.

ERICE
postcode 91016 • pop 29,500
• elevation 751m
The dramatic medieval hill town of Erice is about 40 minutes north-east of Trapani by bus and should not be missed on any account. Settled by the Elymians, an ancient mountain people who also founded Segesta, it was an important religious site associated with goddesses of fertility – first the Carthaginian Astarte, then the Greek Aphrodite and finally the Roman Venus. Today, it has, unfortunately, become a bit of a tourist trap (watch out for exorbitant charges for food and drinks), as well as a centre for international conferences as headquarters of the Ettore Majorana Scientific and Cultural Institute. However, it still manages to maintain a relatively authentic medieval atmosphere, with one sore exception: the town's elevated position has made it a prime location for telecommunication towers, which soar above the medieval skyline, somewhat spoiling the whole effect.

Orientation & Information
You'll have no problems finding your way around this small town – but be prepared for plenty of uphill walks. The friendly and informative tourist office (☎ 0923 86 93 88) is on Viale Conte Pepoli, just a couple of steps from the bus terminus. There's a post office in the heart of town, on Via Guarnotti, while the police station is at the Porta Trapani entrance to town, near the bus stop on Piazza Grammatico.

Things to See
This triangular-shaped town is best explored by pottering around its narrow streets and peeking through the doorways into courtyards. At the top of the hill stands the Norman **Castello di Venere** (Castle of Venus), built in the 12th and 13th centuries over an ancient temple of Venus. It is open from 8 am to 7 pm Monday to Sunday and admission is free. Not much more than a ruin, the castle is upstaged by the panoramic vistas north-east to San Vito lo Capo and Mt Cofano (659m), and west to Trapani.

Of the several churches and other monuments in the small, quiet town, the **Chiesa**

WESTERN SICILY

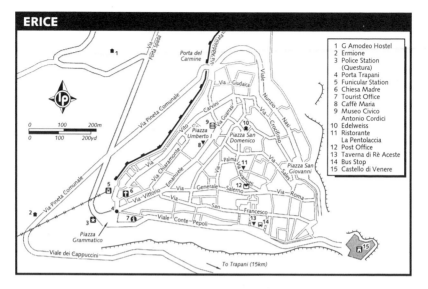

ERICE

1 G Amodeo Hostel
2 Ermione
3 Police Station (Questura)
4 Porta Trapani
5 Funicular Station
6 Chiesa Madre
7 Tourist Office
8 Caffè Maria
9 Museo Civico Antonio Cordici
10 Edelweiss
11 Ristorante La Pentolaccia
12 Post Office
13 Taverna di Rè Aceste
14 Bus Stop
15 Castello di Venere

To Trapani (15km)

Madre, on Via Vito Carvini just inside Porta Trapani, is probably the most interesting by virtue of its separate bell tower with mullioned windows. Built in 1314, the interior of the church was remodelled in neo-Gothic style in 1865, but the 15th-century side chapels were conserved.

At the top of the town's main street, Corso Vittorio Emanuele, is Piazza Umberto I, the heart of the city and where you'll find the **Museo Civico Antonio Cordici**. The museum houses finds from the town's necropolis, including a 4th-century head of Venus. The other worthwhile piece is an elegant *Annunciation* by Antonello Gagini.

Places to Stay & Eat

Hotels are horribly overpriced so, if you can, try to base yourself elsewhere, preferably Trapani. If you absolutely must stay overnight, there is an HI youth hostel, *G Amodeo* (☎ 0923 55 29 64, Viale della Pineta), awkwardly positioned 1km north-west of town and only open between June and September. B&B costs L19,000 and a meal costs L18,000. Otherwise, the options are expensive. The cheapest alternative is *Ermione* (☎ 0923 86 91 38, Via Pineta Comunale), 1km north-west of town, which has cramped single/double rooms costing L60,000/100,000. In the town itself, *Edelweiss* (☎ 0923 86 91 58, Cortile Vincenzo 5) has rooms costing L100,000/140,000.

For a decent meal at a reasonable price, try *Taverna di Rè Aceste (Via R De Martini)*, in a small lane off Viale Conte Pepoli, where you can get away with spending around L35,000. It is closed on Wednesday. The atmospheric *Ristorante La Pentolaccia* (☎ 0923 86 98 99, Via Guarnotta 17) is inside a former 16th-century monastery. It's very touristy, serving up *pasta con le sarde* and other favourites for around L11,000. Otherwise, you can enjoy delicious snacks at *Caffè Maria (Via Vittorio Emanuele)*, just shy of Piazza Umberto I. The *cannoli* (cream horns) are exquisite.

Getting There & Away

There is a regular AST bus service to Trapani (L3500/6000 one way/return, 45 minutes), with nine daily buses Monday to Friday, and four on Sunday. The service begins at 6.30 am and ends at 6.30 pm. In Erice, all buses arrive and depart from Viale Conte Pepoli.

SAN VITO LO CAPO
postcode 91010 • pop 3500

Occupying the tip of the promontory is the pleasant seaside town of San Vito lo Capo, full of beachcombers and sun worshippers in summer, virtually dead in winter. The town is renowned for its splendid beach (at the end of Via Savoia) and for its fish couscous, celebrated at a couscous festival every August. The most noteworthy sight is the fortress-like, 13th-century **Chiesa di San Vito**, about halfway down Via Savoia. If you want to try some good couscous, there's no place better than *Thaam (Via Duca degli Abruzzi 34)*, a North African restaurant just off Via Savoia. Otherwise, Via Savoia is full of pizzerias and other restaurants all priced similarly.

SCOPELLO
postcode 901014 • pop 40
• elevation 106m

Blink and you'll miss it, but it would be a shame: the tiny, two-street hamlet of Scopello, delightfully placed on a ridge high above the coastline, is made up of a square in front of a *baglio*, or manor house, around which the town is built. There is nothing really to do in the town except eat and explore the surrounding countryside, best done if you have your own transport. Still, it's only a 2km walk to the entrance to the Riserva Naturale dello Zingaro (see the next section), and only 1.5km from one of the most idyllic swimming coves on the island, by the old tuna station at the foot of the hill.

Tonnara di Scopello
The tuna processing plant ceased operations in the 1980s, a victim of Sicily's chronic tuna malaise, but its closure has been a godsend for visitors: they are free to enter so long as they respect the site's tranquillity (no radios, no beach umbrellas – basically nothing that might disturb the appearance of the place). Once inside, you will understand why there are restrictions. The place is literally perfect: an old abandoned building surrounded by rows of rusting anchors gives onto a small shingle beach lapped by waters of such an incredible blue that you'll want to take photographs to show your friends at home.

The cove is protected by *faraglioni* (rock towers), jutting out of the sea.

Places to Stay & Eat
The nearest camp site is **Baia di Guidaloca** *(☎ 0924 54 12 62, Località Guidaloca)*, 3km south of Scopello near a lovely swimming hole (the Cala Bianca) and on the bus route from Castellammare del Golfo. It costs L8500 per person. All of Scopello's restaurants and hotels are within a 30-second radius of the main square. *La Tavernetta (☎ 0924 54 11 29, Via Armando Diaz 7)* has seven rooms and charges L60,000 per person; the restaurant below has a tourist menu for L18,500. Next door is *La Tranchina (☎ 0924 54 10 99, Via Armando Diaz 9)*, with well-appointed, modern single/double rooms for L55,000/80,000. The restaurant has a lovely terrace with sea views and a L30,000 menu. Around the corner is *La Torre Benistra II (☎ 0924 54 11 28, Via Natale di Roma 19)*, with rooms for L62,000/83,000, including half board – the restaurant here is the best in town. You don't have to be a guest to eat at any of the restaurants. Alternatively, you can dine at *Il Baglio*, in the main square, which serves excellent pizzas.

RISERVA NATURALE DELLO ZINGARO
A couple of kilometres from Scopello is the main entrance to the Riserva Naturale dello Zingaro (Zingaro Nature Reserve), 7km of pristine coastline flanked by a couple of steep mountains. Established in 1980 after protests against a planned road through the area, the reserve has a series of well-maintained **paths** and six **beaches**. Most people come for the swimming, but the area is rich in plant life and is home to at least 40 different species of bird, including a type of eagle known as *l'aquila del Bonelli*. No kind of motorised transport is allowed in the reserve. It is open from 7 am to 9 pm daily (to 6 pm from September 16 to April 15). There is an information booth at the entrance; admission is free.

Diving
The Cetaria Diving Centre (☎ 0924 54 10 73), in Castellammare del Golfo (see the

WESTERN SICILY

next section), organises dives, classes and underwater tours of the nature reserve from the *tonnara* in Scopello, daily in June and August. For off-season dives, call Vittorio Ballerini (☎ 091 34 17 53), in Palermo.

CASTELLAMMARE DEL GOLFO
postcode 91014 • pop 13,500

Hugging the coast and wholly surrounded by mountains, Castellammare del Golfo is the least attractive of the towns along the gulf, although it does have a pleasant harbour full of cafes and little restaurants.

Guarding the harbour are the remains of a 17th-century Aragonese **castle**. Away from the harbour, the town slopes upwards into the hills, a grid of narrow, uninviting streets and two-storey residential buildings. Although quiet enough today, the town has a history of Mafia connections and bloodshed, particularly in the period following WWII, when it was reckoned to have the highest number of murders per capita of any town on the island. Not surprisingly, the town does not sit at the top of any tourist itineraries. Still, it isn't a bad place to linger for an afternoon, if only to plan your visit to the surrounding area.

There are a couple of hotels in the town, the cheapest of which is **Punta Nord Est** (☎ 0924 3 05 11, Via Leonardo da Vinci 47), where singles/doubles cost L58,000/90,000 (L82,000/104,000 during July and August); however, you're better off moving up the coast to Scopello.

Getting There & Away
Castellammare is well served by buses to/from Palermo, Trapani, San Vito lo Capo (via Scopello) and Segesta, daily except Sunday. All buses go from Via della Repubblica, in the upper part of town. The train station is inconveniently 4km out of town, although a shuttle bus (L1500) ferries passengers to town.

SEGESTA
postcode 91013 • elevation 304m

The ancient Elymians must have been great aesthetes if their choice of sites for cities is any indication. Along with Erice and Entella, they founded Segesta on and around Mt Barbaro (304m). The Greeks later took over and it is to them that we owe the two outstanding survivors: the theatre high up on the mountain, with commanding views out to the Castellammare del Golfo (how did spectators concentrate on the show with such a backdrop?), and the temple.

History
Segesta's history is one of useful alliances. Settled by Elymians, most likely from Anatolia, the city came under Hellenic influence and sought an alliance with Athens in 426 BC. Constantly at war with Selinunte, to the south, it sought Carthaginian help in defeating its rival, and after Selinunte's destruction in 409 BC Segesta continued to benefit from the protection of Carthage against the Greeks of Syracuse (who managed to sack the city in 307 BC). The Carthaginians quickly took back the city, but were repaid during the First Punic War when Segesta was the first Sicilian city to ally itself to the Romans, killing the Carthaginian garrison stationed in the city for its protection! The city went into decline during the Saracen occupation and was eventually abandoned in the 13th century.

Things to See
Time has done to Segesta what violence inflicted on Selinunte, and little remains of the city. On the hill nearest the entrance is the **Doric temple**, dating from around 430 BC and remarkably well preserved. Scholars are in doubt whether the temple was ever completed (it never had a roof) or whether it was left uncovered according to the style of a local cult. It is, nevertheless, a truly wondrous site, especially considering that it has survived a number of earthquakes.

The **Hellenistic theatre** is also in a fair state of repair and is the only structure inside the old city walls to have survived intact. Built in the middle of the 3rd century, it is unique in that it faces north so as to make the most of the extraordinary panorama that spreads out behind the stage, of the hills and the distant Castellammare del Golfo. Nearby are the ruins of a castle and church built in the Middle Ages. A shuttle bus runs every

30 minutes from the entrance 1.5km uphill to the theatre and costs L2000. If you feel up to it, however, the walk up the hill is more interesting, with splendid views of the theatre on the hill behind.

During July and August of every odd-numbered year (alternating with Syracuse), performances of Greek plays are staged in the theatre. For information, contact the APT office in Trapani.

The site is open from 9 am to one hour before sunset daily. Admission to the site costs L4000.

Getting There & Away
Segesta is accessible by AST bus (☎ 0923 3 10 20) from Piazza Montalto in Trapani (L5000, 25 minutes). Between June and September there are buses at 8 am, 10 am and 2 pm daily (mornings only during the rest of the year). Buses depart from Palermo (Piazza Marina) at 7.50 am and 2 pm. Otherwise, catch an infrequent train from Trapani or Palermo to Segesta Tempio; head north-east up the hill – the site is about 3km away.

Islands off the Western Coast

THE EGADI ISLANDS
postcode 91023 • pop 3440
The Egadi Islands (Isole Egadi) are the most accessible of Sicily's off-shore possessions. The archipelago is made up of three small islands – Favignana, Levanzo and Marettimo. The islands have been inhabited since prehistoric times (as shown by the extraordinary cave paintings on Levanzo) and were later the site of a Phoenician-Punic settlement known as the Aegades. In 241 BC Lutatius Catulus routed the Carthaginian fleet near here and the islands came under Roman control. They eventually ended up in Spanish hands and, in the 16th century, were sold to the Pallavicino-Rusconi family of Genoa, who sold them on to the Florio family in 1874; they then handed them over to the Italian state in 1937.

In recent years they have become increasingly popular with foreign visitors, who join the thousands of Sicilian day-trippers who come here in the summer to swim and sun themselves on the beaches. Favignana, the largest of the three islands and easily the most developed, boasts a small town (of the same name) with a number of good restaurants and hotels. Levanzo, whose full-time population numbers 60 is, by comparison, much less developed, whereas Marettimo, the westernmost of the three, can offer little but the wild beauty of its landscape and hidden coves.

Getting There & Away
Siremar runs ferries and hydrofoils to the Egadi Islands from Trapani. A high-season one-way fare to Favignana or Levanzo costs L10,000 on the hydrofoil (20 minutes). The journey to Marettimo costs L22,500. Tickets are cheaper on the slower car ferries. Ustica Lines also runs regular hydrofoils to the islands (L10,000).

For contact details and more on transport options, see Getting There & Away in the earlier Trapani and Marsala sections.

Favignana
Windswept Mt Santa Caterina (314m) dominates the otherwise flat main island. Pleasant to explore, it has plenty of rocky coves and crystal-clear water. Wander around the abandoned **Stabilimento Florio** tuna processing plant *(tonnara)* at the port. It was shut in 1977 due to the general crisis in the local tuna-fishing industry. Lack of funding has blocked plans to turn the building into a complex which would include a school and arts-and-crafts shops. Favignana is also famous for the *mattanza* (ritual slaughter of tuna), which takes place off the coast in May and June.

There is a Pro Loco office (☎ 0923 92 16 47) at Piazza Matrice 8. It's open from 9 am to 12.30 pm and 4 to 8 pm Monday to Saturday, and Sunday mornings between May and September.

Places to Stay & Eat There are plenty of accommodation options on Favignana but during the period of the mattanza, and in August, you'll have trouble finding a bed without a booking. Many locals rent out rooms.

La Mattanza

A centuries-old tradition, the Egadi Islands' *mattanza* (the ritual slaughter of tuna) survives despite the ever-decreasing number of tuna fish swimming into the local waters each year. Schools of tuna have, for centuries, used the waters around Western Sicily as a mating ground. Locals can recall the golden days of the island's fishing industry, when it was not uncommon to catch giant breeding tuna of between 200kg and 300kg. Fish that size are rare these days due to worldwide overfishing of tuna, and the annual catch is increasingly smaller. However, even though the island's fishing industry is in severe crisis as a result, the tradition of the mattanza goes on.

Now that the slaughter of tuna can no longer support the island's economy, it is reinventing itself as a tourist attraction. From around 20 May to 10 June, tourists flock to the Egadi Islands to witness the event. For a fee you can join the fishers in their boats and watch them catching the tuna at close hand – note that you'll need a strong stomach. This is no ordinary fishing expedition: the fishers organise their boats and nets in a complex formation designed to channel the tuna into a series of enclosures which culminate in the *camera della morte* (room of death). Once enough tuna are imprisoned there, the fishers close in and the mattanza begins (the word is derived from the Spanish word for killing). It is a bloody affair – up to eight or more fishers at a time will sink huge hooks into a tuna and drag it aboard. Anyone who has seen Rossellini's classic film *Stromboli* will no doubt recall the famous mattanza scene.

The cheapest option is to pitch a tent at one of the two camp sites. *Égad (☎ 0923 92 15 55)* charges L7500 per person (L9500 during July and August); it is well signposted to the east of town. To the west, the better-equipped *Miramare (☎ 0923 92 13 30)* charges from L16,000 per person. The *Villaggio Quattro Rose (☎ 0923 92 12 23, Località Mulino a Vento)*, also has camping facilities and bungalows. Otherwise, the *Bouganville (☎ 0923 92 20 33, Via Cimabue 10)* has singles/

doubles costing L45,000/80,000. In summer, half board is obligatory and costs L90,000 per person. *Albergo Egadi (☎ 0923 92 12 32, Via Colombo 17)*, just off the main square, has comfortable singles/doubles for L50,000/ 100,000 and offers half board for L110,000 per person. It has an acclaimed restaurant, where you'll eat one of your best meals in Italy at very reasonable prices. Otherwise, there are plenty of other options in and around the square.

Levanzo

The only reasons to visit Levanzo are to spend some time on the beach and to examine the prehistoric cave paintings at the Grotta del Genovese. Otherwise, there's not much else to do save go for a good walk.

There are three great spots to go swimming, all a healthy walk from the town (which is nothing more than a cluster of houses around the port). To get to **Faraglione**, take a left through the town and walk west along the road until you see a couple of rocks sticking out of the water a few metres offshore. It is about 1km. If you fancy something a little quieter, keep going until you get to **Capo Grosso**, on the northern side of the island, where there is also a lighthouse. Alternatively, take a right out of town and walk along the dirt road. Three hundred metres past the first bend the road forks: take the rocky path down toward the sea and keep going until you get to **Calo Minnola**, a small landing bay where the water is crystal clear and where, outside the month of August, you can swim in peace and tranquillity.

Grotta del Genovese The Upper Palaeolithic wall paintings and Neolithic incised drawings at the Genoese Cave were discovered by accident in 1949. Between 6000 and 10,000 years old, the images mostly feature animals; the later ones also include men and tuna. To get there, follow the path across the island, but be warned that it is rough going on your own; you can check with the custodian (☎ 0923 92 40 32), who is available for guided tours (L25,000). Alternatively, you can take the sea route by hiring one of the several sea taxis that advertise in the town's two bars: it should cost you at most L20,000 per person. These can also be hired for trips around the island.

Places to Stay & Eat Levanzo's two hotels are of a similar standard. *Paradiso (☎ 0923 92 40 80, Via Lungomare)*, has single/double rooms costing L45,000/85,000, and just behind it is *Pensione dei Fenici (☎ 0923 92 40 83, Via Calvario 11)*, which charges about the same. These hotels also happen to have the island's only two restaurants; dining alfresco at the Paradiso is a wonderful experience – the stunning views of the sea and coastline come for free.

Marettimo

The most westward island of the three is also the wildest and least-developed. Samuel Butler reckoned this to be the island of Ithaca, home to Ulysses, although most experts agree that the theory is a little far-fetched. There are plenty of good swimming spots around the island; recommended are **Cala Sarda** and **Cala Nera**, on the southern coast. Otherwise, the island is good walking territory.

There are no official accommodation options as such on the island, but locals do rent out rooms; ask at the cafe in the main square and expect to pay between L18,000 and L30,000. There's a *pizzeria* above the town which is open from June to August only; otherwise, *Torrente*, by the port, is open throughout the year and serves up an unsurprising menu of fish dishes.

PANTELLERIA
postcode 91017 • pop 7400

Located 110km south of the Sicilian mainland, Pantelleria is a curious place – a giant, quasi-dormant volcano (the last eruption was in 1891) – whose culture is more African than Sicilian (Tunisia is only 70km away). The island's inhabitants are, surprisingly, less occupied with fishing than with agriculture, thanks to the rich, blackened soil nourished by the volcano. The coast is dotted with small coves and inlets that are perfect for swimming, provided the weather is good.

The island was initially settled by the Sesi, a neolithic people probably from Libya.

Over the centuries it was in Phoenician, Carthaginian and Roman hands before falling to the Moors in the 8th century AD, who named it Bent-el-Rhia (daughter of the wind), the source of its modern name.

The 400-year Moorish occupation has left an indelible mark on this otherwise rugged island, from the typical houses known as *dammusi* to the widespread cultivation of the *zibibbo*, a grape used in the production of the local wine, Moscato di Pantelleria. Even the local dialect is laced with Arabic words, in contrast to that on mainland Italy, which is more heavily influenced by French and Spanish.

Orientation

Apart from Malta, this is the largest of the islands surrounding Sicily, so you'll need to use some kind of motorised transport to get around. Pantelleria town occupies the north-western tip; the airport is 6km southeast of town. Most of the island's places of interest are along the south-western and north-eastern coasts.

Information

There is a small tourist office (☎ 0923 91 18 38) on Piazza Cavour. It is open from 9.30 am to 1 pm and 5 to 7 pm Monday to Saturday, June to September only. Agenzia Rizzo (☎ 0923 91 11 04), on the harbour at Via Borgo Italia 12, has maps of the island. It is open from 5.45 am to 1 pm and 5 to 6.30 pm Monday to Friday, mornings only on Saturday (also Sunday morning from June to September).

Things to See

Pantelleria is less a place to see than to experience. Aside from the 16th-century **Castello Barabacane** (open from 6 to 8 pm daily, June to September; admission free) at the end of the harbour, there is little to see in Pantelleria town: it was flattened during WWII and rebuilt with cube-shaped houses of little interest. More curious are the island's natural phenomena, including the 24 **cuddie**, ancient craters of red volcanic rock surrounding the main volcano – Montagna Grande (836m) – which dominates the cen-

WESTERN SICILY

tre of the island. Also worth checking out are the **sesi**, massive neolithic funeral cairns with low passages leading to the centre. The most impressive of them is the **Sese del Re**, about 15-minutes' walk south of the Cuddie Rosse on the north-western coast. The island was once dotted with these mounds, but over the years most were dismantled and the stones used in the construction of the Moorish dammusi dwellings, whose thick, whitewashed walls and shallow cupolas keep the inside nice and cool, while ridges around the top are designed to catch the rain. Also of interest are the renowned **giardini arabi**, or Moorish gardens, citrus groves built into the mountain-side and protected from the often fierce winds by high stone walls.

On the north-eastern coast, an idyllic spot is the hamlet of **Gadir**, whose small harbour is perfect for swimming. Here you'll also find a number of thermal pools that are renowned for their curative powers.

Places to Stay & Eat

There is nothing cheap here, especially in the summer, when it is best to book ahead. *Albergo Myriam* (☎ *0923 91 13 74, Corso Umberto I*) offers singles for L75,000/95,000 in low/high season and doubles for L120,000/140,000. At *Khamma* (☎ *0923 91 26 80, Via Borgo Italia 24*) singles/doubles cost L70,000/100,000 during the low season. Farther along, the *Port'Hotel* (☎ *0923 91 12 99, Via Borgo Italia 6,* ✉ *porthotel@pantelleria.it*) has singles for L50,000/80,000 without/with bathroom and doubles with bathroom for L115,000. Prices increase considerably between June and August. If you're in a group of three or four, you should consider renting a dammuso:

most bars and restaurants have notices advertising rentals, which can work out cheaper than staying in a hotel.

There is no shortage of places to eat in Pantelleria. Near the Port'Hotel, *Trattoria Dammuso (Via Borgo Italia)* is excellent, with great views of the harbour and a comprehensive pizza menu. Just off Piazza Cavour, *Il Cappero (Via Roma 31)* is where you'll find the local speciality, *ravioli con menta e ricotta*. It is closed Monday from October to April. Outside town, you'll have no problem finding somewhere to eat in the hamlets along the coast.

Getting There & Away

Pantelleria is 20 minutes by plane (L120,000) from Trapani. All boats arrive at Pantelleria town's port; it's a 5-hour trip from Trapani. Plane and ferry tickets can be purchased in Trapani at Salvo Viaggi (☎ 0923 54 54 11), Corso Italia 48, or directly at the airport. In Pantelleria, tickets can be bought from Agenzia Rizzo (see under Information for details).

Tirrenia runs a hydrofoil service on Wednesday and Sunday from Pantelleria to Kelibia in Tunisia (L30,000 one way, around two hours).

Getting Around

Local buses depart from Piazza Cavour in Pantelleria town at regular intervals, daily except Sunday, servicing every village on the island (L900). Alternatively, consider renting a moped, which allows greater mobility. Autonoleggio Policardo (☎ 0923 91 28 44), Vicolo Messina 35, just beside the Port'Hotel, rents 50cc scooters and 125cc Vespas for L55,000 per day. During the off-season, the daily rate drops to L30,000. There is also a weekly rate of L180,000.

Language

While standard Italian may be Sicily's official language, and is spoken almost universally on the island, most locals (over 70%) speak Sicilian among themselves. Sicilian is referred to as an Italian dialect, but is sufficiently different to warrant being termed a language in its own right; even if you're fluent in Italian, you'll find it almost impossible to understand. Luckily, Sicilians will readily revert to Italian when speaking to anyone from the mainland or abroad, although the occasional Sicilian word will still creep in.

Some Sicilians have studied English at school, but English-speakers are generally hard to find beyond the more popular tourist resorts, where staff at hotels, restaurants and tourist offices usually have a basic grasp of the language. Any attempt on your part to get to grips with Italian will endear you to the locals, no matter how many mistakes you make.

Italian

Italian is a Romance language related to French, Spanish, Portuguese and Romanian, all of which are directly descended from Latin. The Romance languages belong to the large Indo-European group of languages, which include English. Indeed, as English and Italian share common roots in Latin, you will recognise many Italian words.

Sicily has a strange relationship with the Italian language. Although it is commonly accepted that modern standard Italian

Speaking in Tongues

Along with all Italian dialects, Sicilian belongs to the Italo-Romance language group. However, centuries of foreign occupation have exposed it to linguistic influences from many and varied sources, including Albanian, Arabic, French, Greek, Norman, Spanish and northern Italian dialects.

The grammatical structure of Sicilian is somewhat different from standard Italian: there's no single verb conjugation for the future tense – instead, Sicilian uses a form akin to 'I have (to do something)'; and the simple past (a literary form only in standard Italian) is used for the past perfect tense in everyday speech. Pronunciation is difficult, and it is commonly claimed that only a Sicilian can pronounce the double 'd' that regularly substitutes the standard Italian double 'l' – the classic Sicilian protestation of sincerity, *La bella madre e veramente* (By the beautiful mother and truly), becomes *La bedda madre e beramante*.

Sicilian is also coloured with a rich range of metaphors and proverbs, some of which date back to the days of Arabic occupation. The English 'All things in moderation' in Sicilian reads *Non essiri duci sinno tu mancianu, non essiri amaru sinno ti futanu* (Don't be too sweet lest you be eaten, don't be too sour lest you be shunned). The Sicilian way to say 'Make the most of what you've got' is *Camina chi pantofuli fino a quannu non hai i scarpi* (Walk in your slippers until you find your shoes).

Sicilians are also known for their epithets, which are used as insults of varying strength in a range of situations. If you want to call someone crazy, you refer to them as *stunato*; if there's an excess of drink involved, it's most likely that they're *scribbi di patata* – literally, taken over by the 'spirit of the potato', a reference to the distillation of some alcoholic drinks from that vegetable. If you want to curse someone, you refer to them as having *u m'al occhio* (the evil eye), and if you *really* want to slander a Sicilian man, refer to him as *cornuto* (with horns), meaning that he is a cuckold. While not an exclusively Sicilian insult, it suggests a loss of honour that is about as ignominious as it gets on the island – so be careful at whom you direct it!

269

developed from the Tuscan dialect, Sicilians rightly assert that the first literature in the 'common vernacular' (Italian, as opposed to Latin or Greek) was produced in Sicily (at the court of Frederick I in the 13th century). Exponents of the Sicilian school of poetry, mostly court officials-turned-poets, were a source of inspiration to many of the early Tuscan writers. After the Middle Ages, works by prestigious writers from the mainland's north, such as Dante, Petrarch and Boccaccio, contributed to the steady elevation of Tuscan as the dominant written vernacular. History shows that Tuscany's status as the political, cultural and financial power base of the nation ensured that the region's dialect would ultimately be installed as the national tongue.

The Italian of today is something of a composite. What you hear on the radio and TV, in educated discourse and indeed in the everyday language of many people is the result of centuries of cross-fertilisation between the dialects, greatly accelerated in the postwar decades by the modern media.

If you have more than the most fundamental grasp of the Italian language, you need to be aware that many Sicilians still expect to be addressed in the third person formal (*lei* instead of *tu*). Also, it is not considered polite to use the greeting *ciao* when addressing strangers unless they use it first; it's better to say *buongiorno* (or *buona sera*, as the case may be) and *arrivederci* (or the more polite form, *arrivederla*). This is true of most of Italy, but in Sicily use of the informal can be considered gravely impolite – and in some cases downright insulting – especially when talking to an older person. We have used the formal address for most of the phrases in this guide. Use of the informal address is indicated by 'inf' in brackets. Italian also has both masculine and feminine forms (usually ending in 'o' and 'a' respectively). Where both forms are given in this guide, they are separated by a slash, the masculine form first.

If you'd like a more comprehensive guide to the language, get a copy of Lonely Planet's *Italian phrasebook*.

Pronunciation

Surprisingly – especially after you hear the near-incomprehensible dialect – a Sicilian speaker's pronunciation of standard Italian is refreshingly clear and easy to understand, even if you have only a limited command of the language. Vowels are pronounced more openly than in mainland Italy, and there is a tendency to emphasise consonants, so that a word like *buongiorno* (good day) sounds something like 'bawn-jaw-rrno'. The French influence also means that in certain parts of Sicily, particularly the west, the 'r' is not as rolled as it is in standard Italian: locals pronounce 'Trapani' the way an English-speaker would, without rolling the 'r'.

Setting aside the vagaries of Sicilian pronunciation and dialect, Italian is not difficult to pronounce once you learn a few easy rules. Although some of the more clipped vowels, and stress on double letters, require careful practice for English-speakers, it is easy enough to make yourself understood.

Vowels

Vowels are generally more clipped than in English:

a	as the second 'a' in 'camera'
e	as in 'day' but a shorter sound
i	as in 'inn'
o	as in 'dot'
u	as in 'cook'

Consonants

The pronunciation of many Italian consonants is similar to that of their English counterparts. Pronunciation of some consonants depends on certain rules:

c	like 'k' before 'a', 'o' and 'u'; like the 'ch' in 'choose' before 'e' and 'i'
ch	hard 'k' sound
g	like the 'g' in 'get' before 'a', 'o' and 'u'; like the 'j' in 'job' before 'e' and 'i'
gh	hard, as in 'get'
gli	like the 'lli' in 'million'

gn	like the 'ny' in 'canyon'
h	always silent
r	a rolled 'rr' sound
sc	like the 'sh' in 'sheep' before 'e' and 'i'; like 'sk' before 'h', 'a', 'o' and 'u'
z	like the 'ts' in 'lights', except at the beginning of a word, when it's like the 'ds' in 'beds'

Note that when **ci**, **gi** and **sci** are followed by **a**, **o** or **u**, the 'i' is not pronounced unless the accent falls on the 'i'. Thus the name 'Giovanni' is pronounced 'joh-**vahn**-nee'.

Word Stress
A double consonant is pronounced as a longer, often more forceful sound than a single consonant.

Stress often falls on the second-last syllable, as in *spa-**ghet**-ti*. When a word has an accent, the stress is on that syllable, as in *cit-**tà*** (city).

Greetings & Civilities
Hello.	*Buongiorno.* *Ciao.* (inf)
Goodbye.	*Arrivederci.* *Ciao.* (inf)
Yes.	*Sì.*
No.	*No.*
Please.	*Per favore/ Per piacere.*
Thank you.	*Grazie.*
That's fine/ You're welcome.	*Prego.*
Excuse me.	*Mi scusi.* *Scusam.* (inf)
Sorry (forgive me).	*Mi scusi/Mi perdoni.*

Small Talk
What's your name?	*Come si chiama?* *Come ti chiami?* (inf)
My name is ...	*Mi chiamo ...*
Where are you from?	*Di dov'è?* *Di dove sei?* (inf)
I'm from ...	*Sono di ...*
How old are you?	*Quanti anni ha hai?* *Quanti anni hai?* (inf)
I'm ... years old.	*Ho ... anni.*

I (don't) like ...	*(Non) Mi piace ...*
Just a minute.	*Un momento.*

Language Difficulties
I (don't) understand.	*(Non) Capisco.*
Please write it down.	*Può scriverlo, per favore?*
Can you show me (on the map)?	*Può mostrarmelo (sulla carta/pianta)?*
Do you speak English?	*Parla inglese?* *Parli inglese?* (inf)
Does anyone here speak English?	*C'è qualcuno che parla inglese?*
How do you say ... in Italian?	*Come si dice ... in italiano?*
What does ... mean?	*Che vuole dire ...?*

Paperwork
name	*nome*
nationality	*nazionalità*
date of birth	*data di nascita*
place of birth	*luogo di nascita*
sex (gender)	*sesso*
passport	*passaporto*
visa	*visto*

Getting Around
What time does ... leave/arrive?	*A che ora parte/ arriva ...?*
the aeroplane	*l'aereo*
the boat	*la barca*
the (city) bus	*l'autobus*
the (intercity) bus	*il pullman/corriere*
the train	*il treno*

I want to go to ...	*Voglio andare a ...*
I'd like a ... ticket.	*Vorrei un biglietto ...*
one-way	*di solo andata*
return	*di andata e ritorno*
1st-class	*prima classe*
2nd-class	*seconda classe*

The train has been cancelled/delayed.	*Il treno è soppresso/ in ritardo.*
the first	*il primo*
the last	*l'ultimo*
platform number	*binario numero*
station	*stazione*
ticket office	*biglietteria*
timetable	*orario*

I'd like to hire ...	Vorrei noleggiare ...
a bicycle	una bicicletta
a boat	una barca
a car	una macchina
a motorcycle	una motocicletta

Directions

Where is ...?	Dov'è ...?
Go straight ahead.	Si va sempre diritto.
	Vai sempre diritto (inf).
Turn left.	Gira a sinistra.
Turn right.	Gira a destra.
at the next corner	al prossimo angolo
at the traffic lights	al semaforo
behind	dietro
in front of	davanti
far	lontano
near	vicino
opposite	di fronte a

Around Town

I'm looking for ...	Cerco ...
a bank	un banco
the church	la chiesa
the city centre	il centro (città)
the ... embassy	l'ambasciata di ...
my hotel	mio albergo
the market	il mercato
the museum	il museo
the post office	la posta
a public toilet	un gabinetto/ bagno pubblico
the telephone centre	il centro telefonico
the tourist office	l'ufficio di turismo/ d'informazione

I want to change ...	Voglio cambiare ...
money	denaro
travellers cheques	degli assegni per viaggiatori

beach	la spiaggia
bridge	il ponte
castle	il castello
cathedral	il duomo/la cattedrale
island	l'isola
main square	la piazza principale
market	il mercato
mosque	la moschea
old city	il centro storico

Signs

INGRESSO/ENTRATA	ENTRANCE
USCITA	EXIT
INFORMAZIONE	INFORMATION
APERTO/CHIUSO	OPEN/CLOSED
PROIBITO/VIETATO	PROHIBITED
POLIZIA/CARABINIERI	POLICE
QUESTURA	POLICE STATION
CAMERE LIBERE	ROOMS AVAILABLE
COMPLETO	FULL/NO VACANCIES
GABINETTI/BAGNI	TOILETS
UOMINI	MEN
DONNE	WOMEN

palace	il palazzo
ruins	le rovine
sea	il mare
square	la piazza
tower	la torre

Accommodation

I'm looking for ...	Cerco ...
a guesthouse	una pensione
a hotel	un albergo
a youth hostel	un ostello per la gioventù

Where is a cheap hotel?	Dov'è un albergo che costa poco?
What is the address?	Cos'è l'indirizzo?
Could you write the address, please?	Può scrivere l'indirizzo, per favore?
Do you have any rooms available?	Ha camere libere/C'è una camera libera?

I would like ...	Vorre i ...
a bed	un letto
a single room	una camera singola
a double room	una camera matrimoniale
a room with two beds	una camera doppia
a room with a bathroom	una camera con bagno
to share a dorm	un letto in dormitorio

How much is it ...?	Quanto costa ...?
per night	per la notte
per person	per ciascuno?

May I see it?	Posso vederla?
Where is the bathroom?	Dov'è il bagno?
I'm/We're leaving today.	Parto/Partiamo oggi.

Shopping

I'd like to buy ...	Vorrei comprare ...
How much is it?	Quanto costa?
I (don't) like it.	(Non) Mi piace.
May I look at it?	Posso dare un'occhiata?
I'm just looking.	Sto solo guardando.
It's cheap.	Non è caro/a.
It's too expensive.	È troppo caro/a.
I'll take it.	Lo/La compro

Do you accept ...	Accettate ...?
credit cards	carte di credito
travellers cheques	assegni per viaggiatori?

more	più
less	meno
smaller	più piccolo/a
bigger	più grande

Time & Dates

What time is it?	Che ora è?
	Che ore sono?
It's (8 o'clock).	Sono (le otto).
in the morning	di mattina
in the afternoon	di pomeriggio
in the evening	di sera
When?	Quando?
today	oggi
tomorrow	domani
yesterday	ieri

Monday	lunedì
Tuesday	martedì
Wednesday	mercoledì
Thursday	giovedì
Friday	venerdì
Saturday	sabato
Sunday	domenica

January	gennaio
February	febbraio
March	marzo
April	aprile
May	maggio
June	giugno
July	luglio
August	agosto
September	settembre
October	ottobre
November	novembre
December	dicembre

Numbers

0	zero
1	uno
2	due
3	tre
4	quattro
5	cinque
6	sei
7	sette
8	otto
9	nove
10	dieci
11	undici
12	dodici
13	tredici
14	quattordici
15	quindici
16	sedici
17	diciassette
18	diciotto
19	diciannove
20	venti
21	ventuno
22	ventidue
30	trenta
31	trentuna
40	quaranta
50	cinquanta
60	sessanta
70	settanta
80	ottanta
90	novanta
100	cento
1000	mille
2000	due mila

| one million | un milione |

Emergencies

Help!	*Aiuto!*
Call ... !	*Chiami ... !*
	Chiama ... ! (inf)
a doctor	*un dottore/*
	un medico
the police	*la polizia*
There's been an accident	*C'è stato un incidente!*
I'm lost.	*Mi sono perso/a.*
Go away!	*Lasciami in pace!*
	Vai via! (inf)

Health

I'm ill.	*Mi sento male.*
It hurts here.	*Mi fa male qui.*
I'm ...	*Sono ...*
asthmatic	*asmatico/a*
diabetic	*diabetico/a*
epileptic	*epilettico/a*
I'm allergic ...	*Sono allergico/a ...*
to antibiotics	*agli antibiotici*
to penicillin	*alla penicillina*
antiseptic	*antisettico*
aspirin	*aspirina*
condoms	*preservativi*
contraceptive	*anticoncezionale*
diarrhoea	*diarrea*
medicine	*medicina*
sunblock cream	*crema/latte solare (per protezione)*
tampons	*tamponi*

FOOD

This glossary is intended as a brief guide to some of the basics and by no means covers all of the dishes you are likely to encounter in Sicily. Most travellers to the region will already be well acquainted with the various Italian pastas, which include spaghetti, fettuccine, penne, rigatoni, gnocchi, lasagne, tortellini and ravioli. The names are the same throughout Italy and no further definitions are given here.

Basics

breakfast	*prima colazione*
lunch	*pranzo*
dinner	*cena*
restaurant	*ristorante*
grocery store	*alimentari*
What is this?	*(Che) cos'è?*
I would like the set menu.	*Vorrei il menù turistico*
Is service included in the bill?	*È compreso il servizio?*
I'm a vegetarian	*Sono vegetariano/a*

Useful Words

affumicato	smoked
al dente	firm (as all good pasta should be)
alla brace	cooked over hot coals
alla griglia	grilled
arrosto	roasted
ben cotto	well done (cooked)
bollito	boiled
cameriere/a	waiter/waitress
coltello	knife
conto	bill/cheque
cotto	cooked
crudo	raw
cucchiaino	teaspoon
cucchiaio	spoon
forchetta	fork
fritto	fried
menù	menu
piatto	plate
ristorante	restaurant

Staples

aceto	vinegar
burro	butter
formaggio	cheese
limone	lemon
marmellata	jam
miele	honey
olio	oil
olive	olives
pane	bread
pane integrale	wholemeal bread
panna	cream
pepe	pepper
peperoncino	chilli
polenta	cooked cornmeal

riso	rice
risotto	rice cooked with wine and stock
sale	salt
uovo/uova	egg/eggs
zucchero	sugar

Meat & Fish

acciughe	anchovies
agnello	lamb
aragosta	lobster
bistecca	steak
calamari	squid
coniglio	rabbit
cotoletta	cutlet or thin cut of meat, usually crumbed and fried
cozze	mussels
dentice	dentex (type of fish)
fegato	liver
gamberi	prawns
granchio	crab
manzo	beef
merluzzo	cod
ostriche	oysters
pesce spada	swordfish
pollo	chicken
polpo	octopus
salsiccia	sausage
sarde	sardines
sgombro	mackerel
sogliola	sole
tacchino	turkey
tonno	tuna
trippa	tripe
vitello	veal
vongole	clams

Vegetables

asparagi	asparagus
carciofi	artichokes
carote	carrots
cavolo/verza	cabbage
cicoria	chicory
cipolla	onion
fagiolini	string beans
melanzane	aubergines
patate	potatoes
peperoni	peppers
piselli	peas
spinaci	spinach

Fruit

arance	oranges
banane	bananas
ciliegie	cherries
fragole	strawberries
mele	apples
pere	pears
pesche	peaches
uva	grapes

Soups & Antipasti

brodo – broth
carpaccio – very fine slices of raw meat
insalata caprese – sliced tomatoes with mozzarella and basil
insalata di mare – seafood, generally crustaceans
minestrina in brodo – pasta in broth
minestrone – vegetable soup
olive ascolane – stuffed, deep-fried olives
prosciutto e melone – cured ham with melon
ripieni – stuffed, oven-baked vegetables
stracciatella – egg in broth

Pasta Sauces

alla matriciana – tomato and bacon
al ragù – meat sauce (bolognese)
arrabbiata – tomato and chilli
carbonara – egg, bacon and black pepper
napoletana – tomato and basil
panna – cream, prosciutto and sometimes peas
pesto – basil, garlic and oil; often with pine nuts
vongole – clams, garlic and oil; sometimes with tomato

Pizzas

All pizzas listed have a tomato (and sometimes mozzarella) base.

capricciosa – olives, prosciutto, mushrooms and artichokes
frutti di mare – seafood
funghi – mushrooms
margherita – oregano
napoletana – anchovies
pugliese – tomato, mozzarella and onions
quattro formaggi – with four types of cheese
quattro stagioni – like a capricciosa, but sometimes with egg
verdura – mixed vegetables

Glossary

AAST – Azienda Autonoma di Soggiorno e Turismo; local tourist office
abbazia – abbey
ACI – Automobile Club Italiano; the Italian automobile club
aereo – aeroplane
affittacamere – rooms for rent (cheaper than a *pensione* and not part of the classification system)
agora – (Latin) marketplace, meeting place
agriturismo – tourist accommodation on farms
AIG – Associazione Italiana Alberghi per la Gioventù; Italy's youth hostel association
albergo – hotel (up to five stars)
alimentari – grocery shop, delicatessen
aliscafo – hydrofoil
Alleanza Nazionale – National Alliance (neo-Fascist political party)
alloggio – lodging (cheaper than a *pensione* and not part of the classification system)
alto – high
ambasciata – embassy
ambulanza – ambulance
anfiteatro – amphitheatre
Annunciazione – Annunciation
antipasto – starter
appartamento – apartment, flat
apse – (English) domed or arched area at the altar end of a church
APT – Azienda di Promozione Turistica; regional tourist office
ara – altar
arco – arch
ARTCT – Assessorato Regionale del Turismo, delle Communicazioni e dei Trasporti; the main Sicilian tourist agency
assicurato/a – insured
AST – Azienda Soggiorno e Turismo; local tourist office
atrium – (Latin) forecourt of a Roman house or a Christian basilica
autobus – bus
autostazione – bus station or terminal
autostop – hitchhiking
autostrada – freeway, motorway

badia – abbey
baglio – manor house
bagno – bathroom; toilet
bancomat – automated teller machine (ATM)
belvedere – panoramic viewpoint
benzina – petrol
benzina senza piombo – unleaded petrol
bicicletta – bicycle
biglietto – ticket
biglietto chilometrico – kilometric card (train pass)
binario – (train) platform
borgo – ancient town or village, sometimes used to mean equivalent of *via*
Brigate Rosse (BR) – Red Brigades (terrorist group)

calcio – football (soccer)
cambio – money exchange
camera – room
campanile – bell tower
campeggio – camp site
canto – quarter
cappella – chapel
carabinieri – police under the jurisdiction of the Ministry of Defence (see *polizia*)
Carnevale – carnival period between Epiphany and Lent
carta d'identità – ID card
carta telefonica – phonecard (also *scheda telefonica*)
cartoleria – stationery shop
casa – house
case abusive – (literally, abusive houses) illegal construction usually associated with the Mafia
castello – castle, citadel
cattedrale – cathedral
cava – quarry (as in the pumice quarries at Campobianco)
cena – evening meal
cenacolo – refectory
centro – centre
centro storico – old town (literally, historical centre)

chiesa – church
chiostro – cloister; covered walkway, usually enclosed by columns, around a quadrangle
cin cin – cheers (a drinking toast)
Circumetna – private train line circling Mt Etna
CIT – Compagnia Italiana di Turismo; Italian national tourist/travel agency
clientilismo (politico) – system of political patronage
codice fiscale – tax number
colazione – breakfast
colonna – column
comune – equivalent to a municipality or county; town or city council; historically, a commune (self-governing town or city)
consolato – consulate
contado – district around a major town
contorno – side dish
contrada – town district
convalida – ticket stamping machine
coperto – cover charge
corso – main street, avenue
cortile – courtyard
Cosa Nostra – alternative name for the Mafia
Crocifissione – Crucifixion
CTS – Centro Turistico Studentesco e Giovanile; student/youth travel agency
cuccetta – couchette
cupola – dome
Cupola – Mafia commission

DC – Democrazia Cristiana; Christian Democrats (political party)
decumanus – (Latin) main street
deposito bagagli – left luggage
digestivo – after-dinner liqueur
diretto – slow through train
distributore di benzina – petrol pump (see *stazione di servizio*)
dolce – sweet, dessert
duomo – cathedral

ENIT – Ente Nazionale Italiano per il Turismo; Italian state tourist office
enoteca – wine shop; nowadays often a basic restaurant with a range of fine wines to taste

ephebus – (Latin) statue of a young boy
espresso – express mail; express train; short black coffee

fangho – mud bath
faraglione – rock stack
farmacia (di turno) – pharmacy (open late)
fermo posta – poste restante
Ferragosto – Feast of the Assumption, 15 August
ferrovia – train station
festa – festival
fiume – river
focaccia – flat bread
fontana – fountain
forno – bakery
foro – forum
fortezza – fortress
Forza Italia – Go Italy (centre-right political party)
francobollo – postage stamp
fresco – (English) the painting method in which watercolour paint is applied to wet plaster
FS – Ferrovie dello Stato; the Italian state railway
funivia – cable car

gabinetto – toilet, WC
gasauto or **GPL** – liquid petroleum gas (LPG)
gasolio – diesel
gelato – ice cream
gola – gorge
golfo – gulf
granita – flavoured crushed-ice drink
grappa – grape liqueur
grotta – cave
guardia di finanza – fiscal police
guardia medica – first-aid station

IC – Intercity; fast train
interregionale – long-distance train that stops frequently
isola – island
IVA – Inposta di Valore Aggiunto; valued-added tax of around 19%

lago – lake
largo – (small) square

latifondo – large landed estate
latomie – small quarries
lavanderia – laundrette
lavasecco – dry-cleaning
lido – beach
locale – slow local train
locanda – inn, small hotel (cheaper than a *pensione*)
loggia – covered area on the side of a building; porch
lungomare – seafront road, promenade

Madonna con Bambino – Madonna with Child (often the subject of paintings, drawings and sculptures)
Maestà – depiction of the Trinity, Christ or Mary enthroned (often the subject of paintings, drawings and sculptures)
mafioso – member of the Mafia
mare – sea
mattanza – ritual slaughter of tuna (in Favignana)
menù del giorno – menu of the day
mercato – market
merceria – haberdashery shop
mescita di vini – wine outlet
metope – (English) sculpted frieze
mezza pensione – half board
Mezzogiorno – (literally, midday) name for the south of Italy
monte – mountain
motorino – moped
municipio – town hall, municipal offices
museo – museum

Natale – Christmas
nave – large ferry, ship
Neapolis – new city
necropolis – (English) ancient cemetery, burial site
Novecento – 20th century
numero verde – toll-free phone number

oggetti smarriti – lost property
Ognissanti – All Saints' Day, 1 November
omertà – code of silence used by the Mafia
oratorio – oratory
ospedale – hospital
ostello – hostel
ostello per la gioventù – youth hostel

osteria – snack bar, cheap restaurant

Pagine Gialle – Yellow Pages (phone directory)
pala – altarpiece
palazzo – palace or mansion; a large building of any type, including an apartment block
palio – pageant, festival
panetteria – bakery
panino – bread roll with filling
paninoteca – cafe
parco – park
Pasqua – Easter
passeggiata – traditional evening stroll
pasta – cake; pasta; pastry or dough
pasticceria – shop selling cakes, pastries and biscuits
PCI – Partito Comunista Italiano; Italian Communist Party (political party)
PDS – Partito Democratico di Sinistra; Democratic Party of the Left (political party)
pedaggio – toll
pensione – small hotel, often with board
pensione completa – full board
permesso di lavoro – work permit
permesso di soggiorno – residence permit
pianta della città – city map
piazza – square
piazzale – (large) open square
Pietà – (literally, pity or compassion) sculpture, drawing or painting of the dead Christ supported (usually) by the Madonna
pinoli – pine nuts
polizia – police
poltrona – airline-type chair on a ferry
polyptych – altarpiece consisting of more than three panels (see *triptych*)
pomice – pumice stone
ponte – bridge
porta – gate
portico – portico; covered walkway, usually attached to the outside of buildings
porto – port
posta – post office
posta aerea – airmail
pranzo – lunch
prigone – prison
Pro Loco – local tourist office

pronto soccorso – first aid, casualty ward
pullman – (English) long-distance bus

Quattrocento – 15th century
questura – police station

rapido – fast train
reale – royal
regionale – slow local train
rifugio – mountain refuge
riserva naturale – nature reserve
rocca – fortress; rock
rosso – red
rotonda – round chamber
ruderi – ruins
rustication – (English) rough-hewn, protuding blocks of stone used in building

sagra – festival (generally dedicated to one food item or theme)
sala – room
saline – saltpan
salumeria – delicatessen that sells mainly cheeses and sausage meats
santuario – sanctuary
scalinata – staircase, steps
scheda telefonica – phonecard (also *carta telefonica*)
servizio – service charge
sindaco – mayor
soccorso stradale – highway rescue
sotto – under
spiaggia (libera) – (public) beach
stazione – station
stazione di servizio – service station, petrol station
stazione marittima – ferry terminal
stele – (English) upright stone column decorated with figures and motifs
strada – street, road
strada provinciale – main road; sometimes just a country lane
strada statale – main road; often multi-lane and toll-free

superstrada – expressway; highway with divided lanes
supplemento – supplement, payable on a fast train

tabaccheria – tobacconist's shop
tavola calda – (literally, hot table) pre-prepared meat, pasta and vegetable selection, often self-service
teatro – theatre
telamon – (English) large statue of man, used as a column in temples
tempio – temple
terme – thermal baths
tholos – rock tomb
tonnara – tuna-processing plant
tonno – tuna
torre – tower
torrente – stream
torrone – type of nougat
tramezzini – sandwiches
trattoria – cheap restaurant
treno – train
Trinità – Trinity (often the subject of paintings, drawings and sculptures)
triptych – painting or carving on three panels, hinged so that the outer panels fold over the middle one; often used as an altarpiece (see *polyptych*)

ufficio postale – post office
ufficio stranieri – (police) foreigners bureau

via – street, road
via aerea – airmail
vico – alley
vigili del fuoco – fire brigade
vigili urbani – traffic police; local police
villa – town house or country house; also the park surrounding the house
vinai – wine bar or shop
vino alla mandorla – almond wine

zona rimozione – vehicle removal zone

LONELY PLANET

Guides by Region

Lonely Planet is known worldwide for publishing practical, reliable and no-nonsense travel information in our guides and on our web site. The Lonely Planet list covers just about every accessible part of the world. Currently there are fifteen series: travel guides, Shoestrings, Condensed, Phrasebooks, Read This First, Healthy Travel, Walking guides, Cycling guides, Pisces Diving & Snorkeling guides, City Maps, Travel Atlases, Out to Eat, World Food, Journeys travel literature and Pictorials.

AFRICA Africa on a shoestring • Africa – the South • Arabic (Egyptian) phrasebook • Arabic (Moroccan) phrasebook • Cairo • Cape Town • Cape Town city map • Central Africa • East Africa • Egypt • Egypt travel atlas • Ethiopian (Amharic) phrasebook • The Gambia & Senegal • Healthy Travel Africa • Kenya • Kenya travel atlas • Malawi, Mozambique & Zambia • Morocco • North Africa • Read This First Africa • South Africa, Lesotho & Swaziland • South Africa, Lesotho & Swaziland travel atlas • Swahili phrasebook • Tanzania, Zanzibar & Pemba • Trekking in East Africa • Tunisia • West Africa • Zimbabwe, Botswana & Namibia • Zimbabwe, Botswana & Nambia Travel Atlas • World Food Morocco
Travel Literature: The Rainbird: A Central African Journey • Songs to an African Sunset: A Zimbabwean Story • Mali Blues: Traveling to an African Beat

AUSTRALIA & THE PACIFIC Auckland • Australia • Australian phrasebook • Bushwalking in Australia • Bushwalking in Papua New Guinea • Fiji • Fijian phrasebook • Healthy Travel Australia, NZ and the Pacific • Islands of Australia's Great Barrier Reef • Melbourne • Melbourne city map • Micronesia • New Caledonia • New South Wales & the ACT • New Zealand • Northern Territory • Outback Australia • Out To Eat – Melbourne • Out to Eat – Sydney • Papua New Guinea • Pidgin phrasebook • Queensland • Rarotonga & the Cook Islands • Samoa • Solomon Islands • South Australia • South Pacific • South Pacific Languages phrasebook • Sydney • Sydney city map • Sydney Condensed • Tahiti & French Polynesia • Tasmania • Tonga • Tramping in New Zealand • Vanuatu • Victoria • Western Australia
Travel Literature: Islands in the Clouds • Kiwi Tracks: A New Zealand Journey • Sean & David's Long Drive

CENTRAL AMERICA & THE CARIBBEAN Bahamas, Turks & Caicos • Bermuda • Central America on a shoestring • Costa Rica • Cuba • Dominican Republic & Haiti • Eastern Caribbean • Guatemala, Belize & Yucatán: La Ruta Maya • Jamaica • Mexico • Mexico City • Panama • Puerto Rico • Read This First Central & South America • World Food Mexico
Travel Literature: Green Dreams: Travels in Central America

EUROPE Amsterdam • Amsterdam city map • Andalucía • Austria • Baltic States phrasebook • Barcelona • Berlin • Berlin city map • Britain • British phrasebook • Brussels, Bruges & Antwerp • Budapest city map • Canary Islands • Central Europe • Central Europe phrasebook • Corfu & Ionians • Corsica • Crete • Crete Condensed • Croatia • Cyprus • Czech & Slovak Republics • Denmark • Dublin • Eastern Europe • Eastern Europe phrasebook • Edinburgh • Estonia, Latvia & Lithuania • Europe on a shoestring • Finland • Florence • France • French phrasebook • Germany • German phrasebook • Greece • Greek Islands • Greek phrasebook • Hungary • Iceland, Greenland & the Faroe Islands • Istanbul City Map • Ireland • Italian phrasebook • Italy • Krakow •Lisbon • London • London city map • London Condensed • Mediterranean Europe • Mediterranean Europe phrasebook • Munich • Norway • Paris • Paris city map • Paris Condensed • Poland • Portugal • Portugese phrasebook • Portugal travel atlas • Prague • Prague city map • Provence & the Côte d'Azur • Read This First Europe • Romania & Moldova • Rome • Russia, Ukraine & Belarus • Russian phrasebook • Scandinavian & Baltic Europe • Scandinavian Europe phrasebook • Scotland • Slovenia • Spain • Spanish phrasebook • St Petersburg • Switzerland • Trekking in Spain • Ukrainian phrasebook • Venice • Vienna • Walking in Britain • Walking in Ireland • Walking in Italy • Walking in Spain • Walking in Switzerland • Western Europe • Western Europe phrasebook • World Food Italy • World Food Spain
Travel Literature: The Olive Grove: Travels in Greece

INDIAN SUBCONTINENT Bangladesh • Bengali phrasebook • Bhutan • Delhi • Goa • Hindi & Urdu phrasebook • India • India & Bangladesh travel atlas • Indian Himalaya • Karakoram Highway • Kerala • Mumbai (Bombay) • Nepal • Nepali phrasebook • Pakistan • Rajasthan • Read This First: Asia & India • South India • Sri Lanka • Sri Lanka phrasebook • Trekking in the Indian Himalaya • Trekking in the Karakoram & Hindukush • Trekking in the Nepal Himalaya
Travel Literature: In Rajasthan • Shopping for Buddhas • The Age Of Kali

LONELY PLANET

Mail Order

L onely Planet products are distributed worldwide. They are also available by mail order from Lonely Planet, so if you have difficulty finding a title please write to us. North and South American residents should write to 150 Linden St, Oakland CA 94607, USA; European and African residents should write to 10a Spring Place, London, NW5 3BH; and residents of other countries to PO Box 617, Hawthorn, Victoria 3122, Australia.

ISLANDS OF THE INDIAN OCEAN Madagascar & Comoros • Maldives • Mauritius, Réunion & Seychelles

MIDDLE EAST & CENTRAL ASIA Bahrain, Kuwait & Qatar • Central Asia • Central Asia phrasebook • Dubai • Hebrew phrasebook • Iran • Israel & the Palestinian Territories • Israel & the Palestinian Territories travel atlas • Istanbul • Istanbul to Cairo on a shoestring • Jerusalem • Jerusalem City Map • Jordan • Jordan, Syria & Lebanon travel atlas • Lebanon • Middle East • Oman & the United Arab Emirates • Syria • Turkey • Turkey travel atlas • Turkish phrasebook • Yemen
Travel Literature: The Gates of Damascus • Kingdom of the Film Stars: Journey into Jordan • Black on Black: Iran Revisited

NORTH AMERICA Alaska • Backpacking in Alaska • Baja California • California & Nevada • California Condensed • Canada • Chicago • Chicago city map • Deep South • Florida • Hawaii • Honolulu • Las Vegas • Los Angeles • Miami • New England • New Orleans • New York City • New York city map • New York Condensed • New York, New Jersey & Pennsylvania • Oahu • Pacific Northwest USA • Puerto Rico • Rocky Mountain • San Francisco • San Francisco city map • Seattle • Southwest USA • Texas • USA • USA phrasebook • Vancouver • Washington, DC & the Capital Region • Washington DC city map
Travel Literature: Drive Thru America

NORTH-EAST ASIA Beijing • Cantonese phrasebook • China • Hong Kong • Hong Kong city map • Hong Kong, Macau & Guangzhou • Japan • Japanese phrasebook • Japanese audio pack • Korea • Korean phrasebook • Kyoto • Mandarin phrasebook • Mongolia • Mongolian phrasebook • North-East Asia on a shoestring • Seoul • South-West China • Taiwan • Tibet • Tibetan phrasebook • Tokyo
Travel Literature: Lost Japan • In Xanadu

SOUTH AMERICA Argentina, Uruguay & Paraguay • Bolivia • Brazil • Brazilian phrasebook • Buenos Aires • Chile & Easter Island • Chile & Easter Island travel atlas • Colombia • Ecuador & the Galapagos Islands • Healthy Travel Central & South America • Latin American Spanish phrasebook • Peru • Quechua phrasebook • Rio de Janeiro • Rio de Janeiro city map • South America on a shoestring • Trekking in the Patagonian Andes • Venezuela
Travel Literature: Full Circle: A South American Journey

SOUTH-EAST ASIA Bali & Lombok • Bangkok • Bangkok city map • Burmese phrasebook • Cambodia • Hanoi • Healthy Travel Asia & India • Hill Tribes phrasebook • Ho Chi Minh City • Indonesia • Indonesia's Eastern Islands • Indonesian phrasebook • Indonesian audio pack • Jakarta • Java • Laos • Lao phrasebook • Laos travel atlas • Malay phrasebook • Malaysia, Singapore & Brunei • Myanmar (Burma) • Philippines • Pilipino (Tagalog) phrasebook • Read This First Asia & India • Singapore • South-East Asia on a shoestring • South-East Asia phrasebook • Thailand • Thailand's Islands & Beaches • Thailand travel atlas • Thai phrasebook • Thai audio pack • Vietnam • Vietnamese phrasebook • Vietnam travel atlas • World Food Thailand • World Food Vietnam

ALSO AVAILABLE: Antarctica • The Arctic • Brief Encounters: Stories of Love, Sex & Travel • Chasing Rickshaws • Lonely Planet Unpacked • Not the Only Planet: Travel Stories from Science Fiction • Sacred India • Travel with Children • Traveller's Tales

LONELY PLANET

You already know that Lonely Planet publishes more than this one guidebook, but you might not be aware of the other products we have on this region. Here is a selection of titles that you may want to check out as well:

Europe on a shoestring
ISBN 0 86442 648 8
US$24.95 • UK£14.99 • 180FF

Florence
ISBN 0 86442 785 9
US$14.95 • UK£8.99 • 110FF

Italian phrasebook
ISBN 0 86442 456 6
US$5.95 • UK£3.99 • 40FF

Italy
ISBN 0 86442 692 5
US$21.95 • UK£13.99 • 170FF

Read This First: Europe
ISBN 1 86450 136 7
US$14.99 • UK£8.99 • 99FF

Rome
ISBN 0 86442 626 7
US$15.95 • UK£9.99 • 120FF

Tuscany
ISBN 0 86442 733 6
US$16.99 • UK£10.99 • 129FF

Venice
ISBN 0 86442 786 7
US$14.95 • UK£8.99 • 110FF

Walking in Italy
ISBN 0 86442 542 2
US$17.95 • UK£11.99 • 140FF

Western Europe
ISBN 0 86442 639 9
US$25.95 • UK£15.99 • 190FF

World Food Italy
ISBN 1 86450 022 0
US$12.95 • UK£7.99 • 110FF

Available wherever books are sold.

Index

Text

Bold indicates maps.